MW01620737
SAFARI PRESS

#2.

ADVENTURE IS MY BUSINESS

ADVENTURE IS MY BUSINESS

Volume II

(1951 - 1955)

Russell Annabel

Illustrated by
Michael Coleman

SAFARI PRESS INC.

P.O. Box 3095, Long Beach, CA 90803
USA

TO THE READER

We promised that all the stories in the Annabel set of books would be previously unpublished in book form; however, we realized that we needed to add six previously published stories to the sequence of "Adventure Is My Business" in order to make this sequence complete. Thus, parts 1, 2, 6, 7, 11, and 12 of "Adventure Is My Business" have been previously published in book form.

Annabel, Russell

Second edition

Safari Press Inc.

1997, Long Beach, California

ISBN 1-57157-064-0

Library of Congress Catalog Card Number: 95-69973.

10 9 8 7 6 5 4 3 2

Readers wishing to receive the Safari Press catalog, featuring many fine books on big-game hunting, wingshooting, and sporting firearms, should write to Safari Press, Inc., P.O. Box 3095, Long Beach, CA 90803, USA. Tel: (714) 894-9080.

TABLE OF CONTENTS

FOREWORD

The following résumé was submitted by Rusty Annabel in 1942. It was kindly given to us by Mr. Jim Rearden of Homer, Alaska.

July 23, 1942
Public Relations,
Fort Richardson, Alaska

Dear Captain Meyer:

Following are the facts you requested about me.

Born:	December 1, 1904, in Seattle, Wash.
Parents:	E. E. Annabel, Louella Russell, both American born of American-born parents.
Education:	Attended grade school successively at Avon, Annapolis and Port Orchard, all Washington cities. High School at Bremerton, Washington. Took special courses in journalism at University of Washington, leaving in 1927.
Residence:	Between 1905 and 1909 my parents resided in Valdez, Alaska, and for a time at Elamar and Juneau. Since 1921 I have maintained residence at Anchorage.
Lodges:	I was for a time a member of the Anchorage Elks lodge but dropped out because of high fees. I am now a member of the Eagles and Redmen lodges.
Employment:	I have been employed in Alaska by the U.S. Forest Service and the U.S. Land Office, and for eight years was a registered guide.
Journalism:	During the past fifteen years I have contributed to many magazines, among them *Field & Stream*, *Esquire*, *Outdoor Life*, *Hunting and Fishing*, *National Sportsman*, *Sports Afield*, *Boys' Life*, *Open Road for Boys*, *Dime Detective* and *Startling Adventure*. I have published one book, *Tales of a*

Big-Game Guide by Derrydale Press, and have two other books in process of publication. I have sold feature material to the *Tacoma Tribune*, *Los Angeles Times Magazine*, *Pasadena Evening Post*, *Memphis Commercial Appeal* and *Portland Oregonian*. I have been employed as reporter by the *Tacoma Ledger* and *INS*, in the latter case working for Courtney Ryley Cooper and Elsie Robinson. I have written radio scripts for KVI, have been string correspondent for the Political campaigns, among them the campaigns of
John C. Stevensen of Seattle,
Senator Lewis R. Schwellenbach,
Congressman Martin F. Smith and
State Representative Clyde Tisdale of Washington.
I am now staff correspondent in Alaska for
United Press Associations.

Sincerely,

Russell Annabel

Murderer in the Trees

Not even the quill-armed porcupine is safe from the fisher—
a cutthroat of the woods with a pelt valued at $200.
I knew that marten could catch red squirrels in the trees.
And I had heard that the pekan could catch marten,
but didn't believe it. So then one morning
Doc Riley and I saw a pekan catch one.
Gentlemen, that was the damnedest thing I ever watched.
—"Shorty" Devereaux, trapper and guide

Suppose you were on a wildlife quiz program trying for the jackpot, and the man asked you to name North America's most mysterious carnivore. Also suppose he considerately gave you the following clues: (1) That the animal is a member of the weasel family and weighs up to twenty pounds; (2) that it is a cannibal and no animal surpasses it in ferocity and bloodthirstiness; (3) that it is the only killer able consistently to prey upon porcupines; (4) that in the trees it is the fastest of all four-footed creatures; and (5) that its pelt is equal to Siberian sable in richness and luster.

O.K., of course it's the pekan, or fisher—*Martes pennanti*, largest of the martens.

But nobody could be blamed for fluffing the questions. The classic natural history books give this savage, lightning-fast cutthroat of the deep woods such brief treatment that writers generally have enthusiastically laid off him. More has been written about okapis, takins, sea serpents, pink elephants, and other rare fauna than about the fisher. The boys (me among them, and I was raised in fisher country) have sort of hated to stick their necks out.

Yet the fisher is no remote never-never beast. Far from it. Fishers actually are distributed from New York state to Washington state, and from the Canadian boundary north to the Land of Little Sticks.

Certainly no other animal on the continent has been a greater genius at keeping his family secrets inviolate.

I figure I ought to know. Shortly after I dog-sledded my first typewriter out onto the fur trails, I began trying to assemble enough information on the fisher so that I could write a passable piece about him. That was back in 1925, and the quest turned out to be one of those things you could make a career of and get no place at all. I'll bet I wrote anyway 200 letters to trappers and game wardens. I interviewed traders and fur buyers all over the North. I carved up fisher carcasses and examined the weirdly heterogeneous contents of their stomachs.

Jim and Frank Barton, a pair of very woods-smart long-trappers operating on the Mackenzie, solved one important mystery for me. They explained how the fisher manages to kill porcupines without getting himself riddled with quills.

Maybe you have heard the various theories about this. The commonest is that the fisher approaches the porcupine from the front—something quite difficult if not impossible to do—deftly places a paw under his chin, flips him onto his back, and slashes his throat. Just like that. But the next time you encounter a porcupine, please imagine that you are a fisher, and try to figure out how you would accomplish the above without getting so loaded with quills you'd resemble a saguaro cactus. I could be wrong, but I don't believe the predator lives that could stay face to face with an aroused porcupine long enough to pat him under the chin.

Then there's the rather special theory that the fisher attacks the porcupine as recklessly as he would a rabbit, ignoring the quills on account of he has in his body a handy substance that dissolves them before they can do him any harm. The bug in this one is that you almost never pelt a fisher without finding a few quills in him, and sometimes it is clear that he has carried them a long, long time.

I was sitting with Jim and Frank on the woodpile outside their summer cabin on a tributary to the upper Mackenzie, a cabin they had built at a little hot spring and where they now had come to plant a garden and boil the winter frost out of their bones, and I said, "Did you guys ever see a fisher kill a porcupine?"

Jim said, "Uh-huh. Sure we have. Two-three times. They kill 'em in trees. Wanta hear about the first time we saw it done?

They said it was on a bitter, crystalline noon in mid-December, with a wind tearing snow plumes off the peaks and a cluster of sundogs glowing sullenly in the hard sky. They had topped a rocky pass between two creek heads, and were slanting down to timber when, in a slope of meadow below them, they sighted the fisher. He was jet-black with a white blaze on his chest, and judging from his size—nearly that of a fox—was a male in his prime. Jim put his binocular on the animal and saw that he was following the deep-wallowed trail of a porcupine.

With their glasses the trappers scanned the wall of timber across the meadow, and presently located the porcupine. He was fifteen feet up on the outthrust limb of a gaunt hangman's spruce, hunched against the congealing wind, paws gathered under him for such warmth as his body afforded.

Almost without slackening pace the fisher flashed up the tree to the hangman's limb. He hung here a moment on the trunk, motionless, paws widespread, watching the porcupine. Then he catfooted daintily out onto the limb until he was just outside the reach of the now wildly slashing tail. He was an executioner sizing up his victim, taking his time, utterly confident of the outcome. You could feel sorry for the porcupine—he apparently knew what was coming, but there was nothing he could do about it. The fisher made no feints. When he attacked, the move was so dazzingly fast, so deadly, and so unexpected that it left the watching trappers openmouthed and bug-eyed. He flowed *under* the limb—safe here from the porky's tail—and all in one beautifully timed movement thrust his triangular head up in a snake-swift slash at the doomed animal's throat.

"That's how he done it," Frank said. "And he didn't get a quill in him, either. We know because we caught him a couple days later in a trap we set at his kill. For a male, he had a fine pelt. We got $60 for it."

It is only in recent years—after the fur farmers finally solved the puzzle of propagating the fisher domestically—that we have had any real knowledge about this formidable animal's domestic life. The female fisher, it was learned, has an incredibly long gestation period. This results from "discontinuous development" of the embryo, growth being arrested for many months. Mating takes place in the spring, late March to early May, with the young not arriving until almost a year later. The litter varies from one to five, three and four being most common. Four to nine days after her young are born, the mother fisher goes out to mate again. It is she who seeks the mating. She is a devoted mother, but at this time, until she finds a male, and mates, her helpless young are forgotten. Here may be the basic reason for the universal scarcity of fishers. The fur-farm female seems to prefer, but only occasionally insists on, monogamy. The male, unless he has been long accustomed to one female, seems to be indifferent as to his consort, and will serve more than one.

On the fur farm, the female, when seeking a mate, is apt to thrash soundly a male she does not fancy (she is only about half as big). The female seems to wear the pants in the family. The male is no hot-eyed Romeo, often has to have his ears slapped by the little female before he sees the light. The male does not defend himself against a female (according to fisher raisers quoted by Robert G. Hodgson, editor of *Fur Trade Journal* of Canada). If permitted to live together throughout the year, a pair apparently will do so amicably.

Old-timers I have known who are acquainted with the fisher in the wilds would dispute, emphatically, some of the observations immediately above. They would probably be right. Fur-farm fishers are not wild fishers, as fur farmers who have live-trapped the latter and gone through a pen-breaking are the first to acknowledge. Although fishers eventually accept captivity well, on the whole, long-friendly males have been known to turn murderously on their keepers without warning and without apparent provocation.

It is a fact that during the greater part of the year in the wild only female fishers associate on friendly terms. You seldom if ever find two males together, or a male and a female. But a pair of females traveling together is a common arrangement. Trappers believe that sisters pair off to form hunting teams, and separate only during the period when they bear and rear their young and mate.

Fishers are fastidious in appearance, but they are not at all fastidious about what they eat. Snakes, toads, frogs, mice, beetles, grubs, rotten birds' eggs—even marten carcasses, which no other animal in the wilds will eat—are welcome provender to them. No doubt their willingness to subsist on all manner of lowly fare is the reason they live far beyond the age when most other highly specialized killers perish. I have taken venerable, gray-muzzled fishers so old their teeth were mere yellowed stubs, yet they were in excellent condition, fat in the hardest part of the northern winter. The fact that their individual survival quotient is high, while their population remains low, seems to confirm that there is a heavy mortality among the young as a consequence of the female coming in heat a few days after her kits are born.

The name "fisher" is misleading because these animals, it is universally agreed, do not catch fish. Often caught in traps baited with fish—customary bait in many areas—it was taken for granted in pioneer days that the fisher also went to the source for this favorite fare. "Pekan," of Algonquin Indian origin, is a better name. Fishers are the outstanding cannibals of the wilds, since they prey relentlessly on their blood relatives, the martens. Much larger than martens, male fishers reach a maximum length of four feet and a weight of twenty pounds. These big weasels range in color from grizzled gray-brown to jet-black, and often have white patches extending from their chests back along their bellies.

Hudson's Bay Company factors in the old days, serving their thirty years in the Canadian wilds, used to hold out the best black female fisher pelts and take them home when they retired to have them made into coats for their wives. There is no record as to how long it took a factor to collect enough matched skins for a full-length coat, but even in those times of abundant fur it must have been quite a chore. Today it would be a fantastically expensive one. In an average good fur market, a top female pelt will bring $200—when one is offered for sale. Such expert fisher trappers as Tom Mould and Bud Gallant, to give you an idea of the animals' scarcity, have taken only three or four fishers a winter during the fifteen years they have been operating on the lower Liard River, where the world's only known concentration of fishers exists. The pelts of male fishers are rougher than those of the females, lacking the characteristic silkiness and sheen of the latter, and sometimes sell for as little as $25.

Like most of the weasel clan, fishers are not smart in the matter of keeping out of traps. White trappers usually take them in No. 1 steel traps set on the ground, with a tip-up pole to hoist the trapped animal into the air and thus prevent the little shrew mice from hollowing out the carcass and ruining the pelt. The Slavie, Athabascan, and Tahltan Indians, on the other hand, take them in deadfalls—and lose plenty of fur to the shrews if they fail to run their lines at least every other day, which frequently is the case. Bait is always used, and the most successful is a spruce grouse or a sizable chunk of porcupine. Of course, no fisher ever was caught in a properly constructed deadfall and got out of it alive, but they often escape from steel traps by wringing off their feet or chewing them off. Yet, despite this mutilation and the lesson it should have taught, they will continue to come to a bait. I have seen a number of three-legged fishers, and once I saw one that had lost three paws in traps. How he had managed to find a living, handicapped as he was, has always been a prime mystery to me.

Northwestern Indians, from the Cascades to the Carcajou Range, have a superstitious regard for the fisher because of his berserker ferocity and his expertness as a killer.

When I was a youngster, the Indian trapper who caught a fisher seldom offered it for sale to white men. It was worth more as medicine. A skin might be passed in trade a thousand or more miles among the Indians, gaining in value as tribe after tribe handed it on until probably it would be well out of fisher country, and some chief or shaman would have it dressed for his medicine bundle. No other animal except the grizzly was accorded greater respect. The Siwashes and Stillaquamishes, whose children I played with from the time I was able to walk, were convinced that eating the heart of a fisher would make a man very brave indeed. But I can supply proof that while this may work for an Indian, it was a failure in my case.

I caught my first fisher on the upper Tolt at the age of twelve, and of course, being indoctrinated to the eyeballs with the beliefs of my Indian playmates, I sneaked a frying pan out of the house, cooked the fisher's heart, and divided it with a youthful savage named Johnny Snoqualmie. I didn't feel any different afterward, and Johnny confessed he didn't either. But we figured that perhaps the medicine just hadn't had time to work. A week or so later, the two of us attended a school play, which made it necessary for us to walk home through the heavy timber after dark. Beside the lonely, pitch-black road was a graveyard. As we came abreast of the place, we saw a light moving toward us among the tombstones. I don't know what the light was. Maybe it was somebody carrying a lantern. Anyway, it was there, and Johnny Snoqualmie and I took off. If I could run that fast today, I would make some track stars look like chumps.

Years later, on Athabaska Lake, I related the incident to the blind Denna shaman mentioned earlier.

He listened, nodded sagely, and said, "Graveyards bery bad at night. A light in a graveyard *damn'* bad. I guess the fisher medicine he scared too."

Trappers, guides, and assorted woodsmen plying their trades in the North country have long known that fishers kill and eat martens, for they find gnawed marten bones and scraps of marten fur with fisher tracks about them. And they find bits of marten fur in the stomachs of the fishers they trap. But the big question always has been—how do the fishers do it? The marten is himself a concentrated bundle of ferocity, fast as chain lightning. He makes his living, for the most part, catching red squirrels in the trees. This itself is incredible enough, when you picture a two-foot marten racing over pencil-size twigs and dodging and twisting among the mazes of branches in pursuit of such an agile acrobat as the squirrel, and catching him. But when you try to imagine a ten- to twenty-pound fisher catching the victorious marten in an arboreal steeplechase, you bog down.

Old Tex Cobb, the dean of northern working woodsmen, expressed the attitude of most sourdoughs toward the matter when he told me, "I know the fishers must catch 'em, but until I see hit happen I'll be doggoned if I'll believe hit."

Only three men, so far as my researches go, have actually seen a fisher catch and kill a marten. One was Bert Sheffield, who trapped the Tutsa River in the Liard country. But Bert isn't around anymore. In 1948 he attempted a bad ford with a saddle horse, and something happened. The horse got out, but they found Bert on a sand bar with a drift log across his neck, drowned. Bert's story of how the fisher he saw caught a marten agrees in every detail, however, with another account that I got from Shorty Devereaux. Shorty says he was making a spring bear hunt with an eastern dude, a doctor named Riley, and that they had climbed to snow line to investigate a line of bear tracks they had picked up with their glasses. The tracks unfortunately petered out on bare ground, whereupon Shorty and Doc, discouraged, sat down with their backs against a sun-warmed boulder to eat their lunch. This was in typical timberline country, a tilted alpine meadowland, with wide-armed spruces standing from 50 to 100 feet apart.

Suddenly, a stone's throw below them, a marten flashed across a rock slide, heading for a tree, with a large black fisher in hot pursuit. The marten reached the tree and went up it as fast as the shadow of a swooping bird. But when he reached the top, the fisher was only a couple of tail lengths behind. So the marten jumped. There was nothing else he could do. He had no opportunity whatever to maneuver. Launching himself out of the twenty-foot spruce, he landed like a cat, and raced for another tree. The fisher also jumped. And when the marten reached this tree, the fisher was so close to him, and gaining so fast, he had to jump before he was halfway to the top. Again the fisher jumped after him. This time the marten, apparently realizing he couldn't outdistance the fisher to the next tree, a good 100 feet distant, whirled back and made a desperate bound up the trunk of the tree he had just left.

The fisher caught him before he reached the first limbs. Shorty says there was no fight, no struggle. The fisher simply shot up out of the winterkilled grass, picked the marten off the tree, and dropped to the ground with his teeth set in the back of the marten's neck. The luckless marten didn't even have time to squall before the fisher's needle-pointed teeth met in his spine and crunched the life out of him.

"That's what Doc and I saw," Shorty says. "Personally, I don't believe a fisher could catch a marten in heavy timber where the marten could maneuver and get out on little branches that wouldn't hold the fisher's weight. But still, I dunno. There's plenty that nobody knows about fishers. When it comes to killing in the trees, I guess there ain't much I'd put past 'em."

Which sentiment, I am sure, all persons who have had business dealings with the wild fisher will heartily endorse.

Trapping Is No Way to Get Rich

Maybe fifty years ago a man could make a living with a trapline in the Alaskan back country. Today it's tougher—unless, of course, he's as lucky as "Baldy" Harris.

I noticed the husky, pleasant-looking tenderfoot lad hanging around the hotel lobby while "Starvation" Smith and I were selling our fur, but because of what was happening to us I didn't pay much attention to him.

We were being scientifically, but not painlessly, sandbagged out of some hard-earned profits that we needed like a wounded man needs plasma. This was shortly after the spring breakup, and we had just come down from the Susitna Basin with a fair catch of high-country marten, mink, and fox. To us the silky, lustrous pelts represented six months' hard work and a cash investment of $1,100, and we knew their market value was at least $3,000. But the buyer we were dealing with, an amiable brigand who knew when to put on the squeeze, offered us $2,500 and said it was positively the best price he could give us. It was murder, but we were in a bad fix. We were broke, in debt, and couldn't afford to shop the States and wait weeks for a check. So we let the guy have the skins. After handing over the money, he bought us a drink and stated sympathetically that it was too bad, really too bad, that the fur market had taken a nose dive just when the trappers were coming out of the wilds with their pelts. Actually, he said, he had paid us more than he should have, and would no doubt be chewed on for it by his boss.

It was the old routine. Page one in the fur buyer's handbook. I had heard it every spring for thirty years. But it works. They get away with it.

Starvation and I went up to our room and had been there about five minutes when there was a knock on the door. It was the tenderfoot. He came in, sat down and spoke his piece, a big, shy kid with freckles and a mop of dynamically red hair, perhaps nineteen, an ex-farmhand for a guess. What he had to say was no surprise after we got a good look at him. He wanted to be a trapper. Like a legion of other restless young buckos from Seattle to Maine, he yearned to settle here on the Alaska frontier and make his eternal fortune hunting and taking fur. He had come north over the highway last week in a beat-up jalopy towing a little homemade trailer in which his outfit was stowed. He admitted he knew nothing about trapping as yet but said that didn't worry him—he was willing to work, and he'd learn. It developed he had $120 to buy grub and transport it, his gear, and himself into the wilderness.

He was a promising brat. I liked his looks. But he had his sights set a mile too high. He told us seriously that he didn't expect to make much the first season. Maybe a thousand dollars—just enough to get by with until he learned his way around and got the feel of things. And he hoped, he said, that Starvation and I would be kind enough to tell him where there was a likely fur pocket for this indoctrination course.

At mention of a thousand dollars, Starvation started as if stabbed with a hot awl. "Gawd a'mighty!" he groaned." "Only a thousand bucks, huh? Now Listen, son," he said. "Listen careful, on account of I'm gonna talk to ya like I was yer pappy. You rustle around an' find yerself a job o'work that'll bring ya in a paycheck every week. Fergit all about trapping in Alasky. Because trapping is as dead as dog mushing—an' it never was much good nohow."

We took turns explaining why following the fur trails was an occupation with no discernible future, but I think the redhead had stopped listening. He was suffering from an advanced case of trapline fever, and when they are that far gone there is nothing you can do for them. They have got to mush back into the big frost on a pair of webs, with the long silence for company and the cold for a teacher, and get it out of their systems the hard way. A lot of them are doing it. Mostly they return disillusioned, broke, and fed to the teeth with the North, and get jobs gandy-dancing on the railroad to earn their passage home.

Of course, big, spectacular fur catches are made by men lucky enough to be in the right place at the right time with a bundle of traps or a roll of snare wire. With suitable liquid priming, any barroom historian in the territory will tell you about them in dramatic detail. They'll tell you about the wild Eskimo who came to Aklavik in a sailing umiak with 1,200 white-fox pelts aboard, for which he received the all-time high price of $65 apiece; about Arthur Berry over on the Kuskokwim, who took 600 marten in three months and sold them for enough to build and stock a trading post; about Joe Palmer who, with a Matanuska Indian named Andrew, took 400 foxes—chiefly silvers and silver crosses—in the Nelchina country one winter and got an average of $100 a pelt for them.

They'll tell you about the lucky exploit of "Baldy" Harris, a one-time partner of mine. Baldy didn't have a trap or snare to his name, yet he took $2,400 worth of fur in ninety minutes, a record so far as I know. He had lost his outfit in a canoe wreck, and lacking the money to buy another, had reluctantly taken a job cutting cordwood for a mining company on Bear Creek. One gray December morning as he was snowshoeing up the trail to his wood yard, ax in one hand and a .22 rifle in the other, he saw a lynx crossing a little brushy gap fifty yards ahead. He shot the animal, and was congratulating himself when another lynx appeared at the same spot. He shot that one, too. A moment later he saw two more and killed them. He had blundered into the setup that trappers dream about, a big cross-country migration of lynx. In an hour and a half he had killed forty of the animals. And his luck held good when he took the pelts to town. The market had skyrocketed and lynx were bringing $60.

But what bemused would-be trappers like the redhead either haven't heard or refuse to believe is that year in and year out few professional trappers clear more than $100 a month during the trapping season. The majority of them, in fact, have to work for wages the remainder of the year to support themselves. I never personally knew one who managed to save any money or who made enough with his traps alone to live better than a cut or two above the standard of a moderately enterprising brush Indian.

One trouble with trapping here is that in Alaska a trapline has no legal existence. It cannot be owned, leased, or hypothecated. Anybody with a license can move in and compete side by side with you for the available fur, no matter how much effort and money you may have expended building cabins and caches, cutting trails, making boat landings and airplane strips, and otherwise improving your district. In the old days it was different, much different. The unwritten law of the wilds, respected by all sourdoughs, gave a man exclusive right to the fur on his line so long as he trapped the area continuously. But today the trapline code is as obsolete as the code of Hammurabi, and your one chance to win out over competitors is to set more traps than they do and set them better.

Just once in recent years have I had the pleasure of seeing a trapline-jumper get his complete and deserved comeuppance. This was in March, the second month of the beaver season, while old Tex Cobb and I were working a chain of ponds strung along a dog-leg creek that spills into Redoubt Bay, down on the storm-lashed west coast of Cook Inlet.

Twenty feet of snow lay on the land. We were able to find the ponds because we had lobbed spruces to mark them early in the winter, but getting at the beavers was something else. You burdened yourself like a packhorse with a shovel, and ice chisel, an empty five-gallon gasoline can, a length of rope, a twenty-foot ladder, your traps, and bait sticks, and broke trail to a pond and set up a project there. First you dug a shaft down through the snow. Next you cut a hole in the ice. Then you patiently maneuvered a set into position on the dark, brush-littered bottom of the pond. You used the ladder as a means of exit from the shaft and to get back into it when you returned to lift the trap. The gasoline can and rope were for hoisting snow out of the shaft after you had dug down to where you couldn't throw it out with the shovel. It was cold, mean, onerous work. Often it took all day to make one set, and then as likely as not a wind would roar out of the mountains and drift the shaft level full of snow before morning.

Then one noon when the ice was thundering and a handful of sundogs hung like hooded lamps in the hard sky, a little red-and-yellow airplane buzzed in across the inlet at low tide and landed on the sand beach 100 yards from our cabin. The pilot, a lanky, tough-looking fellow wearing King Island mukluks and ancient Air Force coveralls, wasted no time informing us why he was here. He was a beaver trapper, he said, and he had scouted this creek from the air last summer, he said, and so now he was going to trap here, period. There was nothing we could do about it. We had put in a lot of work here and had hoped to profit from it without interference. But the law was on the side of the trapline-jumper. We watched him get his gear out of the plane and snowshoe up the trail to the first beaver pond. He stood there a moment considering our snow shaft. Even if our set hadn't been plainly visible at the bottom of it, the lobbed spruce would have been evidence enough that there was a pond here with a beaver colony in it. Obviously the ready-made shaft was a great temptation, and I suppose he was telling himself that, after all, there was no legal reason why he shouldn't make use of it. The beavers were on the public domain and belonged equally to all citizens—and who could claim special rights to a hole in the snow? Anyway, he yielded. He cut a cottonwood bait stick, and a toggle pole, tossed a trap and his ice chisel into the shaft, and stepping out of his snowshoe thongs, descended the ladder we had left in the shaft last evening. Presently we heard him cutting ice. He was making a set next to ours.

I was outraged to the point of speechlessness, but Tex began laughing. "In case ya ain't noticed hit," he chuckled, "the gentleman has made a mistake. Hit's true that the beavers in that there pond are public property. But that ladder shore ain't."

Tex ambled up the trail to the shaft. After making a few disarmingly civil remarks about the weather, he abruptly grabbed the ladder by its top rung and yanked it up. A hoarse, threatening yell floated out of the shaft, but Tex pretended he didn't hear it. With the ladder over his shoulder, smiling happily, he came back to the beach and we returned to our cabin. We could hear the trapline-jumper shouting pleas, imprecations and dire promises of revenge. He yelled that he would have the law on it, and declared that if we possessed even a vestigial trace of guts we would let him out of there and settle this thing like men. He offered to bet money, marbles or chalk that he could lick both of us at the same time. His voice cracking, he hollered that friends of his knew where he was, and that if he failed to return to his base by a certain time they would come looking for him, loaded for trouble.

When his outcries didn't get him anything, he shut up and began trying to devise a means of escape. He must have had a horrible time. He couldn't cut steps in the powder-dry snow, nor could he heap the stuff up in a ramp that would bear his weight. We saw later where he had tried both methods and failed. At last, to avoid refrigeration, he dug a tunnel with his hands fifty feet across the pond to timber, using a rain-formed stratum of crust as its roof and shoving the displaced snow behind him as he moved on. Fortunately encountering a wide-armed spruce tree in his molelike progress, he climbed up it through the smother of snow to the open air. From there he rolled, swam, crawled and floundered through the feathery drifts to the edge of the shaft where he had left his webs. All this took some two hours. Tex and I were in the dooryard sawing wood when the poor chap came stumbling down the trail, a cold, weary, beaten man. Before he wound up the engine of his airplane and took off, he told us we could have his share of all the damned beavers between Tyonok and Bruin Cove, because he was going home and sit on the radiator until he thawed out.

Almost as exasperating as trapline-jumpers are the airborne tourists, hunters and anglers who make free with your cabins and gear in the summer and autumn when you aren't there to discourage them. They chop up your stretcher boards for firewood and sometimes even chop up the floor. They leave the door open and the window shutters off, a clear invitation to bears, wolverine and porcupines to come on in and hold a field day with your provender. They leave your ax and saw on the ground to be covered by snow and lost, shoot holes in the stovepipe, and litter the premises with broken beer bottles on which you ruin your moccasins and your dogs cut their feet. Padlocks won't keep these people out, but my friend "Lobo" Smith has come up with something that will. Last spring before Lobo went to town with his fur, he tacked a message to the door of his headquarters cabin. Addressed to a mythical partner, the message read:

> Dear Bill:
> Red Shirt and some other Injuns stopped here and now the cabin is lousy and so am I. I have gone to town to get something to kill them—the lice, I mean. You better camp in the yard.
> Lobo

Lobo says that when he returned in the fall he found signs indicating that a number of persons had visited the place, but that they had refrained from breaking into the cabin as they used to.

Of all the ecstatic misconceptions about trapping, the greatest is the notion that it is an endeavor requiring almost no capital outlay. Tenderfeet like the redhead at the hotel are shocked, for example, when you tell them that the equipment for a medium-long three-cabin line will cost a minimum of $1,000, and that to fly it into the wilds at the customary bush-pilot rate of $50 an hour will cost an additional $100 to $200. It is a fact that many cheeckakos come North with the optimistic idea that they can live siwash-fashion in tents or brush lean-to shelters, subsist largely on game and fish, and take fur in quantity with a dozen or so haphazardly assorted traps. Admittedly there was a time back in the departed days of plentiful fur when a tough, lucky, weatherproof fellow who knew his business thoroughly could do exactly that. But to make expenses nowadays you need permanent camps, hundreds of traps, and a great deal of expensive supplementary equipment. You need so many things—tools, sleds, dogs, dog harness, snowshoes, stoves, sleeping bags, a boat if you are on muskrat water, maybe an outboard motor—that when you begin buying them your bankroll shrinks like spring snow on a south slope.

If you outfit properly—and you won't accomplish much unless you do—you can count on spending your first winter, and perhaps the second, getting your investment back. That's if everything goes well. If it doesn't you may find yourself in a financial quagmire, unable to claw your way out of it by any amount of toil and smart trapping. As an illustration, take somthing that happened during a bootless trapping expedition I made into the Talkeetnas with "Tip-Up" Williams, one of the most expert sourdough woodsmen I ever worked with.

In mid-August we chartered an airplane and flew deep into the big, sky-busting complex of peaks to scout up a new trapping area if we could. Up to a point we were lucky. While prowling back afoot down the long west flank of the range we hit the jackpot—what promised to be a minor fur bonanza. The cottonwood-bordered creek we were following hadn't been trapped for five years and was swarming with mink. Never except in the lagoons and slow creeks along the rim of the Bering Sea, had we seen such a concentration of the animals. Normally mink are so shy that sighting one is an event, but here we saw whole families running ahead of us on the bars and playing in the slack-water pools.

Tip-Up thought we would take between 60 and 100, and do it in three or four weeks. "We'll clear anyhow $2,500," he asserted confidently, "an' that's somethin' I ain't yet saw stickin' outa barns."

Since there was no lake or gravel bar on which a plane could land, and no snow yet for dog sledding, we backpacked our outfit in from the railroad through brush, blowdown and tundra bogs, eighty pounds to the pack. We repaired two ruined cabins, made our stretcher boards, cut a supply of firewood, and killed a fat bull moose for camp meat. When the season opened November 16, we were ready. In five days, working from daybreak till dark, we put out 150 traps. We made the sets on the creek ice in little spruce-bark shelters that would keep snow off the traps and magpies and whiskey jacks out of them, with twist of wild hay under the jaws so they couldn't freeze down and a handful of duck feathers over them for camouflage. For bait we used a twig dipped in a bottle of scent made by mixing fish oil, shredded beaver castor and the anal glands of mink saved from the past season. They were good sets and we knew they would score. We figured that when we came back over the line we would have so many mink that we would have to sit up nights taking care of the pelts.

But the plans of mice and men have a discouraging history. When we snowshoed in through the cottonwoods to our upper cabin at the end of the fifth day, darkness had fallen and a towering rack of storm cloud was blanking out the stars and the aurora banners. A curiously soft wind had begun to blow in from the south. An hour later, while we were getting some trail grub out of the cache, Tip-Up remarked that if he didn't know it couldn't happen at this time of year he'd be doggoned if he wouldn't say it was going to rain. He had barely finished speaking when a rain-filled gust shotgunned through the gaunt trees and struck me in the face. That was the beginning of such a winter rainstorm as never before was seen in these parts. It was a cloudburst, a ceaseless, battering deluge that roared in on a gale-force wind for three days and nights. The ice went out and the creek backed up into the timber. Six inches of water gurgled across the cabin floor. The woodpile floated away. Our traps were lost and the mink dens were flooded or gouged away by the ice. So far as making any money here this season was concerned, we were a pair of well-plucked ducks. As soon as travel was possible we evacuated the place and retreated to the railroad.

In the order of their value to trappers the important Alaska fur-bearers are the mink, muskrat, beaver, white fox, marten and lynx. Statistics of the Fish and Wildlife Service reveal that pelts of these animals shipped from the territory in the past twenty-year period brought about $28,270,000.

Mink, marten, beaver, and lynx are distributed fairly evenly through the timbered areas of Alaska south of the Brooks Range. The white fox inhabits the coastline and adjacent islands from the mouth of the Kuskokwim River to Demarcation Point in the Arctic. The muskrat, the most abundant and stable of Alaska fur-bearers, is found in heaviest concentrations on the deltas of the Kobuk, Yukon, Kuskokwim and Selawik Rivers and in the triangle of swampy country lying between the upper Yukon and Porcupine Rivers. It is believed that the present muskrat population is about 3,000,000 and that at times it may reach a high of 5,000,000. If I were going to start out again to earn my living with traps I think I would confine my efforts entirely to trapping muskrats, because if there is any big money left in trapping that is where it is.

A resident trapping license, with hunting-and-fishing privileges, costs $3. A nonresident license costs $50 and resident status is withheld until one has spent three years in the territory. A copy of the game laws giving the seasons and limits on furbearers may be obtained by writing to the Alaska Game Commission at Juneau. At present there is a limit only on beavers, ten being allowed to a person.

Newcomers on the fur trails worry a good deal about bad ice, blizzards, avalanches and frostbite, but the hazard that sends a chill jittering up the spine of the sourdough trapper is fire. Despite fiction tales to the contrary, it is the possibility of fire in a cabin more than the threat of marauding wolverines and other four-footed looters that prompts woodsmen to build caches in which to store fur, grub and gear.

In the remote, beautiful Grass Lakes country, the winter I was 18, fire put Tex and me out of business in less time than a hungry hawk would need to finish off a parka squirrel.

We were snaring foxes along the timberline creeks above the spread of lakes, and had been doing all right. The animals were unusually plentiful and as long-haired furs were then in fashion we could see that we had a chance to make some money. Reds were bringing an average of $20, crosses $50 and silvers $200. (Today they wouldn't sell for one tenth as much.) As sometimes happens, the field mice and snowshoe rabbits had reached the peak of their cycles of abundance at the same time, so that the foxes had almost an embarrassment of food and were rearing large litters. We saw them daily working the meadows and the grassy lake shores, and at night the pups practiced their vocal lessons on the ridges behind camp. They were not difficult to take. We would find a populous rabbit colony in a creekside willow thicket where the foxes were hunting and cover the place with a battery of as many as fifty snares. We set the snares so close together, often in double rows, that it was virtually impossible for a fox to enter the thicket without getting into a noose. In one memorable week we took so many of them, reds and crosses, that Tex couldn't pelt them as fast as I brought them in, and Tex is a Rembrandt with a skinning knife.

Then our luck suddenly and dramatically ended.

It was one of those crystalline mornings when mirages make the mountains dance crazily against the sky and it seems the cold of outer space has come down to smite the earth. When I tried to harness our eight dogs in the dooryard after breakfast the snaps and buckles froze to my hands. So I brought the team into the cabin to put the rigging on them. It was a mistake. Our leader, a burly Siberian named Dog, was sitting in the center of the floor keeping watch over the operation when one of his wheel dogs snatched a joint of moose meat from the table. With a roar Dog pounced on the offender, shook him, and threw him halfway across the cabin. That did it. In two seconds we were in the midst of a four-bell canine riot.

The singletree of a lunging, yammering malamute's harness snagged the red-hot Yukon stove, jerking it off is foundation and slamming it with a tinny crash, door open, against the bunk. A glowing cascade of coals spilled out on the puncheon floor, firing a heap of birch-bark kindling and the wild-hay mattress of the bunk. Everything happened so fast that before either of us could reach the water bucket, flames were mushrooming against the ceiling and the tinder-dry moss chinking was ablaze. We got the door open in the blinding smoke and kicked the dogs out, threw our rifles and sleeping bags after them, and fled into the open ourselves with our hair singed and our shirts on fire. The cabin, of course, burned to the ground. Fortunately our fur and most of our grub was in the cache.

In my opinion, the best way for a newcomer to get started trapping in Alaska is to serve an apprenticeship under an expert. But don't ask me how this could be arranged. Frankly, I don't know. But I do know that the eager-beaver understudy will have to work as he probably never did before, sweat out some blue-ribbon hardships, risk life and limb in a variety of interesting ways, and endure the shattering effect of prolonged loneliness and isolation—all for the sake of getting the lowdown on an outdated profession that pays less than ditch digging.

Still, God knows I don't understand it, but the life has a fascination. I can't imagine a worse occupation but it is a fact that the old-timers who quit it most vehemently usually come back to it. Just today I was thinking about a fur pocket I once scouted over on the north slope of the Alaska Range. Fine high country with a slew of game in it. Mink and beaver country. With a tall stand of cabin timber on the shore of a grayling lake as clear as air. I'll bet I could go over there with a partner and a six months' outfit, and. . . .

He Wears a Black Pitchfork

Maybe I'd better start by telling you about something that happened the other day at La Paz, Baja California. A young, fish-loopy Yanqui sportsman was trying to promote a date with a red-headed schoolteacher from Des Moines. They were sitting under a big laurel tree on the sea wall across from the Perla Hotel, and the guy was really turning on the charm. But suddenly the whole romantic project went haywire. Our hero glanced over the lady's shoulder at the glittering blue bay water, and he stiffened as if he'd been stabbed. His jaw dropped and his eyes bugged. He leaped convulsively to his feet, croaking something that sounded like, "Ohmygoodgoshlookatthat!"

Two hundred yards out, a flight of sierra mackerel was heading for the beach. "Flight" is the right word. They were coming in a continuous, swooping, terrified rush. Maybe 1,000 of them—averaging about three pounds each. They were in the air all the while, though they must have been keeping themselves up there by beating the water with their tails. But you couldn't see it. There was a roar as they rocketed in, and then there were sierra mackerel all over the beach.

But the Yanqui angler wasn't interested in sierras. He was staring beyond them. Out at the edge of the shoal water you could see big white, splashing surges and lightning-fast zigzag wakes. Master killers were out there—killers that had herded the sierras onto the beach. And those killers were roosterfish.

A fin broke the surface, close in. It was such a fin as a man would have to see to believe. It consisted of seven pitchfork-like tines. It was glossy black with a bright blue band at its base, and it stuck up more than a foot before the tines tipped over at the top. The Yanqui angler took one look and sprinted for the hotel. When he came back five minutes later, panting, he had a casting rod and a gaff.

The redhead was leaving. She gave the fisherman a disdainful glance. "So long, Romeo," she said, "Mamma told me never to try to compete with fish."

"But baby, listen," our hero protested, feverishly bending on a Japanese feather jig, "you don't understand. Those aren't just fish—they're roosterfish."

The boy had an angle there. He'd discovered a truth about the school variety of roosterfish. The time to catch 'em is when you see 'em. Hesitate, and you'll be skunked. Because the roosterfish, especially when he's in a school, is one of the most erratic and elusive big-game fish we have. He's a silver phantom, a husky, slashing now-he's-here-and-now-he's-gone critter.

A school of them will swarm into a bay or cove. Kill-crazy, they'll churn the place to a lather, splash water ten feet high, and leave the swells dotted with crippled fish. If you get out to them while they're still on their spree, they'll give you marvelous sport. They'll hit cut bait, spoons, feather lures, and plugs. And they fight like tigers, making up to a dozen sizzling runs. With light 3/6 tackle, a thirty-pounder will keep you busy and thrilled for twenty minutes. You'll find him as stubborn as an amberjack and as flashy as a dolphin except that usually he doesn't jump.

Mostly, though, you don't get there soon enough. By the time you've run for your tackle and launched a boat, the rampaging roosterfish have vanished. Just vanished, and for keeps. Once these platinum-sided brutes have left a spot, you'd get no roosterfish strikes if you dragged a lure over that place until you wore yourself out.

In view of which, if you have your heart set on slugging it out with these piratical pitchforks, there's just one thing to do. You charter a boat—a speedboat preferably, so you can cover a lot of water—and go hunting. Take mullet in addition to artificial lures. Take an icebox and stock it with something thirst-quenching. Take suntan lotion. Then cruise the lonely, jewel-colored bays and inlets, and look for fins and big white splashes. Work the glittering reefs and the weed-hung shelves under the cliffs. Follow the birds.

You'll have the time of your life, just as Tommy Jamison, Pete Smith, and I had last June over in the Bacochibampo area, on the west side of the Gulf of California, an exciting body of water discovered by Hernando Cortés in 1536.

One blistering, Aztec-blue morning we eased the *Cazadora*, a sixteen-foot streak of greased lightning, to the foot of a soaring, red, cave-pocked lava cliff at the entrance of San Pedro cove. Tommy, a very nautical, personable guy who runs the sportfishing outfit at Bacochibampo, was at the wheel.

I was mate. Pete was doing the fishing.

Pete, so far as I can discover, is serious about nothing but fishing. Right then he was very serious. This was the first lure he'd dropped into Mexican waters. He let it sink, and we watched it shine as it scaled down into the green-glimmering depths alongside the weedy rocks. He started it in, but something struck short. We saw a flash as the fish turned, but there was no tug on the line. Pete let the lure sink and flutter, then started it in again. This time the fish took it and ran.

Tommy looked at the rod tip and shrugged. "Corbina," he said. The corbina is western Mexico's weakfish, or sea trout. "Bring him in," he added, "we'll eat him for dinner."

Pete tried, but couldn't budge the line. We kicked the boat in out of the glare of the sun, and saw what had happened. The two-foot corbina had fouled the line around a pinnacle of rock. Pete cussed. The bone jig was the only one he had, and it was his lucky lure. He didn't want to lose it; he'd be doggoned if he'd cut the line. Tommy sighed, turned the wheel over to me, and pulled off his clothes. He slipped on a pair of frogman's flippers and a fishing mask, and dived. Tommy glided through the emerald shadows like a merman. Things happened.

As Tommy slanted down, trailing rainbow bubbles, a great dark grouper with a beer-keg mouth drifted across his path. Then a sea turtle that may have been young when Montezuma was emperor, rose from below and headed for the corbina. Then something else came, something that sliced through the water like a bright knife. A second later Tommy shot to the surface. The corbina was out from behind the rock pinnacle, but not by its own efforts. And Pete's reel, on click, was singing a frantic tune.

"Roosterfish," Tommy gasped as he yanked off the mask. "My gosh, he like to ran over me."

It was a roosterfish, all right. He made a brilliant 100-yard run and boomed to the surface. He was a patriarch—one of those old, humpbacked, belligerent cusses that have lairs among the rocks and apparently don't run in schools. He might have weighed fifty pounds. That eerie, black, pitchfork fin stuck up, waggling as he twisted and turned, and he struck repeatedly at the leader with his tail. Pete, tense and hot, was doing his best. He had plenty to do. The sea was pitching the *Cazadora* wildly. There were sharp rocks on three sides of us which the fish could reach in a flash. And the linen line was only six-thread—about eighteen-pound-test. The big fish put on a blast of power and swung toward us in a wild arc on the surface. Then he saw the boat. He whipped around so fast that he made a swash and heave in the green water like a dynamite explosion. Then he was gone, and the line was slack. Pete reeled in. He lifted the leader and took a long, sad look at what was on the end of it.

The front half of the corbina was still there. That hard-boiled old rooster hadn't been hooked at all. He'd simply wanted the corbina, and had been hanging onto it like a bulldog. Then, scared by the boat, he'd bit it in half and departed. Pete issued a solemn oath.

"So help me, I'm going to catch one of those ornery so-and-so's," he declared, "if I have to cruise around on this dizzy ocean for the rest of my life."

When we returned to port that evening, we found storm warnings up. Bacochibampo fishermen were hauling out their boats, and upcountry farmers were taking down their windmills. In the morning a hurricane wind was screaming along the coast. The storm lasted two days, and it served one good purpose. It brought in a lot of fish. On the third day the bays were crowded with acres of mullet, sardines, anchovies, sierras, and bonitos, which meant that soon the big predatory fish would be inshore to gorge.

We took the *Cazadora* roaring out of the harbor at thirty-two knots, rounded the point, and turned into a tiny, nameless bay under chocolate-colored hills frosted with white guano deposits. Here we found sardines swarming in four tight, counterclockwise circles. There were so many of them that the ones on top were actually being crowded out of the water. Over them floated a solid, clamorous cloud of pelicans, terns, and man-o'war birds.

And on the seaward side of the whirlpools was a school of roosterfish. There were thirty or forty, maybe more. Pete threw away his cigarette, pulled off his shirt, and said, "Men, this is it."

Tommy allowed we ought to use live bait, and I thought it was a sterling idea. Since we didn't have a net, he gunned the *Cazadora* through one of the sardine schools. The propeller must have killed maybe a bucketful. Then we turned around and coasted in to pick up our loot.

Screaming ecstatically, half the seabird population of Bacochibampo pitched down out of the hot sky. Pete and I, by working fast, managed to salvage one badly mutilated, canape-size sardine. The yelling birds got the rest. So we went back and killed another batch, and this time Tommy stopped the *Cazadora* in the middle of the school. While Pete waved his shirt at the birds, I picked up sardines.

Dumb, fat, and happy, I leaned over the side. I had my right arm deep in the water, reaching for a half-stunned sardine. Suddenly a great, grotesque something went by like a torpedo. It looked blue. It was maybe ten feet long. It had a head like a double-bitted ax, and a tall dorsal fin that swished within inches of my hand. I saw a white-rimmed, coldly-appraising eye set out at the rim of one of the ax bits. That was all, and that was enough. I executed such a vigorous backflip that I might have shot over the opposite gunwale if I hadn't landed in Tommy's lap.

"What in hell was that?" Tommy said.

"That was a hammerhead shark, and we've got enough sardines, brother," I replied.

I'm definitely no lover of the shark tribe, but what happened in the next few minutes was interesting—in a gruesome sort of way. At least a dozen hammerheads appeared abruptly out of the luminous depths. They surrounded us and the sardines and began to feed. Their technique was simple, but for sharks they had manners. They didn't crowd. While the others rode herd, so to speak, one whipped through the sardines with his mouth wide open. Then he'd stand by while another tore in from the opposite side. It worked out swell for everyone except the sardines. The sharks got their bellies full, the birds got the cripples, and we got a free show.

And if you're wondering what this shark routine has to do with roosterfish, I will explain.

The roosterfish were still splashing around out on the seaward side. So it looked like we had a chance to score. I bridle-rigged a resuscitated sardine New Zealand style behind a 4/0 hook. Pete settled in the fighting chair. Tommy took the bucking *Cazadora* out to meet the feeding roosterfish. Then Tommy slowed the boat to bare steerageway, and Pete fed out fifty feet of line. I threw some chum over. Nothing happened. We turned, came back, and put out a fresh bait. Nope.

Then a fin showed behind the bait. Like marlin and sailfish, roosterfish apparently raise their dorsals only when fighting or going in for a kill. This one came in straight and fast, and hit clean. Pete gave him perhaps three seconds, then socked him twice as hard as he dared with the six-thread line.

Roosterfish don't often jump, but this one did. He came out high and pretty in a shower of gem-spangled spray. He looked like a thirty-pounder. Somersaulting in the air, he hit the water head first, striking at the leader with his forked tail. In less time than it takes to sneeze, he ripped 300 feet of line off the reel. Then he turned. Pete, with a look of exaltation, let the fish run, and Tommy, worried, spun the *Cazadora* and gave chase.

Legitimately this roosterfish was ours. Pete brought him in three times, and each time Pete was ready for the lightning, boat-shy run that is the roosterfish's final ace. The fourth time you could see that the grim old battler was finished. He was on his side, out of gas. I picked up the gaff and grabbed the leader. We were in a trough, and I balanced myself, waiting for the *Cazadora* to lift. Then from somewhere a huge, blue-gray shape flashed alongside. There was a gleam of white, a splash, a thick chomping sound, and a red stain on the water. It was a hammerhead. He'd cut Pete's roosterfish in two with one bite.

Pete wiped his face, and in the strained voice of one who's counted to ten and figures he should have made it twenty, said bitterly, "Now I get it. Now I understand why the International Game Fish Association didn't list a record roosterfish until last year. It's because nobody ever caught one before, that's why."

Many pilgrims have reached the same conclusion, but actually a lot of roosterfish are caught, and there are a lot to catch. Exclusively a West Coast species, the roosterfish ranges from southern California to Ecuador. So far as I can discover, the greatest concentrations are in the Gulf of California, Panama Bay, and the area between Cape Matapalo, Costa Rica, and the Pearl Islands. They are present the year-round. The likeliest spots for them in the Gulf of California seem to be Guaymas, Bacochibampo, and Topolobampo Bays on the west side, and Conception Bay, Puerto Escondido, La Paz Bay, and Cape San Lucas on the east side.

Roosterfish average about twenty pounds, and the record, taken off Peru, was seventy-two pounds. Commercial fishermen report taking some weighing over eighty pounds. No doubt the roosterfish would be better known if he didn't inhabit the same waters as the more spectacular broadbill, marlin, and sailfish, but anglers who go out for him become fans. They cuss him, but they'll tell you he's a champion, a slugger from away back.

Next morning, in the crimson glow of a fantastically boisterous sunrise, we cruised San Francisco Bay, and saw no fish. So we headed over to Guaymas. Here we hailed a Portuguese sailing ship lying at anchor, a sturdy, unlovely old slattern of the seas, worn and battered by years of toil. She was surrounded by an unbelievably large raft of pelicans. The ungainly birds were climbing over one another to crowd against her sun-blistered sides. Tommy explained that the vessel was taking on a large cargo of anchovies and sardines.

The bodies of sick and dead fish that came to the top of the water-filled wells reaching into the vessel's hold, were constantly being floated overboard. That's what the pelicans were after. They were bumming their breakfast.

The Portuguese skipper, a black-bearded, barefoot giant with a red handkerchief around his head, was leaning over the rail and had a tumbler of wine in one fist. He waved at us and bawled, "Hallo. You wan' feesh?"

Tommy hollered back, "Yeah. *Si*. You bet. Roosterfish. You savvy roosterfish?"

The skipper gulped his wine, wiped his mouth on his arm, and showed us a lot of white teeth. He pointed straight down. "Roosterfeesh," he said. "Planty roosterfeesh. Come aboard."

Twenty seconds later the *Cazadora* was alongside. The invitation to board the ship didn't make sense at first, but suddenly it made a lot of sense. We climbed a Jacob's ladder to the deck, and sloshed our way through seawater overflowing from the wells. Moribund fish, en route to the scuppers, bumped against our feet. Then we went forward and gazed over the rail. The pelicans had left a few open patches of water, and as we looked down through them we saw a sight to unhinge an angler's reason.

Fish were stacked up in layers for as deep as you could see. The small fish were attracted by the jettisoned sardines and anchovies, and the big fish were there to prey on the lesser fish. Near the surface was a vast school of seagoing catfish, the largest about eighteen inches. Below them were swift, flashing sierras and corbinas and a few cabrillas and sea bass. Farther down were small sand sharks, and deep down—thirty feet and more—were the big fish. We saw the golden blaze of a dolphin, a tremendous triangle that had to be a manta ray, and a sailfish. It was a fisherman's dream, in Technicolor.

I started to ask where the roosterfish were, but the question stuck in my throat because just then we saw them. They came out of the ship's shadow, down deep. There were about a dozen, swimming in an extended line and slanting toward the surface. They drifted through the hazy blue light, and then suddenly they were gone. It was like magic. Then, 100 feet out, the water erupted in big white splashes. The roosterfish had zoomed up in a surprise attack, and were now giving the works to the surface-feeding catfish. As they moved in closer, I saw how they make those white splashes. They shake a fish to kill it, just as a terrier shakes a rabbit. One of them actually tossed a catfish three feet into the air and caught it coming down.

"Gimme room, men," Pete said, "here's where I score!"

He baited up with a fat sardine and made a nice cast where the action seemed the heaviest. Every pelican on our side of the ship instantly started for the bait. There must have been around 250 pelicans flopping over the water toward Pete's sardine when one that was already in the air pitched down and grabbed it. He hooked himself. Then, panicky, he took off. But he spun right back after flying ten feet. He took off again, tried to climb over the boat, fouled a wing on the lines, and crash-landed on the deck. There he sat, chin tucked in, regarding us reproachfully. The Portuguese skipper, bellowing with laughter, unhooked the bird.

Pete baited up again. This time we fooled the pelicans. Tommy and I hurled bait fish in one direction, and, when the birds scrambled for them, Pete cast in the opposite direction. He dropped the sardine practically in the center of a roosterfish's splash. That did it. There was a gorgeous strike. Pete hit the fish back, and the battle was on.

Forty minutes later, after three of the skipper's crew had taken to a tender so they could shoo away the pelicans with oars and boat hooks, we brought a thirty-five-pounder to the gaff. His pitchfork dorsal was fourteen inches tall. We put him on ice. Then the skipper herded us into the galley and broke out cigars, glasses, and a bottle of amber wine.

It was a swell way to end a fishing trip, and not a bad note on which to end the story. But since I started to tell you about the Yanqui pilgrim under the laurel tree at La Paz, I guess I'd better tell you how he made out. He was a lucky kid. With most of the hotel's guests watching, and traffic nearly stopped, he hooked and landed a nice roosterfish—his first. When he came back with his prize, the redhead from Des Moines was sitting on the porch.

"Mamma was right," she said. "A gal can't compete with fish."

"Honey," he said, taking her hand, "your poppa must have been a roosterfish fan."

Needed: A New Deal for Alaska's Bears

Needless and wanton killing is now seriously threatening the future of the bears of Alaska.

Toward noon on this dazzling, hot July day, the game warden beached his canoe in the slack-water eddy at the mouth of Ten-Mile Creek. He unloaded his gear and was looking for a campsite, when from somewhere close ahead came the loud war whoop of a heavy rifle. Six shots, fired about as fast as a man could work the action. The game warden picked up his own rifle and followed a game trail through the creekside spruces to the rim of a redtop meadow. He had already smelled wood smoke, and so it was no surprise when he saw the camp. There was a mosquito tent pitched under a broad-armed cottonwood, a smoldering bark fire with a kettle hung over it, and a flat-bottomed riverboat pulled out into the grass.

Two men, obviously vacationers from town, were on the strip of sand beach 100 feet distant. They were examining the carcasses of two brown bears lying at the water's edge. Since the bears were wet and there were no tracks on the beach, it was clear they had swum the creek and been met on this side by the hail of rifle slugs. Their pelts were worthless—thin, sun-singed, and so badly rubbed that in places the hide showed. The game warden sighed as he faced the two men. He knew what he was going to hear, knew he was licked before he started, but he had to go through the routine.

"Why did you kill 'em?" he asked.

"Because they were about to attack us or molest our property," recited one of the men. "Page thirteen, paragraph three of the Alaska game laws."

The campers were within their legal rights, for the law states that in such circumstances any bear may be killed at any time or any place in the territory. And of course it is always the man with the gun who decides whether a bear is peaceful or hostile. His decision is final and nobody can gainsay it. You can't read a bear's mind, and if a man interprets a look, a movement, or mere proximity as evidence of dire intent, he can start shooting with the assurance the law is on his side. The purpose of the regulation is good, but it has been abused by spoilers, woods-shysters, and thoughtless characters from the Yukon to Ketchikan.

Then there was the case of the tenderfoot show-off. This one happened on Goose Creek, where I have my backwoods headquarters.

With his redheaded wife plodding behind him, the tenderfoot emerged from the birch-margined trail onto the wide reach of gravel bars at the fork of the creek, heading for the grayling hole where the two streams meet. He had taken only a few steps into the open, however, when he halted so abruptly he stumbled, and motioned excitedly for his wife to move alongside. Fifty yards distant, in a shallow riffle, stood a ragged, high-humped old sow grizzly and her two mustard-colored spring cubs. This was in early August, and the bears were catching spawned-out calico salmon. At the moment one of the tiger-barred, hook-nosed fish came splashing desperately up the riffle, its scarred back half out of water, using probably the last of its waning strength to reach deep water in which to die. The sow grizzly leaped at the fish, set her teeth in its head, and waded ashore with it.

She was strictly a peaceful wildlife neighbor, minding her own affairs.

But the tenderfoot didn't behave as well.

The guy was a phenomenon peculiar to Alaska—a resident tenderfoot. He was a merchant who had been in the territory five years, and who supported the popular theory that residence in a frontier city, plus a few hunting and fishing trips, automatically qualify one as a woodsman and an authority on wildlife. He was a psychological blood brother to the scores of newcomers who, immediately upon establishing legal residence, apply for a guide license for all Alaska, and bitterly cry fraud and favoritism when it is refused. Just now he was bent on showing his wife how casual and sophisticated was his regard for grizzly bears.

"Watch me," he whispered, "make that old bat jump."

While his wife clung to him, prettily frightened, he raised the .22 automatic rifle he carried and fired five hollowpoint, high-speed slugs into the she-bear's ribs. The bear dropped the salmon and whirled, bawling, to bite at her side. Then she fled into the brush, batting the cubs ahead of her. So great was her haste to escape that she crashed into a rotten birch snag, actually knocking it over. The tenderfoot thought this was very funny. He laughed so heartily he had to sit on the creek bank and hold his sides.

"Haw haw haw!" he wheezed. "Did you—haw haw!—see her barge head-on into that—haw haw!—tree? Funniest thing I ever saw in my life, so help me!"

He was still laughing that evening when he came back to the railroad to catch the train to town. When he had related the incident to me, with gestures and sound effects, I at once took my two dogs and a .405 bear rifle and mushed up the creek to warn the anglers camped there that we had a wounded grizzly on the stream. Some of the fishermen had children with them, and several were unarmed. Sensibly, these people broke camp and moved down toward the mouth of the creek. Their vacation was largely ruined, and their resentment toward the trigger-happy tenderfoot was so hot that, if he had still been around, I think they would have done him some violence.

Ten days later the payoff occurred.

My caretaker, old "Starvation" Smith, was working through a wild-rose jungle on the bank of a beaver slough below camp, looking for aromatic red willow to burn in the smokehouse, when suddenly there was a loud crashing in the brush behind him, accompanied by a hoarse roar. Luckily, Starvation has been a professional hunter all his life and is a hard man to take by surprise. As he jerked around, thumbing the safety latch of his .401 automatic, the grizzly broke out of the screening brush and bounded at him. She was fifteen feet distant, coming like a shaggy projectile, mouth wide open, paws reaching. Starvation had no time to aim. Firing by pure instinct and good gun sense, he shot her through the head and side-stepped, and as she rolled past him, shot her again through the heart.

She was the grizzly the tenderfoot had peppered with the .22.

Several of the hollowpoint slugs had gone between her ribs, entering the body cavity. Maggots were in the wounds, and her entrails were literally rotting. She was bloated and she stank. Her agony had been so terrible that she had bitten chunks out of her side. She had come here to the beaver slough apparently to plaster the wounds with cooling mud, and to await death. No more dangerous beast could be imagined. If anybody less alert and expert with a rifle than Starvation had happened past this place, a tragedy would have resulted. And of course a wave of indignation against grizzly bears would have spread over the territory. The animals would have been termed man-killers and obstacles to the settlement of the land, and no doubt—as has happened before—somebody would have tried to jam a bill through the legislature outlawing them.

For half a century since gold-rush days, Alaska has been known as the bear capital of the world. It has more bears to the square mile than any other country, and more species of bears. According to the census, or rather the educated guess, made a few years ago by the Fish and Wildlife Service, there were then around 100,000 of the animals in the territory, representing thirty-odd species and subspecies. Mostly they inhabit unsettled areas where they are not in conflict with human interests. True, they have killed a few head of cattle and sheep here and there, and have made nuisances of themselves raiding the caches and cabins of trappers and other backwoodsmen. Also several men have been killed by them, and others severely mauled—usually after the bears were wounded. By and large, though, they are shy and retiring by nature, and except in very special cases do not deliberately seek trouble.

Certainly the browns and grizzlies top the list of America's glamorous trophy animals, and as such are tremendously valuable assets.

But they are now in bad trouble. With thousands of newcomers swarming into the remote corners of the wilderness—construction men, soldiers, surveyors, airborne vacationers, and military technicians on special assignments—Alaska's bears must have a new deal, or they will be wiped out as were the grizzlies of California and the upper Missouri. Virtually every tenderfoot going into the wilds carries a rifle and has the consuming desire to kill a bear. They kill them out of season, kill females with unweaned cubs, kill the cubs themselves—for no other reason than to be able to boast that they have shot an Alaskan bear. It is meaningless to assert, as many do, that surely there are enough bears to go around. In the first place, the way they are being treated, there aren't enough. And in the second place, readers may recall that only a few years ago the same apologia was being made regarding Alaska's thousands of white mountain sheep and millions of caribou. Now the caribou have been whittled down to a pitiful remnant, and sheep may be hunted only in a few places.

Many old-time Alaska woodsmen, I regret to say, are as guilty as the newcomers in the ruthless, senseless slaughter of bears.

Consider the case of the sharpshooting gill-netter.

I had flown down Cook Inlet with a bush pilot to deliver mail and groceries to a commercial salmon-fishing camp. En route heavy weather closed in behind us, so we decided to spend the night there rather than return on instruments. When we woke in the morning, the tide was at full ebb, exposing nearly a mile of mud flat. And midway out to the surf, beachcombing back and forth across a creek bed, was a huge brown bear. With a great gathering of kittiwakes and other types of gulls hovering about him, he would pause to strike at a school of the myriad fat eulachon, or candlefish, running in the stream, or to dig a razor clam, or to paw through a raft of stranded seaweed in search of crabs, shrimp, or sea cucumbers. He was simply making his living as these coastal brown bears always have, disturbing nobody, as peaceful as the July morning itself.

We were watching the animal with our binoculars when the fisherman came outside the cabin and saw him. The fisherman had spent forty years in the territory. He was a trapper, an expert woodsman as well as a gill-netter, a man who took his entire living from the wildlife resources of the land. But like too many of his kind, he had a phobia against all bears, and never overlooked an opportunity to kill one. During a trip I had made into the Chugaches with him as a youngster, I saw him kill twelve of the animals—ten blacks and two grizzlies. Otherwise he was a fine fellow, good-natured, reasonable, intelligent. Probably more than any other old-timer I know, he understood the need for wildlife management and protection. Through experience and observation he had grasped the principles of the so-called balances of nature, the web of life, the interrelation of species. But he still hated bears.

"Well, well," he said with a broad grin of anticipation when he sighted the brown bear. "So I reckon we'll have us a little target practice before breakfast."

His rifle was a .270, equipped with a $2^{1}/_{2}$-power scope, and he used 130-grain bullets. For long-range shooting, it was a difficult combination to beat. With my glasses I saw the first bullet strike short and shower the bear with mud. The animal reared to his full height, facing us, rolling his head as he tried to see, wind, or hear us. As nearly as I could tell, the fisherman's next shot hit him in the belly, for he fell backward, biting at a spot below his brisket. Then he got up and fled, quartering away from us. Like all gut-shot animals, he traveled in a stiff, wavering lope, back humped. The fisherman, resting the .270 on one of the porch posts, missed the next three shots, reloaded, and dropped the bear with the sixth shot. It had been an utterly wanton, inexcusable performance. The bear's pelt at this time of year was valueless as a trophy. Besides, with the tide coming in fast and a half-mile of treacherous quick-muck between us and the carcass, we never could have reached the spot before the water covered it.

"What was the idea?" I asked.

We had been through this before and so the fisherman knew I was sore, and laughed. "Well, why not kill 'em?" he said. "The big rascals ain't good fer anything. You can't eat 'em, an' the government won't let you sell the skins. Also they're thieves, and—" he grinned at me—"I got a coupla nets out there on the mud with salmon in 'em. I was jest pertectin' m' propity."

Guides, lodge owners, and outfitters, of course, take exactly the opposite viewpoint from the bear haters. They have always ferociously opposed slaughter of the animals because to them bears have a definite cash value. When a guide knows where to find a brown or grizzly when he wants him, he regards the animal much as a farmer regards a crop item to be harvested at some time in the future, and meanwhile to be vigilantly protected. For instance, Leon Shellabarger, the twenty-three-year-old pilot and dude wrangler who operates in the Skwentna River wilds, tells me that he estimates each bear in that region is potentially worth $800 to him. If either he or his father caught anybody shooting Skwentna bears just to see which way they would fall, I am sure the guilty person would find himself in harrowing circumstances indeed. But unfortunately such conservation-minded professionals are sadly outnumbered and handicapped.

"There are just too many screwballs in the woods today with guns," I heard a veteran guide complain recently. "Most of 'em don't live here, and never intend to live here. They don't even buy licenses. But, believe me, they aim to kill a full share of our game before they pull up stakes and go home."

Nearly every sportsman, I suppose, is familiar with the rumor that military personnel in World War II illegally and defiantly killed much game in Alaska, especially bears. Beginning with the Jap landings in the Aleutians and the arrival of troops, the rumor spread through conservation circles, sportsmen's clubs, and editorial offices. It seems to me that now, with another Pacific war on our hands and renewed military activity in Alaska, the old whispers ought to be examined for what they were worth.

As a press correspondent with the armed forces in the North Pacific theater in World War II, I heard most of the talk and had excellent opportunity to evaluate it.

You heard that fighter pilots were machine-gunning grizzlies and giant brown bears in the mountains and on the open tundra of the Alaska Peninsula. You heard that observation planes were used to guide walkie-talkie-equipped gunners to bears in the lowland brush countries. You heard that sea-rescue teams, cruising the bays in army crash boats, target-practiced on bears sighted on the beaches. And you heard that troops in wilderness recreation camps set up by the army used automatic Grand rifles to kill practically every bear that showed itself in those areas.

Undeniably some of these stories were true.

In a storm-battered air force quonset on Adak I heard a young P-38 pilot describe how he killed three brown bears on the high tundra north of Cold Bay. He was a pleasant, likable lad, brought up in a big city, who had never gone hunting. The only bears he had ever seen from the ground were in a zoo. His job was ferrying fighter planes from Elmendorf Field at Anchorage to bases on the Aleutian chain, and the planes were armed. I don't believe he realized what a lousy thing he did when he machine-gunned the three bears. What he needed—what, in fact, all newcomers need who are likely to encounter bears in the Alaska wilds—was a thorough indoctrination course in sportsmanship and the value of wildlife.

"They were in a green flat grazing like horses," he said "and they looked as big as horses. I came in on the deck, out of the sun, and knocked one down the first pass. But he got up again and the three of them ran. But there was no place they could go, no place to hide. When I came back for the second pass, the wounded bear stood up and raised his paws, reaching for the plane. I got him in the sight and tripped the guns and he went down again, and this time stayed down. You guys wouldn't believe how those brown bears can take .50-caliber bullets. I put the other two down in one pass because they had turned and were standing motionless and close together watching me, and finished them the next time I came in. But they died hard—it took a long burst."

Well, nobody knows, or ever will know, how many brown bears were thus killed on the 500-mile reach of Alaska Peninsula brown bear country during the big war. It is a fact that the bear population there appears much lower than around 1943, but this decrease likely has been due to a combination of factors. From elsewhere in the territory, too, at the Japanese war's end came scattered reports from woodsmen indicating that fighter pilots and ground troops with automatic weapons machine-gunned bears they found in open country where there was no brush cover. I personally saw the carcasses of only two bears that apparently had been machine-gunned—a black on the Knik River bars and a grizzly on upper Montana Creek. Whenever I heard that a bullet-stitched carcass had been found, I tried to follow the rumor to its source and either disprove or authenticate it. I never was successful. Usually the chain of hearsay petered out when the original eyewitness account was attributed to some vague character who couldn't be located.

So I believe that the slaughter of bears by army personnel never was even approximately as great as rumor made it appear. And I believe that most of the illegal killing that was done took place in the very early stages of the war with Nippon, where commanders had not yet had time to get the existing problems in hand and make an adjustment between military and civilian affairs.

I know that when the first storm of protest about game killing reached military headquarters, all personnel was at once briefed on the game laws, and officers were held accountable for violations that might be committed by the men under them. After this was done, I visited a number of recreation camps and found no reason to suspect that illegal shooting was taking place. Also I had the opportunity to observe the behavior of soldiers making unsupervised weekend trips into the wilds. These troops without exception scrupulously respected the laws and showed themselves to be sportsmen. After the armistice, a party of sergeants was camped below me in the cottonwoods bordering a trout stream when, one night, a black bear came into the camp, snatched a ham out of the grub box, and knocked down a pup tent in his haste to escape with his loot.

"How come you didn't shoot him?" I asked. "Aw, we could have," the ranking sergeant said, "but hell, it was fun watching him. Anyway, we've got another ham."

Of all the gun-silly newcomers swarming over the North, I am convinced that construction company employees are the most irresponsible. These labor gangs are, or at least were, motley assemblages hired on contract for various government projects, including classified endeavors. They were picked up generally in big-city labor markets, and presumably the only criterion in the screening process at the hiring point was that a man must be capable of a day's work. If any of them ever was officially informed in advance of his arrival that Alaska has game laws, I never heard about it.

Some years ago, for example, a camp of 150 railroad workers was established on Goose Creek, within 300 yards of my house. The impact of this invasion on the wildlife in the valley was tragic, unnecessary, and unprecedented. Some of the men were fine, solid citizens, but among them were a number of typical big-town dead-end kids, tough and swaggering, loudly contemptuous of the backwoods and all its inhabitants. With their first paychecks they bought guns—.22 automatic pistols. The day they got these weapons in their possession, trouble began, and our Goose Creek bears bore the brunt of it.

Close behind the construction camp was a large, open garbage pit, and seemingly every bear that winded it came to investigate the place. After dark as many as a dozen bears would be in the pit at one time, rooting like pigs among the tin cans and heaps of kitchen refuse. They were completely unsophisticated bears, and seldom in their lives had they found such a windfall. One big, glossy black became so tame that he strolled into the mess hall one day, and departed only after a terrified cook had squirted him with a fire extinguisher. But this idyllic state of affairs ended abruptly for them when the shipment of pistols arrived. My wife Dell and I were eating supper the evening the first bursts of gunfire racketed through the dusky timber. In what amounted to a moment of clairvoyance, I told Dell then that it probably wouldn't be safe to go outside again for weeks unless she took both dogs and a gun with her.

Within minutes we heard a wounded bear crying in the birches behind the house, then another one below the house on the creek bank.

It developed that the tenderfoot gunmen had killed two bears and wounded an estimated four. They had placed spotlights on one side of the garbage pit, and waited until the evening's contingent of hungry bears arrived to feed. Then they switched on the lights and began shooting. Naturally they repeated the operation next evening, and this time killed one bear and wounded two. With six wounded bears now in the vicinity, the situation was so serious that I went to the camp superintendent and requested him to put a stop to the shooting. His response was curious.

"I know they're dangerous," he said. "One of 'em growled at me up the track tonight. If they really get tough, I'm going to have to get a rifle and kill all these bears."

Meantime the pistoleers had killed a moose calf and spent hours standing on the railroad bridge shooting salmon—for target practice, they said. In one evening I counted twenty-six fresh-run, ocean-bright salmon lying dead on the rim of the first gravel bar below the bridge. They never were used. Nobody so much as went down to look at them. Hoping it might accomplish something, I had a talk with the gunmen. I pointed out that they were nonresidents, and that to shoot big game they needed a $50 license and would have to be accompanied by a registered guide. I explained that the season wasn't open on bears, and that it was illegal to shoot big game with any gun chambered for rim-fire cartridges. I told them it was against the law to destroy salmon wantonly, and that there was a heavy penalty for shooting moose calves.

For my trouble I was invited to keep out of their affairs.

The climax of this incredible business occurred suddenly a few evenings later. Dell had walked down the track to pick some blueberries. When she was returning, and was just abreast of the construction camp, a bear stepped out of the brush onto the grade. The dead-end kids, it turned out, had already spotted him and prepared an ambush. They were in a safe position, lying in a row on the roof of the office car. As usual, they all opened fire at the same instant, throwing lead as fast as they could work their guns. The bear, a large black, was hard hit and fell to the ties, but lurched to his feet in a flash and headed toward Dell. I don't know whether he was charging or trying blindly to reach cover. In either case, the result no doubt would have been the same if the ambushers on the roof hadn't finished him with a second barrage of slugs.

When I heard about the matter a few minutes later, I belted on my gun, whistled to our eighty-six-pound Doberman pinscher, and went down to the camp and engaged the lads in pointed conversation in which I extended some invitations and made some promises. For some reason, they concluded they no longer cared about the region, and quit their jobs and took the next train to town.

My purpose in writing this piece is not to blow the whistle on any groups or individuals, but to show what has been going on—and is now going on—in Alaska bear ranges. The Fish and Wildlife Service, as I think everyone knows, is doing its best to protect all our game species. But due to a lack of funds, a shortage of trained personnel, and the vastly increased temporary, shifting population, it is faced with a heartbreaking task. The one solution seems to lie in public education in the fundamentals of sportsmanship, together with the acceptance of responsibility on the part of superintendents, foremen, and others in charge of crews working in the wilds.

There will always be plenty of bears in Alaska if they are given a break. Otherwise the animals are headed for the Happy Hunting Grounds. I hope they get a new deal soon.

Moose with the Gunshot Antler

When Buckskin said he wanted to go on an old-fashioned moose hunt, he didn't know what he was asking for, and certainly not that he'd be after the moose with the gunshot antler.

Old Tex Cobb and I called him Buckskin. He was a gray-headed, opinionated, likable little 135-pounder, a retired cotton broker, tough as whalebone, who was convinced that the present generation of big-game hunters was a putty-soft, luxury-demanding lot, most of whom ought to stay home and play lawn tennis. So he asked Tex and me to take him on a real, honest-to-gosh, rugged, old-fashioned moose hunt. We agreed to do it, and this is what happened. . . .

It was raining. It had been raining for three days. A cold, battering downpour with half a gale of wintry wind behind it. The peaks were hidden, the streams were swollen, and the lowering sky was the color of lead, promising still more rain. We had back-packed thirty miles from my homestead on the Alaska Railroad to the headwaters of the south fork of Montana Creek in the Talkeetnas. Buckskin himself picked the place because you've got to walk in—you can't get there either by airplane or packtrain—and because we assured him it was a fabulous moose rutting-ground in late autumn.

On this gray, dispiriting afternoon we were plodding single file along a game trail on the north bank of the creek. In a little meadow 400 yards beyond the brawling stream, two bull moose were fighting. Buckskin dropped his pack and jacked a shell into the chamber of his .300 magnum while Tex and I hastily got out our glasses for a look at the heads.

It was a tremendously exciting bit of primordial drama, what we saw of it. After circling each other at a distance of maybe fifty feet, the two great, dark, rain-wet beasts lunged together head on. So terrific was the impact that the clash of their antlers was audible above the lashing rain and the roar of the creek. They went to their knees, straining forward, rut-swollen necks bowed, scrambling with their hind feet. Then they bounded up and backed away. They danced and shook their heads and sparred, looking for an opening, marvelously fast and light-footed for animals of their size.

All at once I think the smaller of the pair decided he'd had enough, for he half turned as if to flee. This was a mistake. His opponent caught him broadside, lifted him off his feet on his war tines, and flung him sideways into a wash. He scrambled up, in full flight now, with the victorious bull raking his rump viciously—left, right, left—using his antler blades like a two-handed fighter trying hard for a kill. Unfortunately that was all we saw of the battle. Before you could light a cigarette they had crossed the patch of meadow and disappeared into the timber.

"That biggest critter had a good set o' hawns," observed Tex.

"So what are we waiting for—an act of Congress?" Buckskin demanded.

We forded the creek, and it was a mean job. The millrace current came to our hips, and it was liquid ice; football-size rocks were bumping along the bottom. We slanted across as craftily as we could, running on tiptoe when the full force of the current caught us. Buckskin made hard going of it. He didn't have weight enough to keep his feet on the bottom, and I think he would have floated away if Tex hadn't steadied him. A slant of current helped. Pushing against our backs, it slammed us in against a cut-bank, where we were able to grab some overhanging panted willows and drag ourselves out of the stream.

Buckskin was breathing hard and looked a little wild-eyed when we topped the bank. Tex patted him on the shoulder. Tex is craggy and stands over six feet; he has swamp-green eyes and a mane of iron-gray hair. At seventy-eight he is the apparently indestructible dean of Alaska's working woodsmen. His sense of humor is strictly primitive. "Now ye're operatin' like a real old-fashioned moose hunter," he assured Buckskin. "Bridges an' boats are fer sissies, an' don't ya never let nobody tell ya different."

At the rim of the little meadow where the two bulls had disappeared we found signs of further combat—blood, torn-up ground, a lot of hair. But the moose themselves seemed to have departed. We stood there in the head-high redtop grass listening. No sounds of battle. No banging of antlers or crashing of brush. Only the dreary beating of the rain and the wash and tumble of the stream. Presumably the fight was over, or else it was being continued in some other spot. To make certain, however, Tex and I asked Buckskin to remain in the open meadow while we made a swing across the wind. This way, if we jumped the bulls and they fled downwind, they would probably cross the meadow and he would get a shot. It was a good tactic, and it got results—but not the results we hoped for.

Tex and I eased in through the dripping, wind-clawed timber and tried to pick up the bulls' tracks. We didn't have a prayer. There was just too much moose sign thereabout. The wet ground was chopped up with hoof prints like a barnyard. There was dung everywhere, and nearly every bush and tree had shed hair clinging to it. At one point we struck a moose trail paralleling the creek that I at first thought was a road. It was a good six feet wide and twelve inches deep. This, of course, was the main migration trail leading down Montana Creek to the Susitna lowlands. In spring the moose follow it up to timberline, and when freeze-up comes they follow it back down to the big willow-dotted river flats. The only comparable game trails I have ever heard about were those the buffalo made in their seasonal wanderings across the Sioux prairies.

Tex and I stooged around in the wet brush a while, then gave up and headed back to the meadow. Just as we sighted Buckskin, things began happening. Behind us in the timber arose a wild, eerie, hair-raising ululation. As nearly as I can put it on paper, it was a contralto "*mmmm-whooo-uh-ahhh-woooo!*" with a tricky yodel in the middle. This was the love-song of an eager-beaver cow moose in heat, advertising for a boyfriend, and I am dog-goned glad I knew it. Otherwise, to quote the late Rex Beach on a similar occasion, I would have felt like cutting my suspenders and soaring over the treetops.

Buckskin was at a disadvantage. He had never before heard a torch-carrying cow moose sound off. I don't know what sort of dreadful critter he thought was doing the vocalizing. In view of what happened, I didn't feel like asking him. But Tex and I, watching through a screen of wind-whipped boughs, saw him jerk around and stiffen as if he'd been stabbed. He stood motionless a moment, then moved slowly through the tall grass toward the source of the weird cry. You could see he was braced for anything.

He held the magnum like a trapshooter waiting for his target. Afraid he might mistake us for something legally shootable, I was about to apprise him of our presence on the scene when the whole situation went completely screwball.

Out of the timber on the farther side of the meadow stepped a bull moose. I suppose he was the winner of the conflict we had witnessed. Anyway, he was quite a bull. He had a head to make your eyes bug out—sixty-eight inches at least. Wide, flat palms. A jungle of tines, points and pothooks. Beautifully matched brow antlers that gleamed like ivory in the wan light. He paced forward, some 150 feet behind Buckskin, taking it easy. Then the lovesick cow let out another urgent appeal for affection.

That did it. The outsize, wonder-antlered, rut-happy brute shook his head and came across the meadow like a tank on the rampage. Tex and I hadn't had time to form any plan of action at all. As I recall, I had some vague notion that we ought to let the bull get well clear of the timber before we hollered for Buckskin to look around. But that wasn't necessary now. The snare-drum pound of the animal's hoofs and the hoarse "aghrr-uh!" he uttered as he started his rush stopped Buckskin as if he had walked into a stone wall. He spun around, stared an instant in obvious disbelief, then snapped the magnum to his shoulder and fired.

It was a bad shot. As we learned later, the lens of the rifle's telescope sight was wet and covered with grass seeds. Buckskin couldn't find the bull's chest with the post. But at least he stopped the animal. The slug clipped a tine off the leading edge of the right antler, sliced a furrow across the palm and ripped splinters out of the trailing edge. Apparently half stunned by the impact, the bull turned and staggered out of sight and into a wash.

Buckskin had his chance then, but flubbed it. He climbed onto a windfall, chambering another shell, and should have been all set when the bull lurched back into view. But he wasn't. The wet, mossy bark of the spruce peeled under his feet, and he fell sprawling. Before he could get up, the bull had recovered and was on his way, out of sight in the timber.

It could be the animal actually was charging Buckskin; that he intended to demolish him as a warm-up to his projected courtship back in the timber. At one time or another during the past thirty years I have seen bull moose attack not only humans but automobiles, motorboats and locomotives. They definitely are dangerous. In fact, many woodsmen believe the Alaska bull moose is the most dangerous animal on the continent today. Maybe that's true, and maybe it isn't. But nobody would have had any trouble in convincing Buckskin. He was sold.

"That big so-and-so was trying to kill me," he declared when Tex and I joined him.

"Naw, he wasn't," Tex said gravely but with a glint of wicked humor in his green eyes. "He mistook ya fer a eligible moose heifer, that's all. Hit's the way ya climb over windfalls."

We floundered back across the creek and shouldered our rain-sodden packs. Tex had promised he would lead us to a dry, snug campsite—to a cave he had found a decade ago while prospecting through these peaks. It turned out to be some cave. It was about 500 feet above the valley floor, at the bottom of a soaring cliff streaked with veins of limestone. The entrance was ten feet high by twenty feet wide. But I have no idea how far back the cave went into the mountain. I didn't care to investigate, nor did Buckskin or Tex.

One reason was that the blank, echoing emptiness back there gave you the meemies. I had the feeling you could get so badly lost in that unknown blackness that they'd have to send out a search party for you on resurrection morning. Another reason was that the whole floor of the cave was covered with assorted animal tracks, including, believe it or not, moose tracks. It was pretty obvious that we weren't the only tenants of the place. Sooner or later, I figured, some variety of critter was bound to show up that would regard us as intruders. It proved to be a 100 percent accurate hunch, too.

But nothing untoward happened this first night, except that winter sneaked up on us. We built a good fire of cottonwood bark, dried our clothes, and kidded ourselves that a bannock apiece, some rice boiled with bacon rind, and a bucket of tea added up to a feast. We were now so short of grub that unless we made a kill immediately we would be on a rose-berry and Indian-potato diet—a combination of emergency provender that may provide energy for bears and parka squirrels, but is hell on humans. A man can carry only about ten days' grub with him in the Alaska wilds, plus his rifle and sleeping bag, and we had already been out six days. So we ate what we had, banked the fire, and went to bed hungry.

Along toward morning I awoke and smelled winter. I got up and went over to the cave mouth and felt snow underfoot. The valley was ghost-white under a scatter of high stars. The mountain wind rushing along the cliffs now had a different sound. It was sharp and thin and threatening with the music of freeze-up and the coming big cold and the snows.

But the white weather gave us one break. It was bringing the moose down from the secret pockets of the hills. With our glasses two mornings later we saw a network of fresh trails reaching clear across the valley. It looked as if twenty or thirty moose had drifted down into the timber overnight. The animals were gathering here to finish the rutting season before migrating to the Susitna lowlands.

So we barely paused for breakfast. We gulped some tea and squaw bread and hastened forth across the creek—the icy, murderous creek—to do ourselves proud. I figured this was going to be our big day. With so many moose practically in camp, finding and killing a trophy bull should have been a routine matter. Only it didn't work out that way. Our trouble was a snow weighted, boulder-studded, windfall-strewn jungle of six-foot-high wild raspberry bushes. Every fresh moose trail led into this diabolical mess of undergrowth, and none came out. So we had a kind of Hobson's choice to make—we could go in after the animals, or wait for them to come out. Neither move was good.

Buckskin, however, voted for action. And he got it, but not the sort we wanted. We Injuned into the snowy brush with the wind in our faces. With elaborate care we climbed over windfalls and worked around boulders. We plotted each step in advance. We parted the thorny brush with our bare hands and didn't crack a twig, and managed with Spartan fortitude to ignore the snow that fell down the back of our necks. As stalks go, it was a pretty good job, if I do say so myself—but it got us the cube root of zero.

Dead ahead, thirty feet distant, in a hollow behind a bushy-topped windfall, a yearling was bedded down. It had to be a yearling. He bounced up all ears and eyes, stared as if he suspected he was having a nightmare, and let out a snort that would have been credit to a moose three times his size. As an alarm-sounder he was a blue-ribbon wonder. He fixed everything. In two seconds the raspberry jungle was erupting moose. The animals apparently had been bedded down on three sides of us, and they took off in all directions.

A big gray cow tore past so close that I could have hit her with my hat. Then a little mulligan bull with hat-rack antlers, running blind like a spooked cayuse, dashed in on a collision course, saw us at the last instant, and swerved aside so abruptly that he tripped over a hidden log and went to his knees. Buckskin was trying to climb to a vantage-point on a boulder. He was partway up the rock, with Tex boosting him, when a trophy bull slammed past on the trail of the gray cow. It was our belligerent friend of yesterday. As he banked his spread of antlers to clear a spruce snag the gunshot mark across the right antler was plain as a streak of paint.

Buckskin swiveled around desperately from the face of the boulder and, supported chiefly by thin air, tried to get in a shot. He didn't have a chance. Before he could begin to line the magnum, the bull was gone.

"Danged if I ain't beginnin' to understand," Tex remarked solemnly, "why so many o' the real old-time hunters got the hell outa the mountains an' took up saloon keepin'. This sorta life was jest too tough fer 'em."

Buckskin let that one pass.

Wet to the hips, shivering, with snow balling up on our pants and pacs, we headed out across the valley in the direction the stampeding moose had taken. We cut the trail of a grizzly. A flock of spruce chickens boomed into the trees and sat cackling idiotically at us. Somewhere away off on the far rim of the gray day a wolf howled. We slogged on, angling away from the creek now.

Thirty minutes and a mile later, episode number two of the day occurred. We were picking our way through a rose thicket when a thrilling sound brought us to a halt—the sound of antler tines rattling on dead wood. We listened for five minutes, but didn't hear it again. Then suddenly, fifty yards distant, I saw the top of a jack-spruce snag weave against the sky. Hope rose in my bosom. A bull moose was over there polishing his antlers to make himself pretty to the cows and fearsome to his rivals.

This time we didn't risk a stalk. The rose brush was uncommonly dense, and could have trapped us into another fiasco like the one in the raspberry jungle. I tried something else. I got out my belt knife and carefully, gently rattled the bone handle against a dead limb. Nothing happened. I waited a while and tried it again. Nope. But the snag top had stopped gyrating. Then snow crunched on our left.

Out of the barrier of brush strode an ancient bull. If he wasn't the oldest bull moose in Alaska, he was a runner-up for the honor. He was sway-backed, pot-bellied and gray as a marmot. His antlers were mere clubs sticking out from his skull. No palmation. No war tines. A caricature of a head, studded with bumps and warts of bone. But he was doing all right for his years. Behind him in the brush, semaphoring their big ears at us, were two sleek, seal-brown young cows. Buckskin groaned. Lowering the magnum, he picked up a branch and threw it at the patriarch.

"Beat it!" he snarled. "Scram—before you start looking like a trophy bull to me."

We headed for camp. After loading ourselves like pack mules with long shells of dry cottonwood bark for fuel, we climbed the snow-slippery slope to the cave. We built a nice fire at the entrance—a hot, cheerful one that made us forget the freezing white wilderness outside and the mysterious, black, whispering cavern depths behind us. Snug in our shell of light and warmth, we once more dined on rice, bannock and tea. And then we went to bed hungry again. I guess it was around three o'clock when Buckskin shook me awake.

"What's that standing against the cave wall?" he whispered.

He had a good question there. I turned cautiously and took a look, and saw what he meant, all right. Between us and the entrance, in a patch of gloom that the sift of starlight couldn't reach, was a formless blob of deeper gloom. It was sizable. Even allowing for one's tendency to overestimate size in such circumstances, I figured it had approximately the displacement of a telephone booth. And it was moving. You could hear it moving. It brushed audibly against the cave wall. It was breathing in an anticipatory, asthmatic sort of way. It gritted its teeth. Anyway, I think it gritted its teeth; that's what it sounded like.

Then it moved closer, and seemed to be either fumbling with the foot of Tex's sleeping bag or taking an inventory of our grub sack. If Tex never forgives me for this, it was the latter possibility that made my hair stand on end. Those few scraps and odds and ends of grub were more precious than rubies. I touched Buckskin's shoulder to warn him. Finding a match, I lit it with my thumbnail.

Eight feet distant, vast and shaggy in the yellow flare of the match, stood a bear! I couldn't tell what kind of bear, but he was a big one. I mean, he was no adolescent bruin. His eyes glittered green in the matchlight. His wavering, grotesque shadow in the cave wall looked as if it were about to step past its owner and pounce on us. He was standing broadside, looking at us over his shoulder, the way bears often do when in a hard-boiled mood.

What made the situation truly desperate was that the animal had been looting the grub sack. In his mouth he had our sole remaining can of jam. It was peach jam, and Buckskin had been cherishing it. In fact, we had all been cherishing it. We had looked forward to opening that wonderful can of jam the way kids look forward to Christmas. So I guess the action Buckskin took was pardonable. As a rule, no woodsman with a brain in his head would advocate opening fire on a large bear at a distance of eight feet by matchlight in a cave. There is no future in it. But Buckskin felt he had to rescue our jam.

The magnum's report blew out the match and seemed to rock the cave. The bear let out a strangled bawl and fell across Tex's legs. Tex woke up with a wild yell, extricated himself somehow, and fled on his hands and knees toward the back of the cave. I found another match and lit it, but just as I did so Buckskin shot again and the muzzle blast blew this match out too. He scored a hit on the bear, though, and the animal stopped kicking. For an instant quiet descended upon the cave.

Then Tex's voice broke the silence. "If nobody minds," he said querulously, "an' you guys ain't too busy, would ya please inform me jest what's goin' on in here?"

I explained, and we got a birch-bark torch lit. The bear was a black, the biggest one I ever laid eyes on—for a guess, 500 pounds. Possibly he had come to the cave to hibernate and no doubt had been delighted to find a bedtime snack of the white man's grub laid out for him. Tex and I regarded the bear as a heaven-sent boon. For a man on the trail in cold weather there is no better food than fat bear meat. But Buckskin was disturbed. He couldn't find the can of peach jam. In the smoky light of the bark torch he went over the cave floor foot by foot. No can of jam.

Then, when Tex and I had whetted our belt knives and were about to open up the bear carcass, we observed that the animal's entire head had been reduced to a bloody pulp. We knew the magnum was a hard-hitting weapon, but hadn't known it was that hard-hitting. Investigation revealed what had happened. The bear had turned toward us with the can of jam between his teeth, and the first slug had hit the can and exploded it like a bomb in the animal's mouth. When we knew the jam was irretrievably lost, Buckskin was thoroughly disconsolate. So Tex tried to cheer him up in his peculiar fashion.

"Cain't think of a better way to kill a bear," he declared. "Danged if I ain't gonna try hit my ownself. Catch one with a can o' jam in his mouth an' blow hit right through the back o' his neck. You pilgrims sure can teach us sourdoughs some new tricks."

Buckskin muttered something unprintable and went back to bed.

Next morning there was ice on the water-bucket. You could see your breath in the frosty air. But the sun rose big and generous in a flawless arch of sky. With the flood of unstained new light across it, the valley was all diamond glitter and blue velvet shadow. We breakfasted on tea and roasted bear liver, and went down into the valley to look for tracks. There were some fresh ones, made during the night—five or six sets, bulls and cows.

We followed them two miles downstream to a dense island of spruce under a graywacke cliff. Here we were again confronted with a tactical problem. The snow under the trees was crusted and noisy; so if we went in after the animals they would hear us and spook. And if we circled the timber trying to get a look at them, they would scent us and likewise spook. Tex gave me a sidewise glance. He said he hated to suggest it, but it seemed to him the situation called for some moose talk.

Now, moose-calling is a chore that I loathe. It is largely just a stunt; besides, it always makes me feel silly to sit under a tree in some forlorn spot, with an audience, and make with the uncouth grunts, wails and moans of a romantic moose. But today it seemed necessary. It was a slim chance, but the only one we had. Any other stratagem would certainly get us into a repeat performance of the raspberry-jungle mess. So I peeled some bark off a half-frozen birch and made a horn. Then I squatted on the off side of a spruce with the horn an inch or two from the ground, and gave out with the warlock song of an amorous cow advertising for a boyfriend.

I did my best. I tried to imagine I was a lonely wallflower batting around in the snowy timber by myself while all the belles of the herd had mates. Boy, it was a sorry state of affairs, and wasn't there a big, wide-antlered, deep-chested, handsome Romeo bull somewhere hereabouts who would go for a blind date and, if so, hasten this way, Buster, with all possible speed.

"Hey, hold it," Tex whispered. "Either there's a danged pecooliar echo in this timber, or you got expert competition."

We listened with great interest. Somewhere a raven uttered a bell-like "bonk-bonk." The wind cried in the spruce tops and there was the long whisper of mush-ice jamming in the creek. Then, startlingly close, a cow moose sounded off. She was expert competition, all right. By comparison I was Jimmy Durante substituting for a Met star. But she gave Buckskin an incandescent idea. Beaming, he whispered that the thing for us to do was to seek a vantage-point—the top of yonder cottonwood would be ideal—and let the cow call up a bull for us. He made it sound quite feasible. So, with my inborn flair for entangling myself in lunatic enterprises, I agreed to try it. I guess we had reached the point where we were willing to try anything.

What happened was pretty sad. Also humiliating.

We climbed the cottonwood and perched in the topmost branches. No cow in sight. No bull. No nothing. And the cow didn't sound off again. We waited ten minutes, then Tex tossed the horn up to me and motioned for me to make some more moose talk. He wouldn't do it himself because he claims it hurts his throat. Makes him cough. I think he is a liar, but have never been able to prove it. So I was stuck; I had to give out with the moose talk again. And if you think it was crazy, I'm on your side. What bull moose ever heard a lady moose calling seductively from a treetop? But like so many zany stunts, this one at least stirred up some action.

I bawled through the horn—and three moose stepped into view. Two cows and a bull, in a tiny opening a hundred yards distant. They were facing us and gazing upward. I don't know whether moose can properly be said to wear puzzled expressions, but that's the way these three looked to me. I guess they thought some female member of their tribe had gone nuts but good. Then the bull moved forward into a shaft of sunlight, and I heard Buckskin suck in his breath. It was our bull with the gunshot antler.

The cows inadvertently saved their boyfriend. They crowded alongside as Buckskin was lining his sights, and blanked the bull's neck and shoulders. Then all the bull's neck and shoulders. Then all three moose started across the opening toward the timber. Buckskin tried. He held on the bull's hump—about eight inches of target—hoping to put the .300 slug through the animal's spine. It didn't work. The shot went too high. With the crash of the magnum a tuft of hair whipped out of the top of the bull's mane. That was all and that was the end of it. Before Buckskin could chamber another shell, the animals were out of sight in the close-packed spruces. We slid out of the tree and went over for a look to make sure. There was no blood on the snow. No blood or flesh on the bullet-clipped tuft of hair. The bull wasn't even scratched. I asked Buckskin if he wanted to follow the animals, and he said no.

"I'm heading for camp," he said. "The hell with that moose—with all moose. Suddenly I have a grudge against every moose in the world. I don't think I'd shoot a record bull if he came right up and asked me, pretty please."

Came the payoff, the big, wonderful, golden payoff. Thirty minutes had passed. We were mushing somberly back upstream through the snow and had covered maybe a mile. As we topped a little bank at the rim of some cottonwoods, there, about a hundred feet distant, standing under a tree, stone-still, staring at us, was our bull. I think I know why he was here. He had figured we would trail him, and so had run in a circle. And our route home had cut the circle and intercepted him as neatly as an engineer could have plotted it.

Buckskin did all right this time. The little gods of luck were with him, and he couldn't lose. He brought the magnum up like a champion and squeezed it off, and the bull hit the snowy ground so hard that he bounced. It was a good head, a head to be proud of—sixty-nine inches. Perfect formation. A head and a hunt to tell your grandchildren about.

Then it was dusk and we were back in the cave, beside a cottonwood fire, eating bear chops and moose tongue. Tex asked Buckskin if he still favored the real old-fashioned way of hunting.

"Well—uh—sure," Buckskin said. "Y'see, everybody ought to try it—once. Then he'd appreciate airplanes, horses and all such marvelous conveniences of our effete civilization."

Viva Mayheeco!

Beginning—the adventures of a roving Yankee sportsman down Mexico way. You won't forget these tales of a killer whale and a tiger that liked turkey meat!

Everything happens in Mexico. Mexico doesn't have the atom bomb, and it is short on hamburger stands, drive-in theaters, four-lane highways, natural blondes, and other aids and comforts to mankind, which are taken for granted here in our country 'tis of thee. But it has other assets. Especially it has some fifty million of the doggondest, most colorful, and baffling characters who ever delighted a wayfaring gringo and—of course—clipped the poor bemused joker for a few fast bucks.

For example, consider my friend Joselito Alfredo Rudolpho Valdez.

Joselito is a guide and gold prospector. He lives in northern Sinaloa. He is maybe thirty years old and looks enough like a bandit to warm the icy cockles of a Hollywood casting director's heart. Holstered under his cactus-scarred cowhide vest is an old thumb-busting .45 single-action Colt. On his belt he totes a glittering, razor-edged machete that falls just short of saber specifications. He walks with a vaquero's bold swagger and wears jangling, outsize spurs with which, I'll bet, he could gut a buffalo with one swipe. I mean to say, he looks tough and really is tough.

Yet Joselito is a nice guy. Even after what happened I still say he is.

We went turkey hunting together. This was on a sweet, copper-and-turquoise autumn morning in the theatrically broken pine sierras above Joselito's box shaped backwoods adobe hut. It was supposed to be a very special hunt, not for ordinary wild turkeys—no indeed, *señor*—but for royal wild turkeys. *Pavos real.* Now I had never before heard of a royal wild turkey. Moreover I had the dirty suspicion that nobody else ever had either. But Joselito swore they existed. He said he knew right where to find a flock. The distinguishing characteristics of the birds, he informed me, were their uncommon size, the superior flavor of their flesh, and the fact that the gobblers' tails, when spread, glittered with the colors of the rainbow.

"The *pavo real, amigo*, ees the mos' handsome turkey een the whole world," he declared, clapping me on the back, "an' the best to eat, *por Dios*."

He eyed me to gauge the effect of his sales talk and, apparently satisfied, added that the day's hunt would set me back fifty pesos.

I fell for it whole hog. As no doubt, gentle reader, you would have too.

We climbed on horseback for an hour or so, then we tied the horses and climbed afoot awhile. Then we ate a lunch of mashed black beans and *tortillas*, using the *tortillas* as forks, napkins, and supplementary fodder, and then Joselito insisted on a siesta. After the siesta we climbed some more. Eventually, sweating and brush-clawed, we came out on a jagged red crest split by a timbered notch. Here Joselito began to operate. And here occurred one of the most humiliating episodes in my career as a foot-loose sportsman.

Joselito was carrying a sack over his shoulder. Out of the sack he brought a family treasure, a turkey call, which he said had been made by his great-grandfather. The call consisted of a box about the size of a cigar box, made of some dark, glowing jungle wood. Mortised snugly into one side of the box and reaching from end to end was a narrow piece of slate. And cut into the other side were sound holes, intricately formed and embellished with stylized Aztec-type carvings of Indian hunters and strutting turkeys. Sound was produced from the box by drawing a pointed section of turkey wing bone over the piece of slate. The handsome gadget was a collector's item, and Joselito was good with it. He could really make it talk turkey. The flutelike chirps and occasional low squawks he scraped off that chunk of slate sounded just like a matriarchal hen turkey and her brood of half-grown young ones foraging over the crest and trying to keep track of one another.

It wasn't the technique the boys in Alabama, Texas, and Arizona use, but it sounded good. I figured that if there was a turkey on this watershed, royal variety or otherwise, we had a chance for some action.

We got action, all right. Only it sure as blazes wasn't the kind I expected.

An hour dragged past. The sun slid down the brilliant sky. A couple of buzzards looked us over hopefully and went away. A flight of emerald-green parrots streamed overhead, cussing us, and pitched down into the timber. Otherwise nothing happened. I was about to say the hell with it, let's try somewhere else, when I saw something that put icy fingers in my hair.

Directly behind us, in the eye of the sun, was a jagged cockade of lava rock perhaps twenty feet high. Its shadow was moving. As I watched, fascinated, the blob of shifting shadow abruptly took form—the form of a huge out-of-drawing cat. Joselito saw it the instant I jerked around slipping the safety latch off the 12-gauge I was carrying. "*Santa Maria!*" he croaked. "*A tigre!*"

It was some *tigre*. I don't know how big Sinaloa *tigres* grow, because nobody had kept records, but anyway this one was a specimen to write home about. He was scrooched down in a half crouch staring at us. Forty feet distant and twenty feet above us. Of course he was looking for the flock of turkeys he thought he had heard. In return for the privilege of taking the handsome spotted brute's pelt, I would willingly have mortgaged the homestead. But armed only with the 12-gauge and No. 4 shot, I wanted no part of him, believe me. Too many men in these wilds have been mauled trying to kill *tigres* with scatter-guns and assorted inadequate weapons. So I just sat there holding my breath, hoping the critter was a gentleman and wouldn't take advantage of the situation.

He switched his tail a couple of times and showed his teeth and flattened his ears. Then he spun around and vanished instantly and soundlessly. Joselito, suddenly full of bravado, yanked out his venerable .45 and let go a blast after the *tigre*—which came nowhere near the cat but definitely ruined our chances of getting a shot at a turkey on that mountain that day. So we plodded back to camp, neither of us in a conversational mood.

In the morning, deciding I'd had enough, I told Joselito I was leaving, and held out a fifty-peso note. But he shook his head and refused to take it. He was smiling, but his eyes were like polished obsidian.

"It is not enough, *señor*," he said. "Fifty pesos is a fair-day's pay for a man who can call turkeys. But for a man who can call a *tigre*"—he threw back his shoulders and stuck out his chest—"the correct pay is 100 pesos."

Ah, Mexico. I paid him. After all, he had a point. And the episode was educational.

From Sinaloa I drifted over the ancient, palm-plumed port of La Paz, in Baja California, to try for black marlin and sailfish. My fishing luck could have been better, but I am glad I went. Because if I hadn't I wouldn't have met Jesus Escobar, the cop, and the unique experience of being chased ashore—weird as it sounds—practically into the midst of a formal dancing party by a locoed, blood-hungry, jaw-popping demon of a killer whale.

This Jesus—pronounced Haysoos—was a pleasant fellow as Mexican gendarmes go. He was young and spruce, dangerous-looking in a relaxed George Raft sort of way, and probably was honest and an excellent guardian of law and order. But he was uniform-happy—a fact that almost resulted in my hasty departure from this vale of fun, tears, and taxes. Although I never saw the guy in daylight, we soon became fast nocturnal pals. I was staying at the Perla Hotel, and Jesus was assigned to the waterfront block the hotel occupies, working the eight to four night shift. When he came on duty I would get some cold cokes from the cantina and go across the street to the *malecón*—the sea-wall promenade along the rim of the old pirates' beach—and we would sit on the stone bench there under the big *laurel de la India* tree and talk about this and that and watch the girls parade past arm in arm while we drank the cokes.

Jesus aimed to be decorative. He had a streak of ham in him that was strictly from Smithfield. He was meticulous about the hang of his hand-carved gun belt with its polished forward-tilted quick-draw holster sagging under the weight of a .45 auto complete with monogrammed pearl buttplates. He never could get enough glitter on his brass buttons and the blue-enameled police insigne decorating his cap. He wouldn't cross his knees for fear he'd lose the crease in his suntan khaki pants, and he manifestly lived in mortal terror that he would disgrace himself by sweating through his shirt. And he always managed to sit so that the light from the street lamps fell on him to the best advantage.

Tonight two things were happening within our range of vision. There was a society dance on the wide tiled veranda of the hotel—

colored paper lanterns, guitars, *señoritas* in wide skirts and gaudy *rebozos*, *caballeros* in ruffled shirts and peg-bottomed pants. And on the deck of a ship at the end of the municipal pier, 150 yards distant, seamen were slaughtering a couple of steers. The latter project was a thrifty move on the part of the skipper to beat the city tax levied for each beef animal killed ashore. The tide was running out, and we could hear soggy splashes as the butchers threw entrails and other unwanted parts over the stern.

"*Ai Chihuahua*, but it is hot tonight," Jesus grumbled, patting himself worriedly under the arms to discover if the worst had happened and he had sweat-stained his shirt. "How I would like to go swimming."

I hadn't thought about a swim before, but now it struck me as being a heck of a swell idea. So I abandoned Jesus to the promenading *señoritas* and climbed down the sea wall and crossed the narrow sand beach to the water. As I was wearing swimming trunks under my pants, all I had to do was shed the superfluous clothes and wade in. The water was around sixty degrees and felt wonderful. I porpoised around awhile and then headed out toward the end of the pier. At this point I heard a wild yell of admonition from Jesus.

"Come back!" he hollered. "Back to shore, pronto!"

I thought, the poor character doesn't know I'm wearing trunks and is throwing his weight around in behalf of the town belles' modesty. So I shouted back that I was suitably covered and to shut up, *por favor*, before the riot squad was alerted. It didn't get me anything. I saw Jesus leap down the side of the sea wall, pull his gun, and dash toward the water's edge. He was in such a hurry that he stumbled over a chunk of driftwood and fell sprawling, his cap flying off his head into the shadows. Convinced by the drawn .45 that I was really in trouble, I started back to the beach, cussing the thickheadedness of cops in general, and hoping that Jesus had ruined the press of his pretty pants when he fell down.

People were running across the street from the dance now. The music had stopped. I heard a girl scream.

I shouted, "Take it easy. What in the—"

Behind me—close behind me—the bay erupted.

There was a sharp, whistling snort, like the pop-valve of a steam boiler letting go. Something slammed the water so hard that spray flew over me and I felt the concussion against my body. I half rolled and looked back, and there it was—tall as a fence post, black in the reflected shine of the street lamps and the colored lanterns of the hotel veranda—the dorsal fin of a bull killer whale. The animal was headed straight at me. Right then I would have sold out for one cent on the dollar. Killer whales were old acquaintances of mine. I had seen them operate from the Arctic to Acapulco, and didn't need a natural history textbook to tell me they were the most savage, gosh-awful assassins in the animal kingdom. Off the Aleutians I had seen them kill giant baleen whales. On the ice near Point Hope, Alaska, I had seen a killer lunge half his sixteen-foot length onto a floe to grab a basking ring seal. At Chinitna Bay, on Cook's Inlet, I had been a popeyed witness when a pack of killers drove a herd of white beluga whales into a cove and cut them to pieces.

Now when it comes to fast swimming I am no Duke Kahanamoku, but in this desperate emergency I think I would have interested an Olympic swimming coach. I lit out for shore in a ten-beat American crawl I didn't know I possessed. I felt as if I could have passed a dolphin, a flying fish, a wahoo. And I made it. I hit the beach so hard a rock knocked a divot out of my chin, and bounded to my feet like a spooked antelope and sprinted right up the sea wall and into the knot of spectators assembled from the dance.

I didn't know it at the time, but what saved me was the fact that the killer had gone aground. He had followed the blood scent of the slaughtered steers up the tide, then had seen me frolicking about dumb, fat, and happy, and had decided to collect me as an appetizer. But the water was too shallow for him. Jesus, of course, had sighted the fin before I had, and had been trying to warn me. He came up to me now, brushing his pants with one hand and straightening his gun belt with the other.

"What in hell do you carry a gun for?" I demanded. "Why didn't you blast a clip at that varmint to turn him?"

"*Señor*," he replied stiffly, "I fell down—and in the darkness lost my cap."

I wouldn't fool you. That's exactly what he said. He had lost his cap. True, the .45 wouldn't have done any good anyway, and Jesus probably knew the killer was aground, and I was safe, but still, he had been temporarily out of uniform and therefore out of business. It's a wonderful country. . . .

I have always wanted to write a ghost story and I guess this is my chance. The yarn isn't exactly a chiller-thriller, but I think you'll have to admit it's different, and that it has a pay-off as Mexican as frijoles.

It was December again and the ducks and geese had streamed down the Pacific flyway from the high north . . . and tonight was a black night with a million blazing stars, with a thin fog rising in witch shapes from the hostile Yaqui River. I had come over from Bacochibampo Bay for a hunt with Jimmy Robinson. Jimmy is the ineffable, roly-poly, quick-eyed, nervous, cigar-chewing, loud-shirted, name-dropping, orange-gallused scatter-gun genius who conducts a shooting column in the pages of this magazine. This was his first hunting trip here and the country was giving him the works, no holds barred.

We'd had a lousy day. First our sport cruiser had come within a whisper of swamping in the wild maelstrom of the Yaqui bar, the charts of which are as vague as a communist's testimony. Then we had hunted until sunset with no luck. The sky was filled with clamorous skeins of waterfowl, but they were all bound elsewhere. Now, to make a discouraging situation worse, our boat was hard and fast aground in the middle of the channel, and the tide was going out. Jimmy and his wife Clara, and Tommy Jamison, sport fishing director at the Miramar Hotel, and his wife Dinah, were playing poker under a gas lamp in the cabin, trying to forget our troubles.

I was at the stern with Tippy Ral, the mate. Tippy and I were listening to Yaqui ghost wailing on the low, hidden shore.

Anyway local legend said it was a Yaqui ghost. Tippy himself believed it was. But Tippy was in no mood to be impressed by the supernatural. He had drunk water from a spring ashore, which had put his bowels into a remarkable turmoil. He was wan and haggard, and every few minutes would utter a groan of despair and, clutching his belt buckle, dash forward past the card players to the compartment mariners refer to as the head. The spring, he said, was loaded with a mineral resembling epsom salts in effect, and he blamed himself bitterly for not detecting it at the first swallow. Normally Tippy is a lighthearted fellow, a famed singer and guitar player. But tonight he said he expected to perish unless Saint Francis came to his aid—and he rather doubted that Saint Francis would, on account of once before when he was in trouble he had recklessly promised Saint Francis a piece of gold in return for assistance, and never had gotten around to paying the debt.

I tried to concentrate on the Yaqui ghost.

If whatever was keening on the hidden shore was a bird or animal, its voice was new to me. It sounded precisely like a human in the throes of insupportable grief. According to fisherman and

Yaqui hunters, the spook was that of an Indian who had been cut down by a conquistador back in the bad old days when the steel-shirted, black-bearded adventurers from Spain were devaluating Montezuma's empire. This Indian and his young, pretty wife were hoeing maize on the riverbank, the tale goes, when the conquistador rode up and, after expertly appraising the woman, decided that an amorous interlude was in order. So he forthwith ran a yard of Toledo steel through the husband, and with no further formalities took possession of the widow. The lady apparently was no dope. She pretended to acquiesce until she could ease the conquistador's pistol from its holster. Then, placing the muzzle against the back of the luckless Spaniard's neck, she pulled the trigger. The ball shattered his spine and, continuing through, broke hers as well.

The ghost—the Yaqui *espanto*—is said to be that of the murdered husband crying for his wife.

Jimmy, who had just won three pots in a row and so was only mildly interested in the unhappy phantom, looked up casually as Tippy lurched drearily back to the stern, and said, "D'ya think that's really an Indian spook over there putting on a Chloe solo for his ravished wife?"

"No," Tippy replied weakly, leaning against a stanchion. "I think it's a ghost, but he isn't crying because of his wife." Tippy started suddenly and, eyes bugging out, staggered hastily forward again. Over his shoulder he said, "Obviously the ghost is crying, *señor*, because he also drank some of that horrible epsom salts water in the spring over there."

The Old Brown Bear, She Ain't What She Used to Be

Once there was a shaggy, shanty-backed old brown bear who had swaggered up and down the Alaska wilds for maybe thirty years. He was about the size of a brewery horse, tough as a skid-row steak, and powerful enough to shake the living kapok out of the orneriest lion or tiger that ever grew hair. So listen to what happened to him one black night on the Kenai. . . .

This time I was hunting with Buck. We had been over toward Swan Lake for moose, and now were pushing our pack string down Resurrection Creek in a cold late-autumn rain, heading for town. Buck is a dark, volatile little 130-pounder from the Tennessee cotton belt. He is a professional dude who spends six months of the year hunting, fishing or batting around in the mountains with a packtrain, on account of he thinks that's the way a natural man ought to live. His great hope is that someday he will be mistaken for a hoss wrangler or, better yet, a sheepherder. To this end he lets his whiskers and hair grow, wears beat up western clothes and cultivates a Hopalong Cassidy dialect. It doesn't get him anything. All he has to do is ride into a strange town and step down, and the natives rally round and ask who's guiding him, where his camp is located, and would he like to attend the chamber-of-commerce luncheon?

Today we were in trouble. There was supposed to be a trail down Resurrection, but it must have dated back to Little Father Baranof's time, because I couldn't find it. I got the ten pack ponies loused up in a horrible sequence of alder jungles, bogs, side canyons and impossible mud slides. So I slanted back to the creek, and didn't do any better there. To make it worse, the horses were bone-tired and getting rebellious, and dusk was coming on. The rain was plain hell—one of those icy, battering, dispiriting prewinter downpours, part snow at times. With a raw gusty wind behind it, it was stripping the bright leaves from the willows and aspens, soaking through the pack mantles, and starting freshets in every hillside gully. I was wishing I had stayed home as a youngster and made a nice living as a soda jerk or bellhop, when the worst mishap of the day smote us. We got into a nightmarish mess of blowdown, lying crisscrossed at the height of a horse's chest on both sides of the creek.

Buck spurred alongside me, with water streaming off his hat and the wind whipping the tails of his saddle slicker, and said wearily, "Pardner, let us pull the packs off these broom tails and put up camp while we still got some light left. Ah'm plumb beat an' Ah admit it."

Skip two hours to a scene in the tent. It was black dark now, black as the inside of a moose. Buck and I were stoking the whuffing, cherry-red Yukon stove, trying to get some warmth back into our half-refrigerated frames. A single candle stuck on a tin plate flared and fluttered wildly. Rain thundered with unabated force on the bellying canvas and the gusty storm wind screamed down the canyon like a wounded gray lynx. Somewhere out in the darkness the close-hobbled horses were stooging forlornly about in the fallen timber, seeking such miserable forage as the place afforded. One of the ponies, a barn-broke black pinto we sometimes kept tied at camp as a wrangling mount, was so discouraged with the setup that he had already come to the tent several times seeking shelter or sympathy, or both. Buck was afraid he'd blunder into the tent ropes and bring our bivouac down upon us. It had happened on other occasions.

So now, when a heavy body brushed against one of the ropes and made the tent lurch, and a loud snort sounded just outside the flaps, Buck took remedial action. He leaped up, grabbed a frying pan, and gritted, "This time I'm gonna beat that spotted fool's ears off." He lifted the canvas and slipped quickly under it. I heard the frying pan come down hard and solid on bone. Twice. Then I heard Buck yell, and heard a hoarse, startled *whowff-whowff!* Then there was the sound of something like a bulldozer crashing recklessly through the windthrown timber. Buck came back into the tent faster than he had departed. He snatched up his .270, and without a word went over to his sack and got out a flask of brandy. When he had taken the flask down a couple of inches, he stood there pale and scare-eyed, shaking all over. I told him that he hadn't ought to let a little horse trouble get him so upset. "Or *was* it the horse?" I asked.

When he got so he could talk, he croaked, "Listen, did you ever beat a brown bear over the head with a frying pan? He'll come in here and tear us to pieces when the gets his mind made up." Buck huddled there like he actually expected to die. I thought it was a real good act, especially when the bear never materialized.

But next morning I found the eerie thing had actually happened. I saw the tracks in the mud. That big brown got a konking which couldn't have more than parted his head hair.

Moreover, equally strange things happen every year in brown-bear country. Genuinely screwball things not commonly associated with brown-bear temperament. I have seen plenty of them, and so has every other old-timer. The purpose of this piece is to explain the basic reason behind them—which is that the brown bear certainly is America's most maladjusted big-game animal. He is a bundle of what, in a human, would be called complexes and neuroses. If he were a member of our species, and had the dough, he would spend a couple of hours a week lying on a couch baring his innermost self to some expensive guy, in the hope of getting his psyche untangled.

Here's why. From the last glacial period until a couple of bear generations ago, the Alaska brown bear was the undisputed boss of his land. He didn't have to fear anything. And definitely the scattered few puny humans rimming the seacoast and the big rivers with their misery were his least formidable rivals for supremacy. Arrogance and fearlessness were as much a part of him as his pelt. Then came the payoff. Came the rifle-toting American woodsmen. They had already shot seven bells and the ten commandments out of the rough, tough, fighting grizzlies of California and the Upper Missouri. To them the Alaska brown bear was just another long-haired bear, maybe a little bigger than the grizzly but so what?

This awful roughneck breed of killers, looters and pirates gave the brown bear a mean and dirty choice to make. If he stood and fought, he'd get killed. If he ran, his ancient dignity was gone with the breezes. It would have happened to any other fighting animal on the planet. If we'd had a population of man-eating tigers over here, they would have had to learn to scuttle like rabbits and subsist on another diet or, believe me, the fur market at St. Louis would have been glutted with tiger skins until there wasn't another striped cat between the Atlantic and the Pacific. So the swaggering, hard-boiled, three-quarter-ton brown bear has had to learn to run and hide, or else. Because it is against his every instinct, he is a little batty. He can't get used to it. He is erratic, unpredictable, full of indecision, about as positive as a weather vane in a whirlwind.

As an illustration of the brown bear's erratic behavior, take an incident that occurred one summer while old Tex Cobb and I were keel-boating a hunting outfit up Knik River.

With four Tena Indian helpers, we set out from Eagle Butte in late July with half a ton of grub and assorted gear in a 35-foot boat—lining, rowing or poling according to the current and the kind of bottom and bank we had. The Knik is the devil of a river. It is fast and cold and muddy. Hurricane winds scream off the vast ice fields at its head, whirling up Sahara-type sandstorms. The bar points are treacherous with quick muck. The channels shift daily, and the banks for miles at a stretch are timbered and brush grown to the water's edge. Mostly we lined the boat, which is one of the most onerous means of freight transportation known to man.

You rig a bridle to hold the boat in midstream, and head up the bank with the 150-yard towline. You wade sloughs, climb crumbling cutbanks, flounder through incredibly dense alder and cranberry brush, clamber over algae-slippery rocks, and pass the line interminably around diabolically placed bankside cottonwoods. Also you fight mosquitoes. The old-timers who tell time by the sun claim that on the lower Knik in summer you have to throw your hat into the air to clear a swath so you can see it. Of course the bugs aren't quite that bad, but doggone near it.

We passed Cache Point and were crawling up on Hunter Creek, making maybe a mile an hour against a stiff current, when the wind started to blow. You could see the gray-yellow clouds of sand coming, low at first, then boiling high until they blanked out the sun. The stuff hit the cottonwoods like a shower of hail on a shingle roof. Some of it blew in level just above the brush. The rest was stopped by the canopy of glossy cottonwood leaves and fell straight down on us. It went inside your clothes, got between your teeth and into your eyes. Straining against the towline, you had to walk with your head bent and turned to one side, careful to breathe only through your nose.

Tex was bringing up the rear where he could watch the boat. Suddenly he yelled, "Hold it! Sweeper!"

Now a sweeper is a hazard that rivermen have bad dreams about. It is a fallen tree, often a large one, that lies in the current but is still held to the bank by its roots. It may remain submerged and invisible for minutes or hours, like a giant concealed trap. Then suddenly it will jerk to the surface, sawing back and forth, limbs threshing wildly with the deadly power to smash a boat or capsize it in a flash. Our boat was the length of an oar from this one when Tex spotted it. I told the crew to slack off the line, let her drift back. Then we set our feet to hold her until Tex could warp her ashore and adjust the bridle so she'd swing out around the sweeper next time. I guess I let her have too much slack. Anyway, she swung a little sideways and the wind caught her. That did it. With a whip-crack report, the line broke. Downstream went our fall hunt and practically everything we owned.

Horrified, we lit our downstream like a band of spooked antelope. Five hundred yards below there was a wadeable riffle. If we got there first we had a chance. We smashed through a brush jungle, splashed across a slough and tore around a high-piled log jam to a strip of bar that marked the head of the riffle. Here we skidded to an abrupt, bug-eyed halt. Dead ahead in the center of the bar stood an enormous sow brown bear and her spring cubs. Silhouetted against the steel-gray shine of the river, with the sheets of sand blowing about her, she looked like a woolly hangover from the age of monsters. She must have weighed anyway 1,200 pounds. She was hog-snouted, high-humped and pigeon-toed, and had a head twice as wide as this magazine. And she had a grouch on. While the two cubs crowded against her flank, she stood absolutely motionless, watching us, as menacing as a grenade with the pin pulled.

Meanwhile the boat had drifted down almost even with us. In another minute it would be into the riffle.

I have got to hand it to green-eyed, iron-manned old Tex. He had more bear savvy than all the rest of us combined and more guts. In his time he had been in at the death of eighty-odd brown bears, and so naturally he had formed some theories about the brutes. He put one of them into practice now. He was armed with a .30-06 Mauser, but using it wouldn't have solved our predicament. Before he could have put the bear down for keeps, our boat would have been over the riffle and wrecked on the log jam at the next bend.

The ornery cuss of a bear was on the warpath. Her back hair was rucked up and you could see she had murder in her heart. Roaring, popping her teeth, she made a stiff-legged bound toward us. Tex called a showdown. With a yell he sprinted straight at her, waving his arms. The bear bounded forward again and struck the sand with a front paw. Then her nerve broke, but she managed to save face. She swung her head toward the river, saw the boat, let out a hair-raising bawl and charged it. With the cubs at her heels, she plowed into the riffle, launched a sledgehammer blow at the gunnel, bit a piece out of it, and continued on across the river. Tex caught the trailing end of the broken towline and hung onto it until we joined him. I remarked that since bears have poor eyesight, she probably thought the boat was the largest and most formidable enemy closing in on her.

"Oh, shore," Tex said, grinning sardonically. "But the bluffing ol' lardbutt knowed damned well that the boat wasn't gonna shoot at her."

Okay, it sounded like nonsense to me, too. But I have since had encounters with a considerable number of the critters, and I know that they are consummate four-flushers. Not all of them, but most of them. In certain circumstances a brown bear will attack. But if he hasn't been wounded, he'll probably manage to miss you. As proof of this, literally dozens of men have been mauled by brown bears, but mighty few have been rubbed out. I personally know of only three in the past twenty years, which is pretty significant when you consider that in most of Alaska's coastal wilderness brown bears outnumber humans plenty-to-one. Every man I have talked with who had been worked over by a brown bear had the same story to tell—the animal seemed to be in a terrific frenzy to get the matter over with and depart the hell away from there. In short, the big brutes were scared silly of reprisal.

Consider the opinion expressed by Dorg Chicaloosun, a bull-shouldered, moon-faced Tyonok Indian, just after a brown bear finished trying to slap the daylights out of him in a stream channel.

Dorg and I were running a beaver line on the Deshkah, late in the spring season. The streams were open, the snow was gone except for shaded drifts back in the timber, and the cottonwoods and aspens were budding out. On this particular sweet, golden-bright, fragrant morning we mushed upriver to a couple of ponds from which we had already taken half-a-dozen good blanket pelts. Dorg had a year-old pup with him. The pup was a typical siwash Malamute—long-haired, wolf-muzzled, snoopy, with a rickety humped back that angled off to one side so his legs didn't set square under him. Dorg had rather unimaginatively named him Kleega, which in his dialect meant "dog."

We poked along the high stream bank in the wonderful wash of sunlight, both of us lazy-happy with acute spring fever, until we came to the first pond. Here Dorg said he would go down and check these traps if I'd take the next pond. I watched him slide down the grassy bank, lean his rifle against a tree and wade out to a set and reach for the trap chain. The bait stick was down so I knew he'd made a catch. In a moment he found the chain and pulled up a drowned beaver. It was a big one, maybe another blanket. Its orange teeth, broken off jaggedly on the trap, glinted in the sunlight, and its big, scaly, battle-scarred tail flapped loosely as Dorg heaved it back into the dead grass. As I turned to leave, Dorg grinned up at me and shook hands with himself, which meant that the beaver was a blanket and we had made anyhow forty bucks this morning.

I headed on up the trail through the sun-dappled timber, and had covered maybe 300 yards when I heard the Malamute pup let out a series of high, hysterical yelps. Then I heard a brown bear bawl. In case you have never heard a hostile brown bear sound off, I will make affidavit that it is the most marrow-freezing, high-raising, soul-shivering sound to be heard in the game ranges of this continent. It is a deep, full-throated *wagh-h-h!* with plenty of decibels, and vibrations that I'll bet a stone-deaf man could hear. The bear bawled twice, and before he had finished the second vocal effort I was running back down the trail. I knew, as certainly as if I had been there, what had happened. The bear, fresh out of hibernation and hungry, had found the carcasses of the beavers we had skinned at the pond during the past week, and was lying back in a thicket guarding them when the brainless Malamute pup found him and tried to get tough. Then the suddenly spooked pup had run to Dorg for protection, with the bear hot after him.

I left the trail and busted through a screen of birch saplings to the rim of the bank. Two hundred yards distant, nearly the length of the pond, I saw Dorg fleeing out onto the beaver dam. He didn't have his rifle. The crazy Malamute pup was at his heels. And right behind the pup was the bear. It wasn't a big bear—700 pounds for a guess—but it was acting plenty big. Its pelt was cream-yellow, almost white in the downpour of sunlight, and it had a short-nosed, spread-eared head like a Teddy bear. It was reaching for the pup, but having no luck because it couldn't keep its footing on the dam. The dam was an old high one, recently repaired, its top a mere foot-wide streak of black muck littered with slippery peeled sticks. But the bear was so close that the pup apparently figured his time was up, for he let out a shrill yelp of dismay and, somehow, crowded between Dorg's legs. Tripped, waving his arms, Dorg executed a sort of off-balance toe dance, and fell backward off the downstream side of the dam—eight feet down into the narrow leakage spillway. The bear whirled and bounded off the dam to the bank of the spillway, going out of view in the winter-killed grass. It had all happened so fast that, with the sun in my eyes, I hadn't had time to find the animal in my sights.

I didn't see the rest of it, but Dorg told me later he was hip-deep in the soft-bottomed, stinking spillway, reaching for a hold on some willow brush to pull himself out, when the bear jumped on him from behind. He saw the shadow and ducked, and the weight of the bear smashed him down and under. When he came up, the animal had his left foot in its mouth. Dorg was wearing rubber boots, and the bear's teeth were through the rubber and into the instep and sole of his foot. He said it hurt so much he couldn't help hollering. The crushing force of the animal's jaws was just like a steel vise, he said.

Snarling, coughing because of water it had inhaled, the bear shook Dorg's leg and yanked at it as if he hoped to tear it off. Also he kept half-rearing, trying to strike his face. But it didn't succeed because Dorg kept his leg stiff, so that the bear pushed him away each time. Dorg said he knew his smartest bet was to lie still and take it, but, he said, he got rattled, so he pulled his belt knife and made a cut at the animal. The razor-keen blade sliced into the bear's forearm, and the animal let out a bawl, jerking aside so quickly that the weapon was wrenched out of his hand. That was about the end of it. The bear took one more vicious swipe at him, missed, then suddenly let go of his foot, leaped up the bank and vanished.

When I arrived on the scene the bear was nowhere around. Dorg was beat up a little, had swallowed some pond water the wrong way, lost his knife and his boot was ruined. But otherwise he was all right. I told him he was the luckiest guy in the world. I said it was a miracle the bear hadn't caved in his ribs or bitten his face off.

"Huh. He was 'fraid of me," Dorg said with simple conviction as we worked the boot off his injured foot. "Scared plenty, soon as he got some sense back in his head and realized he was fighting a man."

Personally, I am a brown-bear fan. I think he rates with the world's top trophy animals. But it is silly to pretend that he is a dangerous beast in the sense that a lion, leopard, tiger or Cape buffalo is dangerous—it just ain't so. He used to be but he isn't any more. Excepting a few off-beat rogues, brown bears may be considered middling dangerous only when wounded, when guarding cubs, and when they have been come upon suddenly and startled while bedded down in thick cover.

Jimmy Patchell, tough, pint-size, gold-hunting squawman friend of mine, had the atrocious luck one day to hit the jackpot for three of those conditions. He was mushing down the bank of a Cook Inet salmon stream in August, in six-foot redtop grass, when he stumbled upon a sleeping sow bear with two cubs who was guarding a dozen or so calico salmon she had killed in a riffle and brought up here to age. She hadn't winded Jimmy and the sound of the stream had prevented her from hearing him. A squall from one of the cubs was her first warning of his presence.

She reacted to it like a keg of black powder to a match. In one movement she rose up and struck. Jimmy was carrying a .405 but didn't even have time to thumb the hammer back. He sidestepped, started to swing the muzzle toward the bear, and then the pile-driver pawstroke hit the barrel of the rifle and drove it against Jimmy's chest. Jimmy landed on his back in the creek, and the bear and her cubs took off in the opposite direction. Fortunately, Jimmy wasn't hurt. But as an indication of what might have happened to him, the terrible force of the bear's blow had put a two-inch bend in the .405's barrel. Only once before have I heard of a brown bear bending a rifle barrel with its Sunday wallop.

When I met Jimmy the following year in the Cottonwood River country, he was taking no chances. You could hear him coming down the trail two miles distant. He was beating on a frying pan with a club and singing a come-all-ye at the top of his lungs. He didn't aim to surprise any more brown bears. "It's a good system," he said, "but hell on frying pans, so when I get to town this time I'm gonna buy a cowbell an' hang it around m' neck-an' the first joker who calls me Bossy is gonna have a fight."

The brown bear ranges from Unimak Island along the Alaska coast to the Canadian boundary, and is found on many of the adjacent islands. He attains a top weight of maybe 1,800 pounds, which makes him the world's largest carnivore. His tribe is divided into an extraordinary number of species and subspecies by hair-splitting scientists, but he remains the same old brown bear with the same old characteristics, no matter whether you call him the Kodiak bear, the Shiras bear, the peninsula bear, or whatever. Nobody knows how many of the animals there are in Alaska, but for a guess there are probably 15,000.

The largest brown bears apparently are on Kodiak Island, where seven of the first eight record specimens were killed. The open season runs from September 1 to June 20, with a bag limit of one in the Kodiak-Afognak island group and two elsewhere in the territory.

The theory that brown bears miss charges because of poor eyesight, and often seem to be charging when actually trying to get away, is a venerable one. Your reporter freely admits having contributed to it on sundry occasions. But a man ought to have the right to change his mind. What finally changed my mind for keeps was the revealing behavior of a would-be hard-boiled brown bear I met one fine autumn afternoon on Willow Creek. This time I was shepherding the late Fred Hollender, a big, genial, lumbering Teuton from New York whose ambition was to possess the world's finest collection of close-up photographs of big game. By close-up, Fred meant too close. The ineffable character wanted their eyelashes to show. When I picked him up at Anchorage he handed me a rucksack crammed with film packs, and a big camera.

"Now ve go have some fun," he said. "Ve make the animals pose pretty for us, close up."

I guess you could call it fun if you said it fast and had a German sense of humor. We were at the mouth of the tea-colored Willow, where it flows across a reach of gravel into the wide, muddy Susitna. Fred was horsing around with some fresh-run silver salmon, making them jump for the camera. I was taking the pictures, exposing film as fast as I could touch the button and pull a new frame into place. As I turned to pick up a fresh pack, I glanced downstream—and saw three brown bears swimming across a channel from an island. Fred at once broke his leader, abandoning the current salmon to its fate. Snatching up the spare camera, he laid out a plan of campaign. I was to hasten downriver, below the bears, while he remained here. Thus one of us probably would get pictures. It sounded all right. Nonresidents aren't permitted to photograph brown bears unless accompanied by a guide, but I would be close enough so I could cover him with my rifle if he got into trouble.

"But remember," he said. "Ve vant close-ups. Only close-ups."

I got him a close-up, all right. The bears swam into a millrace current rip which swept them some 300 yards below me. They waded out, shaking themselves, and came up the strip of gravel bar toward the creek mouth—shouldering along in typically arrogant, deliberate, go-to-hell brown bear fashion. Like a trio of chicken colonels stalking across the parade ground of a spit-and-polish post. They weren't especially big bears—800 pounds maybe—and they looked so much alike they could have been triplets. I was cached at the rim of the bar in some red willow, kneeling, with my rifle on the ground beside me with the safety off. Just before they came abreast of me, they dropped into single file. Then, a few steps farther on, the last bear stopped to sniff at the sun-dried remains of a salmon. I centered him on the ground glass, cut the focus sharp and tripped the shutter. Now this camera never was designed for surreptitious work. It has a focal-plane shutter and mirror which flop over with a *clunk* that's like dropping a cantaloupe on a concrete sidewalk. The bear heard it and came to attention. He stared at me, and then—don't ask me why—charged like a bull.

His size on the finder sort of confused me. He was only about fifty feet distant, but it looked farther. I thought I had time to take one more picture, then pick up the rifle and work on him if I had to. Chalk up a bad error for Annabel. I shot the picture so close you could see the gleam in his eye—before I could lay a hand on my rifle, he was practically in my lap. But he swerved around me like an all-American quarterback and went tearing off toward the timber, leaving me kneeling there with my eyes bunged out and the beginning of a swell case of shakes.

Ordinarily, at that time, I could have explained his action to almost anybody's satisfaction. Just bad eyesight. Or he really was heading for cover all the while, the innocent so-and-so, and merely happened to get pointed in my direction. Yeah? So I stood up and started back up to where Fred was. At this point I heard a snort behind me, and guess what? Here he came again. I laid the bead on his head and waited. Repeat performance. He came within twenty feet this time, then swung off and hauled ashes into the timber. He had known from the beginning what I was. And he yearned to separate me into pieces the birds could carry away. Only he was a little short on nerve.

As far as that goes, I wasn't doing so well in the nerve department myself. But Fred wasn't worried. He had the reckless courage of the noncombatant.

"Ah, good," he said, hammering me on the back. "Ve got a fine close-up. *Sehr gut!*"

Our old-time Alaska Indians, when they felt particularly full of stuff and vinegar or wanted to outshine somebody, used to tackle the brown bear with a spear. As a youngster I saw some of their bear spears in Alaska Peninsula villages. They were astonishing weapons. I'd make a bet that a look at one of them would give one of the celebrated Masai spearman an inferiority complex. The blade was two feet long and eight inches wide. It was on a ten-foot birch shaft as thick as a man's wrist. Where blade and shaft joined there was a stout crossbar, the purpose of which was to prevent the speared bear from pulling himself up the shaft to where he could get a lethal lick at the spearman. According to my redskin informants, there was a lot of glory in bear-spearing but very little future. If you had to try it, however, you did so according to ritual. First you fasted, then you took a sweat bath. Next you called upon the medicine man and paid off for the protection of the spirits.

This accomplished, you went out to a bear pasture and pounded on a medicine drum until a bear heard you and came over to investigate. You then yelled insults and invited the animal to fight. I am told that you seldom had trouble persuading him. Those bygone brown bears hadn't been discouraged by super slugs capable of punching through a railroad rail as if it were Swiss cheese.

When the bear charged, you set the butt of the spear against the ground and let the animal impale himself on the point. Then you stepped in and whaled him industriously over the head with a stone-headed ax until he gave up the ghost. If you survived the experience, you were quite a guy. You could sit around and brag about it for the rest of your life.

But the old-timers wouldn't recognize today's brown bear. As an illustration, take something that happened last spring, when "Starvation" Smith and I had the rare privilege of watching two of the animals mate. They were 400 yards distant in a grass flat when we spotted them. You could tell which was which because the female wanted to play. She wanted to wrestle. I had a 12-power glass on her, and I will declare as follows—if I could put that match on in public, Gorgeous George and the rest of the muscle boys could take a vacation. The male bear obviously was wrestling only because he had to. He took an awful shellacking. She would wind up and blast him a lick that would have torn a man's head off his shoulders. Then she would roll over playfully on her back, clasp him around the neck, and rake him from his brisket aft with her hind feet. The poor bemused male took it. I guess he figured it was worth it so long as he didn't get permanently maimed.

The actual mating took forty minutes, and that's no typographical error. It might have lasted even longer if Starvation and I hadn't tried to get closer. We eased up the bed of a dry wash, and were parting the grass on the rim when the wind hit the back of my neck. That broke it up. At once the male bear lost interest in everything save getting away from that place. He shoved off like a race horse. The female gave us a long look, and departed on his trail.

Starvation sighed and shook his head. "Brown bears shore ain't what they used to be," he declared. "Why, if he'd had the guts of a shitepoke he'd a bellered at us at least. Dammit, I would have my own self."

But the brown bear is the best we've got. He's a champion. If he's turned a little soft, I guess maybe it's a good thing, because the hunters who come north today aren't quite as rugged as their buckskin granddads were, either.

Adventure Is My Business

PART 1

Beginning—the thrilling real-life adventures of a great American author and sportsman. Here is Alaska at its toughest—the story of one man who had to fight it every inch of the way!

This was going to be a day to remember forever. . . . I woke with the sun in my eyes and knew that I was hungry. I sat up, batting away the white-stocking flies that had found me, and tightened the laces of my pacs. I felt rough. I had no bedding, and could feel the imprint of every rock and pebble I had lain on. From habit, with a sleeve of my jacket—the worn red-checked Mackinaw jacket that had been a Christmas present in another, milder land—I wiped the dew from the long-barreled Winchester leaning against a drift log beside me. Then I stood up for a look at the country.

I was feeling rougher by the minute. But there was something else, too, a mood I had never experienced before—a mood compounded of excitement, curiosity, tension arising from danger, and a kind of wild disbelief. It was a mood that, from this morning, was to stay with me most of the rest of my life.

"What in hell am I doing here?" I thought.

I was fifteen. I was a redheaded, freckled, gangling brat, dead broke and 2,000 miles from what had been home.

The narrow spruce-timbered Alaska valley reaching into the sunrise was still half-drowned in violet shadow. But the peaks, the soaring, snow-patched, glacier-studded, incredibly ragged peaks fencing the valley on both sides, were all ashine in the unstained new light. Ravelings of cold mist drifted along the stream beside which I had slept. I didn't know the name of the stream. Maybe it didn't have a name. But when I came to it last night in the starshot early-autumn darkness, I had heard salmon splashing up a riffle. I could use a fat salmon. I could use any sort of grub. My belly seemed caved in against my backbone. I was so hungry I was rubber-kneed and lightheaded. I remembered that during the night I had dreamt of sitting down to vast, miraculous feasts, gorging myself endlessly. I shut the memory out of my mind. It wasn't doing me any good.

Let me please kill a salmon.

The first riffle was empty, and so was the pool above it. I worked upstream, squinting against the coppery glare now on the water. Along the drab sand bars was a scattering of dead salmon—silvers and dogs, livid carcasses with frayed fins and unsightly bruises, from which ravens had picked the eyes. And there was bear sign, the tracks of both blacks and giant browns, some old, some very fresh. I checked the Winchester. The chamber load and the two top shells in the magazine were softnoses. So that was all right. With the wind in my face, ducking under the wet overhanging bankside willows, I rounded a bend to the next riffle. Beside me a wide swirl broke the water. Then, with a flurry of splashes, a pair of salmon streaked up through the shallows. They were silvers, fresh-run, their sides gleaming rose and platinum. But I failed to catch either in my sights. The light was in my eyes, and I was shivering. I needed a cinch target.

So important was it to kill a fish that I forgot about the fresh bear sign. It could have been a bad error.

I stood waiting under a cutbank, concealed by the drooping willows, watching the dawn-lit water and wishing I could stop shaking. Fifteen minutes or so passed. Then here came another salmon. It was a big hook-nosed male silver, half his back above the water. When he was abreast of me, I cut down on him. The 220-grain .30-06 softnose blasted his life out so abruptly that he turned over on his side without a quiver. I started to wade in after him—and as I did so something like a typhoon ripped through the thicket above me. There was a hoarse coughing grunt, a weaving and cracking of brush. I ducked.

I thought—*sucker!*

Whirling, I had a glimpse of a high-shouldered, mahogany-colored shape racing through the frost-painted willows. It was a brown bear. I suppose that, like me, he had come to the riffle to get a salmon for breakfast. Probably he had been at the point of leaping down to the water after my fish when I fired. He was a monster. When he emerged into full view, galloping up the game trail following the bank, he looked as big as a Clydesdale horse, and no doubt would have weighed as much.

Without thinking, I picked him up in the sights and pulled. It was silly. I needed a brown bear trophy like I needed a grand piano. But I was startled, and this was the first brown bear I had ever seen. I was a cheechako kid still awkward in the North. Gut-shot, the bear spun with a strangled bawl, bit at his flank, lurched off balance, and tumbled over the bank onto the strip of bar. He was so heavy I felt the ground shake. When he got up, I shot him in the chest, then once more behind the ear as he slewed sideways and dropped his head, coughing. The last shot put him down and for keeps down.

He lay with his feet in the water, blood pouring out of his mouth. Although in effect he was dead, his vitality was so tremendous that for ten minutes his eyes blinked and his lungs kept pumping. I watched him, filled with tangled emotions. First I felt a sharp triumph, then shame and regret. He was a patriarch, as noble an animal as could have been found on earth. For perhaps twice my years he had swaggered through this savagely beautiful wilderness, a part of it. He had known the screaming storms, the long, bright summer days, the compelling excitement of mating, the hot lust of combat with other great males of his race. He was admirable and uniquely American.

Now, tricked by a splashing salmon and a flaw of wind, he was dead meat, food for the ravens and wolverines.

I didn't want him. I couldn't carry his pelt where I was going, and I didn't know whether his flesh was edible or not. I thought I remembered having heard somewhere that brown bear flesh wasn't. Feeling low and not proud of myself, I waded out and got my salmon and went down the bars to where I had slept, and gathered rabbit-killed willow brush for a fire. The silver was in good condition, his meat fat and flame-red. I skewered two fillets on green sticks and propped them on a flat rock slanted against the fire. As the edges of the fillets cracked in the heat, juice oozing out, I broke off pieces with my fingers and ate them. I wanted to wolf the fish half-cooked but was so hungry I didn't dare to. So I chewed it slowly, savoring its full sweet flavor. It was the most delicious food I had ever eaten—and the first I had swallowed in two hard days.

Half-an-hour later, with my belly full, I could again think about the mission I was on.

I had the name of a place—Cloud Creek—that I was trying to reach. I wasn't certain I could find it. I knew only that the creek came in from the north to the headwaters of this valley I was following. Old-timers said it plunged through an unmapped, hostile region of sky-busting peaks, impassable glaciers, and alder forests as dense as an Amazon jungle. Up near the source of Cloud Creek, at the rim of a brush-line sheep meadow, a mountain man had a camp. I was looking for this man. I had come from the States to find him.

His name was Tex Cobb.

Three days ago, at roaring, slatternly Old Matanuska, I had learned Tex's whereabouts. I came in on a freighttrain from Seward, arriving after dark, and unloaded at the depot when the engineer stopped for orders. Matanuska was still a camp. It looked like a setting for a low-budget western movie. There was a muddy road and a broken plank sidewalk, and a row of squat log cabins and false-fronted, unpainted frame buildings. Gaunt, fierce-eyed Malamute dogs roamed in the shadows, nosing through heaps of tin cans and garbage. From a two-story building down the street came a blaze of yellow lamplight and the beat of dance music. A sign across the sidewalk said it was Phil Allen's roadhouse.

I took the cased Winchester into the depot office and asked the agent, a fat stubble-faced German with square-lensed spectacles, if he would take care of it until I returned. He gave me a thoughtful look, obviously suspecting I was an escapee from a reform school, but said, "*Ja*," he would.

Then I went down to the roadhouse. The door was open and the blare of noise coming through it was something you could lean against. I edged inside and stood against the wall, bug-eyed and fascinated by the frontier jamboree in progress.

Crowding the big-bore room was a sweating, whooping, rough-and-tumble mob of railroad workers, soldiers, construction men, homesteaders, and trappers—dancing with one another and with Indian girls, breed girls, and a few self-conscious-looking white women. The band consisted of a bass drum, two fiddles, a guitar, and a mandolin. It was playing "Wang Wang Blues." A wiry, white-headed little trapper stomped past with a slender dark-eyed breed girl in his arms. He wore moosehide moccasins and had a frazzled old muskrat cap tilted on the back of his head. The ivory haft of a belt knife jutted from a beaded sheath on his belt. As he whirled the breed girl, he bent half double, shuffling his feet like a Tena ghost-dancer, and let out a wild, high-pitched yell.

"That's Caribou Jack," somebody in the doorway laughed. "Back from two years in the Nelchina country, and loaded for grizzlies."

It was no understatement. The diminutive white-headed sourdough really was loaded for big stuff. When he came past the door again, swinging his partner wide and handsome, a burly construction hand tried to cut in. Caribou Jack shook his head and moved away. The construction hand then made a mistake. Chin stuck out, eyes narrowed with resentment, he grabbed the little trapper by the shoulder and yanked him around. Things happened. The construction stiff looked husky enough to break the old-timer apart. But he never got started. He had as much chance as an ox would have with a timber wolf. Almost on the beat of the music Caribou Jack kicked the man in the stomach, belted him on the chin, and smashed a knee into his face as he slumped to the floor.

In two seconds the roadhouse was the scene of a bizarre and bloody melee. It was a sweetheart of a free-for-all, a battle royal, a Donnybrook with nothing barred.

A chair splintered against the wall a thin whisper from my head, and that was enough for me. I leaped out the door and crossed the street to an observation point in the shadow of a cottonwood. By now the front windows of the roadhouse were smashed. The tin pipe of the oil-drum stove was down and smoke was filling the place. Men were fighting on the sidewalk, in the mud of the street. Curses, yells, and cheers filled the night. The bass drummer came out of the door pushing his drum ahead of him, and a man with his shirt torn off laughed and kicked a hole in it. I don't know how long I had been under the cottonwood watching, when I heard a slight sound behind me. I jerked around—and caught the shine of white hair under a beat-up fur cap. It was Caribou Jack.

"Nice spot to observe th' festivities from," he remarked conversationally. "Slipped out th' back door, m'self. Ain't seen you around before, have I?"

I told him he hadn't. I said I had just come up from the States. On a hunch, I added that I was looking for Tex Cobb.

"Gawdamighty—Tex Cobb." Caribou Jack's voice was sharp. "Now what would anybody want with that long-haired, ornery, miser'ble hunk of original sin? Why, he ain't even hooman." He peered into my face. "You ain't a sheriff with a warrant fer him, are ye?'

"I want to find him, that's all." I hoped I sounded hard-boiled. I didn't realize I was being kidded. I had plenty to learn about sourdoughs. No alfalfa field ever was greener.

But I got information. When Caribou Jack became bored with the fading brawl across the street, he told me about Tex's camp on Cloud Creek. He took me to the edge of town and pointed out the deep notch of a river valley sharp-cut against the star-fretted sky. You could see the phantom-white gleam of a glacier set like a gun sight in the notch. That was where Cloud Creek came in, he said. He said it was a tough trip and asked if I had an outfit, and I admitted that I had only the Winchester, a belt knife, and enough money for supper and breakfast.

"Aw, well," he said, shrugging, "sometimes a outfit jest gits in a man's way. I was in th' hills all last summer with only some salt and .22 shells. Et ptarmigan an' yaller-bellied trout until I started sprouting feathers an' scales." He cuffed the muskrat cap to the front of his head and gnawed at a plug of tobacco. "You'll prob'ly make out all right—one way er another. If ya git inta trouble, maybe Blind Nick'll help ya out. He's somewhere up there in th' main valley."

"So who is Blind Nick, and how would I find him?"

"He'll find you—if he wants to. Blind Nick is a Injun prophet—a shaman—th' only one I ever knew that amounted to a good damn. Stone blind, but I betcha Houdini couldn't put anything over on him. Doggone if he can't even make change with paper money. Seen him do it a dozen times." Caribou Jack spat tobacco juice into the darkness, hitched up his belt, and headed down the street. Over his shoulder he said, "You could git a job as flunky in one o' th' railroad camps. Make yerself some money."

"I'm looking for Tex Cobb."

"Well, say howdy to th' big cuss fer me."

After eating half of the silver salmon, I wrapped the remainder in grass, stuffed it into my jacket pocket, and hit the trail. It was no great shakes of a trail—just a dim trace, probably made originally by bear and moose, that twisted among muskeg bogs and stands of spruce and flaming cottonwoods. I could walk, and I put everything I had into it. Around noon I halted at a narrow, shimmering blue lake for a drink and a rest. A pair of swans were cruising along the farther shore. Above me a beaver was floating a section of birch log down toward a new dam at the lake's outlet. Suddenly the beaver dived, banging his tail on the water. I thought he had winded me, but I was wrong. When he surfaced again he was facing up the lake. He lay partly submerged, only his nose and rump showing. He was watching the bank. So were the swans. Something was on the trail, apparently close ahead and coming toward me.

With my thumb on the safety latch of the Winchester, I stepped behind a spruce and waited.

A strange procession filed into view. First came an Indian boy, maybe ten years old, leading a tall, lean, hawk-faced man at the end of a peeled and painted six-foot length of sapling. Behind them came an Indian girl, a free-striding young squaw about my age, carrying a rifle. Next came six shaggy, wolfish-looking pack dogs, chained together. The dogs were gazing out across the water, trying to spot the beaver they had heard. The Indian boy and the girl were watching the trail. The tall man who was being led had his face turned upward, seemingly searching the sky. I figured that, if I wanted to, I could let them pass without revealing my presence.

Only I couldn't have.

Because just then the man jerked the painted stick, and halted. Facing me, he raised his free hand, palm out, and smiled. "How do?" he said. His voice was guttural and had a chesty, thudding quality like a muffled drum. And now I saw that his eyes were blank, dead-looking, the eyes of a man long blind. I stepped into the open, feeling like a Grade-A, blue-ribbon fool. Of course the man was Blind Nick. But how he had known I was there I'll never understand. He couldn't have heard me. I don't think the boy saw me and signaled with the stick. I'd hate to say what I think. I don't believe it myself except on rainy nights.

I said, "Nick. Caribou Jack said you were up here. I'm trying to find Tex Cobb. He said maybe you would help."

Blind Nick sat down. He got out a carved pipe with a short high-bush cranberry stem and beaded pouch filled with what looked like shredded bark. The boy lit the pipe for him. The smoke was aromatic, like perfume. For a moment or two he puffed without speaking. The six pack dogs had lain down, but their slant green eyes were watching me suspiciously. The boy was sitting beside Blind Nick. Only the girl remained standing. She was looking across the lake, ignoring me. She was pretty—slim, high-breasted and long-legged—with jet-black eyes under fine arched brows. Her glossy hair was in two braids, tied at the ends with red yarn. She wore moccasins, a smoke-tanned caribou-fawn shirt, and faded blue jeans.

The silence began to get me down. So I said, "This is a good country. I am going to stay in it."

Blind Nick's shoulders shook. He was laughing without making a sound. Taking the pipe from his mouth, he said, "Yes, you gonna stay. You gonna stay so long the ravens and wolves gonna know you like their own brothers."

"The heck you say." I knew I was getting the treatment, yet I wanted to hear more. "I'm really going to be around a while, am I?"

Blind Nick let that one drop. "But it's a bad trail to Tex Cobb's camp," he said. "Even for Injuns a bad trail. I think better you take Oolinka"—he motioned toward the girl—"to show you the way." He tossed a sentence at her in the harsh, sharp-angled Tena language.

The girl turned her head for the first time to look at me, meeting my eyes straight and unafraid, like a man. A tingle jittered up my spine as if I had taken hold of a live wire. *What am I getting into now?* I didn't know anything about girls. I had never had a date with one. I had always shied away from them like a morning-frisky cayuse shying from a tumbleweed. As for heading up into the big peaks with a pretty Indian girl for a guide, the idea was too fantastic even to consider. What I didn't know then—and it wouldn't have affected the outcome anyway—was that this girl and the boy were slaves. Blind Nick owned them. They did what he told them to do. That was why the girl was giving me such an appraising look. She thought I was her new boss.

"No," I said. "I couldn't pay you. I'm broke." It was the best objection I could think of.

Blind Nick brushed it off. "I need the boy, but you can take the girl. You don't need money to pay for her." He puffed at the pipe, poker-faced. Then, so help me, he said, "I gotta have bear meat for these dogs. Brown bear meat is the best kind. Makes them strong and brave. Maybe you know where some brown bear meat is?"

That stopped me. But I pulled myself together and confessed that I knew where there was a brown bear carcass. I told him where to find it. He nodded, only half interested in the details. He had me spooked, in spades. Somehow he knew I had killed a brown bear this morning. But how could he have known? The carcass was a good ten miles down valley, and Blind Nick and his entourage had come from the opposite direction. Still—

Meanwhile Oolinka had opened the lead dog's pack and was taking things out of it and putting them into a canvas packsack—salt, tea, a slab of sugar that had been mixed with water and allowed to harden, a blackened kettle.

"No," I said desperately. "Don't worry about me. Thanks a lot, and so long." I stepped around the dogs and started up the trail.

Blind Nick called after me. "Say hello to Tex for me."

I turned to answer, to tell him that I would, and there was Oolinka ten steps behind me, the pack on her back, eyes downcast. She had given her rifle to the boy. I was her new master. I had bought her with a brown bear carcass. I was licked, mouse-trapped, outsmarted, stuck with a girl guide. I had painted myself into a corner. I opened my mouth to make a last feeble protest but the words got lost. What could I do? Throw rocks at her? Whale her with a club? I headed on up the trail, cussing to myself. Let's face it, I was scared.

But Oolinka was all right. She was a champion. She was short on social graces. She wasn't the kind of girl who could tell you the plural of mongoose, but she had loyalty, and she knew these peaks.

There was the cold, overcast morning above the mouth of Cloud Creek on the terrible trail to Tex's camp when she risked her life to save mine. We were in what sourdoughs call a pudding-stone canyon—sheer walls of rotten conglomerate—with barely two feet of boulder-strewn bar to walk on, and the roaring, milky stream hammering past with the velocity of a jet from a fire hose. I looked up and saw a mountain goat on the rim, 500 feet above us. It was a billy, a handsome beast. He was in snow-white full autumn pelage, slick and fat, his needle-pointed black horns shining in the wan sunlight. We needed meat like a wounded man needs plasma. I blew through the sight of the Winchester to make certain it was clear. I put the gold front sight on the goat's chest and squeezed. With the crash of the shot, the billy's legs buckled, and he pitched into space, straight down at me.

Oolinka was behind. She had halted to rearrange the grass padding in one of her moccasins. Out of the corner of my eye I saw her straighten and run toward me, crying a warning.

Then—blackout. The shot had loosened a ton of rocks from the rotten cliff. I went down on my back in the battering stream, pounded by the rockfall, a gone cheechako kid for certain if I had been alone. The next thing I knew, I was on dry land again, 200 feet below the point where I had gone in. Oolinka had draped me over a boulder to drain the water out of me. I was sick and dazed, gagging. Blood was streaming down my face from a gash in the side of my head. I felt like I had been run over by a tractor train. And I knew I had done a stupid thing, and that made me sore. I weaved to my feet, and when Oolinka steadied me I shoved her aside.

"Get the hell away from me."

Then I saw that she was wet from head to foot. She had gone into the water after me. She had managed in some way to pull me out of that savage, millrace current. I was ashamed and wanted to thank her, but didn't know how to do it. So I went back up to the rockfall and got busy gutting the goat carcass. Oolinka knelt beside me, working deftly with her short woman's knife. She kept her head bowed meekly, not looking at me. I felt like all the heels in the world.

Five days later—five days of fog and icy rain—of white-stocking flies, treacherous fords and god-awful hillside alder jungles—of cliffs, snow bridges, and miserable camps with no fuel within miles—we came out of a blue-shadowed spruce canyon into a pretty meadow below a hanging glacier. At the edge of the meadow was a tent with log walls. Behind it stood a stilt-legged siwash cache. A stovepipe stuck up from the tent roof, and smoke was issuing from it. A dog barked. Then I saw a man standing under a gnarled, wide-armed cottonwood. He was skinning the carcass of a white mountain sheep hanging from one of the tree limbs.

He was tall and wide-shouldered, with a black beard and a mane of hair that reached down his back. He wore a blue shirt, tail hanging out, and khaki pants with ragged knees and seat. He stared at us, and scratched his ear with the bloody knife. I saw his eyes flicker to a rifle standing against the tree.

Oolinka said in a low voice, "That is Tex Cobb."

"Hello, Tex," I said. "I've come a long way to find you."

Adventure Is My Business

PART 2

More great true tales of men who fought for life itself in Alaska's wilderness—by one who shared their danger. You won't forget Tex who found a green fortune—and his fighting dog, Smoky.

For me Cloud Creek was the true beginning of adventure. . . . Here I was to make lifelong friends. I was to see one of the earth's most fantastic secret treasures. And I was to learn something about the strength and loyalty of women. . . .

Oolinka and I crossed a lawnlike space of blueberry turf to where Tex stood under the frosted, Indian-yellow cottonwood. To get a better look at us he had stepped back from the white sheep he was skinning. Beside him, watching us intently, was a black, heavy-shouldered water spaniel with a gaze as wise as a man's. Probably neither Tex nor his dog had ever before in these mountains laid eyes on a pair of travelers like Oolinka and me. We were footsore and limping. Our clothes were brush-torn. Oolinkna had been forced to patch her moccasins with green goat hide, the wool only partly shaved off. I had a bandage around my head to keep gnats out of the gash received six days ago in the rockfall. It was a sleeve cut from my underwear.

I said, "Hello, Tex. I"ve come a long way to find you."

"Well, ya found me," he rumbled.

Rough independence radiated from the guy. You could sense peril, humor and intelligence in him, and maybe kindness. You felt after one close look that here was a man you could trust forever but couldn't fool with at all. He was fifty-eight, yet appeared to be twenty years younger. He had swamp-green eyes, a handsome face with lean, bony planes like a chancellor's, wide, loose shoulders that strained his blue wool shirt, and a snowshoe man's powerful legs. He swaggered a few steps to meet us, and shook hands. His big flat-wristed hand was cold and hard. Not callused, just hard. It felt like a paw.

You've got to make him like you.

"From yer looks ya could stand a little grub. Why don't yer squaw cut some steaks?" He nodded toward the sheep.

Oolinka didn't move. She had halted two paces behind and was apparently studying the peaks, her face impassive as if carved from jade. At first I thought she hadn't heard. Then I got it. She wasn't going to work on Tex's say-so. She wanted me to tell her, so I said, "All right, thanks. We'll have some steaks."

She went over to the sheep then and got out her knife. It was one of those wicked little curved knives the Tena women make from a saw blade. Only five inches long, it was sharp as broken glass and bright as silver, with a yellow hand-polished sheephorn haft. They boil a piece of horn until it is soft, then drive the saw steel into it and bake the horn to harden it. She was good with the knife. She made it purr through the meat as she took out the tenderloins and cut the best steaks from a ham.

"Nice. Where'd ya find her?" Tex said appreciatively. I told him. I explained how, unintentionally, I had bought her from Blind Nick, the prophet, with a brown bear carcass. I said I didn't know what to do with her. It didn't seem right, I said, for a girl to be in the mountains with two men. Or with one man either, I added confusedly, when she wasn't married. I was blushing and knew it, and it made me mad. Tex grinned. He tried to hide the grin with his hand and a phony cough, but was too late.

"D'ya mean ya wanta git rid o' her?"

"I guess I ought to. But how would I do it?"

"Well-ll, she's a trim little *klootch*," Tex said thoughtfully. "An' she's a slave or Blind Nick wouldn't of peddled her off. So—if ya wanta sell her, jest say so."

That burned me. I had asked for the remark. But it was so cold-blooded that the steam really climbed in my gauges. You know how it is, you get that hollow, singing feeling deep inside. You are light and easy on your feet. Your senses are suddenly so sharp that little sounds seem loud, and everything that moves is in slow motion. The Winchester was sweet and solid in my hand, and I was conscious of its pretty balance. I fixed my eyes on the third button of Tex's shirt and set myself.

"She isn't for sale. She's free. She goes where she wants to. Or stays where she damn pleases. Starting now."

Then I realized how stupid I was to get hotheaded.

Idiot. Jackass. Cool off fast or you've lost out.

Oolinka had her back to us, listening, poised statue-still, only her braids moving as the mountain wind blew them. Now she turned, came wide around Tex, and showed me the steaks. Her eyes were brilliant, and moist. "Is it enough?" "It's enough," I said. She went toward the tent with the meat, walking proudly as a barbarian princess, chin high, shoulders squared. I can't prove it, but I think she was crying. I noticed that she hadn't put her knife away until she passed Tex. I think now that if I had given her to him, and he had touched her, she would have split him open with the knife like a salmon split for the drying rack.

Tex laughed. It was an honest, belly-shaking laugh, no chagrin or anger in it, and that made me feel better. I decided that maybe, just maybe, I hadn't loused up by talking tough with a gun in my hand.

"So ya come a fur piece lookin' fer me, Redhead. Wanta tell me why?'

Here we go. Tell him. You've rehearsed it for a month.

"Because I'm hunting adventure. I want to write stories for a living—when I've learned to write. And I want to write about Alaska first, if I can learn as much about Alaska as a good writer ought to know. . . . I think you'd be the best teacher."

With my fingers crossed, I told him I was fifteen and broke, and hadn't finished the eighth grade. I had run away from home. My family didn't know where I was. Old "Powder Box" Horton, a grizzled, barrel-chested ex-sourdough who worked in my father's logging camp in the big timber of western Washington, had tried to help me. "If you gotta run off to Alasky," Powder Box had said, "hunt up Tex Cobb. There ain't nobody like Tex. They busted the mold when they made him. The big green-eyed so-and-so is the top woodsman in the territory. He roams the North like a timber wolf, and lives as rough. If he'll take you for a partner, you'll see things nobody else ever saw."

"That's why I came looking for you."

"Be doggoned," Tex said. "Some chore ya cut out fer yerself. Well, hit hadn't oughta take more'n thirty or forty years. But ya oughta start with a good dinner. Let's go eat them steaks. I smell 'em fryin'."

So I didn't know if I had scored or not.

When we had eaten, Tex sat on the woodpile and filled his pipe. I wished that I knew how to smoke. It was a flaw in my character, I told myself, that would have to be remedied soon. Tex's pipe was an outsize, curved-stem affair like a miniature saxophone, and its aroma was like nothing else on earth. He cleaned the stem with a ptarmigan feather, got the cut-plug tobacco burning, and leaned back on the woodpile with a sigh of pure contentment. Oolinka was at the creek washing the dishes Indian fashion, with moss and sand.

"Ya know anything about jewels, Redhead—di'monds, emeralds, sapphires an' sech?"

I said no, I didn't. I had only seen them in jewelry stores. The people I knew, I said, didn't wear precious stones.

"Yeah. Me, too. But I know where there's some whoppers." He pointed with his pipestem to the tangle of peaks above Cloud Creek glacier. "Up there at snow line. Trouble is, they're too danged big to move, an' too hard to bust up. An' most years they're under fifty feet o' snow. Ain't figgered yet what to do with 'em. But somethin' to write about someday."

What could I say except thanks?

I stretched out on the sun-warmed turf, trying to imagine what a jewel too big to move would look like—and what it would be worth. Probably there wasn't that much money. While I was day-dreaming the black water spaniel came over to me. I held out my hand, and he touched it politely with his nose. Then he curled up against the woodpile. I figured he was just a nice, friendly cheechako dog, the kind that'd retrieve ducks for you once or twice a year and loaf in the dooryard the rest of the time. But I was wrong. He wasn't that kind of dog at all. He was a very special dog. Although he weighed only forty-five pounds and normally was gentle as a schoolboy's pet, he was a killer, an ex-professional killer, a canine berserker in disguise.

I want to tell you about this dog now, because his story will help explain Tex. The episode I'm going to relate is not one I witnessed myself. It took place before I had even dreamt of coming to Alaska. But plenty of sourdoughs saw what happened, and they have made the affair one of the colorful legends of the North.

Tex was living at Susitna Station, a trading post and huddle of buildings just above the mouth of the Susitna River. He had just returned from a twelve-month trapping and prospecting trip into the Talkeetnas, and had rented a cabin next to a saloon. He was loaded with money and craved excitement. So one evening, when he heard roars of applause and excited yells on the second floor of the saloon, he at once hastened up there. He says he thought a boxing match was in progress. But instead it was a dogfight. A tinhorn gambler—a weasel-faced, whisky-voiced cheechako down on his luck, by the name of "Solo" Swanson—had come to town with a fighting dog, and was trying to pick up a bankroll. Smoky was the dog.

When Tex shouldered through the door into the smoke and blare of voices, Smoky was in the pit fighting a gray Kuskokwim husky twice his size. The husky knew his business. He fought like his timber wolf ancestors, sparring and slashing—taking full advantage of his superior weight and height, and his protective heavy coat. He kept trying for the spaniel's back. He wanted to get a good hold, shake the little dog, throw him, and pounce for the kill. He was a noisy fighter, snarling like a buzz saw going through a knot. Also he was a doomed fighter.

Solo Swanson was circling the pit, taking bets. "Here y'are, sports. Here's your chance to take some easy money away from o'l Santa Claus Swanson. Two to one on the little dog to win. Two to one. Five'll get you ten—and I must be nuts to do it, sports."

Then something happened in the pit. It happened so fast that the old-timers still argue about it. Smoky, a shifting black ghost, silent as death, broke one of the husky's forepaws. When the husky faltered, Smoky whipped past him and slashed his flank open. Blood spurted and a fold of intestine bulged out. The husky screamed, and spun to snap at his own guts. As he did this, Smoky flashed in and tore the luckless animal's throat out. The sobbing, kicking, dying husky was dragged out of the pit. Smoky remained where he was, watching Solo Swanson. He was bleeding from a dozen cuts. He was weaving on his feet. But he didn't try to leave the pit. He knew what was coming. He wasn't through fighting yet—or thought he wasn't.

"Hard luck, sports," Solo rasped cheerfully, collecting his bets. "But ol' Santa Claus Swanson is a kindhearted guy. So let's give you another chance. Let's fight the little dog again. Even money this time. I got a bulldog outside—"

Above the noise of the crowd Tex shouted, " like hell ya'll fight him again."

Green eyes glittering with rage, the big mountain man stepped into the pit. He knelt beside Smoky, eased a hand out and gently stroked the spaniel's head. Smoky stiffened at the touch. But in a moment he relaxed. Then Tex picked him up. Holding the bleeding dog cradled in his arms, he started for the door. Solo Swanson grabbed his elbow. "Hey, whaddaya think you're doing, fella?" he bleated. With a backhanded wallop that sounded like hitting a plank with an ax, Tex belted the gambler off his feet and over a bench, then went on to the door and down the stairs.

Half-an-hour later, Solo Swanson and two hard-looking friends arrived at Tex's cabin. Tex was sitting on a block of wood outside, rifle beside him, a coil of rope across his knees. He was tying a hangman's knot. "Good evenin," he said to Solo. "I was hopin' ya'd stick around. Seems like this here camp has got real crummy whilst I was away. So I figgered I'd round up some o' the boys an' have a clean-up party. An' you shore are invited—that is, if yer still around."

Solo caught on fast. He gulped, turned pale, and said the only thing he could have said in the circumstances. "Why, the fact is," he declared, "I'm just leaving. Merely dropped by to say so long."

That was how Tex acquired Smoky, the killer—one of the only two authentic canine killers the territory has produced, so far as I know. Oolinka told me some of the story, Tex the rest. In years to come I was to see the terrible little dog in action many times. And I saw him die a hero's death one red day on Hornet Creek. I will get around to telling you about it. . . .

Blue shadows were slanting across Cloud Creek valley now, and the sun was speared on the sharp summit of a peak. For supper Oolinka prepared a brisket stew and sourdough bread. We ate, then Tex climbed into the siwash cache and tossed down blankets and two balloon-silk tarps. "Better turn in an' git some sleep, Redhead. On account of we're gonna hit the trail early—if ya still wanta see them big jewels."

I said I wanted to see them, believe me.

Oolinka had picked up the blankets and tarps. She stood waiting, with the reflected glow of sunset on her face, wearing that unreadable expression again. Tex came down the ladder. "I got m' own bunk in the tent. You two'll have to make out fer yerselves." He left us. I took part of the bedding from Oolinka. I had spotted a nice heap of leaves under a cottonwood. "Find yourself a place to sleep," I told her, and made for the tree.

"All right," Oolinka said.

In the long shadows of daybreak, carrying light stampede packs, we started up to the inner circle of peaks. We skirted a wide, uptorn gravel moraine resembling the cold wreckage of a planet. One at a time, tiptoeing, we crossed crusted snow bridges shaking from the pressure of hidden, booming waters. Then we climbed onto Cloud Creek glacier. It was a tilted ribbon of green ice, mostly smooth, with castellated gray crests sheering close on both sides.

The sun rolled up the brilliant sky and flooded the stark gulches and ravines with light. We had covered maybe five miles when Tex halted suddenly, pointing. Partway up the mountain to our right was a crimson wedge of frosted heather—and feeding on it was a black bear. He was so fat he waddled. His pelt shone like polished jet. Tex put his glasses on the animal. Then he started to check the sights of his rifle. But then all at once he lowered the weapon as an idea struck him that made him grin.

He said something to Oolinka in the Indian language.

She nodded, her lips tightening. I could see she was gauging the distance to the bear.

"We're gonna need meat, Redhead," Tex said. "Oolinka claims you can shoot. So how about lettin' that bear down? We'll take part o' the meat, an' hang the rest in a ice crack."

The green-eyed shaggy old devil had deliberately put me on the spot. Now it was up to me to save face if I could.

I figured the bear was 600, maybe 700 yards distant. A mean and dirty shot, especially as I was using iron sights. I didn't think I could hit him. I'd had good training at home from an uncle, Captain Hardy, who had been a world champion shot. But still—. Suppose a wind was blowing up there. Suppose the crystal-clear mountain air was fooling me, and the bear was half again as far distant as he seemed. Suppose a lot of things. But I had to try. I didn't see how I could get out of it. Tex was lighting his pipe with elaborate unconcern. Oolinka had come over to stand at my left elbow. I saw her flash a look at Tex's back that should have burned a hole in his shirt. Smoky had either seen the bear or winded him, because he uttered an eager, throaty little sound and crouched down, watching the mountainside.

Make it good, bucko. Make it good now. Make it good.

I ejected the chamber load of the Winchester and dumped the magazine. It had been loaded with 220-grain shells. I replaced them with 180-grain stuff that had been factory-fresh when I left the States. Hoping I was right, I jacked the receiver sight up to 650 yards, and double-checked the micrometer mark against a table I had pasted on the rifle's stock. Then I sat down, elbows on my knees, and picked the bear up. It didn't look so good. The bead covered the animal. But I was holding steady. So I blanked the bear with the point of gold and squeezed off the shot. The Winchester barked sharp and clean, the report racketing off twenty square miles of cliff faces. The bear didn't drop. He half turned to face us, as if only mildly interested. I was slamming in another shell and was going to click the sight up to 700 yards and was saying, "Damn it. Damn it anyway," when something like a miracle happened.

As if struck by lightning, the bear suddenly toppled sidewise and came rolling, limp as a bundle of rags and obviously stone dead.

Tex lowered his glass. "Fer gawd's sake, Oolinka, did ya see what this Redhead jest done? He gut-shot our bear instead o' shootin' him through the neck or head. Now we gotta spend a hour or so cleanin' junk an' stuff outa the carcass."

Until I found out otherwise I was pretty darned certain the bear had dropped dead of heart failure. I think I told Oolinka thanks for the compliment. I wanted to pet the Winchester a little myself.

"Aw, well," Tex said, shrugging in mock resignation. "I can hardly remember hit, but I was fifteen oncet myself—I think."

Loaded with bear meat, we went on up the glacier until a complex of yawning indigo-blue crevasses forced us to leave the ice and turn in to a steep canyon. The canyon widened into a saucer-shaped valley. Tex led the way across the valley to a milky streamlet brawling from under a great, gleaming permanent snow field. Fringing the creek was a thicket of dead alders, their gnarled, crooked branches looking like the upraised arms of drowning witches. Probably nowhere on earth could you find a more lost, desolate, forlorn spot. It was cold. It was lifeless. It was a never-never place, the kind of place Indian snow-ghosts are said to inhabit, wailing forever in bitter protest against their fate. Tex dropped his pack, fumbling for his pipe and sheep-bladder tobacco pouch.

"Here we are," he announced cheerfully. "Pick out the million dollars' worth o' jewelry ya wanta tote back."

Then I began to see them.

They were above us on the hillside, great rounded boulders, a half dozen in sight, each weighing tons. They were blue, green, yellow, violet. I went up to the nearest one. It was the color of deep-sea water, partly transparent, with a yellowish mass near its center. Tex joined me. Handing me the camp ax, he said, "Bust off a chunk fer a souvenir." I swung the single-bitted ax as hard as I could. The steel clanged against the stone and bounced back so violently the ax almost flew out of my hand. Not a mark showed on the blue surface.

"Why don't you dynamite them?" I asked.

"Jewelers claim hit'd ruin 'em—flaw 'em so bad the pieces wouldn't be worth haulin' fer road ballast. Doggone if hit ain't a problem. The only chance I see is to find a little one a man could carry. Tomorrow we'll try our luck."

I climbed onto the green stone because it looked like emerald, and I had read that a piece of emerald that would fill your hand would be worth a million dollars. *You wanted adventure and here you are sitting on a billion bucks. If you had this in the States you could hire Rockefeller for your private secretary.* I heard a sound at the back side of the huge gem, and turned to see Tex doing something there that nobody ought to do against the side of a billion bucks.

It was coming dusk. Oolinka had built a fire on the creek bank and was frying bear liver and roasting a rack of ribs. We sat on our bedrolls and ate. When we had finished the liver, we sliced chunks of meat and sizzling fat from the ribs and juggled them in our hands until they were cool enough to put into our mouths. The meat was sweet and tender, like young pork but with the flavor of the blueberries on which the bear had been feeding. Tex said he wished we had brought along a couple of yards of the bear's intestines. The best campfire grub in the world, he said, was bear gut stuffed with fat and roasted over alder coals. It would put hair on a man's chest, he said, and make him bark like a dog wolf in January.

Tex was filling his pipe when Oolinka said to me, "Your left pac is torn at the heel." So I took the pac off and handed it to her. I was learning. From somewhere she had produced a three-cornered buckskin needle and a strip of sinew. Sitting cross-legged by the fire, she stripped a thread off the sinew, moistened it in her mouth, and rolled it between her hands to make it round. Then she threaded the needle and began sewing my pac. Tex looked at his own battered pacs, at the ragged knees of his pants, and sighed lugubriously.

"Reckon ya know the joke about what hit takes to be a sourdough," he said. "Well, ya got part of hit done. You've killed a bear. an' got yerself a Injun seamstress—but ya ain't spit in the Yukon yet. So I guess we better arrange that."

Smoky came out of the shadows and curled up beside me with his head on my knee. I wanted so much to make friends with the gentle, wonderful little demon that I was afraid to move. I didn't want to do anything wrong. But after a minute or two I reached down and rubbed his ear. Smoky sighed comfortably, and raised his head and swiped my hand once with his tongue. I was accepted. I was his friend. Tex was watching amused. His swamp-green eyes were bright in the firelight.

"Yeah, I reckon we gotta arrange that," the towering mountain man repeated. "That's something we gotta get around to pronto."

Adventure Is My Business

PART 3

Continuing—the true and thrilling Alaskan adventures of one of America's great outdoor writers. Here are stories of the courageous men who are fighting on our last frontier.

The wilderness is a heartless jade. She can be wonderful. Also she can be a bum, a tramp. She will promise and promise, then get a kick out of slamming the door in your face. . . . We had been in our blankets maybe three hours. It was a still night with a handful of pale stars showing through a thin overcast. The only sound was the icy tinkle of the creek. Then, with no warning, a storm crept over the northern summits like a gray lynx and pounced, screaming. Wind of tornado velocity hit the camp. The coffee bucket clattered past my head and vanished into the darkness. Pebbles and dead alder branches followed. I stood up to look for shelter, clutching my blankets and the Winchester, and the wind spun me around and hurled me across Tex and Smoky. When I struggled to my feet there was snow in the wind, dry flakes that stung like a sandblast.

"Hit's a williwaw," Tex shouted. "Git up behind one o' them boulders. Where's Oolinka?"

"I am here," she said behind me in the darkness.

Clinging to each other, leaning into the unbelievable force of the wind, the slim, clean-limbed Indian ex-slave girl and I made our way up the hillside to the first of the huge, strange jewel rocks—the blue one from which I had tried to break a chip. The stone back-shelved on the lee side, offering shelter for two persons. I shoved my bedding in out of the wind and went back to the creek for my pack. Tex and I collided again in the clamorous, snow-filled blackness. He was cussing with vigor and variety. I understood why. The snowfall would balk his hope of finding a gem small enough to carry out to civilization.

"Be knee-deep around here afore this lets up," he hollered. "Doggone the lousy luck to hell anyway."

He had found shelter for himself behind a boulder close above the one I had chosen. Passing me, he said, "Now you two stay put. Don't wander around none. A wolf could git lost in this mess." Oolinka had spread my blankets against the rock and placed hers beside them. I stood the packboard up as a windbreak for our heads, slid the Winchester under the blankets, and got in myself. Oolinka was a formless blur in the shrieking gloom, but I could tell from her movements that she was taking off her moccasins and the caribou fawn shirt. I felt good. The drums and trumpets of the great storm wind excited me. It was wonderful being snug and warm with all that elemental fury howling past.

Oolinka touched my arm. "Where will you go when we leave here?"

"I don't know. Anywhere. I haven't made any deal with Tex."

"Can I go too? I will work hard. I can drive dogs, skin animals, cook. I will do what you tell me to do."

That one I didn't want to think about. I didn't know how to answer her. So I asked a couple of questions instead. They had been bothering me since the day on the Cloud Creek trail when Blind Nick traded her to me for a brown bear carcass. "Why were you a slave? Nobody had to be one. . . . And where did you learn to speak English?"

Oolinka moved closer as a savage gust whirled snow under the boulder's overhang. When she spoke her voice was like a sleepy child's. "I will tell you a story," she said.

It was the most terrible story I ever heard.

"My father was second chief at Tyone Village. It was autumn, and we had all gone into the hills above the lakes to hunt caribou. There were ten families. I was eight years old and my brother Ilya—you saw him with Blind Nick—was six. Caribou were very plentiful, and we were all busy. When the hunters brought in meat and skins, even the children helped with the work. We cut the meat into strips and hung it on racks to dry for winter. We pegged down the skins and scraped them until they were white and soft, ready for making moccasins, sleeping bags and parkas. If there was spare time, we gathered blueberries and wild-rose berries, and trapped the little striped squirrels in goose-quill snares for parka trimming. We broke the leg bones of the caribou we killed and stored the rich marrow-fat in rawhide pouches. It was a good time, with much feasting and laughing and singing. It was the best time I ever knew.

"Then one day a stranger—a man of the Ulchana people—came to our camp from the east, where he had been working for white men who were mining gold. He was sick. It was the spotted sickness. He died the first night, and within one week we were all sick. We tried at first to care for one another, but soon there was none left who could walk. A man would drop dead trying to crawl to the creek for water. You would see a woman lying dead with a child trying to nurse from her cold breast. Finally only my brother and I and a hunter named Googla were left. We were very weak, and I think Googla was crazy from grief. He sat beside his dead wife all one day, crying. Then, as the sun went down, he put the muzzle of his rifle in his mouth and pulled the trigger."

"So only my brother and I were left there in the camp of the dead.

"We lay on caribou skins in the tent and heard ravens and wolves looting our food stores and devouring the corpses of our friends. Once a shadow fell across my face from the open tent flaps, and I opened my eyes and saw a wolf standing there. His mouth was open as if he was laughing. He was a black wolf with beautiful, wicked green eyes like stars. My father's rifle was beside me and I tried to lift it, but was too weak. With what strength I had, I pulled back the hammer and fired the gun into the ground. The black wolf jumped aside and went away. The ravens flew up from the bodies of the dead people. But in a little while they were all back. They knew they didn't have to be afraid.

"At first we had water in the tent—a bucketful my father had brought before he died. Then the water was gone and my brother was crying and crying for a drink. I tried to go to the creek to fill the bucket. It was only 100 feet, but after trying all morning, I was only halfway. I kept fainting, and each time the blackness settled over me I thought I was dead. Then I heard voices. I came back from the cold, black place I had been in, and saw three men coming into the camp. One was a tall man with dead eyes who was being led at the end of a painted stick. I had never seen him before but I knew who he was—Blind Nick, the mighty shaman. He washed my brother and me, and fed us, and brought us back to life. He kept us with him. We had nobody else. All our relatives were dead. By the law of my people we were slaves. We owed Blind Nick our lives and he could do with us as he pleased. I know that is not the white man's law. But—but—there were no white men there to save us when we were dying."

"And Blind Nick taught you English?"

"Yes. He said that some day I would belong to a white man and I would need to know his language. He is very wise."

So there was a bedtime story Alaska style. Some day you'll write it, Bucko. Just the way she told it. With the tremendous bellowing williwaw wind for background music, and the snow whirling in out of the blackness—and the sleepy child's voice speaking calmly of stark horror. . . .

The storm lasted two days. On the morning of the second day a grim thing happened. I awoke as a wan, somber dawn was breaking over the valley. During the night the wind-driven snow had formed a high semicircular combing in the lee of our boulder, so that we were in a sort of crystal cave—a natural igloo. An inch or so of snow had sifted in on my blankets. As I was brushing it off, an animal snarled practically in my ear. I jerked around, reaching for the Winchester, but saw nothing. Oolinka was still asleep, head pillowed on her arm, the Hudson Bay blanket snugged close up to her chin, her braids across my chest. Savage storms had no terror for her.

I listened. I think I was holding my breath.

Minutes passed and there was no sound except the eerie screeching of the wind. Then snow crunched audibly, and the packboard at the head of my bed moved slightly. Some animal had burrowed down through the snow to it from the outside of our igloo, and was trying to get at the bear meat it contained. Judging from the snarl I had heard, it was a sizable beast, and not a gentle one. I slipped the safety latch of the Winchester and rose to my knees. As I did so, the head of the animal appeared over the snow combing. It was a furry demon mask—dark little shoe-button eyes, gleaming teeth, round close-set ears. I knew what it was from pictures I had seen. A wolverine. An "Injun devil." Supposedly the craftiest, most ferocious animal in the North.

With another rasping snarl, he grabbed the wooden horn of the packboard and dropped back out of view, tugging and clawing to break the pack free of the wind-stiffened snow. I stood up, shoved the muzzle of the Winchester over the combing, and fired almost in his face. He rolled over with a squall and flipped himself around the corner of the boulder. Before I could pull on my pacs to follow him, Smoky arrived on the scene. Then suddenly Oolinka was standing beside me, knife in her hand. Then Tex appeared from behind his snow-hooded sheltering boulder. Shouting instructions, he came plunging down through the drifts.

"Fer gawd's sake, don't let Smoky tangle with that varmint! Grab him by the tail an' haul him back. An' be keerful yerself. Doggone the dang-blasted lousy—."

The wolverine came back in sight around the boulder, with Smoky raging behind him. I had shot his left eye out and blown a piece of his skull away. He should have been dead but wasn't. He came up the snow cornice with the obvious intention of jumping down into our shelter. I couldn't shoot because of Smoky. Tex couldn't shoot because of us. So I jabbed at the animal with the Winchester, fending him off, and he set his bloody jaws on the barrel of the gun and savaged it, wheezing and coughing. Then Oolinka leaned forward and her knife flashed. The short, curved, whetted blade cut the wolverine's head half off. The dying animal rolled back down the combing, and Smoky took him by the stomach, shook him, and threw him.

"Was that brute crazy?" I asked Tex.

"Naw. He was desprit, that's all. Look." With the toe of his pac he nudged the wolverine's left front leg. The leg ended just below the knee on a scabbed, bloody stump from which jagged bone protruded. "Got hisself into a trap somewheres. Gnawed his leg off and been starvin' ever since."

So he hadn't been a ferocious were-creature after all. He was only a rugged little beast trying to keep alive.

We came to the Knik on a gray noon, after eight days of hard travel. The peaks were white now, but the broad valley had no snow yet. It was a place of bleak, desert-like sand wastes, frozen hard as concrete, margined by strips of spruce and cottonwood. Whispering mush ice clogged the river. It formed on the rocky bottom, broke loose, and rose to the surface. It was soft, watery stuff, but in a night it could freeze solid and lock the river until spring. Tex led the way to a twenty-foot, flat-bottomed riverboat cached in a highbush cranberry thicket. While Oolinka made tea and bannocks for lunch, Tex and I calked the boat with strips of gunny sacking, jamming the burlap into the seams with our belt knives.

She ain't much," Tex said. "Still, if we bail like heck mebbe she'll git us to town."

Tex was at the oars, dropping us down a long ice-filled chute, watching for rocks and deadheads and trying to guess where the channel was, when we saw a man on a bar point at the foot of the fast water. The man sat on a drift log, hunched over, head in his hands. He was lean and gray-headed, and looked like a dude. I mean, he wore the dude uniform—whipcord breeches, high laced boots, gaudy blanket coat. A stiff-brimmed Stetson lay on the frozen sand beside him. Smoke curled lazily from a dying fire back against the timber. A crude raft was moored in an eddy below the bar point. Tex took his hook-stemmed pipe out of his mouth and bawled a halloo that started echoes off the mountainside.

The man didn't reply. He didn't even raise his head. He was now rocking back and forth, hands clenched in his gray hair as if he was going to start pulling it out. Tex shrugged. Keeping his eyes carefully on the man, he eased the boat in to shore. He stepped out, tied the boat to a snag, and swaggered across the bar, rifle in the crook of his arm. Oolinka and I followed. As we came closer, we could hear the man uttering hoarse little panting sounds like an animal in its final agony. It made my scalp tingle. I found myself gripping the Winchester and wishing he would look up, or say something, make any sound except that horrible moaning.

"What's wrong, partner—ya got trouble?" Tex said.

The man muttered something but the words blurred together. He shuddered, lifted his head, and stared at us. His eyes were wild. By a visible effort of will he pulled himself together for a moment. "Toothache," he said, "five days," and hunched forward again, moaning as before. Tex scratched his head. He glanced at the clumsy raft, at the man's siwash camp, at the freezing river and at the sun. Worry was written all over his face.

"Could ya hold out till we git ya down to Matanusky?"

So abruptly that it startled me and I involuntarily raised the Winchester, the man leaped erect, waving his arms. "Pull the accursed thing," he yelled. "Pull it, for God's sake, or do me a favor—shoot me." He slumped back onto the log, writhed off it, and lay doubled up on the sand, pulling at his hair with both hands.

"Sounds like he wants us to pull a tooth," Tex said. "So—."

He went back to the boat and, rummaging through his possible sack, brought out a pair of pliers. "Use 'em fer dequilling dogs," he said. He came back and hoisted the man back to a sitting position on the log, lifting him by the collar of his coat as easily as if he had been a child. Then, tilting the man's head back and holding it clamped under his elbow, he shoved a thumb into the suffering wayfarer's mouth and pried it open. "Which one is hit?" The man gurgled something unintelligible. "Yeah, I see hit now," Tex said. "Hold still." He shoved the pliers into the man's mouth, took a grip on a tooth, and pulled it with a twist and a yank.

The man was beating at him with both fists, pushing him away. He got Tex's thumb out of his mouth, and wailed, "Wrong one! The broken molar behind it!"

"Oh, that one."

Tex pulled the indicated tooth, wiped the pliers on his pants, and shoved them into a hip pocket. He lifted the man to his feet. "Come on, we gotta move. Git into the boat. We'll pick up yer outfit."

An hour later, en route downriver, our new passenger was able to introduce himself.

"I am Chauncey Harrison Swearingen," he said in the deep, affected voice of an old-time Shakespearian actor, "wastrel, spendthrift, and sometime drunkard—the 'sometime' meaning that often I am out of funds. I came up this wilderness river to kill a moose. I hoped to raft the meat back to town and sell it. The money would have paid my board bill at the roadhouse. Also it would have re-established my credit with a certain bootlegger. But I was betrayed by a tooth. It broke on a piece of hardtack." He spat blood over the side, bowed to Oolinka, and held his hand out to me.

"This lad is the Redhead," Tex said. "The girl belongs to him. I'm Tex Cobb."

"Ah, yes. The incomparable Tex Cobb, man of the North, nonpareil woodsman." Respect was in his eyes.

Tex was busy a few moments taking us around a big cottonwood grounded in the center of the stream with an ice jam forming against it. Then he turned his hard green-eyed gaze on Chauncey Harrison Swearingen.

"Ya know anything about books, Chancy?"

"Yes, sir. I have some acquaintance with them. I studied at Oxford, the Ecole Polytechnique in Paris, and at the University of Barcelona."

"Whatever the hell that means." Tex fended an ice cake off with an oar. "Could ya be any help to a feller who's gonna be a writer—he wants to write about adventure—but who ain't finished the eighth grade?'

Chauncey looked at me, quick intelligence in his gray dissipated face, and an age-old weariness. He nodded slowly. "Thus opportunity—arriving down a wilderness river on the edge of winter, with a pair of pliers. Yes, I could help. How much would depend upon the human material. But I could help. . . ."

A bright heliograph flash on shore caught my eye. It was the polished upper surface of a bull moose's antler. Two enormous dark beasts were straining head-to-head in mortal combat. Tex shot the boat to shore. I followed him through the undergrowth. As we came up, I saw a cow to one side, feeding, indifferent to the duel.

The two bulls had backed away, some thirty feet apart. The elderly bull—he had a hayrack of spike-tined antlers—was tricky. He came in straight, then slewed aside, so that his antler caught the young bull off-center. The young bull was thrown off balance. As he sought to recover himself, the patriarch took him squarely in the ribs with both antlers and lifted him off his feet. The youngster landed on his back, all four legs in the air. When he scrambled up, the old-timer was at his rump, raking him right and left. So the apprentice fled. And when he came past us, Tex shot him through the neck.

We camped late one night on a willow-bordered slough, and early in the morning, breaking ice, we went on a few miles to the foot of a bluff where a cabin stood. Tex pushed open the unlocked door and built a fire. We ate fried moose liver and boiled moose tongue, then Chauncey said, "What books have you read, lad?"

I said, "The ones I liked were *Treasure Island, Huckleberry Finn, Martin Eden, the Iliad,* and *Caesar's Commentaries.*"

Chauncey sputtered on a mouthful of coffee. "And you haven't finished the eighth grade? I suspect you suffer from mental indigestion. . . . Tell me, at what point, in your opinion, did *Huckleberry Finn* cease to be a work of art? I mean, when should Samuel Clemens have stopped writing and called it a job well done?"

I was on the spot. But I put my mind on the book.

"He should have stopped when the Negro Sam was kidnapped."

Chauncey was silent a long moment. He said, "I gather I am to be your tutor. We will get you some books. I am a remittance man. In a day or two—or a week or two—I will receive a check, then we'll send for books. Some natural history. A good grammar. Kipling's verse. The Old Testament. Shakespeare's plays. Swinburne. And I think—yes—the poems of Francois Villon." His voice rang sonorously. "Our sad, mad, glad, bad brother Villon. Bird of the bitter, bright, gray, golden morn."

"Nobody asked ya t' pay fer any books," Tex said gruffly. "Jest make out a list o' the ones ya need."

Adventure Is My Business

PART 4

This was the raw North at its rawest—
the great subarctic wolves at work. . . . The boy cheechako
gazes as the devil pack cuts down a moose.

On this hard, beautiful Alaska frontier the ancient dramas of birth and death, greed and kindness, love and hate were not complicated. They were reduced to starkest simplicity. So it was a grand country for a lad with the compelling lust to learn. . . .

We had just finished our first meal after arriving at Tex's lowland cabin, when there was a knock on the door. Tex opened it. An Indian boy was standing there. He said, "The Widder Jones wants to see you."

Tex said sheepishly, "Uh-oh. Yeah. Well, tell her I'll be at her house directly."

The big mountain man spent an hour getting ready for the visit. He shaved off his black jungle of beard, and let Chauncey Harrison Swearingen cut his hair. He doused his face with bay rum, pared his fingernails with his belt knife. Oolinka was banished outside while he took a bath in a tin washtub and changed into a pair of Mackinaw pants which, at least, had a whole seat and knees. "Damn hit," he complained bitterly, "I smell like a dude an' feel nekkid as a skinned bear. But if I hadn't cleaned up here, the Widder would of made me do hit over there—at the waterin' trough. Prob'ly with a wire brush." He put on a beat-up 7X Stetson, which must have cost him anyway the price of two prime beaver plews, and tilted it at a rakish angle.

"Well, let's git goin'," he said, including us all with a sweep of his arm, "an' find out what I've done wrong this time."

Smoky ahead, we followed a narrow, frozen, wagon-rutted road through leafless second-growth cottonwoods. The sun, peering faintly for a moment through the overcast, had still not reached its zenith. Blowing off the white peaks was a wind with a knife in it. Flaws of snow, dry as ice dust, whirled through the bare trees. Everything about the day was melancholy and foreboding, filled with a grim promise—a promise of which all the wilderness was aware. We had just come in sight of a farmstead set in a wide clearing, when a thrilling, spine-tingling sound arose somewhere beyond the waves of timber. It was a long baritone howl. It climbed smoothly up the scale until it became a mere brittle thread of sound. Then it was picked up in the middle distance, and once again to the left, the three voices blending in full choral volume. A sudden excitement gripped me. I had the urge to throw back my head and join in. I felt an eerie kinship with the wild unseen signalers.

That's your first timber-wolf serenade, bucko. That's the song of the North, the song of the big snows and the big frost. And you'll never in your life hear anything that'll give you a greater thrill.

Tex had halted, listening closely. "Now I wonder what those lousy, no-good varmints are up to? Sounds like a king wolf is callin' his pack together. Which means some poor critter'll git pulled down an' et alive today."

The wolf music merged into the mournful whine of the wind and died away. We went on to the farmstead. There was a large two-story frame house, with a cluster of log outbuildings. A roan mule and a pair of fat black work horses stood in the lee of a sod-roofed barn. A buzz saw was set up beside a mountainous heap of firewood. Some red chickens were discouragedly scratching the frozen earth of the barnyard.

Tex knocked on the door of the farmhouse, and a woman's voice told us to come in.

The Widder was a woman for a Viking sea king. All she needed was a raven-winged helmet, a sword, and a shield. She stood almost as tall as Tex. She was full bosomed, square-shouldered, and narrow-waisted. She had cornflower-blue eyes with laughter crinkles at the sides, and a mass of gold-bronze hair bound at the nape of her neck. Maybe forty years old. But you could see they had been good years. Tex introduced us, and she shook hands like a man. Her grip felt as if it could hold plow handles and swing axes. Probably it had. She turned to face Tex, looking him up and down critically. Then she sniffed, and made a wry face, and laughed, "Man, bay rum again?"

The Widder herded us into her kitchen. Sitting in an easy chair beside a big black gleaming range was a character. The guy was skinny and bucktoothed. He wore a shiny blue serge suit and a pink silk shirt with a celluloid collar and flaming bow tie. In one hand he held a slab of apple pie, in the other a cup of coffee. His right foot, heavily bandaged at the ankle, rested on a stool. He grinned, mumbling greetings past a mouthful of pie, while his gaze took Oolinka apart. He had eyes like a rutting billy goat's. I started to burn.

Look out, son. Here's a phony. Here's a country clown on the make. And sure as hell there's going to be trouble.

"This," said the Widder, "is Mr. Harvey Dusseldorf. He is a new homesteader in the valley, and he sprained his ankle trying to do me a favor. So"—she placed an arm on Tex's shoulder and rocked him back and forth, smiling—"you will now please take over the chore. You came home just in time."

"Yeah. Looks as if I did, at that," Tex agreed. His swamp-green eyes regarded her somberly. "What is this here chore?"

The Widder explained. She said she wanted Tex to track down her brown Jersey cow Bessie. It seemed that Bessie had been missing five days. The Dusseldorf character had spent part of four days trailing her, the Widder said. Then he had slipped on the ice of a slough and sprained his ankle. He had last seen the cow's tracks at Spruce Butte. The whole thing was very strange, the Widder said, and she couldn't understand it, because Bessie had never strayed before. So she wanted Tex to start right now, and find out what had happened to the animal.

"Right now, ma'am?" Tex said. "Why, good gosh, I only jest got here. I—."

"Right now. And one more thing. While you're at Spruce Butte, you find out if the Campbells are all right. They're there alone, just the two of them, and Mrs. Campbell is expecting—she's only a girl, and she's my friend—and nobody's heard from them in two weeks."

Tex said sorrowfully, "Well, I guess the Redhead an' I better git started then, dang the luck anyhow." He looked at me. "Oolinka?"

"She will stay here with the Widder." And I looked at Dusseldorf. "I know she will be all right." Then words started to get away from me. "If she isn't—." I was getting light and easy on my feet again and that hollow singing feeling was starting in my chest.

Chauncey, the Widder, and Tex spoke in the same breath. "She will be all right." The Widder put her arm around Oolinka and held her close. At first the slender, jet-eyed, lynx kitten of an Indian girl tensed. Then she bowed her head, relaxing against the Widder's breast. I saw that she was trembling. I think it was the first time another woman had been kind to her since the terrible day her mother died in the death camp above Tyone. I wanted to touch her and say good-bye, everything will be well, but again I didn't have any words like that for a girl.

Outside, with Tex and Smoky, when I picked up the Winchester, I said, "If that guy—."

Tex said, "He won't. His number was up twenty minutes ago. I dunno jest how yet. But believe me, hit was up."

As we left the homestead the king wolf howled again. This time his voice was different. It shuddered only partly up the scale and then broke off into hot, excited yapping. Tex said, "Maybe that's where the trouble is. So we'll head over there, pronto. He's close under Spruce Butte anyway." The green-eyed mountain man headed into the timber at his mile-eating trail pace, his .30-06 Sauer Mauser in the crook of his arm. It was the most beautiful weapon I have ever seen.

The ice-dust snow was feathering faster and faster through the bare branches of the cottonwoods, and a steel-gray haze had hidden the great peaks, when we approached the dark two-dimensional footslopes leading to Spruce Butte. Ahead of us through the close-packed dusky ranks of timber was the white glimmer of a frozen lake. Then I heard the clatter of shelf ice breaking. It sounded like an acre of plate glass giving way. Tex halted. Through the timber, in full flight, came a cow moose. She was an ancient, ribby, sway-backed old bat, and she was terrified. With her mulelike ears laid back tight against her head, she was traveling at a plunging gallop—and when a moose gallops it is really frightened. Tex let her pass. Then he moved fast toward the lake shore. I guess he knew already what was going on out there. When we busted through the final frost-killed thicket of head-high cranberry brush to the margin of the nameless lake, we beheld a sight to make every woodsman's blood pressure soar.

Trapped by seven Alaska timber wolves—the largest and most deadly timber wolves on the planet *(Canis lupus pambasileus)*—

was a moose spring calf. So savage are the giant northern wolves when they kill in packs that even an Alaska cow moose will abandon her calf when they attack, as this cow just had. The seven wolves were playing with the calf. The doomed young beast would probably have weighed 500 pounds, and it could have fled at race-horse speed, but in its frightful predicament it was hypnotized. It simply stood there, head down, feet braced wide, eyes rolling, ribs heaving, frozen by the instinctive knowledge that it was only seconds from the most horrible death a wild animal may expect. Tense Smoky lay quiet at a low command from Tex.

Apparently only casually observant, the seven killers sat in a loose circle about the trembling calf. Two of the wolves were silver-gray, one was brown, three were black with dirty white markings on chest and belly—and the seventh was a giant white wolf that blended into the dusky whiteness of the ice like a phantom. He was almost as large as a Shetland pony, a ghost shape with dragging tail and high-held head with open grinning jaws from which puffs of white vapor rose into the frosty air.

Tex said through gritted teeth, "That's Whitey, the blasted king wolf of the Knik. I knew hit when I heard the dirty so-and-so howl two hours ago." Tex found himself better footing and raised the beautiful Sauer Mauser.

All right, son, you've wondered if this paragon of the North could really shoot. You never knew a man who could make that shot. Not in this light. Not at that distance. It's got to be 300 yards. Now we'll see.

The king wolf was partly hidden behind the calf. Just sitting there. Tex wanted so badly to blast this snowy-pelted killer of the Knik that he sacrificed the calf. While he waited for a clear shot, a black wolf flashed in and, so easily that at first I thought nothing had happened, cut the calf's left hamstring. At the same time the brown wolf took the calf from the side. He grabbed the calf's entire flank between his jaws and wrenched, bracing his feet on the ice and pulling back, and then in an instant the calf's entire paunch was torn open and the brown wolf was still bracing his feet and moving backward and shaking his head with two yards of intestine strung between him and the calf, and now suddenly the snow was red with blood and the calf was dead on his feet and did not yet know it.

Tex said, "Damn hit, damn hit, anyway."

And then he put the Sauer to his shoulder and began shooting. I never would have believed it, and I had been trained most carefully in the matter of shooting by a champion of the world. . . . So the thin-barreled .30-06 blasted, and the white wolf spun on the ice like the *fiffolet*—the snow devil of the Tena people—and then he was lost in a blue shadow in which his pelt blended so perfectly that nobody—I mean nobody—could have caught him in iron sights. So, faster than the beat of a raven's wing, the Mauser bolt rattled and the hot ejected cartridge hit me in the face, and it was still in the air when the brown wolf, that had hamstrung the calf, was down on the ice kicking, with his back broken. I took a step ahead for a better look at this phenomenal shooting, and Tex's hard elbow caught me in the ribs as he slammed another cartridge into the chamber, and then the Sauer crashed again, and a black wolf pitched straight ahead onto his brisket and lay there without a movement. Meanwhile the other members of the killer pack had streaked so far across the lake that they were safe.

There it was, bucko. Now you've seen it. You've seen a champion in action. Never forget it.

Tex said, "The bastards ain't worth pelting. And there's no bounty on 'em."

Then Smoky whined and I heard something coming through the snow crusted timber behind us. I whirled with the Winchester up. Suddenly Tex was beside me. Through the transparent turquoise woodland shadows came a slender, free-striding, lynx-footed figure. It was Oolinka.

I said, "Why are you here?"

"Blind Nick told me to follow you. So I came."

"Are you still taking orders from Blind Nick?"

"No."

"Then why did you follow me?"

"He said you would need me." The pretty, probably sixteen-year-old Tena girl was avoiding my eyes. Tex was pointedly moving beyond earshot.

Because there was something I wanted very much to know I asked, "How did he tell you?"

She said, "He is able to tell me things like that, but I do not know how he does it. I only know that he does. I have not seen him. Nobody else has told me. I only know that this is so. So I came. And whenever else you will need me, I will come.

"Once Blind Nick told me the story of Ruth," Oolinka said. "He told me, 'Whither thou goest, there will I also go—.'"

Tex came toward me. He said, "Just a small piece of advice, Redhead—if she thinks Blind Nick told her to follow you, maybe it would be a purty good idea to hold still. On account of I've got a feeling myself—a fancy one—about this whole thing."

So we went on, the three of us, through the whispering dry snow and now the wind was making wild warlock music through the gaunt trees. Somewhere in the wintry valley there was a sick king wolf. Somewhere—maybe still alive—was the Widder Jones's cow Bessie. And somewhere ahead under the silhouette of Spruce Butte, which looked like a piece of black cardboard posted against the close gray horizon, was a little family of cheechakos, probably in trouble.

Then the quick-eyed Indian girl said, "There is the Campbell homestead—and I think they have trouble, as Blind Nick thought."

In the raw new clearing ahead stood a clumsily built spruce-log cabin so recently raised that no weeds had yet taken root on its dirt roof. No smoke issued from the new wire-guided tin stovepipe. A black-and-white spotted Holstein cow mooed forlornly from a pole corral below the cabin. From somewhere behind the corral dashed a skinny yellow mongrel dog that showed his teeth and began yapping ferociously until he saw Smoky, the gentle but terrible little berserker ex-professional fighting dog. Then the mongrel became silent and obviously fearful, tucking his tail between his legs and hastily departing back whence he had come. Otherwise there were no signs of life at the homestead.

Tex said, "I don't think we're gonna like this."

He knocked on the hand-hewed plank door. Inside we heard a sound that was a cross between a moan and a whimper. Tex pulled the babiche thong of the latch and shoved the door open. Across the single large room, on a bunk made of plain spruce planks, lay a woman. She had dark hair and blue eyes, and perhaps ordinarily she was pretty. But now she was wild-eyed and haggard. and her face was contorted with pain. Only a red wool blanket protected her from the cold of the unheated cabin.

Tex stood the Sauer beside the door and crossed the room to her.

She looked at him with wide, unseeing eyes. Then she moaned, "The pains—the ragged, tearing pains—are coming every five minutes. My husband went for a doctor, but has not returned." She tried to speak again but the words were lost as pain caught her once more and her body arched and shook convulsively under the red blanket.

On a homemade chair beside her bed was a nickel-plated clock, a pitcher of water and a pencil and sheet of paper with figures written on it. Tex glanced at the figures and said, "Well, I ain't no sawbones, but hit appears to me that Alasky is gonna have another citizen practically at once."

What happened in the next thirty minutes was something that probably every fifteen-year-old youngster should witness.

A child was born. Tex and Oolinka took charge of the matter. I built a fire in the cast-iron cookstove and kept it going with such furious energy that the pipe was red halfway to the roof when the baby uttered his first mewling squall.

Oolinka said, "It is a man-child, and he will be strong and healthy."

"How do you know?" Tex said.

Oolinka looked at him in wide-eyed surprise. "Because when he was born he fought me, and he sought his mother's breast like a hungry wolf puppy—as you saw and heard yourself. . . . The woman should have meat broth, I think."

There was no meat in the cabin. Through my mind flashed the irrational thought that maybe I ought to go out and kill the spotted cow. But Tex had a better idea—an idea that could have occurred only to a sourdough of his experience and ability. He searched through the kitchen cupboard and found a flat loaf of cornbread and went outside with it. There he crumbled the bread in his hands and broadcast the crumbs across the dooryard. He picked up a length of remnant fence wire that was lying in the yard, snarled the wire in his big hands and stepped back into the doorway. In a moment a flock of little fat snowbirds pitched into the yard and began greedily eating the crumbs. Then he stepped forward quickly, and when the startled birds whirled up at sight of him, he hurled the tangle of wire through them. A dozen or so fell, crippled and fluttering. He picked them up and brought them into the cabin in his hat.

By this time I had enough hot water on the whuffing cherry-red stove to scald a large hog. So Tex dropped the snowbirds into a pot of boiling water, and presently fished them out with a spoon, after which he rubbed off their feathers and pulled off their legs and heads, and tore out their entrails with a practiced gouge of a horny-nail thumb. Then he dropped the small denuded carcasses into another pot of boiling water and said, "In jest a moment now she'll have meat broth."

Two hours later, into the shanty lurched a gaunt young cheechako. Without a word he stumbled to where the woman and infant lay. . . . Almost he had not come back. He had been trapped by running ice on an island.

Supplies and a doctor were needed at the cabin. We struck out in starlight, soon had better light, the brilliant northern aurora. After a couple of hours we came to another homestead.

"Harvey Dusseldorf's place," Tex said. Light came from a small window but Tex went straight to the barn—a logged-up hole in a hillside. Tied inside was a brown Jersey cow—Bessie. Oolinka laughed, the first time I had seen her laugh.

I said to Tex, "How did you know the Widder's cow would be here?"

"Because all tenderfoot characters on the make fer a gal like the Widder try to play hit smart—and they ain't so smart. That guy jest rustled the Widder's cow and then pertended to look fer the critter—and pertended to sprain his doggone ankle so's he could set hisself in, he hoped. Only he made one little mistake." Tex's wide shoulders shook in silent mirth. "He should of brushed the brown cow hairs off'n those blue pants o' his. . . . I told ya his number was up with the Widder. We'll say we found the cow in the woods. Won't that leave him in a fix?"

COFFEE

Adventure Is My Business

PART 5

The Redhead hits the fur trail. . . .
The great snows come, he grapples with a black bear,
and a K.O.'d lynx revives to savage life on his back.

We had hit the fur trail, and now the great snows were upon us. Daylight was but a brief blink of brilliance above the saw-toothed mountain horizon. Seven sundogs glowed in the hard slate-gray sky, and it was cold. I do not know what the temperature may have been, but it was as if the absolute cold of outer space had descended to smite us.

Tex glanced back from the gee pole of the leading dogsled, and with an exaggerated shiver, said, "Doggone if hit ain't cold enough to freeze the ears off'n a brass monkey." We were on the wide, barren, ghost-white bars of *Knah-Kutnoo*—River-Where-We-Dry-Meat. We had two teams of siwash Malamutes, six dogs to a team, hooked up two abreast, Nome style. Tex was breaking trail with one team. Oolinka followed with the second. I snowshoed at the rear, observing the exasperating art of dog mushing. On Tex's sled, swathed to his ears in a wolf robe, huddled Chauncey Harrison Swearingen, who was accompanying us to tutor me in literature and the stubborn malleability of the English language.

Oolinka said to me, speaking through her teeth, "These siwash dogs are not good dogs. They are fat and lazy." She banged the lash of a fifteen-foot caribou-gut whip beside the ear of her lead dog, making it sound like a rifle shot. The dog stretched out, tightening his trace, and looked back interestedly, recognizing a master hand with a whip.

When the tall flare of sun-death was fading in the south we turned off the bars into a point of spruce timber. Presently we entered a clearing in which squatted a low, square log cabin. Blown snow had drifted it under to the eaves, so that you could easily have mistaken it for a snow-hooded mound or boulder. Tex and Oolinka halted their teams in the dooryard, far enough apart to prevent the savage wolf-ancestored Indian dogs from getting into a bloody battle royal. Then the big green-eyed mountain man turned to me, tugged at the icicles fringing his jungle of beard, and motioned with a gauntleted hand to the snow-masked door of the cabin.

"This is headquarters cabin, Redhead. You an' Oolinka git a fire started whilst Chancy an' I unload these here sleds."

The Indian girl and I slid down the wind-stiffened drift blocking the cabin door and entered the black interior. From the pocket of her caribou-fawn parka Oolinka brought a wax candle which she carried for emergency fire building on the trail, touched a match to its wick, and stuck it on a window ledge in a pool of its own wax. The flickering yellow light revealed a scene of havoc. The single large room looked as if a tornado had spent a weekend in it. Bedding, cooking gear, clothing and items of grub were strewn in wild confusion over the puncheon floor. The plank table was overturned. The tin Yukon stove lay on its side, half hidden by fallen lengths of pipe.

I said, "What did this?"

"A bear did it—a black bear, I think." Oolinka picked up a milk can from the floor and held it close to the candle, showing me tooth marks through the tin. "The bite is too narrow for a grizzly or a brown bear," she said, and bowed her head as if she had made too forward a statement.

Together we set the stove up and rejointed the pipes. Oolinka then went outside to bring our box of trail grub, and I got out my belt knife and whittled shavings from a stick of dry spruce wood. At this point I received a shock. I was touching a match to the shavings when, from somewhere at the shadowy rear of the cabin, there came a deep resonant snore. At first I didn't believe it. I thought my ears must have played a trick on me. But the snoring continued, rhythmical and full-throated. I reached for the Winchester, and slipped the safety latch. Across the entire back end of the cabin, raised some four feet off the floor, was a split-pole bunk covered with a mattress of wild hay and fluffy-white mountain goat skins. The snoring seemed to come from beneath this bunk. I knelt, trying to analyze the sooty shadows.

The snoring was no auditory illusion. Something was under there, all right. Staring hard, I could make out the shape of a large animal curled up against the cabin wall. *Watch it, son. Watch it now. This could turn into a gosh-awful mess.* I picked up a stick of stove wood and hurled it at the animal. The creature grunted, stirring sluggishly. Then it came half erect—and a ray of yellow candlelight fell across it. I saw that the animal was a black bear, a grandfather of black bears. One of those 600-pounders that you hear campfire yarns about but seldom see. Moreover he was coming out from under the bunk, and he wasn't snoring now, he was popping his teeth and rumbling his battle snarl. I guess he figured he was cornered and was going to have to fight his way out of here. Anyway, here he came, so the next move was mine. In this light I couldn't use the receiver sight of the Winchester. So I pointed the barrel by instinct and pulled.

Everything happened.

The muzzle blast blew out the candle. I had time to chamber another shell, shove the muzzle toward the unseen animal and fire again. Then I was down under a coughing, bawling, sobbing avalanche of bear. And then suddenly above me I heard Oolinka's voice—and heard the thud and whisper of knife steel driving into living flesh. I wasn't hurt, and so was able to roll from under the animal and relight the candle.

When the wick flared it revealed a scene straight from the Age of Stone. Lips drawn back from her teeth, eyes slitted in a mask of fury, the Indian girl lay across the carcass of the giant black bear, driving her wicked short-bladed woman's knife repeatedly into the animal's heart. The bear was dead. Probably I had mortally wounded him with my first shot. But Oolinka hadn't waited to find out about that. She had again been willing to risk her life for me.

That was your second lesson in the strength and loyalty of women, bucko. Don't forget it.

Back at Matanuska, Oolinka had stayed with the Widder Jones. I had wanted her to continue staying there. Because to me it did not seem right for a girl to accompany three men on a trapping expedition. I mentioned this to Tex. The mountain man gave me an amused sidewise flash with his swamp-green eyes. "Better take her along, Redhead. Every trappin' outfit needs a Injun or Eskimo seamstress. You ever try to sew a busted moccasin seam yerself? An' what's more, these gals are the world's best camptenders. They know how to take off pelts, drive dogs, split wood, an' cook after their fashion. Take her along. Ya won't be sorry." We were standing in the Widder Jones's kitchen. I said to the Indian girl, "Do you want to go?" She said, "Yes. But I will do what *you* say."

So here we all were. We had given Oolinka half of the twenty-foot-wide bunk, and had hung a blanket partition around it. To further mark off her quarters, Tex had placed a heavy spruce log across the bunk.

There were so many things to do. We had to break snowshoe trails, put out sixty miles of traps. We had to saw wood. We had to replace much of the tundra-moss chinking between the logs of this headquarters cabin and three smaller line cabins to make them proof against the marrow-searching cold. We had to make stretcher boards on which to dry our furs—splitting lengths of straight-grain spruce into inch-thick sections, then whittling the boards into shape and smoothing them with a piece of broken glass. We had to kill meat for ourselves and the dogs, at least 150 pounds a day.

And once the trap line was established, we had to follow it every day from dawn until dark, even when blizzard winds were howling down the bars of *Knah-Kutnoo*. It was savage, grueling work for both ourselves and the dogs. We had to contend with treacherous ice, avalanches, and always the terrible cold. There were days in this crystalline atmosphere when the mountains danced and reeled drunkenly against the sky and seemed about to topple into the valley. Again, the weird snow mirage, which the Tena Indians call the Light of Delusion, would cast its luminous blue glow over the valley, and you could not distinguish the sky from the earth, so that there were no longer any depressions or elevation and you could not see the snow at your feet.

But we were making money. A migration of lynx was passing through the region, and had halted in the red willow thickets of *Knah-Kutnoo* to hunt rabbits and ptarmigan. And this year the pelts of the gray, hairy-footed, tufted-eared animals were selling for the highest price in a decade. They were listed at $85 apiece. For weeks we took as many of the big cats as we could skin—as many as a dozen a day.

Coming in from the trap line after dark, bone-tired, we would still have to work until midnight or later. Oolinka would be repairing moccasins, darning socks, mending dog harness and cooking food in five-gallon oil tins for the twelve yammering Malamutes. Tex, because he was an expert, would take charge of keeping our snowshoes in repair. We all worked at taking off pelts, and at cooking and sawing wood. Often when the night was half gone, one of us would be kneeling in the starlit snow dragging a crosscut through a white spruce log.

In his spare time Chauncey Harrison Swearingen tutored me. The gaunt, gray British remittance man was good—as I know now. Using a high-school grammar, he taught me the parts of speech, which he called the tie-ribs of language. With him he had brought more than 100 pounds of books, selected by him and paid for by Tex. He was a classicist, yet he appreciated all good writing, wherever he found it.

He admonished me never to be trapped into becoming a literary snob. "Classics, lad," he said, with a wry smile, "usually are recognized only a century or so after they are written—when their subject matter is dry as Pharaoh's bones."

He taught me to read Lafcadio Hearn for color, Jack London for his gusty eagle-spirit of adventure, and Somerset Maugham for his precise technique.

Pointing a bony finger at me for emphasis, he said, "If you wish to become a really good writer, lad, with the word power to describe anything from a deification to a dogfight, read everything—and read with a pencil in your hand. When you find a phrase that pleases you, set it down in your notebook. At first you will have the uneasy feeling that you are preparing to become guilty of plagiarism. But after a few years, when you've collected a few thousand sharp, dramatic and colorful phrases, you will become aware that they turn up in almost every top author's writing."

The lean man with the life-worn face smiled at me across the candlelit table. "The only way to acquire language, lad, is to get it from the masters who went before us because that is the way they themselves got it." He poured himself a cup of tea, and watched me while he stirred sugar into it. "And there is only one way to learn to write, that is—write." So I wrote.

But there was a difficulty. Our winter's outfit was short one important item. Tex had purchased the grub, gear and camp equipment. Chauncey Harrison Swearingen had selected a compact library of representative literature. Oolinka had dickered with the Indians for dog harness, moccasins, gloves and parkas. But nobody, including myself, had remembered that if I was going to learn to write I would need writing paper. In the 1,000 pounds of outfit we had freighted in, there was not one sheet of it. So, with a few soft black pencils which I had had the wit to bring, I wrote my stories this winter on the only available substitute—toilet paper. By candlelight, on the split-pole table, when I was free from chores, I wrote voluminously. I wrote novels, plays, short stories, vignettes, farces, verse—practically every form of literature that Chauncey Harrison Swearingen made me acquainted with. I took episodes from the *Iliad* and Shakespeare, and tried to turn them into short stories. Chauncey read them carefully and his criticisms were gentle but pointed.

Tex, on the other hand, was fascinated by my tales. Of course the toilet paper could not be wasted so after I had written on a roll of it, I would re-wind it on its cardboard core. Each time Tex retired to our outdoor privy, he remained there so long reading that he would return half frozen. Warming himself at the Yukon stove, he'd say through chattering teeth, "I jest got interested in findin' out whether them Greeks ever did ketch up with the lousy Trojans that kidnapped that gal Helen. Nearly froze to death. How'd hit turn out anyhow?"

Then I met Blind Nick again—a strange meeting. On a blue midnoon Oolinka and I were mushing up *Knah-Kutnoo*, heading for the carcass of a moose which Tex had killed yesterday. Our job was to freight back to the cabin as much meat as the six dogs could pull. By the time we sighted the landmarks Tex had given us, the sun was rolling low on the horizon.

Oolinka stopped suddenly. Apprehension had come into her face. After a moment she said, "Something has happened." Her head was turned to one side as though listening to a summons audible only to her. "There is trouble ahead," she said.

She cracked the lash of her whip over the back of the lead dog, heading him toward a point of spruce timber. As we approached the snow-weighted javelin spruces, I saw the flicker of a campfire in the gloom. When we were within fifty feet of the fire, Oolinka abruptly overturned the sled and ran ahead. The camp was at the foot of a huge boulder. Between the fire and the face of rock, lying in a sleeping bag made of mountain sheep skins, was an Indian woman and a child. They gazed dully at us, neither of them moving. The woman was about twenty-five, child—a girl from her braids—probably eight. You didn't have to be a sourdough to see what was wrong here. This was a starvation camp.

On the snow lay the skin of a Malamute pup, and beside the fire were the pup's gnawed bones, carefully cracked and the marrow extracted.

Oolinka knelt by the sleeping bag and spoke in the swift, hard-syllabled Tena language. The woman replied weakly.

Oolinka said to me. "These are people of the Goat-Eater Tena. Twelve days ago her husband started across the river with their dog team to stalk a band of goats on a cliff. He has not returned. She waited for him all this time, but now she thinks he is dead. She thinks he went through the ice or was buried by an avalanche. They are very hungry. All they have had to eat was the meat of a puppy her husband left tied in camp."

There were tears in Oolinka's eyes. She had been through this herself. While she built up the fire and raked coals out to cook on, I went back to the sled for our grub box. An hour later the woman and child had been fed and were asleep. Oolinka and I had planned to load our sled with moose meat and return to the cabin tonight after moonrise, but now the project had to be abandoned. So we made camp for ourselves.

Toward morning the fire burned low, and I went out to the edge of the timber to search for a dead spruce. The moon was up and the tall flare of the aurora blazed in the North. I found a dry windfall and had just raised the camp ax to chop off a length I could drag, when I heard webs coming on the sugar-dry snow. I stepped back into the shadows of the timber and stood motionless, waiting. In a moment, across the auroralit snow, came two Indians. One was a boy, the other was tall and wide-shouldered, and his face was turned upward as though he was searching for something in the sky. The boy was ahead, and leading the other at the end of a peeled wand. My scalp tingled.

I said, "Blind Nick."

Before the prophet could reply, Oolinka came out of the timber, striding swiftly on her long webs. She stood close to me, her shoulder touching mine, and said to Blind Nick, "They have been fed. They are safe." She turned to me. "Could I take the dogs tomorrow and start for Matanuska with the woman and her child?"

"Yes."

Blind Nick touched me on the arm with a caribou-gloved hand and said, "This is a kind thing you are doing. I know that you need the dogs on your trap line, and that not having them will cause you the loss of much fur. But these two people are in trouble and need help badly. Your kindness will never be forgotten."

As a result of Chauncey Harrison Swearingen's teaching, I had become very language conscious. So I said, "You speak beautiful English, Blind Nick."

The prophet's smile, revealed by the many-hued aurora lights, was gentle. "I was not speaking English. . . ." Then he and the boy turned and mushed back down *Knah-Kutnoo*. Heading for town? For a camp they had made somewhere below us? For a rendezvous with other Indians? Who could guess? Blind Nick was a great shaman, and he moved mysteriously.

One bright, windy Sunday morning at headquarters cabin I got Tex into a fantastic predicament.

Tex was cooking breakfast, moose steaks, sourdough hot cakes and tea, when I remembered a lynx trap I had set the day before at the farther rim of a small lake behind the cabin. It occurred to me that I could go look at the trap and return before breakfast was ready. So I pulled on my parka and trotted out across the lake. I had bad luck. Near the shore I stepped through a muskrat's air hole, getting my right leg wet to the knee. As the temperature was around thirty below zero, any experienced trapper would have returned at once to the cabin. But I went on to the trap. There was a lynx in it, a big one—held by one toenail. I drew my .22 pistol, laid the sights on the lynx's head, and pulled. Nothing happened. Hastily examining the gun, I saw that the firing pin had stuck. My right foot and leg were freezing. I had to return to the cabin in a hurry. Yet if I left this lynx, his first lunge against the trap chain would set him free. So, desperately, I threw the gun at him. It hit him in the face and he went down.

Ten seconds later I was sprinting back across the ice with the lynx over my shoulder. I had some more bad luck. When I was midway across, the animal suddenly revived. I did the only thing I could have in the circumstances. Holding him by his hind legs, I spun like a ballet dancer, and banged him down full length on the ice. The big cat stiffened and showed his teeth, then went limp. Again I hoisted him onto my shoulder and made for camp. On the shore of the lake stood an ancient abandoned Indian cabin. As I drew abreast of the place, hard luck once more smote me. This lynx must have had his full complement of nine cat lives, for abruptly he uttered a bubbling snarl and began clawing at my back.

With my foot and leg freezing, I didn't have time for further argument with the rugged brute. So I resorted to a stratagem. I kicked open the door of the old cabin, threw the lynx inside, pulled the door shut and departed. When I entered our headquarters cabin Tex took one look at my ice-encrusted leg, and got busy. With his belt knife he cut the laces of the moccasin and pulled it off. He probed my foot with his hard fingers, and nodded.

"It ain't froze, but hit'll be damn sore fer a coupla days. What happened?"

I told him. But because of the blazing anguish in my foot, I omitted an important detail. I neglected to explain to Tex that the lynx was still alive. After he had eaten his breakfast, Tex lit his pipe and said, "Reckon I'll stroll out and git that lynx afore he freezes solid. On account o' I do hate to skin a doggone frozen lynx."

He left the cabin. Five minutes later he returned. His drill parka was in ribbons and he was bleeding from a wonderful assortment of cuts and scratches. He looked at me reproachfully and said, "Redhead, iff'n you were a son o' mine, danged if I wouldn't whale the everlastin' daylights out'n you. Why didn'tcha tell me that ornery cuss was still alive?" Tex went over to the washbasin and began mopping blood off his face. Over his shoulder he added, "The varmint was sittin' upon a rafter when I opened the door. He landed on my haid clawin' with all four feet. Had to strangle him with m' bare hands—an' b'lieve me, that ain't no pastime fer any man who yearns to keep his good health."

The winter wore on and then suddenly it was spring. And there came the morning when Tex said, "Snow's goin' fast. Guess we better light out o' here—an' quick—if we wanta beat the breakup."

I said, "Where are we going?"

"Well-l, I sorta figgered we'd hit the beaver trail." He grinned behind his mask of beard and his swamp-green eyes were bright. "But I think we reelly oughta drop down to Matanusky fer a spell first. Ya cain't tell, the Widder Jones may of lost that doggone old Bessie cow again."

Adventure Is My Business

PART 6

". . . It was the skeleton of a man, both shattered wrists caught in a rusted bear trap. Nearby was a jar of gold." The Redhead gets a gruesome lesson in the grim life of the Alaska frontier.

Now it was May and the sun had returned. We were mushing into the Talkeetna country, hunting beaver water. It was two o'clock in the morning, and the snow was crusted iron-hard, the dogs running on it as easily as if it had been a paved highway. They wore moosehide moccasins to protect their feet from the gritty ice crystals. They hated the moccasins and would cringe and snarl when we tied them on, but still they were happy and willing, because this was the time of year when every living thing in the North has a resurgence of vitality. The bitter, gloomy seven-month winter was ended, and this was the beginning of spring.

Oolinka and Tex were driving. On Tex's sled rode a new recruit to our nomad company—a dark-eyed, volatile little southern sportsman named Buck. Chauncey Harrison Swearingen was not with us.

Chauncey Harrison Swearingen was dead.

He met his end pathetically but in a manner that might have been foreseen. This is what happened.

We had gone south to the raw, roaring new boom camp of Anchorage, at the head of Cook Inlet, to sell our furs. After a day of haggling with a fat, crafty-eyed, cigar-chewing buyer from New York, Tex and I were sitting in the back room of a cigar store with the three elder giants of the North: The Malamute Kid, Gordon

Bettles, and Moosehide Charlie. Our hostess—the owner of the place—was The Oregon Mare, a sporting woman notorious throughout the frontier. Appropriately, the girl who worked as her assistant—a chemical blonde from Utah—was called The Utah Filly. When the sourdoughs saw that these nicknames startled me, they recalled equally colorful ones that had been applied to Alaska's adventuresses. There was The Black Bear, who had an understudy called The Cub, and there was The Flame of the Yukon, The Cheechako Rose, Sweet Marie, The Beef Trust, The Tin Fiddler, Nellie the Pig, The Kaiserine, Kitty the Bitch, The forty-Horsepower Swede and The Calcimine Kid. The sourdoughs had a story to tell about each woman. It was lusty talk and good talk, loaded with the color and drama of the North. I was wishing I had a notebook and pencil, when there was a knock on the door.

It was Chauncey Harrison Swearingen.

Gray-faced and weaving, the remittance man came into the room. The neck of a bottle stuck out of his parka pocket. "Been celebrating a bit," he informed us. He rested a shaking hand on the table for support, and looked at me. "I'm off to the post office, where a package awaits me. I believe, lad, that its contents will be of lasting benefit to you." He left, lurching through the doorway with a farewell wave of his hand.

It was the last time we saw him alive.

Outside a May blizzard was screaming through the icy streets. When the sourdoughs and I departed, such a blast of snow-laden wind struck us that I was spun half around and had to catch hold of the door casing to remain upright.

We rounded a corner into a street where a line of new frame buildings broke the force of the gale. Then, out of a shop entrance ahead came a slender, dark-eyed, obviously expensively dressed girl. She was beautiful. Moosehide Charlie whistled appreciatively, and Gordon Bettles muttered, "Fer gosh sakes, who's that? Ain't she a honey?" She had halted on the sidewalk, apparently waiting for someone still in the shop. Then, as we drew closer, the door opened and the Widder Jones came out. She put an arm around the beautiful girl's shoulders—and suddenly I received one of the great surprises of my life.

Because the dark-eyed girl on the snowy sidewalk, with the wind whipping her dress against her straight legs, was Oolinka.

The buxom Widder greeted us heartily. "Hi," she called through the wild orchestration of the storm. "How do you shaggy trail-hogs like the way I've got this lynx-kitten dressed up? And look what the beauty parlor's done to her. Didn't know they had one in the camp. But they have, and it's all right—a gal can get a job done there." The Widder looked proud of herself, and she had a right to be. Tex and I had asked her to come to town to buy white girl's clothes for Oolinka. And as I have tried to make clear, the result was pretty spectacular and heart warming.

Oolinka turned to me and said shyly, "Look, I have shoes with high heels behind." She touched her hand to the glossy, raven-wing hair spilling breast length beneath a red, sequin-spangled little turban hat, and said, "But I think I liked my braids better."

We went to the hotel, and then to a restaurant for dinner. The town marshal came in out of the storm, batting the snow off his martenskin cap. He said to Tex, "Didn't you have a trapping partner named Swearingen?"

"Yeah," Tex said. "Why?"

"Well, he's dead. Froze in an alley. We just found him." The marshal reached inside his parka, brought out a package, and placed it on the table. "I guess you'll know what to do with this. It's nothing valuable—just a coupla books."

The books were Spencer's *Philosophy of Style* and Darwin's *The Origin of Species.* They were to become invaluable to me. From the first book I learned the painstaking precision, judgment, and taste that must go into the construction of a good sentence and paragraph. From the second I had my first glimpse of the vast and complex interrelation of all life upon the planet, and of the continuous pattern of growth and experimentation marking nature's progress toward an unguessable goal. This was my legacy from the frozen hands of Chauncey Harrison Swearingen, the life-beaten exile who could help others but could not help himself.

So now we were on the beaver trail, mushing swiftly eastward into the great triangle of flat country lying between the Susitna River, Goose Creek, and the soaring fence of the Talkeetna snow peaks. The transparent blue spring darkness had faded, and although it was only 7:30, the morning sun was already booming up above the southeastern summits.

Tex said, "There's beaver water two miles ahead. Found it last year. An' we won't git there none too soon, because when the sun hits this crust hit'll go to pieces in ten minutes. A ptarmigan couldn't walk on hit without boggin' down."

We came to a chain of beaver lakes winding through low hills studded with second-growth aspens whose bark was already beginning to show its summer green. These were warm lakes and the beavers had been out feeding. All along the shores of the first pond were felled trees, mounds of yellow chips, and the padded-down network of their haulways. "There's some old settlers in that pond," Tex said, "some sure-enough blanket beavers. Jest look at the height o' them stumps an' the size o' the chips." We made camp on ten feet of snow downwind from the first dam, where there were dead aspens and cottonwood bark for fuel. While Oolinka fed the dogs and began cooking our supper, Tex took a half-dozen No. 4 toothed single-spring traps from his sled, and said, "Redhead, you an' Buck come on, an' I'll show you how to plant a beaver set so's hit'll git ya a plew."

In against the bank of the pond was a place where many haulways converged at a hole in the ice. Tex thrust the handle of his camp ax into the black water and probed the bottom. "Jest right. There's a frozen mud shelf down there, half an ax handle deep. Ya see, the way to make money is to ketch big beavers. An' the way to ketch big beavers is to plant yer trap deep enough so's small beavers will swim right over hit. But the big one'll step on the pan." Kneeling on the ice, the mountain man spread the jaws of the trap and notched the trigger. Then he lowered the trap by its chain onto the mud shelf.

Tex took a short length of wire from his parka pocket, and fastened the ring of the trap chain to an underwater root. "Sometimes—'specially in shallow water—ya gotta tie a rock to yer trap chain so's a beaver will drown when he gits caught. Or else you can drive a pole into the mud bottom an' put the ring on hit so hit'll slide down an' hold yer beaver underwater. But neither is necessary here. This is a hind-foot set—an' no beaver ever stuck his hind foot full into a No. 4 toothed trap an' got out o'hit."

With the ax he cut a four-foot length of aspen sapling, peeled it, and stuck it into the snow at the edge of the open water. Then he reached into his parka pocket for a beaver castor. The castor was a meaty object about the size of an egg, with the good aromatic perfume of cottonwood buds. Tex rubbed the peeled stick vigorously with it. "Castor is a beaver's callin' card. So now any beaver that sticks his head out'n the water anywheres on this pond is gonna smell this an' think a stranger has arrived, an' he'll come over here in a hurry to investigate."

Buck said, "Doggone if I don't feel like a professional already."

We had met Buck in the hotel at Anchorage, where he was staying until he could find a woodsman who would guide him on a spring grizzly hunt. His doctor, he told us, had ordered him north to the frontier. With engaging candor, he said he guessed he had inherited too much money and had been spending it on loose and riotous living until his nerves had begun vibrating like banjo strings. So he wanted to head into the wilds, away from night clubs, blondes, and racetracks, and stay there until he got himself in hand again. If he killed a grizzly, he said, that would be swell. If he didn't, that would be all right too.

"Well, ya can come with us if ya want to," Tex had told him. "We're gonna be plenty busy peelin' beaver plews. But there'll be a grizzly or two around, I reckon, an' if ya can shoot I figger ya ought to git yerself a trophy."

That was how Buck became a member of our party. He proved to be a good and valuable recruit. Through him I was to get into the dude-wrangling business. And we were to be fast friends for years, adventuring in most of the game ranges of the continent.

We put out twenty traps, and for ten days took beaver from this chain of ponds as fast as we could skin them and lace the pelts into alder hoops to dry. Then we moved into the mountains, to the lake-dotted headwaters of a clear-water creek the Indians call Nolletana—Stream-Running-Through-Bald-Mountains. Here I had an experience that will haunt me all the days of my life.

I had left our camp with Smoky at three o'clock in the morning to scout ahead for beaver water. Intending to be gone a day or two, I was carrying my sleeping bag, six traps, and some grub. In the violet half-light, walking without webs on the crusted drifts, I crossed a little packsaddle pass, and dropped down to the brushy head reaches of a nameless stream. The south slope of this valley was bare of snow partway to its summit. I was making my way through a stand of gnarled dwarf cottonwoods, watching the partly open stream for beaver lodges, when I came upon the tumbled, moss-grown remains of an ancient cabin. The spruce logs were so rotten you could kick them apart. I guessed they had been cut at least fifty years ago. I passed the cabin, following a game trail that paralleled the creek. Presently Smoky turned off the trail to examine something in a snow-bare opening. I went over to see what the little fighting dog had found, and beheld as gruesome a sight as a woodsman ever laid eyes on.

In the opening, both shattered wrist bones caught between the jaws of a heavy, rusted, hand-forged bear trap of antique design, lay the skeleton of a tall man. The bones had been there a long, long time. Moss had grown over the skull, and the little shrew mice had scrimshawed the weather-whitened ribs. The trap chain was fastened to a dead cottonwood with an old-fashioned square spike which had been driven into the tree to its head. Fifteen feet distant, leaning against another cottonwood, was a Sharps rifle, its rotted stock covered with moss, and its barrel and breech eaten by rust. On the ground beside the rifle were four decayed strips of hardwood—the frame of what had been a siwash packboard. Upon them lay two clamps such as trappers use for setting bear traps. And between the clamps lay a quart-size glass jar filled with gold. Some of it was wire gold, with pieces of ruby quartz clinging to it. It was jewelry gold, the kind of gold that prospectors dream about but seldom find.

I at once headed back for camp, scouting through the timber as I went. Near the ruins of the cabin I found something I had missed before—the skeletons of eight dogs chained to trees. Obviously they had starved. All the way over the packsaddle pass and down to Nolletana, my mind was filled with the thought of the agony and despair the old-time sourdough must have felt when he stumbled into his own bear trap and knew that his only release would be death. And I thought of the eight chained dogs howling their helplessness to the bleak mountainside. And I wondered where he had found his fruit jar of jewelry gold.

At camp, when I had told Tex, Buck, and Oolinka about my discovery, Tex took the jar of gold and spilled some of the nuggets into his hand. "Hit's sunburnt gold, and hit ain't traveled far. That old-timer made hisself a real strike." Tex sighed covetously. "We'll git over there one o' these days an' see if we can locate hit."

But beavers were our immediate concern. From two o'clock in the morning until around nine, while the snow crust would support us, we ran the traps and made new sets. Then we would eat breakfast and sleep an hour or two. After that we worked until dark, taking off pelts, fleshing them, and stretching them to dry. A man can handle only about six beavers a day, and we were crowding ourselves to the limit. But it was pleasant work in the spring sunshine, also very profitable work, and I was learning many curious and useful things.

For example, Oolinka showed me how to prepare that celebrated trap-line delicacy—boiled beaver tail. And one morning in the foothills I learned something about beavers so unique that probably not one trapper in a thousand knows about it. I saw a large beaver running on his hind feet. I have no theory as to why he was traveling in this manner. I can only certify that he was doing it—and that he scared me half to death.

Another morning I discovered a beautiful piece of retributive justice at a large beaver lake at the end of my line. Two bald eagles had a nest in a tall cottonwood overhanging the lake. They had nested early and their eaglets already had hatched. Because these snowy-headed predators were killing beavers, I had tried time and again to get a shot at them. But they were too crafty. They apparently knew about rifles, and they stayed out of range. The beavers themselves, however, took care of the killers nicely. On this particular morning, when I returned to the lake, the cottonwood with its eagle nest no longer stood against the sky line. During the night the beavers had gnawed it down, and it had fallen into the lake and the eaglets had drowned—a swell payoff for the many beaver kits the parent eagles had pirated from this colony.

Then one bright noon we were sitting in camp under the shoulder of a steep mountain, all of us fleshing wet beaver pelts, when Oolinka raised her head and pointed with her short woman's knife. "Grizzly," she said. The animal's deep-wallowed trail led down through the snow from a cave entrance at the base of a blue cliff halfway to brush line. He was maybe 1,000 yards distant. Tex picked up Buck's binocular, and after a moment said, "That's a good bear. He's in full winter pelt, jest out o' hibernation, he ain't rubbed, an' he's got that yaller, Swede-blond color I always liked. Fer a grizzly he's big, too. Doggone if I don't think his hide would square ten feet."

Then suddenly the blond grizzly lay flat on his belly on the forty-five-degree pitch, forepaws extended, and let gravity have its way with him. With astonishing speed he tobogganed down the mountainside until he crashed head-on into a jungle of tough mountain alders. The impact would have killed any ordinary animal, but to this grizzly it was apparently just fun. He regained his feet and headed obliquely around the mountain, in our direction. Buck, hot-eyed and eager, picked up his .270.

Tex said, "The crust is gone. You couldn't walk 300 feet in this slop. We'll git him in the mornin'. He ain't goin' nowheres. Jest keep yer shirt on."

At two o'clock the next morning, carrying our webs, both of us still half asleep, neither of us speaking, Buck and I headed out across the now-frozen crust toward the spot where he had last seen the bear. It was not dark—the snow was reflecting the starlight in a kind of turquoise glimmer. Within twenty minutes I found the grizzly's deep trail. It led into a stand of dog-tail black spruces. Here we found where the bear had slept beneath a windfall. From this point on there was no trail. Like ourselves, he was traveling on the crust.

We sat somberly under a spruce until the tall saffron-and-crimson glow of sunrise flooded the mountain crests. When the sunlight reached across the flat, I was able to make out the marks of the grizzly's long winter claws on the drifts. We took the animal's trail, and had followed it some thirty minutes when, from somewhere up ahead, came the most terrifying sound that may be heard in the northern wilderness—the deep, hoarse roar of a charging grizzly. Intermingled with it was the clatter of hoofs on the icy crust. We hurried ahead.

A gaunt, gray, sway-backed cow moose was fleeing desperately from a grizzly whose pelt was the blond color of burlap sacking. The bear had overhauled her and had raised a paw to sledge-hammer her down, when beside me Buck's .270 blasted. I heard the solid whoop of the 150-grain slug smashing home through bone and muscle. Then the bear went down on one shoulder with a choking bawl, clawing at the snow. Remembering Tex's parting instructions, I stepped back and said, "Keep shooting." I needn't have spoken. Buck kept shooting, all right. He shot the .270 empty, then reloaded. But the bear was dead.

The grizzly's pelt was long and silky, with a golden glint, the kind of trophy sportsmen would come half around the world to take.

Adventure Is My Business

PART 7

The growing Redhead enters the land of Salmon Clubbers, kills a man—a notorious Eskimo murderer— and falls in love with a beautiful countess—a tiger huntress with mocking and fascinating cross-eyes.

Tex, Buck, Smoky, and I were now in the Land of Salmon Clubbers. Ahead of us was peril, excitement, humor, and pathos. Here I was to meet the lovely, tempestuous, cross-eyed Hungarian Countess Tanya, and kill the Eskimo outlaw Klootuk. In any case, I believe I killed Klootuk. Nobody ever saw him again after the smoke-filled, flame-shot night when I laid the sights of my .30-06 on him and pulled. . . .

I must explain that Alaska had two clans of sourdoughs—the Rabbit Stranglers and the Salmon Clubbers. They feuded, and each faction told great, gusty, defamatory lies about the other. The Rabbit Stranglers roamed the trackless interior country and, it was claimed, lived exclusively on the skinny carcasses of snowshoe rabbits, which they snared in willow thickets with their moccasin strings. They were described as being only approximately human, and so ornery that they grew bark on their chests, had three rows of jaw teeth and seven coats of hair, and milked female grizzlies to get cream for their coffee. The Salmon Clubbers, on the other hand, inhabited the wild sea frontier, where it was alleged they won subsistence by clubbing sore-backed salmon to death in the riffles of streams. It was declared that they often grew scales, and that during the spawning season their noses became hooked and their teeth grew long and pointed.

Our expedition to salt water was Buck's idea.

The intense, eager little Southerner had fallen in love with the North. On the beaver trail he had become healthy, and tough as rawhide, and now he yearned for adventure. He pored over maps of Alaska, locating the many blank areas, and speculating happily as to what might be there. Also, he collected rumors about the back-of-beyond—and there were plenty to collect. Practically every sourdough you met contributed some gaudy ones.

There were yarns of unknown beasts that had been sighted, of a lost tribe of Pygmy-size people somewhere beyond the Kobuk, of a tropical valley in the Liard country, of a mountain of pure jade near a half-mythical place called Shungnak, of a strange species of white ibex in the glacier-studded Chugach range above Prince William Sound, of an island off the Shumagin group populated by blond women—colorful tales brought in by moccasin telegraph, typical of this great and as yet largely unexplored land. Some were subsequently found to be based on fact, some were sheer fantasy, but to Buck they all were wildly fascinating. He was like a lad in a toy shop. He couldn't make up his mind which rumor he wanted to play with first.

That is, he couldn't until he heard about Klootuk the Killer and the giant rainbow trout of great Lake Iliamna. Then he was sold hard and fast. Tex and I weren't. We didn't like it. But just the same, one pretty summer morning we found ourselves camped on the beach of Iliamna, deep in the Land of Salmon Clubbers.

We had cruised down Cook Inlet in a Kodiak power dory to Iliamna Portage. Here we had hired a band of Kenai Indians to pack our outfit over the portage and help us construct two canvas canoes. The region appeared to be deserted except for a family of Eskimo reindeer herders who, at sight of us, hastily broke camp and disappeared into the hills with their reindeer. The Kenai packers also were eager to quit our presence. The moment the canoes were completed, they collected their pay and headed back across the portage. It was a most somber welcome into a supremely beautiful and promising place—the handsomest country I had yet seen.

"We sure ain't popular around here," Tex said, checking the sights and loading of his Sauer. "I smell plenty o' trouble. Got a funny sort o' feelin' between m' shoulder blades, like as if somebody was fixin' to pull a bead on me."

"Aw, let's find those giant rainbows and the blazes with Klootuk," Buck said. "I can hardly wait. D'ya reckon they're really here?"

They were here all right.

We mushed up the beach to the mouth of a wide clear-water creek margined by shoulder-high grass. The sun was overhead now, and in the downpour of light the great lake lay calm and lovely as a sheet of polished cloudy amethyst. Gulls and terns circled above us. A mallard arrowed past. A half-mile up the beach a brown bear shambled out of a brush clump, caught our scent, and fled back whence he had come. Then, out in the middle of the creek, a fish jumped. He came out high and straight as a post, batting the water with his tail. He had a stripe down his side as broad as my hand, deep rose against buffed platinum. I thought he would go at least thirty inches. I had caught some rainbows, some that I thought were pretty good, but I had never seen one like this monster.

"Oh, holy smokes!" Buck said in a hoarse whisper. "Get outa my way, please. Gimme room."

Nobody was in his way. We watched him tie on a polar bear streamer and cast it over the spot where the fish had jumped. For three casts nothing happened. Then, at the next try, a rainbow took the fly and boomed up out of the water with it. Buck set the hook while the fish was in the air, and thereafter was very busy. The rainbow performed every acrobatic maneuver of which a trout is capable. He ran, jumped, pinwheeled, and swapped ends. He gave us everything he had for ten minutes, then lay over on his side, gills pumping wearily, and let Buck bring him in. In the course of the afternoon, Buck took twelve more. The smallest was fourteen inches, the largest thirty-one inches. We killed a medium-size fish for dinner, and went back to camp.

Tex had been telling us what he knew of the legend of Klootuk. Klootuk was a notorious Eskimo outlaw who for years had been waging a one-man war against the whites. He was said to be a squat, broad-faced, immensely powerful man, with slant eyes as depthless and full of hate as a wolverine's. He never came to civilization for supplies. He didn't have to. Such grub and gear as he needed he took from the outfits of venturesome trappers and prospectors who came into his country, and who he bushwhacked. We had no law organization in the North to make a proper investigation of the disappearance of the men he killed. There were only a scattered few United States marshals in Alaska's vast wilderness area, they were all political appointees, and there was probably not one competent woodsman among them. When a man vanished, it was easier to say he had gone through the ice, been killed by a brown bear, or simply had wandered off into another part of the territory than it was to make a search for him in Klootuk's country. So the outlaw held his domain, and lived high on the white man's grub.

"That Klootuk is jest a gut-eatin' savage, but he's tough," Tex said. "I sure hope we don't have no trouble with him."

Purple dusk had drowned the valleys and the lake was pure turquoise. We sat by the dying coals of our campfire, jackets pulled close against a cold wind off the peaks. Buck and Tex got into their robes and went to sleep, but I sat up a while longer, watching the midnight sun roll along the mountain horizon. Smoky lay beside me, and I stroked his head. I was lonesome, probably because Oolinka was not with us. We had left her with the Widder Jones, and it had been a sad parting. When I told the ex-slave girl that she would have to remain at the Widder's, she stood before me, head bowed, saying nothing.

"Well, so long," I told her. "You'll be all right. The Widder'll take care of you."

"But how will I know if you need me?"

"I'll be O.K. Don't worry. So long, Oolinka."

"Good-bye," she said. "I will ask Blind Nick to make magic for you and your rifle."

Maybe she did. If so, it was good magic.

I had got into my sleeping robe, with Smoky's head on my elbow. I was just dropping off to sleep when suddenly the little fighting dog jerked up his head and growled. I listened but couldn't hear anything, nor could I see anything moving on the dusky beach. Smoky's nose was working, and I thought perhaps he had winded a bear. So I went to sleep. Perhaps an hour later the sharp smell of smoke awoke me. I sat up, took one incredulous look upwind, and yelled to awaken Buck and Tex. The entire hillside above us was ablaze. The season was late here, and there was a heavy mat of dead grass under the new green growth, as inflammable as tinder. The flames were mounting treetop high, showers of sparks were falling on us, and smoke was whirling through the trees in hot, choking clouds.

"Gawdamighty," Tex shouted, "git this outfit loaded into the canoes. We gotta shove out onto the lake."

I was carrying gear down the shingle beach when, a quarter of a mile up the lake, ghostlike in the flamelit smoke, I saw a canoe with a man in it. He wasn't paddling. He was just sitting there in the smoky shadows watching us. I did something then that I've never been able to explain. I should have warned Tex and Buck. I should have let Tex handle the matter. Instead, sixteen-year-old kid that I was, I sprinted up the beach, Smoky running ahead of me. I had my rifle. A naked sand point jutted out into the water. I ran to its tip end, and found myself within 100 feet of the canoe. The man in the canoe gazed at me across the flame-spangled water, and laughed—a hoarse animal sound, with no mirth in it. The firelight glinted on the barrel of a raised rifle. Then I realized what an idiot I had been. I was backlit by the blazing hillside. I had no cover. I was out of breath. In short, I was a sitting duck, practically a dead apprentice sourdough.

For I realized now, of course, that the man in the canoe was Klootuk the Killer.

His rifle blasted, and I heard the wasp-whine of a slug past my ear. So I raised up my .30-06 and found him in the sights. But I had never shot at a man, so at the last instant I dropped the sights and put a slug through the canoe. Klootuk laughed again, and stepped overboard on the far side of the canoe. The water was so shallow that his head and shoulders showed above the gunwale. I dropped to the sand, jacking a new shell into the chamber. If he fired again, I didn't hear it. I picked his chest up as best I could in the tricky firelight and pulled. Klootuk yelled, and dropped from sight. That was enough for me. I fled back to the timber. When I knew I was safe, I turned for another look. The canoe was sinking. Klootuk was not in view.

Tex and Buck came running up the beach. Tex took me by the shoulder and spun me around to look at me. His face, blackened by grass soot, was grim. "What in hell d'ya think yer doin', Redhead? Who was in that canoe—Klootuk?"

"I guess so. He shot at me. So I shot back. I think I hit him."

"Yeah. The lousy varmint tried to burn us out. Too many guns in camp fer him, so he used the old Injun trick, a grass fire. I hope ya busted the gizzard out'n him. But listen, if ya ever again go into a deal like that on yer lonesome, without hollerin' fer help, I'll whale the britches off'n ya if hit's the last thing I do. Ya hear?"

I said I heard. I was getting scared now. My knees were shaking. That first slug of Klootuk's should have blown my brains out. If I had any brains. I suspected now that maybe I didn't have any.

Iliamna was behind us. We had fished a week, then had recrossed the portage to Cook Inlet. Tex said, "We'll cruise up the coast to Redoubt Bay, then angle across the Inlet to Kenai Village. You two'll git a lotta fun outa Kenai. Hit's a real heller of a town, this time o' year. Ever'body makin' money hand over fist fishin' salmon fer the canneries. Dances ever' night an' plenty o' purty gals. More fun than playin' games with them overgrown Iliamna rainbows."

At Redoubt, while we were waiting for weather in which it would be safe to cross the Inlet in our dory, we had a strange adventure with a pod of beluga whales. I'll have to tell you about it some other time. On the long run to Kenai Village, Buck shaved and washed his shirt, and Tex combed the tangles out of his long hair and beard. It was clear they were thinking about the dances and those pretty Kenai girls.

All Kenai Village smelled of fish. Cannery boats were unloading the day's catch of salmon, the oilskin-clad crews spearing the silvery fish out of the holds with a single-tined tool called a pew, and tossing them on conveyors. The beach was littered with fish heads, guts, and skeins of bright-carnelian eggs. Incredible clouds of kittiwakes and other kinds of gulls hovered over this free lunch.

We walked up the road to town, and, as we passed a white cottage on a rise of ground, Tex halted, squinting against the sun. In the back yard of the cottage, a large man was hoeing strawberry plants. The man had white hair and a long white beard. He wore a blue robe that reached to his ankles, and a crucifix dangled at his waist from a gold chain. Tex turned to me, a glitter of humor in his swamp-green eyes.

"That's old Bishop Antonin. Visitin' the local Russian priest. Ya better go on up there, Redhead, an' make yer peace with him. Give him a contribution fer the church. Hit's the best way to git along in this town. Buck an' I'll see ya later."

So I went up to the cottage and leaned on its white picket fence until the bishop saw me. This close to him, I realized he was an even bigger man than Tex, with the most piercing blue eyes I had ever seen. When he spoke, his voice sounded like a deep note from an organ.

"Good evening, my son. I have heard about you from one of our Eskimo reindeer herders who crossed the Inlet yesterday.

Something about a fire in the night. I think perhaps you have done a good thing for this part of the territory."

I was startled, practically stampeded, but I remembered Tex's admonition. "I—well—that is, I just stopped by to make a contribution to your church," I said. I fished a $10 bill out of my pocket and held it out to him.

The bishop took the bill and smoothed it in his hands, his eyes filled with laughter. "I suppose you plan to attend one of our dances tonight, and don't know a nice girl to invite. Also I suspect that Tex Cobb advised you to make this gift to the church. Well"—he leaned his hoe against the fence—"come into the house. Who knows what my develop?"

Something developed, all right—something that was to take me around the world before it was finished by death.

When I entered the cottage, the first person I saw was a girl. But she was unlike any girl I had ever seen. She was sitting on a couch with her feet tucked up under her, and she wore a bright peasant skirt and blouse. Her face was elfin, her coloring creamy brunette, and she was cross-eyed. I had always thought that cross-eyes were a disfigurement, but this girl's cross-eyes were fascinating, intriguing and all the other synonyms in the dictionary. I stood there awkwardly, conscious of my rough clothes, my shaggy mop of hair, my callused hands. I knew I was blushing but couldn't do anything about it. The bishop introduced us, and in a vague sort of way I gathered that the girl was a countess and that her name was Tanya.

The rest of my visit was a sort of golden blur. Later I recalled having eaten some strawberry shortcake. And I remembered hearing the bishop explain that the countess was a sportswoman who hunted big game. He showed me a newspaper clipping from New York that described how she had killed a man-eating Bengal tiger during a recent hunt in India. I don't know whether or not I asked her to go to the dance with me, but I must have, because presently I was leaving and she was asking me to come to the cottage for her at nine o'clock. Her voice had a wonderful foreign lilt and her eyes were mocking but not unkind.

I went through the town walking about six inches above the sidewalk until I saw Smoky lying outside a restaurant. Tex and Buck were at the counter eating ham and eggs. I sat down beside them. I was still seeing those mocking eyes and hearing that voice. And I was wondering how old she was. Twenty-one, I guessed.

Suddenly I was furious because I was only sixteen. It was a dirty trick played on me by a malign fate. I resented it. I—.

"Fer gosh sake, what's wrong with ya, Redhead?" I heard Tex say. "Ya lost yer hearin'? I asked ya three times how ya made out with the bishop."

Buck leaned sideways and looked into my face. He laughed and slapped me on the back. "Leave him alone," he told Tex. "Can't you see the visit was a big success? The poor guy is in love."

I guess I was.

The dance proved to be one of the outstanding social functions of my life, in several respects. I knew how to dance, but only in backwoods fashion, with plenty of action and no finesse. I whirled the countess and swung her, and skipped about the floor, and hoped I was doing all right. It seemed to me that I was. Most of the other men were cannery hands and fishermen, heavy-foot characters, many wearing rubber boots. I thought they were pretty dull. Several came up to us and asked the countess to dance, but each time she refused. I was feeling pretty good. Obviously she preferred me. It occurred to me that perhaps I was mature for my age.

But I was still a brat, as I presently discovered.

We were sitting on a bench against the wall during an intermission, and the countess said abruptly, "You and your friend Mr. Cobb are woodsmen and hunters, no?"

I said we were, and managed to shove my chest out a bit.

"Well, then, could I hire you to guide me on a trip into the Alaska Range? I will have horses shipped from the States. I want to see the country there, and hunt white sheep and caribou when the season opens."

I swallowed my heart, which had somehow climbed into my throat, and said, "Of course we'll go. Just tell us when."

At this moment a burly cannery hand wearing a red shirt and smelling of moonshine hooch and lilac de France came across the floor and said, "Sis, I'm claiming this next dance." The countess shook her head. He said, "Aw, come on, honey, don't give me that treatment." He reached down, took her hand, and pulled her to her feet. I hit him. It was a good blow that jarred my whole arm and shoulder. But the cannery hand didn't even stagger. He stepped back, grinning, a trickle of blood running out of the corner of his mouth.

"Come on outside, hard guy," he said, "and let's get this settled."

Here's where you get the beating of your life, Bucko. This oaf is too big for you and too strong. He's really going to clean your clock.

I went outside with him. I had to. We squared away, and a circle of men formed around us to watch the slaughter. I heard one or two say it wasn't a fair match, but nobody did anything to stop it. The cannery hand lunged at me, both fists swinging. I side-stepped and moved back. As I did so, I felt something hard prod me in the back, and heard Tex's voice say, "Take hit, Redhead." I reached around, and the butt of Tex's stag-handled .45 slid into my hand. The cannery hand was coming at me again like a bull, head down, arms flailing. This time I stood my ground. When he was close enough, I belted him over the head with the barrel of the gun. He fell like a tree, and a split second later Tex whisked the gun out of my hand. I don't believe anybody saw what I hit the man with.

Then the countess stood before us. She took my arm, and I introduced Tex. The big mountain man's green eyes were sparkling, as he allowed he was pleased to meet her. "So this is what caused the battle," he said.

"We're going to guide the countess into the Alaska Range for sheep and caribou," I said. "A long hunt."

"Well, I'll be doggoned," Tex said.

Adventure Is My Business

PART 8

Unforgettable are these true tales of Alaska in its wildest, roughest days. Here is a beautiful cross-eyed countess who rode and shot like a man; a crazed sourdough with a gun in his hand; a Tena medicine man whose magic called up Death.

Alaska's sourdoughs maintained that the northern wilderness was a swell place for Swedes and bears, but hell on horses and lady dudes. Tex always added a line to that. Whimsically, he pointed out that the back-of-beyond could also be pretty doggoned rough on honest, hard-working dude wranglers. He knew what he was talking about. He'd had plenty of experience. During the long pack trip we made with Tanya, the beautiful, cross-eyed Hungarian countess, we had troubles enough, for example, to dismay a half-dozen expeditions.

A snorty bronc named Popcorn caused our first difficulty.

Tanya, Tex, and I were standing in the horse corral out behind Black Carlson's roadhouse on the north slope of Broad Pass. It was a perfect, azure midsummer morning, drowned in chill mountain sunlight. A morning fresh as the dawn of creation. A morning designed for peace and tranquillity—except for one thing. Tanya was having a temper tantrum. She and Tex had clashed, whereupon the countess had exploded like a block of TNT. I had never heard anything like it. I didn't know girls ever threw their weight around in such dramatic fashion. So I was just standing there with my mouth open, undecided whether to flee, take part in the conflict, or pretend to be deaf and blind. "I tell you, I *will* ride Popcorn!" Tanya was raging. "Lady, I say ya ain't!" Tex growled for the third time. "Get out of my way!" Tanya gritted. She was ominously slapping her leg with a rawhide quirt.

With us in the corral, crowded against the spruce-pole fence, were twelve desert-bred cayuses that had been delivered to us today from Pendleton, Oregon. The shipper had guaranteed them to be sound of wind and limb, and undeniably they were. But there was a catch to it. For I doubt that a wilder, crazier string of short-grass broomtails ever was sawed off on an innocent purchaser. They were a wrangler's blue-ribbon nightmare.

They kicked, bit, struck and pitched. They were outlaws and they looked the part. Some had Roman noses and the rest were jug-headed. They all had too much white in their eyes. If you so much as started toward them with a rope or halter, they shied away as if from demons.

The best looking—and orneriest—of the lot was Popcorn. He was a pin-eared, short-coupled, proud-cut 1,200-pound appaloosa gelding—a chestnut roan with freakish dollar-size white spots all over him. After one look at the spectacular brute, Tanya enthusiastically chose him for her personal mount. So Tex and I tried him out—or anyway started to. Tex flipped a loop of Manila rope over the horse's head, and I took a twist on an ear and held the animal while the mountain man eased a saddle and bridle onto him. But before Tex could toe the stirrup, Popcorn yanked free of me and came unglued like a tornado. For five minutes he wamped all over the corral, sunfishing, fence-railing and swapping ends, bawling louder than a gut-shot grizzly. Then he tried to climb the fence, only to fall backward with a crash that should have broken his spine, but didn't. Now he was standing in a far corner, sides heaving, glaring at us.

"Dang hit, be reasonable," Tex pleaded with Tanya. "Popcorn would toss ya so high the birds would build nests in yer pockets afore ya hit the ground. As yer guide I'm responsible fer yer safety, an' I say ya ain't gonna git yer neck busted ridin' that locoed bronc."

Tanya's face was paper-white and her dark eyes were flashing. Biting her lower lip, she catfooted closer to Tex. Never since we first met at Kenai had she looked more beautiful. Slim and high-breasted in jodhpurs, boots and a red shirt bearing her crest in gold thread on the left pocket, she confronted the towering mountain man. "Listen to me. My father was a colonel of Hungarian cavalry. There was no better horseman in Europe. He taught me. Almost since I knew how to walk, I rode with him. So, please believe me, I need no advice about horses from you or any other dog-mushing Alaska backwoodsman." She raised the quirt. "Now get out of my way, or—."

"Ma'am, you hit me with that thing," Tex blazed, "an' I'll take ya over my knee an' give ya the damndest spankin' ya ever heard of—an' that's a promise."

Tanya swished the quirt back for a full-armed slash across Tex's face. I moved in fast. Before she could bring the wicked little whip down, I was between them. I knew that if she struck Tex he would carry out his threat. And I didn't want anybody manhandling Tanya, not even if she deserved it, which she certainly did now. "No," I said. "If you've got to hit somebody, hit me. Go ahead." She stared at me, her face unreadable, and I saw her hand move. *Here it comes, son. She's going to cut you up with that rawhide, and it'll hurt the rest of your life.* But then something happened that I suppose was typical of countesses, or typically feminine, or maybe just typically Tanya. Anyway suddenly she was crying and laughing in the same instant, and her arms were around me. I stood rigid as a post, hands at my sides because I didn't know what else to do with them. The one clear thought in my mind was that the perfume of her hair was the grandest I had ever known or would.

"But perhaps I do need a spanking," she said against my shirt. "Darling, would you like to spank me?"

Nobody else had ever called me darling. It stampeded me. As I remember, I mumbled something incoherent in a voice that didn't sound like mine, and backed away. Popcorn helped me. He was trying to climb the fence again, and that gave me something to do, an opportunity to recover my reeling senses. I picked up a reata as if I knew how to use it, and headed for him. Behind me Tex let out a shout of laughter. I knew I had made a poor showing, and hated myself for it. As I closed in on Popcorn, hating him too, I wondered miserably how long it was going to take me to get over being awkward in the world.

We spent ten days at Black Carlson's place. I practiced wrangling technique and the intricacies of the diamond hitch while Tex reformed our string of outlaws. He gave them what he called the

Injun treatment. It was drastic but quite successful. Since we couldn't risk our outfit on the animals, he packed them with rocks, 250 pounds to the horse, and let them buck themselves silly. When they were too weary to pitch any more, he picketed them to stout pins driven into the ground, and kept them trotting in circles. They lost weight. They'd groan in the mornings when we cinched the sawbuck saddles onto them. After a day or two they were so stiff they moved as if their legs were made of wood. But the work was good for them. They quit trying to throw the packs. The hostile look faded out of their eyes, and they no longer watched for a chance to kick your head off. By the end of a week you could flap a slicker at them, yelling, and they'd hardly flinch. They were now trailworthy. And surprisingly, Popcorn was the best horse in the string.

"Reckon I gotta admit hit," Tex informed Tanya one morning at breakfast. "That there appaloosie is all right. Tried him out thorough the last coupla days. He reins purty, he'll stand, an' he handles his feet like a billy goat. Ride him if ya wanta."

Popcorn proved to be better than just all right. Somewhere, sometime, he must have been somebody's top saddle mount, and then later probably fell into bad hands and turned wild. Now, with the rough edges of resentment worked off, he became a gallant, faithful cayuse, plenty smart, and tough as sun-dried babiche. He was what old-time riders call a "free" horse. Ask for it, and he'd give you everything in him. He was to demonstrate this to us at a place called Red Butte Pass. With Tanya's clever hands on his reins, he made the most desperate, dangerous downhill run I ever saw— and saved Tex's life. . . .

At last, in the towering flare of a carmine sunrise, we broke camp and rode eastward toward the hunting country with the tremendous snow-striped peaks sheering above the trail, and with unguessed adventure again ahead—some of it fated to be pleasant, some very grim. There were only the three of us, and Smoky. Buck had left us at Anchorage, heading down the coast with Caribou Jack to discover if there was any truth in the rumor that sky-blue bears roamed the glacier moraines at Yakutat. I didn't know where Oolinka was. When Tex and I arrived at Matanuska with Tanya, the ex-slave girl disappeared. The countess and Oolinka met only once, at the Widder Jones's farmhouse. So far as I could tell, nothing untoward happened. But during the evening Oolinka walked into the timber and didn't return. I felt low about it. I had done nothing wrong. But still . . . a sense of guilt gnawed at me. I wondered if Blind Nick, the prophet would understand that Oolinka was a free soul, and if she chose to leave without explanation, that was her affair and nobody else's.

Otherwise, I was never happier. Day after day we wound through the deep blue-shadowed passes of the range, topped lofty summits, and followed up emerald-glimmering valleys where probably horses' hoofs had never before rung on rock. Trail life became a routine. We made camp and broke camp; packed the horses and unpacked them. I was wrangler for the party, and I especially liked one nighttime phase of the chore. This was when we were in mosquito country and it was necessary to keep a smudge fire going all night for the horses' protection. The animals would graze until they could no longer endure the incredible swarms of bloodthirsty pests, then would race to the smoke for relief. But you had to watch them or they would back into the embers and burn their hoofs. So I would lie on my sleeping robe beside the fire, Smoky with me, and read and endeavor to write stories.

I was now studying the northern tales of Jack London, and marveling at them. When I finished one, I tried to reproduce it from memory in the hope of catching some part of London's vocabulary and superb sentence rhythm. Or I lifted out a character and substituted one of my own. Or I changed the setting. Or, to develop a sense of timing and climax, I would read a story half through, and attempt to complete it. Often, the next day, I would be so sleepy I'd doze in the saddle. But it was wonderful. I knew with redoubled assurance that this was the whole reason for my existence—to find adventure and learn to write about it.

One night Tanya left her tent to visit me. I was holding the horses in a bunch-grass flat above a lakelet which the midnight sun had turned to a sheet of pure gold. Tanya sat beside me on the sleeping robe and looked at the London story I was struggling with. It was *The Faith of Men*. She read part of what I had written, then put the manuscript down and gazed into the wind-fanned coals of the fire. Presently, in a curiously sad voice, she said, "Some day, when you have become a writer, will you write a story about Tanya? And will you please make her a good girl—a little temperamental, a little lost, lonesome and foolish, but still a good girl?"

I said I would try. Thinking about putting her on paper excited me. I began making notes for a story about a beautiful, cross-eyed, madcap countess who was sad because she feared people would not understand she was a good girl. I was so interested I didn't notice when Tanya left me to return to camp.

Came Red Butte Pass and bad trouble.

We were angling down the rim of a deep, crooked canyon, following a game trail that twisted among huge boulders and clumps of stunted wolf willow. Tex was in the lead with the bell horse, with a couple of turns of the lead rope around his saddle horn. Tanya had ridden ahead and climbed a steep, rocky hillside to take photographs. I was at the rear, watching the packs and keeping the train closed up. The day was hot, the sun blazing out of a cloudless sky, not a breath of breeze blowing off the peaks. I saw Tex fill his pipe and scratch a match to light it. Then everything happened. The burning match head broke off and fell into his lap, setting fire to the frayed end of the lead rope. Tex slapped at the flame with his hat to put it out—and ignited his horse's mane. It was a mishap that wouldn't happen once in a hundred years, but it had happened now and it spoiled our pack trip.

Bawling, Tex's horse sank his head and came undone expertly and with abandon, pitching high, wide and handsome. The bell horse, crowded from behind and frightened, slammed past Tex on the left side, and his rope slipped over the cantle of Tex's saddle and snapped taut against the small of the mountain man's back. It was the worst mix-up I ever saw a rider get into—the rope was fouled on the horn. Some 1,100 pounds of horse-flesh were lunging against each end of it, sawing the Manila into Tex's spine. And the canyon rim with its sheer, dizzy drop-off was only a few feet distant. I was powerless to help, as the packhorses were milling ahead of me, blocking the trail. There was only one thing I could do. Thinking I might be lucky enough to free Tex by cutting the rope with a bullet, I slid the Winchester out of its boot. The bell horse was down now, on his back, kicking and groaning, with his head over the brink of the canyon. I saw Tex's hand flash back to his knife, but the rope was across the haft of the weapon, holding it in its sheath.

I tried a snap shot. It wasn't good enough. A cut strand jumped up from the rope but the other two strands held.

Then, 100 yards up the mountainside, I saw Tanya hang her spurs in Popcorn's ribs and race down the steep, rock-studded slope. She rode like a Valkyrie, and she had a noble horse under her. The appaloosa hurdled boulders, jumped washes, sat on his haunches and slid down a treacherous stringer of scree. I don't know how he kept his feet under him, or how Tanya stayed in the saddle. The run they made actually was a controlled fall. Popcorn hit the trail and skated to a halt, his shoulder against the rump of Tex's plunging horse, the lead rope under his neck. Tanya carried an engraved, silver-hafted Hungarian knife. It flashed in the sunlight, and the rope parted.

When I reached the scene, the countess had snubbed Tex's mount to her saddle horn, and was holding the wild-eyed cayuse with one hand while she supported Tex with the other. The mountain man sat slumped forward, chin on his chest. The back of his shirt was blood-soaked. Raw flesh showed through the torn cloth.

"Can you ride?" I asked him.

"Got to," he muttered. "Git me down to timber, Redhead, an' make camp. But take hit easy—I can't move m' legs."

It was a day and night to date time from. When we reached timber at the headwaters of Red Butte Creek the sun was behind the peaks, and Tex was barely conscious. Tanya and I lowered him from the saddle and got him into a sleeping robe. Then when I had unpacked the horses and buckled the hobbles onto them, we pitched a tent over the mountain man. Tanya washed his rope-torn back and bandaged it, using most of the tape and gauze in our first-aid kit. Tex kept mumbling that he couldn't feel his legs. His face was flushed, and his swamp-green eyes were glazed with pain. During the terrible ride down the canyon rim, he had vomited into his beard. Tanya heated more water and washed off the slime, working as tenderly and capably as if she were a professional nurse.

Outside the tent, she said, "Do you think his back is—?"

"How could it be? He wouldn't have been able to ride." I hoped I was right. But I had the sick feeling I was wrong.

I sat with Tex the first half of the night while Tanya napped by the campfire. I was leaning against a stack of pack-panniers, my robe around my shoulders, when a metallic click awakened me. I opened my eyes, and froze. Tex had lifted himself on one elbow. And he had the Sauer Mauser in his hands, pointed at my chest. The click I had heard was the safety latch. "All right, Hempstead," he grated. "Fill yer hand. This time ya ain't got a cinch like ya had when ya dry-gulched my brother. But go ahead. I'll give ya a chance't, ya mangy polecat." He swung the Sauer's thin muzzle to one side.

He was delirious, and I knew he was going to shoot. Leaving his rifle within his reach had been suicidally stupid. I didn't have a prayer of getting the gun away from him. His finger was on the hair trigger, and I was too well aware that, so long as he could see, he could shoot the buttons off my shirt without half trying. So I sat there, motionless, waiting for the muzzle to swing again. Waiting for a slug to crash through my ribs.

At this point, out of the corner of my eye, I saw Tanya step into the tent.

Tex saw her too. Craftily, with the rifle steady on my heart, he turned his head slightly. Then abruptly he went to pieces. "Mary!" he groaned. "Fer gawd's sake—Mary! They lied to me. They told me ya were dead an' buried." He dropped the Sauer and tried to sit up, but a spasm of agony caught him and he fell back, panting. Tanya went to him and took his head in her lap, smoothing his mane of hair. He said, "Mary!" once more, and lost consciousness. By this time I had the rifle. I took it outside. I was shaking and, despite the chill of the mountain night, sweating as if I had run a mile. I felt that from here on I would exist on borrowed time.

Our mountain men of the North were tough. They were powerhouses of vitality. A man of a softer breed, injured as Tex was, almost certainly would have died or been permanently maimed. But Tex licked it. Within ten days he was able to sit up. Feeling had returned to his legs and he could move them. But he was a cantankerous patient. We tried to keep him on a diet of tea, hot canned milk, dried fruit and squaw-bread toast. After several days he refused it, growling balefully at us. The hell with such invalid fare, he said, he wanted red meat and fat sheep-brisket stew. So I rode up a side creek to a hanging glacier, located a band of white sheep, and killed a young ram. That night we had brisket stew for supper. Tex ate half a kettle of it. Then he belched and, wiping the grease off his mouth, declared that if doctors only had the brains to feed their patients properly, be doggoned if the hospitals and grave-diggers wouldn't soon be out of business.

While we were waiting for Tex to recover, I succeeded one evening in making a double-barreled fool of myself.

Since Cloud Creek, I had wanted to learn to smoke. It occurred to me that now was as good a time as any. So I carved a birch knot into a pipe bowl, and made a willow stem for it, burning a hole through the willow shoot with a hot wire. I filled the pipe with Tex's high-powered cut-plug tobacco, lit it with a coal, and sat comfortably by the fire to enjoy a treat. The first few puffs were marvelous, the smoke fragrant and pleasant on my tongue. I felt grownup, a man in my own right. I could hardly wait for Tanya to come out of her tent and see me performing in adult fashion. Then came the payoff, and it was rough . . . .

Suddenly I was dizzy and sick. My knees had gone weak and my stomach felt as if somebody was rowing a boat in it. The pipe fell out of my mouth. I wanted to get out of sight so I wouldn't disgrace myself, but when I tried to rise, the ground swooped up and smacked me in the face. I was crawling toward a brush clump, gagging, when Tanya ran to me with a gasp of alarm. *If she laughs at me, I'll pull out of here and never see her again. Or kill myself if I don't die before I get the chance.* The countess didn't laugh. She held my head while I was being very sick. The pipe was lying there by the fire, so of course she knew what had happened. After a while she brought me a drink of water, and swabbed my face with a moistened handkerchief. I hadn't known anybody's hands could be so kind.

"Now I have two patients," she said. "And you know, a patient is always supposed to fall in love with his nurse. . . . Shall I tell you about the time I first smoked? I was ten, and it was my father's pipe, a great carved meerschaum with a cherry-wood stem. It made me so ill that I dropped it, and it broke. My father punished me by taking my pony away from me for a month. . . . Growing up can be a terrible business, no?"

It wasn't necessary to fall in love with her. That had happened when Bishop Antonin introduced us at Kenai.

Now it was autumn and the hunting season was open. One evening Tex said to me, "We gotta git the countess a coupla trophies. The way things are, hit's your job. So git goin' in the mornin' an' see what ya can do."

I was loaded with luck. I found Tanya anyhow 5,000 caribou the first day.

We were riding across a terraced alpine meadow ten miles from camp when our horses halted, ears turned forward, blowing softly. Not a living thing was in sight. But after a moment I heard rocks rolling, and a sort of low, muted thunder, and a confused clattering and clicking. The sounds seemed to come from a green canyon that slashed the meadow 300 yards above us. We halted, and tied the horses in a clump of frosted willows. Then, out of the canyon, heading obliquely down the slope, trotted a ribby caribou cow. Behind her came other caribou, then still others, then a dun tide of the animals. Their clashing antlers were like a forest. The snowy capes of the bulls gleamed in the sunlight. It was the big caribou migration of this region. I don't know how many were in the herd. Maybe 5,000. Maybe twice that many.

"Tell me which one," Tanya whispered.

I tried to choose a head. I think I decided on at least a dozen, and each time either lost track of the animal or saw a better head coming out of the canyon. Finally, afraid that if I didn't make up my mind we'd lose out altogether, I pointed out a big bull on the near side of the herd. He was a magnificent beast, with a tall, branchy hayrack of antlers so polished that they reflected the sun in bright mirror flashes. Tanya raised her rifle. With the crash of the shot I heard the softpoint bullet strike home.

When we went over to the kill, leading the horses, the herd split around us, two torrents of gray-brown bodies streaming past, ankle joints clicking, antlers clattering and banging.

"They are attacking us!" she said.

They weren't, but it looked like it. The herd had turned at the foot of the meadow and was now coming back toward us at top speed. It was a maneuver I had never before witnessed, but Tex had told me about it. The caribou were curious to know what our horses were. They wanted another look at them, wanted to get their scent. We mounted, and watched the herd thunder past and circle downwind.

In five minutes the caribou were gone, vanished as mysteriously as they had arrived. Tanya took a deep breath.

Then it was September. Southbound geese were clamoring across the sky. The rabbits and ptarmigan were turning white. A hard frost had turned the blueberries sugar sweet. Tanya killed a forty-inch ram one windy noon on a snow-dusted ledge behind Red Butte—and when we returned with the meat and the trophy Tex rode out to meet us. He was taking it easy, bracing himself with his hands on the pommel, but still he was up there and was grinning widely because he had surprised us.

"Figgered I'd better quit loafin'," he said, "on account o' hit's time to git outa these peaks. Snow's gonna fly mighty soon—an' we sure have got a long way to ride."

That evening green and violet aurora lights flared in the northern sky. The wind off the peaks held the bite of approaching winter, and the rising moon was frost-white. We were roasting a rack of fat sheep ribs over red-willow coals. Tanya moved closer to me.

"In October I am going to Africa to hunt. Will you go with me—the same job you have now? You could learn to guide there, and some day write about it." In the firelight her face was eager and it seemed very young, not old enough to be the face of the Tiger Countess. "I would take my attorney to see your parents. Please think about it, and let me know when we reach Anchorage."

I said all right, I would. And I did. I thought about the offer all the long hard way back to Black Carlson's, and during the train trip south. I didn't think about much else. I worried and cudgeled my brains to the point where I lost sleep and, I believe, weight. And I was still undecided when we unloaded the outfit at Matanuska.

As we had to make an arrangement regarding the horses, Tanya stopped off with us, taking a room at Phil Allen's roadhouse. She could sell the string, if a buyer could be found, or else pay someone to winter the animals. Matanuska was one of the best places in Alaska for wintering horses, but nevertheless they would need constant care, and the going cost was steep—$90 a head. But that wasn't my problem. My burning problem was whether or not to abandon the North, just when I was getting started in it, and head across the world to Africa.

Tex was no help. When I asked him one day at the roadhouse what I should do, he shrugged his craggy shoulders.

Tanya kept glamorizing Africa.

That night we walked out to the horse corral in the early starlight and sat on the top rail listening to the horses eat their ration of clover hay. With her shoulder touching mine, she said, "Beneath Kilimanjaro there is a yellow plain dotted with herds of game animals to the far horizon and beyond. Lions hunt here. And sometimes the tall black natives with their shining spears and painted shields hunt the lions. You will love it. It is a land of adventure and drama—the great land God set aside for sportsmen. Please come with me."

"I'm still thinking about it," I said.

Then, in a flash, I knew to whom I would go for advice. Next morning I arose at daybreak and headed for Blind Nick's cabin on Rabbit Slough. I was lucky. When I came in sight of the cabin, smoke was curling from a hole in the roof. The prophet was home.

Blind Nick said in his deep, thudding voice, "Come in."

I entered, standing for a moment in the doorway to let my eyes become accustomed to the gloom of the single room. Blind Nick was alone. He sat cross-legged on the puncheon floor beside a dim fire built on a circle of blackened rocks, an otter robe over his shoulders. The cabin was bare as an anchorite's cell. It had no chairs, no bunk, no table. Blind Nick shoved a hand from under the otter robe and motioned for me to sit down.

"I came to ask about Oolinka," I said, "and about something else."

The prophet nodded. At his right knee was a bundle of dried grass tied with a babiche thong. He took a handful of the grass and dropped it on the coals of the fire. At once the cabin became filled with a haze of aromatic smoke, sweet smelling and heady as perfume.

"Oolinka is on Maclaren River with Chief Nelchina Stepan and his family. They are drying caribou meat and blueberries for winter. She will stay there until spring." He placed another handful of the sweet grass on the coals. "She is sad. She is one of those born to be sad. Not like you."

I wanted to ask him if he was speaking English now, but didn't dare. So I said, "I have a job—to go to Africa." No sooner had I spoken the words than the question seemed foolish. What could a blind Tena medicine man know about Africa. Probably he had never even heard of Africa. If you described an elephant to him he would no doubt think you were joking. He'd think a lion was an overgrown, off-color lynx with a mane and tail. "Well, I just thought I'd ask you about it."

"The answer you want is in your own mind," Blind Nick said. "In a little while you will know what it is."

He drew the otter robe closer about him. The red coals of the fire seemed to glow brighter. The perfumed smoke eddied and coiled. It assumed strange, shifting shapes, gradually forming such a heavy bank above the fire that the prophet's form first blurred, then became indistinguishable from the shadows. Then something weird happened.

Maybe I fell asleep and dreamed it. I don't know. I don't even want to guess. Anyway, the firelight grew still brighter. It grew tall and wide. It took on the hot colors of a mighty sunrise—as sunrise over an alien land. Cutting the flame-tinted fan of radiance now was the violet silhouette of a big snow-topped mountain. Beneath the mountain was a yellow plain with dusty grass, flat-topped trees, clumps of thorny brush.

I was walking in advance of a half-naked black man, a slow step at a time, my rifle ready. Close ahead was a small island of the thorny brush. There was a lion in the brush. I couldn't see him but

I knew he was there. And I knew he was wounded. I kept moving forward. Then, fast as the blink of an eyelash, the lion charged from the right. I put the Winchester's sights on his head and pulled—and the shell misfired. The lion was in the air now, paws outspread, teeth gleaming in the new light. This was death. There was no time to do anything but take the charge and die. . . .

"Have you decided?" Blind Nick asked. The scene had abruptly faded and the sweet smoke was streaming up through the hole in the roof and I could again see the prophet. He was watching me closely, his lean hawk face creased in a sympathetic half smile. "I would have tried to advise you," he said. "But what could a blind Indian medicine man know about Africa."

I said I had decided. I said, "Thanks," and stood up and went to the door and departed. I was bewildered, I had a headache, and my eyes hurt. An hour later, at the roadhouse, I found Tanya in her room writing a letter. She gave me a searching look and arose.

"I was writing for reservations for us," she said. "Should I?"

"Not for me. I'm not going."

"What happened?" Her voice was low and her eyes were wide and very dark.

I told her. It must have sounded dumb and I guess it made me seem pretty superstitious, but I had been as undecided as a tossed coin anyway, and now I was dead certain I was not going to light out to Africa to get killed by a lion. Not even in the name of adventure. Not even to please a beautiful countess with whom I had fallen in love.

The pen broke in Tanya's hands and ink spattered her blouse. For an instant I thought she was going to throw the pieces at me. Then she smiled, a slow, rueful smile. "I should have known better. I told you I was a little foolish." She put a hand on my arm. "Perhaps next time?"

"Maybe."

"So . . . tomorrow I will leave. The horses are yours. A gift. And please be especially kind to Popcorn. But that Blind Nick, that prophet—when you see him again tell him I hate him, and ask him what was in that sweet-smelling grass," She faced me, straightening her shoulders. "Now let's go and take a last walk together—a long one."

Adventure Is My Business

PART 9

Learning to call up a kill-crazy bear within rifle range, twice saving the life of the same spitfire girl—it was all in a day's work for the Redhead. For his job lay on Alaska's fur trails.

It was early blue-hazed autumn again, I was nineteen, and Tex and I had returned to Matanuska after a hard year of chasing rainbows in the Kuskokwim country—beautiful rainbows but barren of pots of gold. . . .

We were waiting for a frost. We planned to spend a month or so hunting black bears for the fur market, but there was no use starting out until we had a frost. It always took a few days of sharp weather, and an almighty lot of frost-sweetened blueberries, to put the proper gloss on a bear's pelt. So we were just marking time. We stuffed ourselves with store grub, the kind of grub we had dreamed about in the wilds—canned peaches and tomatoes, pickles, sardines, cheese, strawberry jam, oranges—until even Tex's copper-lined stomach protested. We read yellowed and tattered newspapers to find out what had been going on in the world. We went visiting. And we slept late every morning. This last was something Tex insisted on. When he was in town, he declared, he aimed to sleep as late as he pleased, by the holy old Mackinaw, and he didn't want anybody or anything to disturb him.

So he was fit to be tied one sunny Saturday morning when our eight sled dogs, chained in the dooryard, abruptly set up a crazy, hysterical yammering that could have been heard in the next township. The big mountain man didn't wait to pull on his pants. He surged out of bed, clad in baggy-kneed red underwear, and banged the cabin door open so violently that it rattled on its hinges.

"*Hya-aar! Chook!* Ya-mangy, cross-bred, siwash bacon thieves," he bellowed. "Shet up, damn ya, afore I frail yer worthless hides to door mats."

He snatched up a gunny sack, probably the heaviest instrument of punishment he had ever used on dogs, and waded into the team, striking right and left with the sack and roaring curses intended to scorch a Malamute's hair right down to the epidermis. I had followed him outside to witness the performance. This turned out to be a grievous error, mainly because my costume was as disreputable as his. I was wearing only a pair of drawers with most of the buttons missing and with a sizable hole in the seat.

"Take that, ya lousy, miser'ble, slant-eyed, slumber-destroyin' varmints," Tex was hollering as he brought the sack down in two-handed swipes. "An' that. An' th—."

At this point we both realized we were not alone. From the road forty feet below the cabin had come a horrified gasp and a chorus of soprano giggles. I spun around—and felt as if I had been hit with a bucket of ice water. Staring up at us from the road was our new Matanuska schoolmarm and eight of her girl pupils. I suppose they had arisen bright and early to go on a nature hike. Or on a picnic. Or something. Anyway, there they were.

I had never met the schoolmarm but I had seen her. I knew that her name was Susan, that she was twenty-three, and that she had recently come north from Oregon. She was pretty. I mean, pretty all over. She had soft, curly dark-auburn hair and gentian eyes you could drown in and feel no pain. She wore slacks and a turtle-neck sweater. And whoever coined the term "sweater girl" could have had Susan in mind. As we stood there on the hill, frozen motionless, Tex holding the gunny sack upraised for another wallop at the dogs, the wild hope flashed through my mind that maybe this was all part of a ghastly dream. But it was a short-lived hope. Trim and indignant, the morning wind blowing her cap of curls, the schoolmarm was regarding us as if we represented some unspeakably low form of animal life.

"Barbarians," she exploded. "Come along, children. Don't look at them."

Tex and I fled into the cabin. Some introduction.

That did it, bucko. You're finished socially around here until the school term ends. How in hell could you dare ask her for a dance after this? Or to go for a horseback ride? Or to let you walk her home from school? She wouldn't give you a pleasant hello. Starting now you're the bare-butted laughingstock of the countryside.

I was exploring the seat of my drawers to discover how big the hole really was. It was pretty big. Too big. "She was right," I said. "I guess we are barbarians."

"Yeah," Tex chuckled. He was over being angry with the dogs. His primitive sense of humor had been tickled. He stretched out on the bunk, hands behind his head, swamp-green eyes bright with laughter. "Doggone if I ain't got a notion to go back to school, Redhead," he said. "On account o' I got a idea that dark-sorrel schoolmarm could teach a feller a whole heck of a lotta things."

A week later I encountered Susan again.

Bored with doing nothing while we waited for a frost, I rigged us some tackle and Smoky and I went fishing. The season's last run of silver salmon was coming into Spring Creek slough from salt water. There was a horde of the fat ocean-bright fish. They filled the green pools and the long gravelly riffles where they had their ancient spawning beds. There were so many of them that they actually bumped into your boots when you waded a ford. I found a wedge of bar under some brilliant overhanging willows, and tied on a No. 4 Colorado spinner. Just above me was a deep, wide pool. I cast the bit of brass obliquely across the current, let it sink partway, and started it in. Before it had moved ten feet a husky female silver struck. She was a champion. She came out cartwheeling. And she kept coming out, banging the water with her tail, shaking herself until she became a blur of motion in the sunlight. When at last she tired I brought her in, drove my belt knife through her gills, and took her up into the grass. She was a six-pounder, bulging with her twin skeins of carnelian eggs. Just the right size to make a salmon dinner for Tex and me. I knelt in the grass, sliced off the fillets, and skinned them.

Then Smoky growled.

The little black fighting dog was facing upstream. He had winded something or somebody. Because this was brown bear country, I picked up the Winchester and checked the chamber load. But it wasn't a bear. After a little I heard brush slapping against a pair of rubber boots. A branch broke. Rocks rolled. Whoever was coming down the trail was no Indian or white woodsman. In fact, I don't think I ever heard anybody make more noise in the timber. Presently I saw who it was. Susan. She came striding along in a bouncy heel-and-toe sidewalk gait, passed without seeing me, and halted on the bar from which I had fished. I knew it was ungallant not to let her know of my presence. But I couldn't think of anything to say. I guess I was scared of her. So I just sat there, fifteen feet distant, in plain view, and watched her prepare to give the salmon a workout.

She tied on a Polar Bear Streamer, ran out some line—almost snagging my ear—and began dropping the fly across the pool. The gal could cast. And she got action. At her third or fourth try I'll bet twenty salmon boomed up at the lure. The pool boiled. You could hear the beat and flurry of the fishs' tails as they drove to the surface. A great hook-nosed male won the race. He shot full-length out of the water, closed his wickedly toothed jaws on the fly, and headed for the bottom. Susan socked him with everything her leader would stand, and thereafter was very busy. The salmon was probably a six-year-old. Around ten pounds. Now at the very peak of his life, he was as fast, powerful and belligerent a fish for his weight as the salmonoid tribe could produce. He proved it. He jumped ten times. He went crazy and beached himself on the opposite bank, but managed to somersault back into the water. Then, getting crafty, he made a blazing run downstream and around a brushy bend.

The line fouled on the splintered end of a long out-thrust snag.

"Oh, damn," Susan wailed. Her difficulties had only begun. Obviously intending to crawl out on the snag and free the line, she backed toward its butt end, off the bar now, knee-deep in fast water. When she reached the willows she reached around and took hold of a stout limb to steady herself. Ten seconds later she was a schoolmarm who needed a friend. The limb she was clutching supported a yellow jacket's nest the size of a Japanese lantern. I had seen the first shock of a yellow-jacket red-hot stinger jar a tough woodsman off his feet. Susan took at least three stings in the same instant. She screamed and dropped her rod, slapping her face and neck. Then turning to flee, she slipped on an algae-slimed rock and fell. The current rolled her. Deep water was close below.

I sprinted down the bank, waded out to my waist, and grabbed her coat collar as she floated past. She fought me all the way to shore. Her fishing cap was down over her eyes, and maybe she thought a bear had her. I don't know. Anyway, I dragged her into the shallows, then took her in my arms and carried her up the bank. She twisted around against my chest, yanked the cap off, and looked up at me, a wounded-panther glare in her eyes. I wanted to tell her it was all right, that she was safe now, but she didn't give me a chance. She wrestled violently out of my arms and backed away, stumbling in her water-filled boots. From her expression I gathered she wished it had been a bear instead of me.

"Y-you again," she said through chattering teeth. "Yes, ma'am. The barbarian. Only with more clothes this time."

She let me pull off her boots and wring out her socks and coat. Her sweater clung to her like a second skin, and she knew it and was embarrassed. So I put my caribou jacket over her shoulders. Then I went downstream and found her rod. The big mule silver had won his fight. He was gone. He had got a good solid pull against the snag, and the leader had snapped. Now all he had to do was to fertilize a nest of eggs and complete his destiny by dying. When I returned to Susan she was trying to powder her nose with a wet powder puff. She gave that up, and tenderly examined a yellow jacket sting which looked as if it was going to close one eye. Suddenly she turned and gave me a dirty look.

"You were here while I was fishing," she accused. "Spying on me."

"Yes ma'am." I wanted to add it was lucky for her, but didn't.

"I hate snoops," she said. "But . . . thanks for pulling me out of the water. Thanks for the use of your jacket. I'll have it returned." She picked up her rod and headed for town. Over her shoulder she said, "Good-bye!"

Came a chill, star-fretted night with geese clamoring overhead, flock after flock, gray voyagers down from the freezing arctic, southbound for California and Mexico. In the morning the dooryard grass sparkled with frost. So it was time for us to move too. Time to light out for the black bear country. Time to go to work. While Tex cooked breakfast, I brought in the horses, tied five at the cabin, and hazed the others over to the Widder Jones's pasture. As I was shutting the gate, the Widder came out of the house with a cup of coffee for me.

"If the schoolmarm wants to go riding," I said, trying to sound offhand, "you could let her take Popcorn. But don't tell her I said so. She hates my insides."

The Widder laughed, and slapped me on the back so hard that I spewed coffee six feet. "I like her myself. Of course, she's a spunky cheechako gal who needs a little taming. But the country'll take care of that."

"If she doesn't buffalo the whole country first," I said.

We were camped on *Knah-Kutnoo*, in a stand of wind-twisted spruces below the shattered blue-green wall of the glacier. This was the true home of the black bear, his own wild, generous freehold. In the streams were fish for the taking. The wide sand bars were covered with red-flowering pea vine, the sweet roots of which he dug in the spring. And above timberline, countless acres of them, were blueberry meadows and saskatoon thickets. The ice fields kept him cool in the heat of summer. In winter there were dry rocky crevices where he could sleep undisturbed while storm winds raged and snow drifted deep above him. It was his great, happy domain and he thrived in it. But he had an enemy—the pelt-hunter with a rifle.

Tex and I were spoilers here, game pirates, although this did not occur to either of us.

There was no bag limit on black bears. Someone in power had decided the animals were harmful predators, and protection had been denied them. So you could kill as many as you were able to, and sell the pelts legally. Tex and I intended to make a notable killing. Between now and freeze-up, we hoped to take enough skins and fat to pay our winter's grub bill, with maybe enough left over for a week of fun in Anchorage. But it was hard, bloody work. You ate before daybreak. Then you saddled up and rode the bars, always looking for an easy kill. If a bear was feeding too high on the range shed, you passed him by because you didn't want to spend a whole day on the chance of getting a shot. You were killing for money, and time was against you. Any day now snow would fly, and the *Knah-Kutnoo* bears would vanish as if they had never been. So you hunted from sunup till sundown. You ripped off pelts and let the blood dry on your arms. You climbed mountains till you hardly knew how to walk on level ground. And you hopefully estimated your profit.

Sometimes a kill would be dramatic. Like the time Tex taught me how to call a bear into rifle range.

We were riding down a boulder-choked moraine trough that opened onto the *Knah-Kutnoo* bars. Sand was blowing on a stiff east wind, and I was trying to eat a bear-meat sandwich. Finally deciding I was getting more sand than meat and bannock, I said the hell with it, threw the sandwich away, and dismounted at a streamlet to rinse the grit out of my mouth. My horse was a line-back dun named Shotgun, a tough, smart cayuse that had learned to spot bears like a pointer spots quail. As I knelt at the water's edge, reins in my hand, I felt Shotgun pull back, then heard him blow. Looking around, I saw that he was standing with his head high, ears turned forward, interested in something out on the open bars. Tex hadn't noticed the horse's actions. He was busy filling his pipe. I stalled a moment or two, then saw the bear. He was a medium-size black, about 700 yards distant, upwind. He had just come out of a wash, and was heading for an island of timber on our right.

"Are ya gonna drink the creek dry, Redhead?" Tex asked impatiently.

I said no. I was only watching that fine bear out there, and wouldn't it be a good idea to make a fast ride to the timber and cut him off? I didn't often sight game before Tex, and when I did it was fun kidding him. Most mountain men were peacock-proud of their keen eyesight, and Tex wasn't any different.

"Huh?" Tex swiveled his head in three directions before he saw the bear. "Oh, yeah. That one. Well, no hurry about hit. We'll git him." I knew he was sore because his nose and ears, almost the only parts of his face not covered by his jungle of beard, were flushed. He lit his pipe with exaggerated care. "O' course, I could make him come over here an' ask to git shot. Hit'd save time, an' maybe teach you somethin', if possible."

I said that would be a trick I'd like to see. And Tex said, all right, just watch and listen.

We rode down into some frost-yellowed dwarf cottonwoods at the rim of the bars, and ground-tied the horses. The bear was now straight out from us, shambling along in the blowing sand. If he knew where he was going, he was in no hurry to arrive there. He turned aside to sniff a clump of pea vine. He dug something out of a bank and ate it. He sat down and leisurely scratched an ear. He was taking his own sweet time—and the mountain man went to work. He pressed both thumbs against his lips, and uttered the anguished, high-pitched scream of a mortally stricken snowshoe rabbit.

It was a good trick. It worked.

At once the bear whirled, and reared to his full height. I had my glasses on him and saw his nose working as he tried the wind. It wasn't hard to figure out what he was thinking. He thought that a fox, weasel or maybe a marten had waylaid a rabbit somewhere over here. Also he thought that if he could locate the spot, and reach it in time, there was a good chance he could steal the carcass. Bears don't get many rabbits to eat. They aren't fast enough. In the timber the most agile bear would bat his brains out against trees trying to follow a twisting, dodging, long-legged snowshoe. So this bear was so eager he was practically slobbering. Tex gave the rabbit scream again. Instantly the bear dropped to all fours and came slamming across the bars—thirty degrees off course.

"Damn hit," Tex growled. "Is that fool bear stupid!"

He started to repeat the call, but I stopped him. I wanted to try it myself. I put my thumbs to my lips as he had, and let out a terrific rabbit scream. It started too low, and it ended in a squawk, but the bear got his direction from it, all right. He came straight at us now, traveling so fast that his hind feet were reaching past his nose. Tex knelt, and thumbed the safety latch of the Sauer. He waited until the bear was 100 feet distant. Then he made a beautiful head shot. The bear went over in a high somersault, kicked a couple of times, and died. Tex was grinning as he reached for his knife. He had gotten even with me for sighting the bear first. He had taught me a good one.

It was night, and we were sitting by a little campfire under the overhang of a shadowy cliff. Between us the loin of young bear was roasting on a willow spit, its fat hissing and flaring in the red coals. Tex was cleaning the Sauer. I was fleshing the pelt of a big sow bear we had killed that afternoon in a high-bush cranberry thicket. Neither of us felt like talking. We were dog-tired. For thirty days we had prowled this rough reach of wilderness, taking time out only to eat and sleep. We had killed twenty bears.

"Ya know what I wish I had," Tex said. "A big, thick, juicy beefsteak."

We didn't wait for daylight. We saddled up in the snow-filled, predawn darkness and hit the trail. Tex was so happy to be moving again that he burst into song.

But he wasn't so happy next day, nor was I. Something had happened that was to worry the blazes out of us. With the wind at our backs, we were drifting down toward the Jim Creek sand dunes. The snowfall had ceased now, but the sky was still overcast and the first mush ice was running in the river. Suddenly Tex raised his arm, pointing. A runner was coming up the bars.

"The Widder sent me," Hurry-up Joe said. He wasn't panting, his breathing was as even as mine. "She tol' me, find Tex. Bad trouble at Matanuska. The schoolteacher, she got lost. Rode a horse somewhere yesterday, don' come back. All day. All night. Lost somewheres."

It was coming on midnight when we rode into the Widder Jones's dooryard and snow was blowing again. We stripped the packs off the leg-weary horses and stumbled into the house. The Widder fed us, and I ate without knowing what I was eating. I was too intent on what she had to tell us. This was Sunday. Susan had ridden out on Popcorn early Saturday morning. She hadn't said where she was going.

At the cabin I tried to sleep, with no success. I kept thinking there ought to be some way of figuring out where Susan had gone. But I couldn't come up with anything. My mind went around like a weasel in a brush patch. Pictures came to me. Susan hooking the silver salmon. Striking at me as I carried her out of the water. Standing in the road that morning, the wind blowing her curls. . . . Then I had an idea. I hit the floor in a flash and reached for my clothes.

I reined in at a dark cabin behind the roadhouse and got down and knocked on the door. It was Bill Swanson's cabin. He opened the door, saw who I was, and asked what I wanted. I said, "Bill, your daughter went on hikes with the schoolmarm. I know because I saw her one morning when Tex and I were having trouble with the dogs. Wake her up, Bill. Ask her where Susan went most often."

Bill disappeared into the house. When he returned he said, "Maybe you got something. The kid says she went to Lookout Bluff every Saturday or Sunday."

Lookout Bluff was above the river, five miles from town. I made it there as fast as I could push the trail-worn Shotgun. With the snow-laden wind clawing at me, I rode down through a fringe of skinny balm-of-Gilead cottonwoods to the rim of a cutbank. Shotgun was getting interested now. He raised his head and whickered. In a moment I smelled wood smoke. Then, at the foot of the bank, I saw the glow of a fire. I tied Shotgun and slid down a twenty-foot gravel pitch. A figure, swathed in a saddle blanket sat in the shadows.

I said, "It's me again. The barbarian."

"Yes," she said. She stood up. "I'm all right. But Popcorn"—she pointed into the darkness—"is hurt. He fell with me. And then—then in the snow I couldn't find the trail back."

Popcorn was down, groaning, piled up against a windfall. It was clear what had happened—Susan had tried to put him down the bank. He recognized me and tried to get up, but I sat on his neck while I felt him over. I found it—his left foreleg. I sat there with him a while, remembering a lot of things. Black Carlson's. Tex's Injun treatment. Tanya's Valkyrie ride at Red Butte Creek. Then while I petted him and talked to him, I laid the muzzle of the Winchester against his temple. Susan was still at the fire. I gave her the food I had brought and put the blanket around her. Neither of us said anything. While she was eating I went around to the other side of the fire and lay down to wait for daylight. Maybe I went to sleep. Anyway, after a while, I realized that Susan was standing beside me.

"Smoke was blowing over there, and sparks. Could I lie down here?"

"On the same side of the fire with a man you said was barbarian?"

"You could be a kind barbarian. Besides, I wanted to tell you I'm sorry. About Popcorn. It was my fault." There were tears in her voice. She sounded lonely, frightened and forlorn, and she had reason to.

I said, "All right," and she began spreading the blankets.

Adventure Is My Business

PART 10

*Alaska had plenty to offer the Redhead—
all of it on the tough side. Wasn't it tough to see
a kid's dream ruined for ten ounces of dust?
Even stranger were the adventures with Short-Card Montague,
who shot one caribou too many; and the mysterious cabin of
Whisky Bill that suddenly walked off one freezing night.*

I hit Fairbanks around noon, this dazzlingly bright spring day, mushing on the last of the winter's snow. I put up my dogs at French Louis's Malamute Hotel, checked in at the Nordale myself, and headed down the main street looking for some excitement. I had come in from five months on the fur trails with Tex, and I craved fun, action and companionship. I didn't have to look far. A block from the hotel I rounded a corner toward Chena Slough, and bumped into two old friends—Caribou Jack and The Oregon Mare.

"Hiyah, Redhead, where the hell ya been the last coupla years?" the pint-size white-headed sourdough hollered. He grabbed me around the waist and whirled me across the sidewalk in a two-step. As usual in town, he was a spectacle. He wore an electric-blue silk shirt with a mustard-yellow tie in which sparkled a diamond sunburst pin of about .45 caliber. His Mackinaw pants had red and green checks five inches across. His satin-soft Sitkan deerskin jacket was decorated on both sleeves with his monogram and the Alaska flag in dyed porcupine quills. All he needed was neon. "Come on, join us," he said. "We got a party down the street. Celebratin' the breakup, or something."

The Oregon Mare, gray-eyed and stately, wearing more mink than a top trapper likely would take all winter in good mink country, said in her soft, precise voice, "Yes, come with us. Cap Northway is in town. He's a steamboat man, and I want you to meet him. He's a character for you to write about some day."

Thus fate operating on a spring morning. Thus I met the incomparable Northway, riverboat skipper, would be empire builder, and pioneer of the Yukon Basin.

We turned into a pool hall that had been a saloon before Volstead, and went through it to the back room. Sitting around a poker table in a noisy bull session were Cap Northway, Gordon Bettles, the Hootlinanna Kid, Blueberry Bill, the Malamute Kid and Smokehouse Ole Hogan. Northway was short, white-headed and roly-poly. The Santa Claus type—until you saw the sharp alertness in his steel-blue eyes, and noticed that his knuckles had been broken and rebroken. When I shook hands with him it was like taking hold of a chunk of granite.

The Oregon Mare winked at me over her shoulder and said, "Cap, tell us a steamboat story. One with a moral." Cap said all right, he would. He said he knew one with a hell of a moral.

"I had the old *Beaver*," he said. "A fine boat. Seventy feet long, plenty of power, and she'd run on a good heavy dew. Also I had a cargo of baled hay, grub and lumber for some crazy stampeders down the river. But I needed an engineer. I needed one bad. So I hired a joker I didn't know, one Hungry Thompson. I never met anybody like him. Always eating. First at the table and last to leave, and bumming handouts from the cook between meals. When he came aboard here at Fairbanks, doggoned if he didn't have half a smoked salmon in one hand and a loaf of bread in the other. Mouth so full he had to swallow three times before he could say good morning. Everybody in sight was laughing at him, and that made me sore.

"'Mister, that doesn't look so good,' I said.

"Hungry didn't realize he was being bawled out. 'Well, it ain't so good, either,' he said, sniffing at the salmon. 'These blasted Tanana Injuns never did smoke salmon so's a white man would enjoy it.'

"I should have hustled him right back down the plank. Because a few days later the so-and-so put me out of business. When the cook wasn't looking one morning, Hungry raided the galley and swiped a pound of spoiled bologna sausage the cook intended to throw overboard. He ate it. Maybe he didn't notice it was spoiled. Or maybe he didn't care. Anyway, in an hour or so cramps tied him in knots. The way I heard it, he was humped over the reverse lever like a praying pilgrim at Mecca, popeyed and sweating. Suddenly he had to go. I mean, he had to go. So he yelled to the fireman to take the throttle, and lit out at a staggering run for the head.

"Meanwhile, I was taking the *Beaver* down through that bad chute below Moosehead Point. It was tricky work. The river was high, running like the milltails of hades, and there was a lot of heavy drift. Snags and trees that would rip your bottom out in two seconds. I guess I was dropping her down pretty fast, because I never was a hand for slow bells. Anyhow, we came skyhooting around a bend—and I saw the thing that gives pilots nightmares and makes 'em white-headed. Grounded crosswise of the stream was a cottonwood about four feet through. A big old skinned-up brute of a cottonwood, its branches waving and thrashing in the current. There was a chance that I could sneak past it close in against the left bank. But I had to lose some speed. So I rang the engine room for full power astern, spun the wheel, and started praying.

"Well, of course the fireman was at the throttle, and the poor cuss got the bell signals confused. He gave me full speed ahead. "Gentlemen, we hit that grandfather of cottonwoods with the most awful crash you ever heard. The bow caved in. The hog stays snapped and the stacks came down. Our deck load of baled hay and lumber flew in all directions. In the engine room the main steam line broke. The fire door clanged open and blazing cordwood rolled all over the deck. You talk about a situation. We were sinking, afire, without power, and the boat was filled with scalding steam. By a miracle we got ashore. But the *Beaver* and her cargo were lost." Caribou Jack scratched his head, looking puzzled. "Yeah, but where's the moral?" "The moral," Cap grinned, "is that you should never trust an engineer who's full of baloney."

The guy was wonderful. He really had it. I knocked around with him several days, doing the town, and discovered he could produce more fascinating ideas per hour than anybody I had ever known. He said he was going to build a chain of trading posts on the rivers. At the posts he would plant vegetable gardens and berry patches, so that, with fish and game, they would be largely self-supporting. He would bring in portable sawmills. He would comb the North for experienced prospectors, and grubstake them. Eventually, when flying machines became a little more reliable, he would import one and use it for winter fur-buying trips. He foresaw the future of the North—aviation, agriculture, syndicate methods of prospecting, and the enormous value of strategic wilderness spots.

(At Northway on the Tanana there is a giant B-36 air base. It is located on the site of Cap's first trading post. But when I visited it last year, not even the commanding officer knew for whom it was named. Cap died too soon.)

One night a week or so after our first meeting, I was asleep at the Nordale when Cap banged on the door. I told him to come on in. He shoved the door open and leaned against the wall, hands in his jacket pockets, chewing on the stem of a battered corncob. A roughneck's version of St. Nicholas. "I just had an idea," he said. "You want to go into business with me—as a full partner?" I said, "Yes."

He said, "Well, all *right*, partner. You don't have to be so argumentative about it." He hit me over the head with a pillow. "G'wan back to sleep. We got work to do tomorrow."

Steamboating was a wild, free life and I loved it. We roamed beautiful rivers with music in their names. The Yukon, the Tanana, the Innoko, the Koyukuk, the Iditarod. All this vast spread of waterways was fresh and unspoiled, filled with drama and color, a marvelous primitive world for a lad who wanted to write. I doubt that even Mark Twain could have improved on some of the characters we carried as passengers—or on the strange, violent and pathetic things that happened to them. There was a Short-Card Montague, a gambler who once took passage with us from Ruby to Nenana. Montague was a type specimen of his profession. He was tall, dark and elegant, with fine hands and quick, flashing eyes. He sported sideburns and wore black broadcloth, snowy linen and glossy British-made boots. I think he changed his shirt two or three times a day, for otherwise it couldn't have remained so immaculate. According to rumor, he was a dangerous man, supposed to have killed several men in gunfights in the States. Because of his reputation as a killer, the miners and traders we were carrying shied away from him. He was treated with much respect and obviously enjoyed it. Then he had the bad luck to run afoul of Cap Northway.

We were operating the *Delta*, an eighty-foot craft we had bought at a bargain from a defunct California firm. On this particular rose-tinted autumn morning, Cap and I were in the wheelhouse making large plans for the boat, when suddenly the mate touched my arm, pointing. A quarter of a mile upstream a migration of caribou was about to ford the river. It was the great northern herd. I wouldn't even guess how many caribou were in it. Cap thought there must be 100,000, but how could you tell? They covered the tundra back to the crest of the first hill, a mile distant, and more were coming into view. Polished antlers and white manes gleaming, the close-packed ranks poured over a bar into the river and struck out across. They swam in such tight formation that their bodies touched and their antlers seemed intertwined. In mid-channel the current bellied the long line downstream, so that presently there was a deep arc of swimming caribou reaching from bank to bank. Tufts of hair floated past us. You could smell the animals, a good familiar ammoniac smell like a horse corral on a rainy day.

Cap eased the *Delta* into an eddy, putting her so close in against the bank that brush overhung the bow, and held her there with power while we waited for the tremendous herd to cross. "There they go, Redhead," he said with almost a note of awe in his voice. "Alaska's wild cattle. Her antlered host. The far travelers—heading for the Endicotts, the Bering and the Arctic shore. Think of the people waiting for them in all the lone, lost places. And think what would happen if the herd didn't arrive. There'd be famine. No meat in the caches. No skins for clothing and sleeping bags. No sinew for sewing. I tell you, Redhead, the caribou are the territory's most valuable single asset."

We had twenty-two passengers aboard, and they had crowded at the rail to watch the herd. Suddenly a rifle began blasting. I couldn't see who was shooting, but I saw a little caribou cow roll over, her back apparently broken, and come floating down toward us. She was still alive, arching her neck desperately to keep her nose above water. I could see her eyes roll as strength failed her. Her head went under. She raised it once more, coughing, knowing that this was death. Then she gave up and drowned. The rifle blasted again, and a fine bull lunged straight up out of the water, to fall backward across another bull. Their antlers locked, and both came spinning down the current. Cap said to the mate, "Take the wheel, mister."

We elbowed through the knot of passengers, and saw who the rifleman was—Short-Card Montague. The gambler was laughing as he shoved a fresh clip of shells into a pretty little 6.5 Mannlicher. A dead caribou bull dragging a live one to its doom seemed to be his idea of high comedy. Cap moved up beside him. With deceptive calm, looking more than ever like a benign Santa Claus, he said, "Now, that's a handsome firearm. Mind if I look at it?" Montague handed it over, still laughing. After pretending to examine the weapon, Cap dropped it over the side. Montague stared, eyes widening. Then he struck quick as a cat, both hands. I guess the tinhorn really was dangerous.

But he fanned the air. And Cap belted him bowlegged. I never did find out where Cap had learned to slug, but it must have been in a rough school. His rock-hard fists slammed the gambler against the rail left to the face, right to the heart—caught him again on the bounce, and sent him sprawling to the deck. Groggy, blood streaming from is nose, Montague sat up. He shook his head to clear it. Then his right hand flashed under his coat and came out with a short pearl-handled gun. Cap was ready for that. He kicked the gun out of the gambler's hand, picked it up, swiped the luckless tinhorn across the face with it, and tossed it overboard after the rifle.

You could see that Montague wanted to continue fighting. It was in his eyes. But he was a gambler, and the percentage was too rough. So he assumed an aggrieved attitude. "What's this all for?" he muttered.

Cap told him. "It's for the ghosts of 10,000 caribou slaughtered by bums like you—and for the good people who could have used those caribou." He headed back to the wheelhouse, giving the other passengers his most cherubic smile.

Then there was Bunny (I will call her), who played a part in one of the most awful experiences of my life.

She came up the plank at Iditarod, where we had unloaded cargo for the trading post and the Otter Creek mines. She was carrying a suitcase, and was slim, blonde and beautiful in a tailored powder-blue outfit. She walked like a dancer. Even carrying a suitcase she seemed to be moving to music. I would have avoided her. I had been under the boiler all morning calking a leaking seam, and was covered with bilge muck, soot, and rust stains. I had tried to wipe the muck off my face with a piece of waste but had only rubbed it in. I looked like an end man in a minstrel show. The last type I wanted to meet was a honey blonde with a Pavlova walk. But before I could escape, she pinned me down with a smile.

Her voice was low and it had temple bells in it.

She said, "I am a seamstress but I can cook. I want to work my passage to Nenana or Fairbanks."

"We've got a cook," I said.

"Forgive me, but I think you haven't. He's going to quit today to work at one of the mines. I overheard him promise the foreman he would."

She moved closer, and she smelled good. I don't know what it was, but it smelled expensive, and it actually made me dizzy. I realized all at once that it had been two long months since I had seen a pair of sheer-silk stockings. My judgment went to pieces in a flash. "All right," I said, trying to sound like a rough steamboat operator. "Stow your gear somewhere. If the cook quits, you've got a job."

The cook did quit, and Bunny took over the galley.

But that evening something bad happened. We had aboard a prohibition agent, a pot-gutted, fish-eyed character whose hair was artificially waved and who used cologne. He had been snooping around the lower river posts trying to catch somebody with a moonshine still. His name was Horace. When we were several hours out of Iditarod, running by searchlight and what was left of the midnight sun, Horace buttonholed me on the main deck. He wore a smile like a wave on a swill barrel.

"I just got a look at your new cook," he said. "Did you know she's been working as a—uh—sporting girl at Otter Creek and Iditarod?"

So she lied to you, son. But take it easy. She couldn't very well have told the truth. Anyway, you hired the gal. So stand up for her. And cut this smirking oaf to size.

As stuffily as possible, I said, "the lady's background is her own affair. She was hired as steward and cook. That makes her a ship's officer. I hope everybody treats her as such. . . . And they damned well better."

That made Horace sore. He departed in a flouncing nancy-prancy gait, and of course spread the word all over the boat. The result was that I soon began catching surreptitious grins from the passengers, who seemed to get a huge kick out of the mistake I had made. Cap was superbly innocent. He just didn't know a thing about it. He did find occasion to mention, though, that dinner had been excellent. I went for a walk around the deck. Paprika Carlson, our burly, towheaded Iditarod-Innoko pilot, was dropping us down fast. The exhausts were snorting sharp and clear, and the paddles were bucketing as if they enjoyed it. As I rounded the stern I saw Bunny coming toward me. I halted, but she went past without speaking. By the reflected glow of the running lamps I saw that she was crying.

A few days later I met my private Gethsemane. It was something I had subconsciously known would happen somewhere, some day. I think I had been dreading it since the time I visited Blind Nick in his gloomy cabin in Rabbit Slough—the time he let me see pictures in the sweet-smelling smoke.

We were on the Yukon, and Cap had tied up at a tiny settlement to take on cordwood for fuel. It was a dreary, weather-beaten, poverty-stricken place, and a lowering sky and a hard rain-laden wind didn't improve its appearance. There were a couple of sagging cabins. A gaunt salmon-drying shed with smoke rising from the eaves. A fish wheel creaking in the current. Three or four little birch-bark canoes pulled out on the bank. The usual gang of lean Malamute dogs yammering at the boat. We had moored under a cutbank on which cordwood had been stacked for sale. The deckhands rigged a tin-lined chute from the top of the bank to the fireroom door, and began heaving the seasoned, pitchy lengths of wood into it.

Cap came up to me and said, "The cook wants you to see if you can buy a fresh salmon or two. . . . I dunno why she didn't ask you herself."

I knew why. I said, "Tell her I'll run her errand." Paprika came with me. If I had known what was going to happen, I wouldn't have gone into the settlement for all the gold along the Yukon.

We crossed a belt of timber and slid down a grassy slope. In the smoky gloom of the open-sided salmon drying shed a woman stood at a plank table splitting salmon. Her back was to us. She wore a shapeless dress of faded checked gingham, a man's old felt hat, and beat-up Holy Cross moccasins. Her black hair was in two braids, tied at the ends with red yarn. Beyond her, in a papoose board hung from one of the shed's uprights, was a sleeping child. We stood a moment watching the woman work. She was good. She was an artist. In fact, I had seen few men, and only one other woman, who could use a knife as well. The other woman was—.

A chill jittered through me and my heart felt as if a hand had closed over it. Now I knew the set of those shoulders. I remembered too well the way those glossy braids swung when she moved. I started to back out of the shed. I wanted to get away from there unseen. But Paprika was already speaking.

"Hiyah, sis," he said. "You got a couple salmon we could buy?"

The woman turned—it was Oolinka. But not the neat, trim lynx-kitten of Cloud Creek and the bear trails. The once clean planes of her face were blurred. Her eyes were dull. She had an angry bruise on one cheekbone. There were finger marks on her throat. The front of her dress had been torn to the waist and fastened together with pins. She flashed me one wide-eyed look of recognition, and as plainly as if she had spoken it said, "Loose no more demons upon me." Then she turned her back to us and resumed splitting salmon. I got out of there. Paprika started to argue about the salmon but gave up and followed.

"What happened? You look as if you'd seen a ghost."

"Maybe I did. How long has she been here?"

"Oolinka? About six months. She's old Thirty-Forty Jackson's woman. He bought her somewhere over in the McClaren country. She was some kind of an Injun slave, and a chief's wife got mad at her and auctioned her off. Thirty-forty claims she cost him ten ounces of dust. . . ."

I was sick when I went to my cabin.

I knew that Bunny was there. For an age, whenever I battled up through the feverish darkness, she was there—holding me while she gave me something out of a spoon, washing me, replacing the covers I threw off. Four days later I came out of it. We were tied up at Ruby. Cap was standing over me.

"Where's Bunny?"

"Well-l, she left us. Most faithful nurse I ever saw. But when we knew you were going to pull through, she quit and went ashore to wait for another boat. She left a message. She said please don't hold it too much against her, and that she'd see you again some day."

Then there was Whisky Bill, a sourdough who unwittingly saved the *Delta* one freezing night on the Tanana.

We had come up from the lower Yukon, making for Fairbanks with passengers and a cargo of fancy-pack canned salmon. It was the last run of the season. Shelf ice was forming, and the Tanana was so low that in places you could almost have waded it. When we reached Nenana, Cap was worried. "This is going to be nip and tuck," he said. "Doggone river could freeze tonight. If it does, we'll lose a steamboat."

So I went below. the fireman pointed to the cordwood stacked against the bulkheads, and shrugged. "Green wood. No heat in it."

The passengers got the idea fast. It was a long weary walk to Fairbanks. Cap put the *Delta* in to a bank, and twenty-odd of us went ashore with lanterns, saws and axes.

"There it is, boys," he said. "There's wood that'll make steam, by the yumped-up yimminy."

He was pointing to a brand-new cabin made of peeled and seasoned spruce logs. The cabin was unfurnished and had never been occupied. The floor was still littered with chips and sawdust. We eyed it covetously. I said, "Yeah, but we can't steal a man's cabin." The Swede said, "Aw, we'll find out who owns it and pay him. Come on, men, pull her down." They pulled it down. Within three quarters of an hour every log was stacked in the fireroom.

We arrived at Fairbanks in the morning.

The payoff came a month later. I was looking for an electrician to do some work on a generator, and had been told I'd find him in a bootleg joint down toward the Pioneer Hotel. He was there. While we were discussing the job, Whisky Bill came in.

"Gentlemen," he said, "I have just had an awful experience. Either I have gone nuts, or the whole country has. Maybe both. You all know I'm a woodsman. A damned good one, too. Or anyway I thought I was. Last summer I went downriver and built me a cabin. Figured to trap there this winter. But when I went back last week, I couldn't find the doggone cabin. It's gone. Or else I forgot where it was. But how in blazes could a woodsman misplace his cabin?" Whisky Bill gulped another double shot. "And that ain't all. This morning a big Swede I never saw before stopped me on the street, handed me $500, and went on without any explanation at all!"

Adventure Is My Business

PART 11

Blind Nick warned the Redhead of two things—the potent medicine of Te-kun-day and the golden wolf. But even the Redhead, who knew Blind Nick's power, did not realize this was to be the strangest adventure of his whole career.

Somewhere on the near edge of the bitter, starfretted night the king wolf howled. He had a strange, eerie voice. Once having heard it, you would recognize it anywhere. He had been caught in a snare belonging to old Lobo Smith, the master wolf trapper, and in escaping the wire had injured his throat. Now when he howled, his voice broke in the upper register, ending in a sort of harsh strangled yodel.

Tex sat up in his fawnskin sleeping bag and stared out across the frozen river. "That's yer friend," he growled. "Spooky-soundin' cuss, ain't he?"

I've got to try to pelt him this winter," I said. "I promised Blind Nick."

"Maybe some day ya'll learn not to make silly promises," Tex said and lay back down, pulling the fawnskin over his head.

I had abandoned steamboating—selling my interest in the boats and equipment to Cap—and had returned to trap and hunt with Tex. After seeing Oolinka at the poverty-ridden fish camp, and seeing what life had done to her, the Yukon had lost its magic. I didn't care if I never saw the river again. Cap didn't try to talk me out of leaving. I guess he had pulled up some stakes himself in his time, and had felt heartsick over the lousy things fate does to people. . . . He borrowed some money from Gordon Bettles and The Oregon Mare, paid me off, shook hands, and said to come on back and join him any time I got tired of murdering poor defenseless wild animals for a living.

At Matanuska a chain of events began which I will never fully understand. Maybe I don't want to understand them.

Snow was blowing through the streets when the train pulled in. I got off and headed across the platform, feeling in my parka pockets for my baggage checks. As I entered the big double doorway of the baggage room, someone standing in the shadows touched my arm. It was Blind Nick, the prophet. He stood leaning on a painted staff, tall, gaunt and erect, a smile lighting his lean hawk face. His blank, lifeless eyes were fixed a foot above my head.

I said, "*Cheemai*—hello, Nick. Were you waiting for me?" I was kidding, because nobody, not even Tex knew I was arriving on this train. But the joke backfired.

In his thudding, chesty voice, the shaman said, "Yes. I was waiting. When you trap with Tex in the Susitna country this winter, I want you to do something for me."

I hadn't even known we were going to trap the Susitna. But I pulled myself together and said, "What could I do for a shaman?"

"You could kill a wolf for me. He is a king wolf. White trappers have called him the golden wolf. You will know him by his color and his broken voice." Blind Nick raised the painted staff as a barbaric sovereign might have raised his scepter. "Kill him for me, please. . . . And when you meet Te-kun-day on the Deshkah, buy his wolf medicine, then throw it away without using it."

I said all right, I would make a project of the golden wolf if our trails crossed, and the hell with Te-kun-day and his wolf medicine. Then I went over to the baggage counter, claimed the Winchester and my packboard, and headed up the snowy road to the cabin. The sled dogs tied in the dooryard saw me and began yowling. Then Smoky loped down off the hillside to meet me. Always polite and reserved, the little black fighting dog touched my leg with his nose, wagged his tail once in greeting, then escorted me to the cabin, trotting the regulation ten paces in advance. I knocked on the door, and Tex said come in. He was sitting at the oilcloth-covered table, clad only in red underwear, with a huge bowl of mulligan stew before him. Like most sourdoughs and all Indians, he hated hellos and good-byes. His swamp-green eyes gave me one critical look, then he waved toward the mulligan pot on the cast-iron stove.

"Shed yer pack an' help yerself."

"Same stew you had when I was here a year ago?"

"Sure. Hit ain't quite ripe yet, but hit's improvin'."

Toward evening the big mountain man said, "Ya better put on a clean shirt an' shave—if ya growed anything to shave up there on the Yukon—on account o' somebody wants to see ya over at the Widder Jones."

So I put on a gaudy Hudson Bay shirt colored like a rainbow with a cramp, and went through the practically unnecessary motions of shaving. Then we mushed out across the wind-scoured cottonwood flat to the Widder's farmstead. Tex hadn't said who wanted to see me. Across the big, warm, spice-smelling kitchen, seated demurely in one of the Widder's heavy birch chairs, was Susan, the auburn-headed spitfire schoolmarm. She wore beaded Tena moccasins, a plaid skirt, and a green sweater that fit her like a marten pelt fits a stretcher board. The Widder picked me up with one arm, and gave me a rib-cracking thump on the back. Then she backed away, shaking her head sadly.

"You must have grown up," she said. "You smell like shaving cream. Thank God you didn't use any of Tex's bay rum."

As soon as I could, I maneuvered to a chair beside Susan. I hadn't seen her since the snowy night under Lookout Bluff when she was lost, and I found her huddled by a fire, with Popcorn behind her with a broken leg. I could still feel the gallant appaloosa's silken temple under my hand when I laid the muzzle of the Winchester against it, and hear the crash of the shot. Susan was watching me with an odd look in her gentian eyes—a shadow of pain, and of anticipation, I thought. "Have you forgiven me—because of Popcorn?" she asked.

I said I had. I said there were a lot of worse ways a horse could die. He could grow old and be sold for dog food. He could get rolled in a river and drown. He could get stuck in a bog and be eaten alive by mosquitoes. Popcorn had been doing his best to the last, I said, and he had been among friends when the .30-06 slug sent him to horse heaven. The Widder and Tex were at the other end of the room, pointedly not listening. I knew something was coming, but I couldn't figure what.

Susan said, "I have a present for you. It's all I can do in repayment. I hope you like it. I think you'll receive more affection from it than you've ever had."

That one stopped me. I didn't say anything. I just sat there.

The Widder served coffee and cake, and we played the phonograph, and I danced a couple of times with both women, and I could see that Tex was laughing at me, and I was beginning to get sore at him for it. After a while Susan put on a jacket and went outside. When she returned, she had a dog with her. At least it looked like a dog. It was different from any creature I had ever seen. Take a long-legged cub bear and a sheep and put them together, and it would give you a rough idea. It was woolly from nose to rump. Its feet were shaggy as a lynx's. If it had eyes, you couldn't see them. It weighed about sixty pounds, and judging from its movements, it was a pup. Maybe a year old. Also—the animal was purple.

I said, "For gosh sake, what is it?"

Susan said, "Look on his collar."

There was a brass plate. Engraved on it was: "My name is Woolly. I am a Briard, and I come as a present to the Redhead. I was born in France, where a cathedral was erected to my ancestors for bravery. Keep me with you and I will love you and guard you while I live."

What could I say at the moment except thanks? Anyway, that was how Woolly came to live among us. He was a strange dog and a good dog. And within a few weeks he was to figure in a weird adventure.

In our snow camp beside the frozen Susitna the fire had died to a handful of red birch coals. The trees were popping like pistol shots, and the river ice was hooting and grumbling. Woolly, the purple Briard pup, was under the flap of my sleeping bag, crowding against me, and whimpering in his sleep. I petted his shaggy head, and he woke up and swiped my hand with his tongue. During the two weeks we had been on the trail, a curious thing had happened. Smoky, the canine berserker that all dogs feared, had adopted the pup. It was almost ridiculous, the way the old dog watched over him. They played in the snow, and Smoky let the still awkward Briard roll him over and chew his ears. You could see that the hard-boiled Malamute sled dogs were astonished by the spectacle. All eight of them couldn't have put Smoky off his feet.

But the pup did it, growling ferociously, and Smoky liked it. I think now that he may have been teaching Woolly the deadly tricks of combat that had made him famous. Maybe also, through some unexplained animal sense, he had a presentiment of the frightful thing that was soon to take place.

I was dropping off to sleep when the king wolf howled again, this time behind us on the spruce-timbered river flat. Then in reply came the full chorus of a large pack. As it climbed to top volume, echoing through the somber spruces, it seemed to make the ground shake. I had heard wolf song many times, but it still sent a shiver through me and made my neck hair lift. I sat up, my hand on the cold breech of the Winchester. It sounded as if there were at least thirty wolves out there, and they weren't the scrubby wolves of the southeastern rain forests. These were the Susitna wolves—*Canis lupus pambasileus*—largest of their race. I had pelted old dog wolves on this river that weighed upward of 170 pounds.

"Gawdamighty, what a place to try to sleep in," Tex grumbled. Then he said in a different tone, "Uh-oh, hear that? They're gonna make a kill."

In a moment I heard it—racing hoofs smashing through the wind-crust. The pack had located a moose yard and stampeded the herd. The wolf song had changed now. It had become a high-pitched hysterical yapping—the hot blood-cry of a pack streaking in to a certain kill. In the still, crystalline night, sound carried so easily that we heard the moose go down. There was a frantic thrashing of hoofs, a deep agonized groan, then a gurgling cough as blood from the torn jugular filled the dying animal's throat. After that there were sounds of feeding—snarls, the crunching of bones.

I said, "Let's go over there and—"

"Take hit easy," Tex said. "Go on back to sleep. In the mornin' I'll show ya somethin'."

He wasn't fooling. We got up when there was light enough to shoot, left the dogs in camp. We pushed our way through a fringe of brittle, frozen willows, and there it was—a bloody, trampled, urine-stained, hair-littered space the size of a city lot. All that was left of the moose were his vertebrae, skull, hoofs and a scattering of leg-bone splinters. Judging from the skull and hoofs, the animal had been a bull in his prime, that had only recently shed his antlers. At this time of year he probably would have weighed a thousand pounds. And since the maximum capacity of a wolf's stomach is around twenty pounds of meat, there must have been at least fifty wolves in the pack. That is not a record by any means. A mail carrier once sighted a gang of 300 wolves on the ice of Minchumina Lake, over on the north slope of the Alaska Range. But still, fifty wolves hunting together under a king wolf is an almighty lot of wolves.

Tex was looking very pleased with himself. He motioned to me for absolute caution, and checked the sights and chamber load of the Sauer. Then he made a circle of the blood-stained opening, catfooting over the wind-crust on his long Susitna webs. Presently he found what he was looking for, the trail of the departed pack, a confusion of paw prints on the quarter-inch of powder snow topping the crust, heading toward a stand of javelin spruces on the riverbank. He reached out a big mittened hand, drew me closer, and whispered in my ear.

"They're on a meat drunk. So stupid ya could kill 'em with a club. All we gotta do is git in the middle of 'em."

Whatever a meat drunk was, I had never heard of it.

We had the wind and the ice was making a lot of noise, so it wasn't a tough stalk. We eased into the timber, walking abreast, a slow step at a time. Then I saw a wolf curled up against a windfall, a huge black brute, tail over his paws and nose like a sleeping malamute. Just beyond him was a second wolf, a gray one, smaller. He saw us and stood up clumsily, slant green eyes staring vaguely. His stomach bulged. As I raised the Winchester, he whirled, staggering, then stopped to vomit. I shot him through the shoulders. At the same instant the Sauer blasted, and the black wolf died in his sleep, his brains sprayed over the snow. Shadowy forms were moving all about us now. I hurried ahead, passing up two easy shots. I had covered maybe fifty yards when I saw him—the golden king wolf. He was red, almost sorrel, and he was the biggest wolf I'd ever seen. I'd have bet his pelt would measure ten feet. But I couldn't get a clear shot at him.

He floundered toward the river, breaking through the crust, always keeping windfalls or snow-weighted brush between him and me. I was too eager. I stepped over a fallen spruce, my eyes on the wolf—and a snow-concealed limb stub hooked the toe filling of my right web. I went down hard and the muzzle of the Winchester rammed into the snow. A couple of minutes were wasted while I cleared the barrel. The golden wolf reached the ice. There was a narrow channel between the bank and a cottonwood island, and in the center of it was a streak of black overflow water with frost fog rising from it. Desperate, the king wolf waded the overflow. When I reached the rim of the bank he was just disappearing into the cottonwoods.

I went back to Tex, cussing myself. The mountain man had killed two more wolves, and was leaning against a spruce putting an edge on his skinning knife. "Ain't no use follerin' the rest of 'em now," he said. "They've puked their guts empty an' they'll prob'ly run fifty miles afore they settle down. Whatcha do, git yer legs braided cheechako style an' fall down?"

Two days later we arrived at the mouth of the Deshkah. On the top of the high south bank was a tumble-down settlement occupied by a fading clan of the Susitna-Tena. A cluster of crudely built cabins, a few sod-roofed underground barabaras, some drunkenly leaning caches. Several ragged long-haired Indians were fishing through the ice for ling cod, squatting in the lee of piled-up snow blocks, jigging their lines at the end of short sticks. As we turned the dogs in from the ice of the main river, one of the fishermen came to meet us. He had the lean frame of a snowshoe Indian and the face of a wild man. His eyes had the Mongolian slant, his nose was high-bridged and pointed, and his chin and flat cheeks were covered with a wispy beard. The striking thing about him, though, was a blaze of snow-white hair across the top of his head.

"My name Te-kun-day," he said, his eyes shyly sizing up our outfit. "Chief here, me. Shaman too. You got tobacco? I like trade wolf medicine. Good wolf medicine."

Blind Nick had said to buy the guy's medicine. So I said, "Sure. Give him some tobacco, Tex."

When the dicker was completed, we went on up the Susitna. The medicine consisted of a small moosehide bag tied with babiche. As soon as we were out of sight of the village and the fishermen I opened the bag. In it were two dried ptarmigan feet, a ball of owl dung, a dozen or so of the strangely shaped bones to be found in a whitefish's head, and a black pebble that looked like flint. I dropped the junk back into the bag and threw the bag as far as I could off the trail.

"What's Blind Nick got against Te-kun-day?" I asked Tex.

"Aw, hit's a medicine man feud. Te-kun-day is jest a ambitious faker tryin' to muscle in on Nick. He don't amount to nothin'. Damn if I know why Nick don't fergit about him."

That could have been the worst piece of judgment Tex was ever guilty of.

Our headquarters cabin for the Susitna was on an island of spruce at the head of a long lake three miles west of the river, near where Hornet Creek enters the lake. It was a good comfortable cabin of heavy logs, with two store-bought windows, a stove with an oven, and a door you could pass through without bending double. By contrast with some of the makeshift huts we had operated from, this cabin had all the comforts of home. We killed a fat moose, strung a brush ptarmigan trap across a narrow arm of the lake, and got busy boiling our traps and breaking snowshoe trails.

In a week we were all set, and it looked as if we'd have a good season. There was a lot of marten sign on the ridges, and fox and lynx were prowling the willow bottoms for snowshoe rabbits and ptarmigan.

"This is the life," Tex said with satisfaction one evening. We were lying on the big wild-hay-mattressed bunk, reading, a moose-tallow *biche* burning on a shelf between us. Smoky and Woolly were playing on the cabin floor, and as usual Smoky was down and the purple Briard pup was mauling him unmercifully. "Hit's the peacefullest life in the doggone world—"

Only it didn't last long.

Came a night of wind and stars, with a huge full moon floating above the ridges. We had skinned our day's catch and put the pelts on the stretcher board. Tex was washing a shirt. I was weaving new babiche foot-filling into my webs. The Briard pup, that had been asleep behind the stove, got up, yawned, shook himself, and scratched on the door. I let him out. Some ten minutes later Smoky went over to the door, walking stiff-legged. He cocked his head, listening, then suddenly snarled and clawed the door planks with both front paws. His back hair was rucked up and his eyes were wild. I snatched up the Winchester and opened the door to find out what was going on. Smoky went past me like a black streak, making for the lake. Tex, barefoot and in his underwear, whirled on me.

"Fer gawd's sake, Redhead, get out there—quick."

I stepped into the hitching of Tex's webs and ran through the timber to the edge of the lake. I wish I could forget what I saw. One hundred yards down the lake, in against the shore, was a tangle of drift logs. Smoky was standing there, a lone black shape in the frosty, spectral moonlight—and racing toward him over the ice was the wolf pack. I cut down on the leader, recognizing his great size. I had him fair in the sights despite the tricky moonlight—and the Winchester missed fire. Before I could jack another shell into the chamber, the pack flowed over Smoky, a ton or so of wolf fury. It was over in ten seconds. I fired into the edge of the pack, heard a wolf squall. Fired again, and saw the golden wolf break out of the tangle and race for timber. I rolled him over with the next shot but he regained his feet and vanished into the shadows of the spruces. The other wolves headed across the lake, preferring to take their chances on the ice, where they had footing. I emptied the magazine at them but didn't score.

Tex passed me, wallowing through the snow since he had no webs. When he reached the ice he sprinted to the log jam. I followed and we stood there looking at what was left of Smoky, the wonderful, terrible, gentle little fighting dog. He was torn apart, strewn over the snow. Tex picked up the tail and wiped the blood off on his underwear sleeve—the most pathetic gesture, I think, I have ever seen. I was trying to think of something to say, when a muffled snarl came from under the log jam. Then there was a scrambling sound, and Woolly emerged. I think I know what happened. I think the pup chased a rabbit under the jam, and the wolves, making a sweep across the lake, saw him and closed in. And Smoky, inside the cabin, heard the wolves, and went to his protégé's rescue.

Popcorn's death brought us Woolly, and Smoky died to save him. Thus life on the frontier, and adventure.

I went back to the cabin and finished repairing my webs. Then I made up a light stampede pack. Fawnskin sleeping bag, some raisins, ten pounds of meat and five pounds of tallow, an ax, two extra pairs of socks, a box of ammunition.

Tex said, "Where in hell d'ya think yer goin'?"

"I'm going to take his trail. I hit him. Now I'm going to follow him as long as I can find his trail. Take care of my dog."

"Maybe ya got a chance if ya can keep him off'n the ice. Yer younger'n I am. But listen, if ya catch up with the devil, do me a favor—gut-shoot him, will ya? So's hit'll take him a while to die."

A day and a half later, as purple dusk was pouring across the wide valley, I sighted the wolf. This was on the barrens west of the Deshkah. There was ten feet of snow here and he was making hard going of it. For the first four or five hours he had bled, but that had long stopped. He was lunging into the drifts, and twice I saw him fall. He knew I was on his trail. He kept looking back. I knew he was trying to reach the ice of the Deshkah, so I used all the strength I had.

I came down off a high bench, and when I reached the bottom the wolf was about 500 yards distant. I put the sights on him and pulled. . . . He died with his lips curled in a snarl, gut-shot. And as I stood looking at him, weaving on my webs, I saw a white blaze across his forehead, such a mark as might have been made by a bullet scar.

When we returned to Matanuska in the spring, I went down to Blind Nick's cabin on Rabbit Slough.

I said, "I have a present for you," and handed him the king wolf's pelt. Blind Nick held it across his knees.

"I bought some wolf medicine from Te-kun-day," I said, "and threw it away. We did all right without it."

"He won't sell any more wolf medicine," Blind Nick said. "He's dead. He went hunting one day—and didn't come back."

Adventure Is My Business

PART 12

The Redhead had come to the Lost People, looking for furs to buy. Instead, he found a great Arctic tragedy—a village slowly starving and that only he could hope to save from sure death.

Brant racked the single-engine, open-cockpit plane over on its left wing and hammered on the fuselage with a gloved hand to attract my attention. "Something down there," he shouted above the howling of the slip stream and the roar of the engine. "Is that it?"

The guy had quick eyes. We were cruising the shore of a frozen brush-rimmed lake, deep in the Arctic, and I had told him what to look for and he had seen it first. A tracery of sled trails converged on a flat above the head of the lake. Where the trails met, there was a cluster of low mounds like outsize beaver houses. Near the mounds were many small dark spots, and they were moving. They were chained sled dogs. And the mounds were the roofs of the underground dwellings—*innies*—of a village of Nunamuits, the Lost People, or Inland Innuits. I signaled Brant to go down and circle the place. He nodded and pushed the stick forward.

For two hours, since leaving Bettles Village on the Koyukuk, we had been searching for this place. It was the first time an airplane had been here. There were other planes in the territory, but if the pilots had ventured into the icy, storm-beaten Endicotts, they hadn't found this village. The flight north had been fantastically wonderful. The earth below was in shadow, deep luminous blue, but the horizon was aglow with the light of the hidden sun. And the arctic mirage was working its strange magic. The ragged

Endicott peaks alternately dropped from sight below the rim of the world and boomed up in unbelievable shapes. They were gigantic mushrooms, purple and two-dimensional. They were huge ships without sails, adrift in golden light, cut off completely from the planet. They were a cosmic bridge, their tops joining perfectly, climbing to infinity. And far behind us to the southward, sheering above turquoise emptiness, the massive bulk of McKinley shone pure saffron like a pilot's guide beacon home.

We roared full-throttle over the village and I got a good look at it. When Brant glanced back questioningly, I motioned for him to land. He kited back downwind over the lake, turned, and dropped her in prettily, the skis touching lightly as blown cottonwood bloom. We taxied to the shore beneath the village and sat there watching and waiting, half frozen despite our flying suits and parkas. Men were coming down the bank toward us now. Most of them had rifles but some carried spears. They were short, squat, fur-clad people, almost pygmy size. They halted in a group on the ice 100 yards distant, and stood motionless as statues, staring at us. Brant rolled his eyes heavenward and cut the switch.

"I hope the hell they're friendly," he said in the sudden quiet. "That's probably what they're hoping about us."

I had come down to Anchorage in late February to sell my furs. I pocketed my winter's earnings and headed down the street looking for a barbershop. My hair hadn't been cut since September and it hung to my shoulders. I had to wear it tied back from my forehead with a moosehide band, Indian fashion, and was self-conscious about it. People on the street stared at me, and the girl clerks in the shops did a double-take as I passed, and laughed. Also I was painfully aware of my snowshoe gait. I had been on webs five or six hours a day all winter, and it would take anyhow a week to learn to walk in the short nervous steps of these city folk with their low shoes and rubber heels. I imagined I was as awkward as a bull moose on a suspension bridge.

I found a barbershop and there was an empty chair, so I went in and sat down. The barber, a bald skinny character I had seen around Matanuska once or twice, looked at me and shook his head in fake dismay. "My gawd, you're as shaggy as Tex Cobb," he said. You don't expect to get all that mowed off for just the price of one haircut, do you?"

"Next time I'll give you a break," I promised him. "I'll make a contract job of it and advertise for bids."

In the chair next to me was a slight blond man with a towel over his face. He wore choke-bore whipcord pants, Strathcona boots and a factory-made buckskin shirt. The pants were oil-spattered and he smelled of gasoline. He lifted a corner of the towel and regarded me with an inquiring wood-smoke-blue eye. The scrutiny lasted until his barber impatiently replaced the towel.

"I'll bet," the man said, "that I know who you are. You're the Redhead, Tex Cobb's partner. And for a while you were Cap Northway's partner."

I said it was a fact, I couldn't deny it, and he said his name was Brant, and forgive him for not getting up and shaking hands. "My wife told me about you," he said. "She used to know you. I've been hoping you'd come to town."

"Why?"

He let me have it with a rush, no preliminaries.

"Look. I'm a pilot and I've got an airplane, but it isn't paid for. I'm broke. Spent all my money flying gasoline up the Koyukuk to Bettles and caching it there. Intended to buy furs this spring on the Arctic slope. I was dumb. I thought it was a cinch way to make a stake. But now I'm out of dough, the company threatens to take the plane back, and hell, I don't know anything about buying furs anyway." He paused for breath. "Why don't you go into the deal with me? You put up the money to buy the furs, take it back off the top when we sell, and we'll split the rest."

That was a honey. I had never ridden in an airplane. I had never ever seen one. But still . . . it sounded exciting. It would be something to write about, if I ever learned to write. Also it would be a heck of a welcome change from snowshoeing and mushing Malamutes.

"Come over to the hotel after a while," I said.

I was in my room reading a book of Chekhov's short stories when there was a knock on the door. It was Brant. I had been wondering what he looked like without lather or a towel on his face. He looked all right. A small bony face, weather-burned to the texture of saddle leather. Direct eyes with a wind squint at the corners. A fighter's cheekbones. Maybe twenty-five. There was a woman behind him in the corridor. He stepped back and took her arm.

"My wife," he said. "I guess you two have met."

You could have floored me with a ptarmigan feather. It was Bunny. Canary-blonde Bunny, beautiful Bunny, who had cooked for Cap and me aboard the *Delta*, who had lied to me about her profession, and who had nursed me through flu and pneumonia and then disappeared, leaving a message asking me to forgive her and saying she'd see me again some day. I mumbled something, I don't know what, and they came in. We sat there a while talking about airplanes and fur buying, and speculating as to whether aviation would ever become important in Alaska. Then the bellboy came up and said there was a phone call downstairs for Brant. When the pilot had gone, Bunny came across the room to me in that well-remembered dancer's walk, as if she was moving to music that only she could hear.

"Help him, Redhead," she said. "He's in trouble. I love the guy, and I haven't lied to him. Help him, and I'll do anything for you."

"All right, I owe you something—my life, I guess. I'll help him."

With the Arctic wind clawing at us, Brant and I climbed out of the cockpits and, while the twenty or thirty skin-clad Innuits watched impassively, cut holes in the ice and tied the plane down. Then we headed up toward the group. As we approached them, their manner abruptly changed.

Laughing and shouting, they came to meet us. In the lead was a stooped, wrinkled patriarch with a great scar down one side of his face.

"We are glad you came to visit us," he said in English. "We were afraid because we had never before seen anybody fly." He nodded toward the plane, smiling. "We didn't know whether or not it was alive. Now we see it is something you made. The white men are very smart."

"Some of them are," I said.

We went up the bank to the village, passed a couple of hundred yowling sled dogs, and came to the central cluster of *innies*. Children peered at us from behind the mounded roofs, and women's faces showed in the low entrances. The scar-faced patriarch touched my arm, and said, "You can stay in my home if you wish, and your friend in the home of my cousin Ahpigaluk." He pointed to a grinning square-faced man with a butcher-knife haircut who wore a carved bone plug in the lobe of his left ear. I said, "Happy lodgings, Brant. See you later." The pilot looked worried. He didn't like the idea of being separated. But he departed with cousin Ahpigaluk.

Inside the tunnel-like entrance to his *innie*, the patriarch took off his caribou parka, beat the frost out of it with a stick, and hung it on a peg. So I did likewise. Only I had underwear and flying suit under my parka, whereas my host had nothing under his. The one room of the *innie* was about twenty feet across, circular, with a domed, timbered roof. There were two bunks, or sleeping ledges, covered with wild hay and caribou skins. The only light came from a smoke hole in the center of the roof and from a tiny fire of willow brush burning on a circle of blackened stones.

Sitting beside the fire were two women, both naked to the waist. One was ribby and dried up, very old, obviously the patriarch's wife. The other was a girl, nineteen for a guess. She was a gold-bronze Venus in miniature, a toy woman, with glossy jet hair and liquid almond-shaped eyes showing just a hint of the Asiatic slant. She was watching me, not shyly and out of the corner of her eyes as most Tena girls would have, but with frank interest, no pretense at all.

The old man said, "My name is Ikpikpuk. I am named for the river. This is my wife, and this is my daughter. Her Innuit name would be hard for you to say, but it means Cloud Woman. She learned to speak English at Pilgrim Springs mission. Are you hungry?"

I said yes, I was hungry.

The girl hung an iron kettle over the coals, went outside and returned presently with a small frozen whitefish. In the kettle were two pieces of meat, each about the size of my fist. After a while she took the meat out of the kettle with a knife, placed it on a wooden platter with the whitefish, and handed the platter to me. The meat was tough and stringy, practically jerky. You could tell it had hung in the cache a long time. I ate it, then ate the whitefish. Few of the old-timers I knew would eat raw frozen fish, but once you become accustomed to it, it is good. It tastes to me like coconut. I became aware that while I was eating, my host and the two women had not spoken, and that they had kept their eyes averted.

Suddenly a ghastly thought struck me.

This is a hunger village, bucko. That stringy meat. That lone little whitefish. Just as sure as hell you've eaten the last food this family had. That's why they couldn't watch you.

"Have you had good hunting?" I asked.

The patriarch, siting cross-legged with his back against one of the sleeping ledges, looked at the floor, examined his hands, then said, "We can't find the caribou. They should have come here a moon ago from the northwest, but they didn't. My son went to search for them fifteen days ago. He didn't return."

"Your dogs?"

"We have tried to save them for the hunting if the caribou came. But. . . ." He shrugged.

This was the great tragedy of the North—failure of the caribou migration. When the herds are present, there is a time of plenty. When they aren't there is famine and death—no meat in the caches, no food for the dogs, no skins and sinew for clothing. In this village the dogs were doomed. The weaker ones would be killed to feed the other dogs and the people. Eventually, if the caribou didn't appear, all the dogs would be killed. And that would be the end of the village, for without dogs an Innuit is helpless.

I said, "I think tomorrow we will find the caribou."

I went outside and hollered for Brant. I didn't know which *innie* he was in. But presently he came out of one of the tunnel entrances, pulling on his parka. I said, "Brace yourself. You'll have to go back to Bettles for a load of gas. We're going to look for the caribou herds tomorrow."

Brant studied me a moment, rebellion in his woodsmoke eyes. Then he spread his hands in resignation. "Well, I guess the engine's still warm. I'll take off now and come back in the morning. And to think I had a good job as a soda jerk, and quit it to learn to fly."

It was night. Outside in the bitter blue half-light that passes for darkness in the Arctic, the starving dogs were howling their interminable wrongs. Only a handful of willow coals remained on the cooking hearth. Ikpikpuk and his wife went to bed, pulling off their pants and mukluks and covering themselves with a caribou robe. I had brought in my sleeping bag. Cloud Woman unrolled it and spread it on the other ledge. I slid into it and undressed, and pretended to go to sleep at once. Let's face it, I was worried. Arctic mushers had told me some gaudy stories about the customs of primitive Innuits.

Well, there were only two sleeping ledges. I was at the back side of this one, crowded against the wall. Minutes passed. Then Cloud Woman lay down beside me. She sighed, and snuggled into the soft-tanned skins like a sleepy kitten. We hadn't exchanged a word since my arrival. But I knew she was going to speak now.

So I tried a snore, a fine resonant one. It didn't get me anything.

"Do you have a woman?" she said. Her voice was low and warm, with a lot of timbre in it, like a deep note on a cello.

I said no, and Cloud Woman said why? I said, various reasons.

"It must be nice to have red hair," she said.

"It can get you into trouble. . . . Go to sleep." Then I had a brilliant idea, a truly sterling thought. "I've got to dream about where to find the caribou tomorrow."

That made sense to her, even though she had attended a mission school. "Oh, I understand. . . . I hope it is a fine dream."

I could have commented on that, but didn't. I went to sleep with the forlorn wails of the hungry dogs in my ears.

Brant came in at what would be called dawn in any other latitude. Here it was just a wash of gold on the southern horizon. We unloaded the tins of gas, filled the tanks, and took off immediately. We flew northwest along the stark, barren north slope of the range. It was a land almost empty of life. We saw a red fox. We saw five wolves. We saw a wolverine. That was all for a hundred miles. So we edged in closer to the mountains and turned east. Half-an-hour later we sighted a long narrow lake. On the lake was a network of trails. We went down for a look. They were caribou trails, fresh, headed east—the trampled highway of a vast herd.

We barreled along another ten minutes. Then I sighted the herd up ahead. Brant saw it at the same instant, and looked back at me, grinning, and shook hands with himself. It was a herd to tell your grandchildren about. Everywhere you looked now there were caribou, thousands of dun-colored spots in the shimmering azure light. The animals were on the march, heading toward the deep gap of Anakhuvuk Pass, which would bring them within easy striking distance of the village hunters.

When we landed, everyone came out on the ice to meet us, men, women and children. Cloud Woman ran ahead of the others. She was wearing a sik-sik-puk parka with ermine, white wolf and polar bear trimming that would have sold for plenty in a New York fashion shop. She ran as if she weighed nothing, as if the wind was blowing her. I was tying down a wing. She reached out and touched my shoulder.

"Did you have a caribou dream last night?"

"Yes." Who would say no?

"Was it a true dream?"

"Yes."

She bowed her head. When she straightened she was biting her lip and her eyes were wet. She turned and said something in Innuit. There was a dead silence. Everyone stood motionless. Then a hundred or more voice shouted, "*Hai-eee—tuktu.* The caribou. . . ."

That night the people ate the last of their food, and there was a dance on the hard-packed snow of the village. It was a barbaric spectacle, something straight out of the Stone Age. Fires of willow brush blazing. Three old men beating hypnotic rhythms on caribou-stomach hoop drums. The fur-clad dancers posturing and stamping, cracking their voices in the cry of the wild goose. Each dancer carrying a pair of ceremonial gloves in his left hand, for a reason, according to Cloud Woman, that nobody remembered.

But later, in Ikpikpuk's *innie*, there was a curious atmosphere of gloom. The patriarch and his wife sat huddled in a corner, not speaking. Cloud Woman was somber and preoccupied.

I said, "Is there trouble?"

Ikpikpuk said simply, "My son is dead. And I am too old to hunt."

So he had trouble, all right. It was sort of like having to starve to death in a restaurant. I spread my sleeping bag and got into it. When I undressed and laid my clothes on the foot of the ledge, Cloud Woman took the Hudson Bay moccasins and went over the seams carefully for rips. She was sitting on the floor with her back against the ledge, her head almost against mine. The firelight on her upper body would have fascinated a da Vinci, a Phidias.

I said, "I will hunt for you."

Cloud Woman turned her head and looked up at me, and I never want anybody to look at me that way again. It isn't good to have a human soul offered to you in one glance, not if you're a foot-loose woodsman with ideas as to what you want to do with your life. Ikpikpuk said, "I will go feed my dogs so they will be strong tomorrow." That meant the weakest dog would die to feed the others.

Cloud Woman put my moccasins back on the ledge and stood up, facing me. "I will make the hunt with you," she said.

In the morning I had trouble with Brant. I was helping Cloud Woman harness Ikpikpuk's dogs, when the pilot came up to me and said, "This was supposed to be a fur-buying expedition, not a hunting trip. And these people haven't got any fur. They haven't got anything. They're a poverty-stricken outfit, but good. So I'm going to buzz out of here. Get your gear together, partner."

I was tempted to let him go. But then I remembered the promise I had made Bunny. I remembered the four days on the *Delta* when I was sick and how, each time I fought up through the feverish, choking blackness, she was there, doing something for me. So I knew I had to get rough with this cheechako sky hawk who hadn't been in the North long enough to recognize opportunity when he had it in his hands.

"I'm going on the caribou hunt," I told him, "and you're going to stay here until I get back. I'll tell you why. There's an old man in the village with a rifle. You start that plane engine to take off, and he'll put a bullet through it. Don't think he won't."

Brant was still glaring at me when Cloud Woman banged her whip over the heads of Ikpikpuk's dogs.

We met the vanguard of the caribou only thirty miles from the village. It was an absurdly simple hunt. The Innuits closed in on three sides and took stations on high ground. Cloud Woman and I left our dogs on the side of a blackspined ridge which the wind had blown partly clean of snow, anchoring the sled with a three-pronged steel grappling hook. We climbed to the crest and saw the point of the herd less than 600 yards distant. There was a snow mirage, so that the animals seemed to be swimming toward us in pure blue light. The fog of their breathing hung above them in a cottony drift. We lay down on a frozen drift and I handed Cloud Woman a box of shells. She knew her business. She arranged five shells on the palm of her gloved hand and held her hand at my right elbow. We waited. Then a gunshot sounded somewhere ahead on the flank of the herd.

I shot the Winchester hot. In the next few minutes I dropped fifteen caribou. That was enough to keep Ikpikpuk and his dogs and family the rest of the winter and into the summer. Cloud Woman helped me gut them. Guns were crackling all about us—more guns, I thought, than I had seen hunters in the village. I mentioned this to Cloud Woman.

"There are three other villages of our people," she said. "We sent word to them. They will come to our village tomorrow for a feast."

Brant was still glowering when Cloud Woman and I returned. He glowered all through the twenty-four hours of feasting and dancing, hardly speaking to me. But when the celebration was over and the hunters of the four villages were ready to begin freighting their meat home, something happened that changed his attitude. Cloud Woman and I were sitting on the side of an *innie* roof watching some children trying to repeat one of the dances they had seen their elders perform, when Ikpikpuk came over to us.

"If you would like to buy furs," he said, "the people have some ready."

I said I would like to buy some furs. Then Ikpikpuk and the headmen of the three other villages brought out such a store of pelts as few buyers have ever seen at one time. Bales of furs. White and red fox, lynx, marten, wolverine, beaver from the lower rivers, ermine. Lustrous, shining furs. They spilled them on our caribou skins for me to examine, and I bought until I was out of money. Normally these people traded at the coast, Cloud Woman said, but they hadn't made the trip for two years.

Brant said, "Good gosh, if we only had some more dough." But he was so happy he couldn't stop smiling.

Cloud Woman said in a low voice, "The furs would be waiting if you come back for them."

"I'll come back," I said.

I thought of a lot else that I wanted to say—but I didn't say it.

She was still standing there, watching me, when I walked over to where Brant was waiting.

"For a while there, I figured we weren't going to get furs. Any furs," he said. "The way things were going. You know what I mean?"

"Yeah—I know what you mean," I said. "Well now you've learned something."

Well, I thought, you kept your promise to Bunny. She said her boy was in trouble and you helped him out. Just plain luck, that's all.

We got into the plane. I looked back. Cloud Woman was still there, watching me.

Adventure Is My Business

PART 13

Finding himself lost in Alaska was a tough break for the Redhead but it wasn't the worst —it was the bear who stole his food!

When Brant and I returned from our second flight to the Arctic village of the Lost Innuits for furs, Buck was in town. The eager little Southerner had come north to make a brown bear hunt with Caribou Jack. They had chartered a gas boat—the *Agta*—and hired a skipper, an ox-shouldered, ambling, heavy-footed Russian-Aleut breed named Simeon. Then at the last moment Caribou Jack had an attack of appendicitis. Buck and I went to the hospital to visit him. He was fit to be tied, sore as a bear with a faceful of porcupine quills.

"This butcher shop is the damnedest place I was ever in," he beefed. "A cheechako nurse comes in here ever' five minutes or so, an' sticks a thermometer in my mouth, or gives me a bath, or rubs my back with alcohol, or takes my pulse, or some other fool thing. An' they don't feed ya nothin'. My gawd, I tell ya I'm starvin'. If they hadn't swiped my clothes an' hid 'em, I'd light outa here so fast ya couldn't see me fer dust."

Buck said, "Well, take it easy. The Redhead and I'll go find a brown bear. When we come back, you'll be good as new. Then we'll pick out a nice blank spot on the map, and see what's there."

"I'll be underground before then," the sourdough growled. "Starved plumb to death. By gosh, I hope you heartless fellers get hungry yourselves some time."

We did. Within the next few days. Plenty hungry.

It was a wild and dirty night on Big River. A cold rain. No stars. Ghostly ravelings of mist blowing through the black bankside spruces. With Woolly, the purple Briard, between us, Buck and I were bedded down under a tarpaulin on the cabin roof of the gas boat. We had spent the best part of a week upriver looking for a trophy bear, but hadn't found one. So now we were heading back down to Cook Inlet. Simeon had insisted on making the run at night. Don't ask me why. It could be that Simeon was not very bright.

Buck said worriedly, "The guy's got her wide open. If we hit anything, the old orange crate'll dissolve in a shower of splinters."

"He won't hit anything," I said. "He wants to get home to his wife and kids. He's a jealous husband and is afraid his wife might say hello to one of the neighbors."

Was I an optimist.

Some twenty minutes later, as I was getting nicely to sleep, Simeon made an error in navigation. He cut a bend too sharp, and grazed the point of a submerged sand bar. The *Agta* had a V bottom. So when she hit, she whipped over at least thirty degrees. Buck, Woolly and I didn't have a chance. We shot off the cabin roof, over the rail, and into three feet of water that was practically liquid ice. The *Agta* righted herself and kept on going. I grabbed Woolly, got my feet, and helped Buck up. While we fought clear of our sleeping bags, I hollered louder, I'll bet, than I ever had before. But Simeon had the engine racket in his ears, and was probably worrying about his neighbors. Anyway he didn't stop. The stern light disappeared around the next bend.

"I don't believe it," I said. "I'll wake up in a minute and find out it's just a bad dream."

The situation had the raw material for a nightmare, all right. There we were, hip-deep in the icy water of a wilderness stream. No outfit. Not even a rifle. Rain beating down and a hard wind battering at us. The nearest town forty miles distant—on the other side of Cook Inlet. I didn't even know whether we could get ashore. If there was a channel between us and the bank, we were licked. I let my soaked sleeping bag float down with the current. No use hanging onto it. Even in a warm cabin it wouldn't dry in less than a week.

"Well, anyway, we got our shoes on," Buck said. "Reckon we can get ashore? This cold water comes about six inches too high for comfort."

We were lucky. We got ashore without any trouble. I tossed Woolly up the bank, and blundered around in the windy gloom until I found a spruce windfall. There were some pitchy limbs, and I had my belt knife and matchsafe. In a few minutes we had a good fire burning. We stood over the blaze, clothes steaming, and considered our predicament. I thought Simeon would miss us in a short while, and come back upstream. But Buck said no, he wouldn't. He said Simeon wouldn't miss us until morning, when he'd be well out on the Inlet. Then he wouldn't know where he'd lost us, so he'd return to Anchorage and report that we'd gone overboard in the Inlet and drowned.

Morning came in bleak, gray and rainswept. No *Agta*. We had got a little sleep, but I was feeling stiff and rocky. Buck groaned when he moved, and his face was pinched and blue under a stubble of beard. I knew where there was a cabin forty miles down the coast. It belonged to Beluga Jack, a sourdough who was currently serving time for making moonshine. It was almost certain there would be grub in it, and maybe a rifle. Also maybe there'd be a dory at the place. If there was a dory, we could step a sail in it and light out for Kenai or Point Harriet. So we headed for the coast and Beluga Jack's cabin. There was still spring snow under the timber, wet sloppy stuff, several feet of it in spots. I broke trail, with Buck plodding grimly behind.

"What would Tex Cobb do in a case like this?" he asked.

"He'd do what we're doing. Only he'd cuss more. He'd scorch Simeon's ears off at fifty miles."

"I gotta take some lessons from him," Buck said.

Woolly was plowing ahead through a rain-rotted drift. Suddenly he halted, growling. I eased forward. There in the snow was a brown bear's trail, deep wallowed, so fresh that pieces of snow were still crumbling into it. I looked around for a couple of trees we could climb. Without the Winchester, I had never felt so helpless. We stood motionless for a while, listening. Brown bears out in the snow are touchy animals. Their feet are tender from hibernation, their stomachs probably aren't working right yet, and there isn't any green vegetation to provide their needful spring physic and tonic. So I didn't want any part of this one. His trail led to the left. I angled off to the right. But we had covered only 100 yards or so when I heard a crunching sound. Woolly was bristling, walking stiff-legged. The crunching came from a brush-screened opening close ahead. I side-stepped, trying to see into the space.

Buck whispered, "There he is—and I wish he wasn't."

He was a giant, a mahogany-colored brute with black legs and a yellow forehead. And he was lying across the carcass of a moose. There was no blood on the snow, so presumably it was a winter-killed moose. He was biting into the side of the carcass, feeding. So powerful were his neck and shoulders that when he took a mouthful of flesh and tore it loose, the whole carcass moved. The crunching I heard was his teeth shearing through the heavy ribs.

We backtracked, stepping softly. But the bear heard us. He stood up over the carcass and roared. In the North there is no more blood-chilling sound. The vibrations are so terrific that, at close range, you can feel as well as hear them. Buck fled, and Woolly and I fled right behind him.

Out of breath, we leaned against a tree, panting. Buck said solemnly, "I hate that bear. Even more than Simeon, I think."

"Me, too."

Around noon next day we reached the shore of the Inlet. Huge blocks of ice were piled along the high-tide mark, but the tide was out now and there was good walking on the exposed sand. We found a dead goose, and I examined it carefully, but it was too high. I mean, it was really rotten. It was so rotten that Woolly wanted to roll on it. An hour later, though, on a rocky point, we found a colony of green and blue baby crabs, an inch or so across. I collected a hatful of them. Behind the point was a cove in which drift from all the North Pacific had collected. There were great cedar logs from southeastern Alaska, surf-beaten planks, part of a ship's life preserver, lengths of bamboo, a couple of Japanese glass net floats. I hunted around until I found a dented and rusted five-gallon can. Then we built a fire and boiled the crabs.

There wasn't much meat, but the soup was good. I could have drunk five times my share. In fact, I think it was the best soup I ever tasted.

We slogged along the beach the rest of the day. Woolly chased a rabbit but didn't catch it. I found some fiddlehead ferns that were pushing up through the leaf mold on the south slope of a point, and we ate them raw. Tex and I had often eaten fiddleheads for greens in the spring, and had learned to like them. But they made Buck sick. He lost them and his crab lunch as well. He was becoming rubber-kneed, and that worried me. If he played out, I'd have to go on to Beluga Jack's cabin alone. And if there was no grub there, I probably wouldn't have strength enough to come back to him.

The sun slid down to the white, jagged crests of the Aleutian Range. I was looking for a place to camp, when we arrived at the bank of a sizable creek. The tide was full now, and hair seals were bobbing in the rollers off the stream's mouth, ten or fifteen of them, their heads gleaming like polished metal in the slant yellow light. Suddenly I realized that they were fishing. A run of fish was entering the stream, and the seals were feeding on them. It was too early for salmon, so the fish had to be hooligan (eulachon), a species of oversize candlefish which the Indians often dried and burned in winter for illumination. And I remembered how Tex and I had once killed some seals for dog food in a creek like this when the hooligan were running. A number of seals had followed the fish some distance upstream when the tide was full. When the tide ebbed we had stationed ourselves on a skinny riffle and clubbed the animals as they struggled down past us.

I said to Buck, "Cut yourself a club. We're going to dine on seal liver and roast flipper tonight."

"I will certainly cut a club," Buck said.

We located a riffle and sat beside it under a dripping spruce. The sun went down, the tide turned, the moon came up. The sky had cleared and it was cold. But, although we were both shivering in our wet clothes, I didn't dare build a fire. If any seals had gone upstream and they scented wood smoke, they'd ghost back down immediately underwater and we'd never get a chance at them. The water dropped until the riffle was only ankle-deep. Leaving Woolly on the bank, we waded cautiously into the stream, not speaking, making no splashes. The moonlight was almost as bright as daylight. Somewhere above us, beyond the next grassy high-banked bend, I heard a seal snort. Buck planted his feet on the algae-slippery rocks and raised his club. It was a two-handed length of alder sapling with which he could have stunned a bull. I saw the seal come around the bend, head shining in the moonlight. He was close in against the bank, gliding along effortlessly.

Then there was movement in the grass above him. A great dark shape rose into view—a brown bear—and launched itself like a projectile out over the bank. The seal let out one terrified blat, a high-pitched "*Maw-w-w!*" Then the bear had him between his jaws and was wading ashore. The great animal leaped up the bank, agile as a cat, and disappeared into the moon-silvered saw grass. The whole thing happened as fast as that. Buck said,

"Well, I'll be eternally good gosh darned." Of course our project was finished.

"You know, I dislike that bear even more than the other one. Even more, by gosh, than Simeon."

"We'll come back someday and pelt him."

"If it takes all my life, and all the money I can raise and borrow."

Next morning we had some luck. We found two dead hooligan on the beach. They were pretty smelly, but not too far gone. So we hastily built a fire and cooked them. They were wonderful. We ate everything—heads, fins, livers, hearts and eggs. We even chewed the bones and swallowed them. Then, a mile or so farther on, I saw a clam spurt. This was razor clam country, and the razor clam is a tricky character, so we tiptoed back and sharpened two sticks to serve as shovels. Then we stalked the spot where the clam had spurted. The jet of water came up again, and I dashed in, drove my stick into the mud, and pried. Luck was with me. I got him. He was a fine, fat, beautiful clam, six inches long. We removed him from his thin, brittle shell, cut him in half, and ate him raw. Then we looked around for others. But apparently he was the only clam on this beach. If he had any neighbors, they were too smart to spurt.

I said, "After all that grub, it ought to be a breeze to make it to Beluga Jack's cabin."

"Yeah," Buck said without assurance. "But I've been thinking about that goose. We should have brought it along. Maybe it wouldn't seem too doggone rotten to us now."

The sun was going down in a bank of incandescent cloud, and Buck was staggering, when we came to the slough on which Beluga Jack's cabin was located. The place was concealed, and I had trouble finding it. We scouted the near bank of the slough without seeing an ax mark or a foot of trail. Then we crossed over, wading to our armpits, and scouted the other bank. Woolly found the cabin. He left us, and began barking furiously in the dusky timber to our right. We went over to him. The cabin squatted beside a cache in a tiny clearing. On the porch roof was a big yellow porcupine, and Woolly was trying to tear the porch down.

"That's the most beautiful sight I ever saw," Buck said.

"The cabin?" "No. The porcupine," he said, picking up a long pole from the woodpile. "And if a bear tries to take him away from us, I'll fight the cuss with my bare hands."

The cabin was large and well equipped. Beluga Jack had been a prosperous moonshiner and beaver trapper, and he enjoyed comfort. The cast-iron stove would have pleased a chef. There were eider-down quilts on the two bunks. The cooking gear was heavy aluminum, and the dishes were chinaware, the first I had ever seen in a backwoods cabin. There was plenty of grub, stowed in large tin containers so the mice and squirrels couldn't get at it. I built a fire, browned the best cuts of the porcupine, and placed the meat in a Dutch oven with a can of tomatoes and one of peas. Then I made biscuits and stirred up some gravy in the frying pan.

"I have found a rifle," Buck announced. "It is some rifle. D'ya reckon I could kill a bear with it?"

The rifle was a .45-90, an ancient piece, octagon barreled, without a speck of bluing left on it. But the bore was clear and the action worked.

"Maybe—if you had some shells," I said.

"I've found some shells too. Ten of 'em. Made about the time the Klondike was struck, I should judge."

The shells were dark with age, and you could see they had been handloaded. Only heaven knew what kind of powder was in them, or how much. "You could go outside, shut the door behind you, and try one," I said. "If you don't come back, I'll eat this porky mulligan myself."

"We woodsmen," Buck said with dignity, "don't waste our ammunition on target practice."

We ate, and dried our clothes, and that night there was rain on the roof and a wind crying under the eaves, and it was swell. In the morning, before Buck awakened, I climbed into the cache and found a shovel and a hooligan net. I set the net across the slough, and went out onto the strip of beach the tide had exposed. There were plenty of clams here—one of the reasons, I suppose, that Beluga Jack had chosen the spot to locate in. I dug a bucketful. Then I headed up the slough throwing rocks into the water. The surface swirled. The net floats bobbed. I waited a few minutes, and pulled the net in. I had fifteen hooligan, averaging ten inches long.

Back at the cabin, I made coffee and biscuits, fried some of the clams, and baked a half-dozen hooligan in their own fat. Buck woke up, swung his legs over the bunk, and yawned luxuriously.

"I just had a silly dream," he said. "Dreamt we got lost overboard in a river, and didn't have anything to eat but two sick fish, some baby crabs and a rotten goose."

"How'd you make out?"

"Well, at the end of it I was chasing Simeon over a mountain with a dull ax."

We stayed at the cabin all day, resting up. Buck took the .45-90 apart and cleaned it. I read some yellowed magazines in which the women in the illustrations wore bustles and buttoned shoes and had pompadour hairdos. The next day we went bear hunting. There was brown bear sign on the beach here, and along the slough, but Buck said he wanted to return to the seal stream. He had, he said, important unfinished business there. So we made up a couple of packs and headed back up the beach. We arrived late, and set up a siwash camp under a giant spruce, near a spring 100 yards or so in from the beach. I had brought along enough hooligan netting to make a dip net, and also a small shovel of the type the sourdoughs call "clam gun." So next morning we got busy filling our larder. Later, when the tide was nearing its ebb, we went up the creek to the riffle.

Armed with clubs, we took up our stations as before. And also as before, we presently heard a seal blow somewhere upstream. Then another. In a moment, here they came. They were in the deep water of a pool, but they had covered only a few yards when they hit the head of the riffle. Their backs were out of water, and they were twisting and turning to avoid the rocks. Buck raised his club, and said, "This time we're really going to have seal liver and roast flipper for supper." The seal that came down my side of the stream was a little gray cow. She halted ten feet distant, raised herself on her front flippers, and looked at me with the kind of liquid dark eyes that a chorus girl would like to possess. So I made a wild swing at her, deliberately missing her by a foot. She went past with a flirt of her back end that slung a bucketful of water in my face.

Buck wasn't doing so well.

The seal on his side of the creek was a huge bull weighing maybe 200 pounds. I don't think I ever saw a larger bull, or an ornerier one. When he saw Buck in his path, he reared up, snarled, and showed his teeth. It was a fine set of dentition. I'll swear his canine teeth were two inches long, and sharp as needles. Buck, with a do-or-die look in his face, stepped in and swung his club. I guess I'd neglected to tell him that to kill a seal you've got to hit it on the head. You can't even slow one down hitting it anywhere else. There's too much blubber under the thick skin. Anyway, Buck hit this one across the rump. It sounded just like hitting a sack of potatoes with the flat of a canoe blade. The bull flashed past him, and as he did so snaked his head up and tore one of Buck's pants legs off from the knee down.

"Well, I probably wouldn't have liked seal liver anyhow," Buck said. "And roast flipper sounds like a mighty primitive dish."

We hunted up the creek all day but didn't sight a bear. Next morning, though, we got a break. When I went out to the beach for an armload of driftwood fuel, the tide was full out, at least a half-mile of tidal mud exposed. And at the edge of the water, nosing along in the mud, were three brown bears. They were having a time. They waded into the water, rolling and splashing. They wrestled in the mud. They chased one another. As nearly as I could figure, the trio consisted of a big male and two smaller sows. I know that doesn't sound reasonable for a spring group, but still, the two smaller bears were too large to be yearlings. Anyway, there they were, and one was a trophy bear.

The trophy bear pigeon-toed across the final step of sand, rolling his mud-plastered shoulders arrogantly. Buck was kneeling, the .45-90 cocked and ready. When the bear was maybe 100 feet distant he reached the first spears of grass. Buck was very literal. He waited until then before he pulled. The ancient rifle went off with an ear-shattering crash. There was a lance of flame, a cloud of white smoke, a hoarse bawl from the bear. I side-stepped to see around the drift of smoke. The bear was down, kicking. The other two were fleeing into the timber.

We were still camped on the seal stream, drying the bear pelt in a frame because we had no salt. It was midafternoon and we were taking a nap. Suddenly Woolly began barking on the beach. At the same instant I heard an airplane's engine. It was coming in low and fast, and was so close I knew it would pass us before I could reach the beach and make a signal. I tried, though. I pulled my pacs on and sprinted out through the brush, tripped over the trailing pac strings and fell sprawling. By the time I had picked myself up, the plane had passed overhead. Cussing myself, I went on to the beach. Buck had joined me now. The plane was a mile south, skimming the beach. Presently a wonderful thing happened. It turned in a shallow bank and came back. It was a single-engine twin-cockpit job. The pilot side-slipped in. The wheels touched, and she rolled to stop fifty feet from us.

Brant was the pilot. He waved at us from the front cockpit. "Saw that purple, mop-headed dog," he said, "so I figured you were around here somewhere."

He said Simeon had reported us lost overboard and drowned, but that his wife Bunny and the old-timers didn't believe it. Tex, he said, was coming down the Inlet in the *Agta*, skippering it himself, and Caribou Jack. Starvation Smith and Lobo Smith were aboard. He'd fly out at once, he said, and give them a compass course to our camp.

"Bunny said she'd divorce me if I didn't find you," he said. "So I've been trying hard. . . . You want to send a message back to her?" I said, "Tell her I love her and will thank her when I get back."

"Me, too," Buck said. "And tell her we'll bring Woolly along. Everybody ought to see at least one purple dog."

Adventure Is My Business

PART 14

The Redhead stirred up trouble
when he took on a kid who wanted to kill a grizzly—
and a bird who talked out of turn.

It was August, and I was at the headwaters of Bird Creek, camped in a beat-up cabin, doing assessment work on one of Tex's mining claims. Bird Creek is a lonesome place. It is walled by giant peaks that boom straight up from the valley floor. Over the tops of the peaks sprawl glittering tentacles of the enormous Chugach glacier system. Even in summer the sun rises late above the eerily broken crests, and sets early. The only sounds you commonly hear are the moaning of wind in the dwarf cottonwoods, and the sullen roar of the battering, milk-white creek.

I had been here alone forty-five days. The work was dreary and uneventful. Stripping moss and earth from the vein to expose it. Drilling holes with a single-jack outfit. Planting dynamite shots. Shoveling away the debris after the shots. Cooking and sawing wood and washing my clothes. Most young people in the present year of our Lord will fail to understand the true meaning of loneliness in a place like Bird Creek. No radio, no television, no newspaper, no mail delivery. Just yourself and the big peaks and the mournful music of wind and water, and the wilderness closing in on you day after day, reaching for you.

I'd probably have gone a little bush-happy if two friends hadn't joined me. One was Squeaky, a striped, bright-eyed little parka squirrel. The other was Pete, the screwball magpie. Squeaky arrived by choice and took up residence under the cabin floor, because he realized I was a soft touch for raisins and pieces of bannock. But poor Pete was literally blasted into my company, short a good part of his feathers. I had put five heavy shots in the face of the short prospect tunnel, touched off the fuses, and ran for cover. While I was standing behind a tree fifty yards distant, I saw the magpie alight at the mouth of the tunnel. All magpies are born thieves, and I suppose Pete thought I had something edible in the tunnel that he might make off with.

He found out. I hollered at him, but he only flirted his long tail and stepped a couple of feet into the tunnel. Then the sixty-percent dynamite began blasting. Pete might just as well have been standing in the mouth of a cannon. The first explosion blew him straight out into the air. He landed in a spruce top a good forty feet distant, and tumbled to the ground. When rocks had ceased whistling past me, I went over to him. He was alive. He didn't have any right to be, but he was. I brushed him off, straightened his feathers, and put him in the pocket of my packboard. That night I took him home.

I had always heard that magpies could be taught to talk, and in the next three weeks I discovered it was true. In fact, Pete didn't have to be taught. He learned by himself. When he had recovered from the blast, he became such a terrific thief that I had to keep an eye on him whenever he was in the cabin. He'd pick up anything he could carry—a spoon, a cartridge, a buckskin needle—and fly away with it. So when I saw him cocking his eye at something, I'd say, "Look out, mister. I'm watching you."

So one day I had some shiny ore samples on the table. Pete flew in the door, alighted on the table, and began sidling toward the samples. I raised my hand as if to slap him, and he squared away at me like a fighting cock, and said, "Look out, mister. I'm watching you."

It was a very cute trick, and it got cuter.

In early September old Frank Lee rode up the creek leading an extra mount. I've got to take time here to tell you about Frank. He was one of the great bronc-stompers of the old West. He had ridden Midnight, Five Minutes to Midnight, Rabbit, Steamboat, Jumper—all the good ones of his time. He stood six feet and was wide as a door, with gun-blue eyes, heavy hands with cracked nails, a broad strong face, and thick lips in which a brown-paper cigarette was permanently plastered. He could neither read nor write, but he could make money, and he could get more work out of a horse than any man I ever knew. He could take the laziest, most gold-bricking, tourist-ruined horse in a string and make him walk six miles an hour flat-footed without using spurs or a quirt.

Frank once told me a wonderfully comical story about himself. He had just sold a string of horses, and had got on a train at Fargo, North Dakota, heading for Idaho. This was in the early days, I don't know what year. Anyway, he rattled his spurs back to the dining car. The only available table was occupied by two schoolteachers who were eating a frugal breakfast of toast, coffee, and orange juice. Frank sat down opposite them, and a waiter brought him the menu. Since this was a deluxe train, the menu was a lengthy one. Frank looked at it helplessly. He couldn't read a line of it, and wasn't even sure he had it right side up. Until today his eating had been done at cow-camp chuck wagons and in frontier short-order joints. But he was hungry and he aimed to buy himself a good meal. So, when the waiter returned for his order, Frank said with attempted nonchalance, "Just bring me some of all of it, please."

One of the schoolteachers had a mouthful of coffee, and she was so startled she sprayed coffee all over the table and Frank as well. Horribly embarrassed, Frank gazed around the car. At the farther end, on a highboy, was a large silver bowl of fruit. With some wild notion of salvaging his dignity, Frank pointed to the fruit with one hand while he mopped coffee off his face with the other, and said to the waiter, "Bring me that, too, will you?"

"Well, there was a feller sitting across the aisle," Frank told me. "He was husky, with glasses and a mustache, and a lot of white teeth. He'd been reading a newspaper. But he put the paper down and laughed until he had to wipe his eyes. Then he called the waiter back, and said, "Bring the cowboy a bottle of champagne, too. I think he could use it."

"You know who that feller was?" Frank asked me. "He was Teddy Roosevelt. No wonder he made a good president, huh?"

Today, when Frank rode up Bird Creek looking for me, I was at the prospect, single-jacking another round of holes. So he hobbled the two horses, shoved them out on a pea vine flat, and made himself at home in the cabin. When I returned toward evening, the old-timer was sitting on the bunk wearing a baffled expression. Even after we had talked for half-an-hour or so, he still seemed preoccupied and puzzled. Finally I asked him if anything had gone wrong.

"Well, I dunno," he said. "I sorta hate to tell you about this, but here's what happened. It's the truth, so help me gawd. I come in here a coupla hours ago, and sat down at the table to eat a sandwich. But I had just unwrapped the sandwich when a parka squirrel jumped up on the table, squeaked at me, and grabbed half the sandwich and ran behind the stove with it. I picked up a chunk of wood to throw at the cuss, but just then a fat magpie flew in the door, and said. 'Look out, mister. I'm watching you.' Anyway, somebody said it, and there wasn't nobody else around!"

I explained about Pete and Squeaky.

Frank said relievedly, "Well all right. I thought maybe I was going balmy." He rolled another brown-paper cigarette. "I got a job for you. And I don't think you're gonna like it."

He told me what the job was, and it was a little special, all right. A Midwestern grain broker named Ed Webley had come north with his fourteen-year-old son Johnny for a big-game hunt. Frank agreed to outfit them, supply horses, and hire a guide for young Johnny. He was going to guide Webley senior himself. Then, at Frank's headquarters ranch at Eklutna, Ed galloped his horse into a weed-hidden abandoned well and sprained his knee. But he wanted son Johnny to go ahead and make a hunt. For white sheep, bear, and maybe goats and moose.

"Why don't you guide him yourself?"

"Well-l-l, I ain't as young as I used to be," Frank said, looking uncomfortable. "And this Johnny, he—uh—he's kinda hard to handle. Skinny kid with red hair and freckles. Has the damnedest habit of getting into trouble. He was racing with Ed when the old man's horse fell into the well. . . . Well, shucks, I dunno anything about kids. I thought maybe you would. . . ."

It sounded interesting. Anything would have. I was absolutely tired and sick of pounding a drill on the head with a single jack. I was weary of being alone. I was fed up with Bird Creek. So I said, "All right, you just hired a guide. Fifteen dollars a day and expenses. Thirty days' work guaranteed. And if the Biological Survey says the kid's too young to hunt without papa, you fix it up."

"It's already fixed," Frank said. "I got him a special license."

When we got off the mixed train at Eklutna and rode in past the Indian village and through the stand of huge cottonwoods to the ranch, somebody was in the corral trying to rope a horse.

Frank took one look and his face twisted as if he'd bitten into a lemon. He said, "That's him." The boy wore black angora stovepipe chaps, boots with California heels and a playing-card trim, straight-shank spurs with sunflower rowels and jingle-bobs, a red squaw-catcher shirt, and a Stetson with the crown punched in Texas fashion. He had a hard-twist rope and was swinging a loop wide enough to snare a mastodon. The one horse in the corral was a glossy black gelding that was obviously pretty tired of the whole thing. Sweating, rolling his eyes, he was racing around the corral, crowding the fence, dropping his head each time he saw the loop coming.

"Didja ever see anything like it?" Frank moaned. "That horse'll be rope-shy the rest of his doggone life."

The kid made a dozen or so more casts. Then he scored. The big loop sailed out and part of it hit the fence but the rest went over the black's head and tightened over his chest and withers. Apparently Johnny had seen some roping in the movies. Anyway, he leaned back, dug his heels into the corral dust, and snubbed the rope around his hip. But he didn't weigh quite enough. The black gelding kept right on going. Johnny skidded ten feet, the hard-twist rope burning through his bare hands. Then he went down hard on his back and was rolled over and dragged with his face in the dust. He lost the rope and sat up, spitting mud and glaring at me.

Frank and I put up our mounts. I looked over Frank's rigging. I told him I wanted gear for three pack animals. Sawbuck saddles with Humboldt pads. Double cinches. Hurry-up buckles instead of tie-latigos. Breast straps and breeching. New lash ropes and cinch ropes. Canvas panniers. An extra set of shoes and nails all the way around. Sweat pads as well as blankets. A can of wool fat and a block of graphite blacking for saddle galls if I put any on the horses, which I didn't intend to do. And a can of buhach powder and one of axle grease to use as a mosquito repellent.

"O.K. O.K.," Frank grumbled. "The stuff I haven't got, I'll get. Good goshamighty, we used to work 'em barefoot and with Injun saddles and deerhide pads. But you guys today. . . ."

We went up to the big, square, peeled-log house to meet Ed Webley. Out of the corner of my eye I saw that young Johnny had got hold of his reata again and was working along it, hand over hand, trying to reach the black's head. Frank didn't pay any attention to him. So I didn't either. Webley was a stooped, patient-looking, white-headed guy. Hobbling with a homemade diamond willow cane, he came across the living room floor to meet us. He was sizing me up but good as we shook hands.

"This is your boy's guide," Frank said, sounding like a man who had suddenly rid himself of the weight of the world. "He'll take him out, give him a hunt, and bring him back."

"Can you do that?" Webley asked me. "Johnny is—um—a rather spirited boy. A bit headstrong on occasion, too. I want him to make a hunt but I've got to be certain he'll be safe."

At this moment a high wild yell sounded at the corral. Frank jerked the door open. Johnny had got hold of the black gelding's head, led him out the corral gate, and mounted him bareback. He was now fanning the horse with his hat and raking him fore and aft with his spurs, yelling like a Tena buck at a salmon dance. I guess the black was a pretty good horse. He took it as long as he could. Then he sank his head and did an easy sunfish toward the house. Johnny was delighted at the first jump. He grabbed the black's mane, lost his balance, and clamped both arms around the horse's neck. Then the black swapped ends and Johnny soared through the air and landed on his head.

Ed Webley said, "Do you still want the job?"

We shipped to Whitney Station on the railroad, then rode up Ship Creek Canyon to where the valley fans out. There was plenty of snow on the peaks and the little side streams were freezing. I found a campsite in a clump of stunted junipers under Indian Creek Pass, and got down and began stripping off the packs. Johnny had been sulking all day. He was riding the black, whose name was Comanche, and I had warned him about using his spurs on the horse. But he had persisted. Hollywood horses never walk. They only gallop. The slow gait of our packtrain bored him, and he kept spurring ahead, whooping and hollering. When he had done this four or five times, I crowded him into a cutbank, made him dismount, and took his spurs away from him.

"When my father hears about this, you'll be in trouble," he raged. I said, "Listen, Buster. I ought to take you home now. But that would be too easy on you. I'm going to let the country take care of you—and believe me, it'll do a job."

So he was still sulking while we were making camp under Indian Creek Pass. I hobbled the horses, pushed them up onto a bunch-grass bench, coiled my ropes, stacked all the rigging and covered it with the pack mantles. I pitched the 10x12 tent and set up the

Yukon stove. I built a fire in the stove and put on a kettle of water. I cut juniper boughs, made a double mattress at the back end of the tent and unrolled our sleeping robes. I opened the pannier of trail grub. Then I went up the slope of the pass to a clump of dead junipers and selected a couple of pitchy trees for a night fire. All this time Johnny had been sitting on a rock watching me with a contemptuous expression. I wasn't doing things the way the movie heroes did them. I guess he thought I was a 14-carat phony.

I had raised the camp ax to trim the first tree before I cut it down, when I caught a glimpse of movement 200 yards around the slope. It was a bull moose. A nice one. He had been bedded down under the overhanging boughs of a flat-topped juniper, and something—maybe the rattle of the horses' hobble chains on the flat below—had alerted him. His head looked good. It would go anyway sixty-five inches and it was branchy, with good wide palms and heavy well-matched brow tines. He hadn't seen me, and I don't think he had seen the camp. He seemed to be watching the horses. I faded back down the hill, picked up the Winchester, checked Johnny's Springfield, and said, "Come on, pal. You're going to make your first kill."

The bull was angling up the hill, taking it easy. Once he stopped to fight a bush, dancing around it, raking with his antlers and striking with his forefeet. His neck was swollen with the rut, and as he moved along he uttered deep, hoarse grunts. It was an easy stalk. When we were within 150 yards, I told Johnny to take him. I told him to hold on the point of the bull's shoulder and to keep shooting as long as the animal was on his feet. The kid could shoot. He was cool as an icicle on an igloo entrance. The 220-grain softpoint hit with that solid *whoomp!* That means it's struck home where it'll do the most good. The bull halted, dropped his head, and spread his feet, weaving. Johnny slammed a new shell into the chamber, but before he could fire again the bull's knees buckled and he went down, stone dead.

We admired the head, then I got busy taking off the cape. I was tired—that's the only excuse I have for what happened. Johnny was sitting on a fallen juniper watching me work. The light was going fast and I wanted to finish and get back to camp and cook dinner. Fried liver, gravy, bannock, and a can of peaches for dessert. I could already taste the thick slabs of moose liver I was going to cook, and was figuring on boiled tongue for breakfast, when it struck me that Johnny was unusually quiet. So I looked around to see what he was doing—and he was nowhere in sight. I decided he had returned to camp, and went back to work. Suddenly, somewhere on the other side of Indian Creek Pass, a rifle blasted. In a moment of what amounted to pure clairvoyance, I knew what had happened. While I was working, the ornery redheaded brat had taken a sneak. He had crossed the pass—it was a low summit.

Only a couple of hundred feet above the spot where we had killed the bull—and had found a game animal of some sort and cut down on it. I went up the hill like a spooked mountain goat. There was snow on top and Johnny's tracks were in it, leading down the other side. In a moment I spotted him. He was moving across the slope below me, heading for a circular clump of alders, holding the Springfield ready. I scanned the alders, looking first for movement, then for color. At first there was nothing. But then I picked up an off-color spot at the center of the clump. As I stared at it, it gradually assumed form. A chill shivered up my backbone. It was a grizzly, crouched beside a lichen-shaggy boulder. I yelled at Johnny but I guess he didn't hear me. He kept right on, walking in an intent crouch like Kit Carson closing in on a band of redskins. Obviously the bear was wounded—that explained the shot. And there is one thing that the most reckless woodsmen do not do—page one in the book of things not to do—you don't follow a wounded brown bear or grizzly into a brush patch.

I tried to put the Winchester's sights on the bear. Nope, I knew I couldn't make the shot. The distance was too great and the light wasn't good enough.

So I headed down the slope, really traveling. I smashed through junipers, hurdled boulders, leaped over washes. My favorite belt knife, a handsome weapon with a carved fossil-ivory haft, given to me my Caribou Jack, bounced out of its sheath and I never saw it again. I was almost within effective rifle range when Johnny entered the alders. A cold wind was blowing off the ice fields, and after shooting the bull moose, Johnny had put on his saddle slicker to break the bone-searching chill. Now, as he moved in through the tangled, inter-fretted alders, the grizzly suddenly stood up and charged—and Johnny tried to raise his rifle. But the slicker was too tight and he couldn't bring his arms up. In the next couple of seconds I thought about a lot of things. I thought about Ed Webley. I thought about Johnny's mother.

Because of the run I had made, my heart was banging and I was panting like a steam engine. But I brought up the Winchester to do the best I could. Then Johnny's Springfield crashed. The kid had simply held it out like a spear and pulled it off. But the shot was good. The bear somersaulted, thrashed in the alders a moment, and died. I walked on down the slope, feeling anyway 100 years old. Johnny was leaning against an alder trunk. His face was so white that he seemed to have three times as many freckles as before.

I said, "Johnny, for heaven's sake. . . ." He said, "I won't do it again. Honest I won't."

So I put my arm around him. I was remembering the day on Cloud Creek when I stood against Tex with the Winchester, and I was wondering if Tex had felt about me as I felt about this redheaded kid. And I decided he probably had. And I was remembering Tanya and Smoky and Popcorn and Susan, and now it was clear to me that on a frontier the wild ones turn out to be the best ones.

I said, "Listen. Bird Creek Pass is the next one above here. We could cross it in the morning, and go down to a cabin I know about. Would you like to meet a parka squirrel named Squeaky who'll steal the grub off your plate if you don't watch him, and a magpie named Pete who can talk plainer than any parrot you ever heard?"

Johnny looked up at me and the orneriness was gone out of his face. He said, "Gee, yes!"

Adventure Is My Business

PART 15

The Redhead had faced many perils in the Far North—but none like this one. It was to keep a date with Death high on a stark peak in Alaska.

So years had passed. I was selling stories now. Not for much money—pay-on-publication stories. You got a swell thank you letter, and a request for more stories. But the check came in a year later, and usually it was for $35. I was trapping beavers and guiding big-game hunters to support myself. But on this azure and copper morning when I stepped off the mixed train at Matanuska, I wasn't thinking about beavers or sportsmen. I thought I had never felt so completely despondent. I asked the station agent if Blind Nick was in town, and he said yes, the prophet was. So I claimed my rifle at the baggage room and headed out through the cottonwoods toward Rabbit Slough. This was why I was feeling low. I had taken part in a tragedy. Let me explain.

I had been in Hollywood signing up sportsmen for Alaska hunts for old Frank Lee. When the job was done, I returned to Seattle to take the boat to Seward. I took a cab to the New Washington Hotel and went in through the lobby, and Kay English, the switchboard operator, smiled at me and then gave me a significant look which I didn't understand. I went past her and was registering in when someone touched my shoulder. A grand well-remembered voice spoke in my ear.

"Redhead. I have been trying to find you. They said you were in Hollywood but would return soon. So I have been waiting here hoping they were right."

It was Tanya, the cross-eyed Hungarian countess. I couldn't speak. I was so glad to see her that I was choked up, my voice gone. Through my mind went these scenes—the day at Kenai when I found Bishop Antonin hoeing strawberries behind the white picket fence and gave $10 to his church, and he took me into his house and introduced me to Tanya, and the fight at the dance that night when I belted a roughneck cannery hand over the head with Tex's .45, and the day at Red Butte Creek when Tanya made her Valkyrie ride down the mountainside on Popcorn to save Tex.

She said, "You're a big boy now. Could you have a drink with Tanya? It's a special occasion. We're going on a sheep hunt—my last one." I managed to say, "All right, I'll have a drink."

In her room I said, "I thought I was tied up with hunters for the rest of the year. But. . . " Something in her face had warned me. The old bright mocking light was there, only there was something else. "Why is this your last sheep hunt?"

She raised her glass and smiled at me, and then spoke one of the most terrible sentences I have ever heard.

"Because I am going to die," she said. "On the best doctors' authority. So will you please guide me?"

"I will guide you," I said. I mean, I managed to get the words out, but I guess it didn't sound like me. "Why are you going to die?" "Cancer. Incurable."

Tanya had come from Hungary to America after the crash of her family fortunes to do the only thing she knew how to do—dance and ride horses. She had married here—well. But she had too much spirit, I suppose, and so made a career of roaming the earth hunting dangerous game or combating dangerous terrain. Now she was dying. My bright, mocking, beautiful Tanya had the seeds of death in her, and she wanted one more hunt in the crazily tangled Alaska peaks for white sheep before the brutal thing killed her. I sat there with the glass in my hand and felt that old hollow singing feeling start in my chest. I will tell you what I wanted to do and I know it was silly, but I wanted to stand against that cancer with my rifle in my hand for only two seconds. I was a primitive off the fur trails and that was the only way I knew how to settle with any enemy.

Tanya read my face. "Don't feel bad about it," she said. So we camped at the mouth of a stream called Salthorse. A good campsite, one of the prettiest I have ever seen. A park. Level ground, grassy, the spired spruces far apart. No brush. The great mountains sheering straight up on both sides. The stream thundering past over the huge rocks, so that if you shut your eyes and listened you could hear what the Tenas call the voice of the rapids. The place was inaccessible to horses, so we hired eight backpackers, husky lads who could walk all day over rough country with 100 pounds on their packboards. We made Tanya a good camp. We pitched her tent beside a clear-water spring. We cut feathery spruce-bough tips and stood them on end for her mattress. We made a rack of peeled poles for her clothes. We kept a bright smokeless fire of rabbit-killed willow burning outside her tent flaps. And we tried not to be sympathetic, because Tanya was not one who needed sympathy and she would have resented it.

I spent two hours the first morning scanning the peaks for trophy rams with my glasses. Since this was a special hunt, I had brought two binoculars, an 8-power Zeiss and a 16-power Bausch and Lomb. With the 8X I spotted a white object on the top of a high whalebacked ridge. It could have been a rock, or it could have been a patch of snow. I kept watching it, and after a while it moved. It was a ram. A good one. This was the beginning of the rut—late September—and he had left the younger rams and mastheaded himself on a summit. When he got ready, he would come down and select his harem. I put the 16-power glasses on him to make a check on his head. I figured it would go 15 1/2 inches in basal circumference by maybe 43 inches around the outside of the curve. The tip of the left horn was broomed. I don't know—nobody knows certainly—why rams broom their horns. Maybe it is because they interfere with their side vision. Anyway, they rub them against rocks, and wedge them in crevices, and pry off pieces of the amber-colored tips. This one's left horn was broomed, but not badly.

Tanya was standing behind me. She said, "Is it a good ram?" I said, "It is a good ram. A trophy for a king—or a countess." "So we will make a stalk for him," she said.

Something had been worrying me, and I had hesitated to bring it up. But now I had to. "Can you climb? I mean, would your doctors approve of this? It's a tall mountain."

Tanya laughed at me. "Where would you like to die? Answer me truly." "On the side of an Alaska mountain. Climbing for a big ram." "So we will make a stalk for him," she said.

There is a trick to climbing. You must do it rhythmically. Almost like a dance. You move slowly. You keep your hands on your hips, or else keep your arms folded, so that your chest will be open to expand. A slow step at a time. Easy, easy. And you keep climbing. Maybe a rest every twenty minutes or so. But not a long rest. And you try not to work hard enough to sweat. And also you do not drink the temptingly cold water from the many snow-fed streamlets tumbling down the mountain.

This climb took two hours. During this time we had not seen the sheep. We came out on the summit and Tanya was doing all right. Her feet were steady and her breathing was good. I was carrying her rifle and mine slung over my shoulders by the sling straps. Now I checked her weapon—a .270—and handed it to her, chamber-loaded and with the micrometer sight zero for 200 yards. One hundred and thirty grain open-point bullets. The sheep should be, I figured, less than 300 yards distant, if he hadn't moved.

But I was worried about the weather. Tatters of mist were blowing across the summits, and the sky had a blank, gray overcast. There was no sun and there was that feeling and smell in the air that meant snow. Ahead of us, jutting up from the crest, was a red, broken formation of rock like a giant rooster's comb. When we came to it, I found that the talus which had crumbled from the up-jut was in slab formation and that it was the bane of sheep hunters—a type of shale that rings like phonolite when struck.

This stalk had to be a success. So I whispered, "Tanya, take off your shoes."

I don't know why, but that delighted her. She sat down and laughed silently until she cried, but took off her pacs and handed them to me. I tied the laces together and hung the pacs around my neck, along with my own. We then went up the side of the cockscomb pinnacle to its summit, walking easily, watching the tilted slabs to avoid moving them and causing them to clank. But my hunch about the weather was correct. Snow was blowing when we came out on top. Small dry flakes driving on a slow wind. The ram wasn't in sight but we found his bed—a rounded depression in an area of fine scree. A lot of dung. Some shed hair. I placed my hand in the bed and it was still warm. I could even smell the animal. He had been gone only a few minutes. Tanya looked at me and her eyes were bright and excited.

"Where did he go?" she whispered. "That's the silliest question I ever heard you ask." "I feel silly," she said. "I feel wonderful."

I put the 16-power glass on our camp in the valley. Our backpackers were good men and I knew they would be watching. And they would have seen which way the ram had moved. A curious thing was happening down there. Somebody had a white cloth—a dish towel, no doubt—tied to a long pole, and was waving it violently to the right. I handed the glass to Tanya, and said,

"Look." Suddenly she began to cry. She said, "I know. They want me to make this last kill so much. They are trying to help."

I said, "Cut it out. Nobody can shoot with her eyes full of tears." "Who's crying?" Tanya said. "Show me that ram."

I stalled a few moments by giving Tanya her pacs back and putting on my own. Then we moved to the right. On that side was a wildly eroded pitch. Points and buttresses of rock. Crooked ravines. Naked of vegetation. And the snow blowing. I heard shale clatter below us, and knelt, pulling Tanya down beside me. We waited. The wind whined among the bare rocks. The snow was hitting us in the face. I took the .270 and checked the sights again to make certain. Tanya remained motionless. Her hands were steady. Her breathing was all right. Then, with the suddenness of a magician's trick, a ram appeared before us. He came from around a boulder and stood with his feet braced, thirty feet distant, staring at us, black nostrils distended, pin ears forward, eyes wide. But he wasn't a trophy ram. His horns wouldn't have gone better than 12 by 20-inches. I put my hand on Tanya's arm, holding the .270 down. At the movement, the little ram struck the rock with a forehoof and fled over the summit. Came another ram. Then more. All went through the same routine. And all were baby rams. Not a trophy head in the lot.

I put my glass on the camp. The snow plastered the lenses and I had to clean them with a piece of tissue. I tried again through the blowing snow. This time I saw the white flag on the pole. Whoever our well-wisher was down there, he was trying hard. He was moving the pole straight up and down. So the big ram was somewhere directly beneath us. Ten feet below the crest was a ledge, a tricky ledge, about three feet wide, tilted, and slippery with snow. I eased down to it, then motioned for Tanya to follow me. We balanced ourselves there while I scanned the mountainside. Minutes passed. Then I caught a glimpse of movement 100 yards below us. It was the big ram's rump. He was standing behind a boulder, believing himself, I suppose, to be completely concealed. Now, I had seen mountain goats do that, but never a sheep. This sheep was a crafty operator or else he was not at all alarmed.

I said to Tanya, "Get ready to shoot."

She didn't reply. Then I saw that her face was so white that her lipstick was a crimson slash and her dark eyes were like jet. She was weaving on her feet. I took hold of her and brought her to her knees. But I saw I couldn't hold her. Not on this windy shelf. So I pulled her against me, found a handhold in a rock crevice, and took a leg-scissors around her body. I waited a moment, then tossed a rock down the slope. The ram reacted as I had hoped. He hadn't been behaving craftily. My guess is he had just been bored with the company of the younger rams. Anyway, he did what all sheep do when they are alarmed—he headed for the summit, for height, for the only real safety mountain sheep know. I let him come on until he was fifty feet distant.

Then I said, "Take him."

The .270 blasted. The ram never knew what hit him. He crumpled and fell, rolling and bouncing, a limp tangle of head and legs. Far below, at camp, I saw the white cloth on the pole waving in wild congratulation.

Tanya said, "Well, that's the end," and put her head on my shoulder.

So I headed out through the naked cottonwoods to Rabbit Slough and Blink Nick's cabin, and I was feeling pretty low. I went down the frost-flowered mudbank of the slough. I passed a little birch-bark canoe pulled out on the bank. I passed the cache. I passed a couple of yowling sled dogs tied before brush-roofed kennels. I hailed the cabin and then knocked on the hand-hewn plank door. Nick's deep, thudding voice said, "Come in." So I went in. The prophet was sitting before his open fire in the center of the gloomy, windowless room, an otterskin robe over his shoulders.

I said, "I just heard. She is dead." He said, "Now you will go to many far places. You will leave many beautiful things behind you. You will have many regrets. But you will do what you set out to do." I said, "Are you speaking English now?" He said, "What difference does it make? Should I say, 'Too bad she die—I bery sorry because you my friend?'" I said, "Nick, stop it. Where is Tex?" I hadn't seen Tex in two years but now I needed to see him.

Nick's lean hawk face showed a smile in the red light of the fire. He said, "This is where you started. You look up the bars of Knah-Kutnoo and you will see a gap against the sky and the white shine of a glacier. On the left side a creek comes in. It is named Cloud Creek. Somewhere on Cloud Creek you will find Tex Cobb. If you have any trouble finding your way, there is a Tena shaman called Blind Nick who may help you."

I said, "Thanks," and picked up the Winchester and left.

I Ought to Hate Porcupines

Even experienced woodsmen will tell you lots of things about porcupines that aren't so. Here Mr. Annabel sets the record straight, including the answer to that ancient puzzler, how do they mate?

In woodsy circles the belief has been current probably since the late Pleistocene that the porcupine is a dull, uncomplicated character, too brainless to step in out of a cloudburst. Which is a four-bell libel. Actually the porky is a smart cookie. He has a higher I.Q. than many of the predators who yearn to dine on him. Moreover, you hear that the porky is valuable only because a hungry wayfarer in the wilds can always kill him with a club. That ain't so, either, believe me. Then, too, you are told that the porky never, never throws his quills, on account of it is a physical impossibility for him to do so. Shucks, gentlemen. I've *seen* porkies throw their quills—and if everybody will hold still, I'll presently tell you about it.

In my opinion less is known about the porcupine than about any other small animal common to our North American forests. He really is a mysterious critter, even if he doesn't look the part. For example, listen. . . .

It was a bitter early December night on Knik River in Alaska. The snow-hooded spruces were ghostly under a whitewash of moonlight and the wild flare of the aurora. Old Tex Cobb and I, scouting for fur sign, had bivouacked for the night in an ancient, half-ruined cabin which squatted at the rim of a tiny clearing. It was a spooky, bat haunt of a place—and it got spookier. We had been in our sleeping bags maybe half-an-hour when a series of weird sounds arose outside. There were moans, groans, squalls, grunts and a deep chesty booming. Then something, or somebody, wailed what sounded like, "Oh, dear. Oh, dear. Oh, dear." To me the voice was almost, but not quite, human. Tex, who had batted around in the northern wilds for forty years, thought it really was a human voice.

Surging out of his split-pole bunk, the big black-bearded mountain man grabbed his rifle and hastened across to the single window. "By gosh, somebody must be gittin' kilt out there," he said as he scraped frost off the cracked pane with his thumbnail. I don't know why he didn't head out through the door, unless it was because he wanted to see what ghastly thing he was up against first. I was busy getting into my pants and moccasins.

"Well, what's out there?" I asked him. "Is it a secret?" "Take a look fer yourself," he said. "If I told ya, ya wouldn't believe me."

I guess he was right. What I saw when I joined him at the window was one of the rarest sights a woodsman is likely to behold. In the snowy, moonlit dooryard, standing upright, dancing, and singing the eerie duet that had awakened us, were two porcupines. As we watched, they stamped their feet, rocked their shoulders, advanced and retreated, moving rhythmically as if to music. It was a sort of grotesque parody of a siwash salmon dance. Also it was a mating ritual. In a moment one of the porkies—the female, we later discovered—became aggressively affectionate. She dropped to all fours and crowded the male, rubbed noses with him, patted him on the forehead and swapped ends friskily before him. But the male was reluctant—and you couldn't blame him, all things considered. He was the one who, every now and then, whimpered, "Oh, dear. Oh, dear. Oh, dear." I know this is going to be rough for readers to swallow, but fortunately for my reputation, it has been reported before now by some pretty solid observers.

"I gotta wait up to see what happens." Tex said, reaching for his pants. "This is somethin' I've wondered about all my doggone life."

He wasn't alone there. What woodsman hasn't wondered about the mating technique of the porcupine? Aside from the idiosyncrasies of blondes and the alleged perfidy of fur buyers, it is easily the North's most popular topic of campfire conversation. More theories have been advanced on the subject, and probably more gaudy lies told, than about any other wildlife activity. I even heard my friend Starvation Smith declare that porkies weren't born at all. They were hatched from eggs, he said, like platypuses. It stood to reason, he said, because he had once caught a baby porcupine in a rabbit snare and it had quills as sharp as devil's-club thorns. Of course, he said, he hadn't yet figured out how the eggs got fertilized, but he was working on it.

But tonight Tex and I got real low-down. We had ringside seats, so to speak, at the mating of these two moonstruck, vocalizing dancers. Before I tell you what happened, I want to comment on sundry other facets of porcupine character. Maybe it'll help make this and the quill-throwing matter more believable.

Most woodsmen hate porcupines, and with good reason. Dominated by a passion for salt, a porky will gnaw to pieces anything containing even a trace of it—that is, anything his orange-colored chisel teeth will cut. Porkies have ruined enough of my gear to outfit a sizable expedition. They have ruined ax handles, canoe paddles, snowshoes, gunstocks and shoe-pac tops. One night on the Tonzona, a big yellow cuss of a porky gnawed all the skirting off my saddle, a brand-new $80 Hamley. Another time, in the Wood River country, a salt-hungry porky pup cut both horns off a record-crowding white sheep head that I had salted and tossed onto the cabin roof to cure. Still another time, on the Matanuska, a miserable night-prowling porcupine ate a section out of the painter of my dory, which I had brought up from salt water and moored for the night in an eddy. Result: I lost a boat and most of my outfit. Things like that cause you to run a temperature every time you see a porky or hear one mentioned.

The Alaska railroad management once found out about porkies and salt, to its embarrassment. Intending to smart up that part of th railroad crossing the northern Kenai Peninsula, the maintenance engineer got authority to import a large number of Douglas-fir ties from the state of Washington. The Kenai was then unquestionably the porcupine capital of the world—and the fir ties had been floated in salt water. What happened was inevitable. Within a couple of weeks, apparently every porky on the Kenai was camped along the railroad, banqueting on the wonderful salty ties. In one evening I counted sixty of the animals in one mile—all busily scrimshawing railroad property. The unfortunate engineer was kidded so mercilessly about his porky ranch that I think it preyed on his mind. Anyway, he departed from Alaska, and the last I heard of him he was running a motel in California—in an area where no porky had ever been seen.

Old-timers tell a story about Jack Filce, one of the North's elder sourdoughs, who came out to the railroad this same summer for his first train ride. Some time after the train pulled out, Jack asked the conductor to show him to the men's room. He entered the cubicle, and gazed down through the porcelain bowl at the blur of ties whipping past. He had observed earlier the remarkable assemblage of porkies along the track, and now he stepped back into the aisle, shaking his head in refusal.

"Aw, no you don't," he declared to the delight of his fellow passengers. "You don't get me onto that thing. It'd be just my luck we'd run over one of them damned porkypines."

Every Alaska musher spends a good part of his time profanely de-quilling sled dogs. But I'll bet I am the only one who ever had to de-quill a horse. It was a pleasure, too. Gunn Buckingham had hired me to guide him on a five-month packhorse trip westward along the wild north slope of the Alaska Range. We bought ten horses sight unseen at Seattle and had them shipped north, and one turned out to be an outlaw. He was a blue-roan, proud-cut, 900-pound gelding, appropriately named Snorty. He was hammer-headed, pin-eared, ewe-necked, paddle-footed, shanty-rumped and snake-eyed. His specialty was kicking. He could kick backward and forward like a mule, and sideways faster than a brockle-faced range cow. The first morning I put the rigging on him, he kicked my hat off. And every morning after that for the next two weeks, he kept trying for a better shot.

Snorty got his comeuppance on the Chedolothna. We were camped beside a rocky lake under the great white mass of Mt. Foraker. The horses were just below camp feeding on yellow-flowering pea vine, and I had gone out to make certain they were all right. Snorty was rattling his hobble chains toward me along a caribou trail, when suddenly he came face to face with a big black porcupine that would have weighed anyway forty pounds. Typically, Snorty played it dirty. I don't think he had ever seen a porcupine before. He stretched out his head as if to sniff noses with the porky, then whirled like a flash and let go with both heels. He was a sharpshooter, and he connected solidly.

The porky sailed fifteen feet into some snow brush, and Snorty took off across the country, bucking and bellowing. He was probably the most surprised cheechako cayuse this part of the territory had ever seen. When Buck and I hazed him back to camp and threw him, we found 150 quills in his heels, most of them driven into the bone. The necessary surgery took most of the afternoon, and what with one thing and another, it was a salutary experience for the roan. I am pleased to state that never again during our association did he offer to kick at anything. As for the porky, the episode didn't even affect his appetite. When I saw him at sundown he was twenty feet up in a spruce, talking happily to himself as he gnawed bark off the tree.

There are two main races of porcupines on the continent, the Canada porcupine *(Erethizon dorsatum)* which ranges throughout North America and as far west as Minnesota and Hudson Bay; and the yellow-haired porcupine *(Erethizon epizanthum)* which inhabits western America from the mesquite thickets of Arizona to the spruce forests of the Arctic range in Alaska. Porcupines mate between October and mid-December, and their young are born between early April and March. Usually there is a single offspring. In weight, the adults vary from eight to forty pounds. The animals subsist chiefly on the inner bark of conifers, but also eat the bark and tender terminal shoots of such deciduous trees as willow, birch, beech and oak. Despite their reputation for stupidity, scientific tests have shown that porcupines learn faster and adapt themselves more quickly to new conditions than many of their enemies. In short, they just *look* like morons.

The porky's natural enemies are the fisher, lynx, wolverine, coyote, cougar, wolf, and the black and grizzly bears. When attacked, he has only one defense tactic. He turns his back to his foe and lashes out with his muscular, heavily quilled tail. He is startlingly quick with it, and once he gets in a good lick, the animal he hits is in trouble for a long, long time. The black quill tips are not dissolved by body juices, but continue to work into the victim's muscles and organs because they are surfaced with hundreds of vicious little barbs. I know that they cause death, but, strangely, they apparently do not cause infection. I have pelted scores of animals that were riddled with quills, but have not once found festering.

As for that matter of the porky's ability to throw his quills, I'd better give you a specific instance. It was spring and I was coming down Montana Creek, in the Talkeetnas, with a load of beaver pelts on my back and a little gray Tahlton bitch trotting ahead of me. The dog's name was Kloon and she was a wonderful animal, the best I ever owned except for one thing—she spent her life looking for a porcupine she could whip. Today, as I was floundering through knee-deep muck at the edge of a beaver pond,

Kloon suddenly flashed down the trail, yelping like one of her blood-hungry wolf ancestors. She had sighted a porky. She cut the porky off from the tree he was heading for, and began dancing around him, looking for an opening. When I arrived on the scene, muck-stained, angry and out of breath, she knew I was going to break up her sport. So she whipped in and made a pass at one of the porky's front feet, intending to throw him, wolverine fashion, then rip open his belly if she could. But the porky was fast, too. He swiveled around, rump toward her, tail lashing wickedly. He never touched her, but a spray of loose quills flew out, and one struck Kloon in the left eye. That was the end of the fight, and the end of Kloon's eye.

It wasn't the first time I had seen a porky throw quills, nor was it the last. But, of course, in every case throwing them was accidental on the porky's part. He was just doing his darndest to stick some quills into his enemy, and the whiplash action of his tail caused a few to break loose and fly through the air. I have actually seen quills travel a couple of feet and stick into my moccasins. All of which, I suppose, is the basis of the old myth that porcupines can hurl their quills with the accuracy of .22 bullets.

But to really appreciate what a fearsome customer the porky can be, a man ought to face him at eye level, close up, as most of his meat-hungry foes must. I had this experience one pretty moonlit night in the Yellowjacket country, and I think it put anyway half of the gray hairs in my once auburn locks. Tip-Up Williams and I were scouting for trophy sheep in advance of a hunting party, and had camped for the night under a wide-armed white spruce on the bank of a mountain streamlet. I had been asleep an hour or so when I was jerked abruptly awake by two untoward circumstances. There was a weight on my chest that didn't belong there—and practically in my ear was the sound that woodsmen hate most of all to hear in camp, the sound of a porky's teeth at work. Frontier experience and training saved me. I didn't sit up. I just opened my eyes—and froze, horrified.

Sitting on my chest, his tail an inch from my throat, was a porcupine, a big, black, blunt-nosed so-and-so, shoe-button eyes glinting in the moonlight. He was gnawing at the wooden frame of my packboard, which stood against the tree at my head. I had carried salt for curing trophies on the packboard, and I suppose the frame was impregnated with the stuff. Anyway, the porky seemed to think it was marvelous. He was practically smacking his lips. I was almost afraid to breathe. In the moonlight the animal's quills were like ivory needles. They looked at least five inches long, and probably were.

I rolled my eyes toward Tip-Up, and saw that he was awake, but he hadn't moved or spoken. He knew that I was in as much danger as if a grizzly had been standing astride me. When on the trail Tip-Up always carried an old thumb-busting single-action Colt, the type the pioneers called the Peacemaker. It lay between us on Tip-Up's caribou-skin jacket. Now his hand eased out toward it. He slid the gun out of its holster an inch at a time, and cocked it so expertly that the hammer didn't make the slightest click. Meanwhile the porky had turned to one side to get a better bite at the packboard, with the result that Tip-Up was in his range of vision.

Tip-Up couldn't raise the gun to sight without alarming the porky, so he tilted the muzzle, not lifting his hand. I did some fast sweating. Tip-Up could shoot, but in moonlight nobody is that good. Not without a lot of luck. He could wound or miss the porky and cause me to get a faceful—maybe my eyes full—of quills. He could miss the porky and hit me. Or he could be lucky as a smokehouse mouse and kill the porky stone cold dead and everything would be swell. The bore of the .45 looked as wide as the mouth of a culvert. I held my breath and waited. Then there was a dazzling lance of flame and a blast of sound. The shot was good but not quite good enough. The porky fell sideways across my face, shot through the neck, but before I could duck, the dying animal's tail swiped me once on the top of my head.

While I wiped blood and brains off my face, Tip-Up lit a candle and rummaged in his sack for the pair of pliers which are standard equipment for northern woodsmen in porcupine country. "I won't muzzle ya, if ya'll guarantee not to bite," he said. In the next twenty minutes he yanked thirty quills out of my scalp. If you want to know how it felt, I'll tell you this—ever since then I've had a knot in my stomach when I had to de-quill a dog. I know what blazing agony the poor animal goes through.

I said earlier that the legend that the porky is valuable only because he is the one animal a hungry wayfarer in the wilds can count on killing with a club is pretty much baloney. In the first place, the man would have about one chance in a hundred of finding a porcupine, even in porcupine country. A roster of the men who have saved their lives in modern times by killing porkies could be written, I'd bet, on a very small sheet of paper. In the second place, the porky is really valuable for another reason—

he keeps down the population of many harmful predators, especially wolverines and, in the North, coyotes. And in the third place, to get back to that club business, it is no cinch to kill a porky with a club.

Tex Cobb and I discovered this to our discomfiture one crystalline, subzero day on Sheep River.

We were heading out to the railroad from our trapline, to spend Christmas and New Year's in Anchorage. Because we were in a hurry and it was hard snowshoeing, we carried only one rifle and light stampede packs. We would, Tex said, eat game mostly—ptarmigan and such. He carried the rifle, slung Alaska-style over the left horn of his packboard. The second day out, he lost the bolt. Brush caught the knob, I guess, and opened the bolt, and it shook loose and fell into the snow. He didn't miss it until late in the day. "Aw, well," he said, "what's the difference? We'll find a porky today or tomorrow, an' everything'll be fine. We'll eat high all the way out. "That's the good thing about a porky—a man can allus kill one with a club."

Famous last words.

Purple shadows were slanting across the range next day when we struck the deep-walled trails of two porcupines. We had followed the trails about a quarter of a mile when they separated. One went down into a stand of tall spruces, and the other angled up toward a ragged rimrock. Tex took the first, I took the latter. I had the camp ax. I would have staked my share of our fur catch that within a half-hour I would be skinning a fat porcupine. And I would have lost. When I sighted my intended victim, he was within ten feet of a tall slender spruce, and he had heard the crunch and squeal of my webs. He was galloping, heading for safety. I got in one lick at him with the ax as he went up the tree, but missed. I thought, well, hell, all I've got to do is cut the tree down. So I went to work. The frozen spruce was hard as bone, but I kept hacking at it, and after a while it creaked loose from its stump.

When the swirling snow settled and I could see, I began looking for my porcupine. Only I couldn't find him. He had been some thirty feet up in the tree, and I figured the fall probably had killed him and buried him in the ten-foot drifts. So I took off a web and, using it as a shovel, started digging on both sides of the tree's trunk. It was mean, onerous work, but I kept at it. I had shoveled maybe a ton of snow when, behind me, I heard the rattle of claws on frozen bark. There was my porcupine—climbing another tree. The tough, indestructible thus-and-such had burrowed dazedly through the snow until he came to the bare space under the tree. Then he had started climbing again. This tree was a monster of its species for this part of the country, at least two feet through.

"Well, what the hell?" I told myself. "Tex has killed the other porky anyway. So who cares about this one?"

I backtracked and took Tex's trail. It was dark when I met him coming down from the rimrock. I mean, the sun was below the peaks. It never gets really dark in the high North in winter. There was enough light so I could see that Tex wasn't carrying a porky carcass.

"Damned porky went into a cave," he said mournfully.

"Well, why didn't you go in after him?" I asked.

"Believe hit or not," Tex said, "there was a doggone bear in the cave."

Until last year I always supposed that no animal of approximate size could slug it out tail-to-tail with a porky and win. I was wrong. In October I went up into the Pequot Lakes country, in northern Minnesota, with an editor named Herb Mueller and an outdoor-calendar artist named Rog Preuss. Herb and I were interested in catching some of the region's famed walleyed pike, while Rog was concerned with finding picture subjects. We rented a resort cabin on the shore of a beautiful emerald-green lake, and set about our respective projects. Herb and I did all right—the fishing was swell. But Rog was as unhappy as a beaver with a loose tooth. He had come up here with a big high-priced assignment from his agent, but couldn't find a scene he thought was good enough.

He had to have something different, he told us. Something with humor and drama. Something in the wildlife field that hadn't been painted before. What in hell, he asked us, would that be?

He found out a couple of nights later. We were playing a few hands of gin rummy on the kitchen table when we heard a flurry of activity on the porch. The rattle of claws, a thumping sound, a querulous chattering and grumbling. We went to the screen door to investigate. The yellow glow of an electric light hung in a dooryard spruce revealed a remarkable sight. On the bare planks of the porch, rump to rump but several feet apart, stood a black Canada porcupine and a husky summer-fat skunk. The skunk lived under the cabin. We had heard about him from the resort owner, who complained bitterly that he had tried all summer to figure out a way to liquidate the animal without rendering the cabin unfit for human occupancy. The porky was a transient, but his business on the porch was obvious. Our canoe paddles stood beside the door, and of course their sweat-stained maple shafts had attracted him.

I guess each animal was confident of his prowess. Anyway, the porky backed toward the skunk, tail lashing, and the skunk stood his ground. Suddenly both combatants let go. The porky missed—he wasn't quite close enough when he started his rush. But the skunk didn't miss. He not only sprayed the porky, but also the screen door and most of the porch. The last we saw of the porky, he was fleeing across the dooryard, sneezing, blundering into trees, and falling over his own feet. The skunk retreated with dignity to his home under the cabin, and we hastily moved our possessions out via the rear window. With the aid of the apologetic resort owner we were establishing ourselves in another cabin, when all at once the light dawned on Rog. He had his calendar subject.

"And I even got a caption," he told us happily. "'Two tail-happy champions in battle of the scentury,' Get it?"

So Tex Cobb and I were standing at the frost-flowered window in the tumble-down cabin on Knik River, watching the two sex-struck porcupines out there in the moonlight and the aurora glow. It was around 20 below in the cabin—practically as cold as it was outside—because the moss and rabbit-hide chinking had long ago fallen from between the logs. But we had stuck it out, determined to get to the bottom of the secret of the porky's love-life if it took all night. The male porky by now seemed convinced that all was well. He hadn't said, "Oh, dear—oh, dear—oh, dear," for nearly a quarter of an hour. The female, apparently realizing he was reassured regarding her intentions, had flattened her quills and tall back ruff so that she appeared to have shrunk one-third in size. She stood passive, her terrible tail turned to one side. Then suddenly it happened—and a thousand colorful campfire tales collapsed. Because there was nothing at all extraordinary about the mating.

"Shucks, I'm dissap'inted," Tex growled, heading for his bunk. "I was beginnin' to think I was gonna learn somethin' important."

I guess that ties it up.

Brawn, As in Bruin

Just how strong are bears, anyway?
The author has some surprising answers.
Take the case of the brown bear that unburied the moose.

One pretty spring down at Chinitna Bay a slope-backed, crate-headed old brown bear with a heart full of larceny tried to steal a whale from Simeon Nicolai and me. That's right, a whale. Of course, it was dumb of him. The logical place for a bear to eat a whale is where he finds it, without complicating the matter with transportation problems. Still I've got to give the animal credit. He may not have been bright, but what he lacked in brains he made up for in brawn and self-confidence. When Simeon and I blew the whistle on him he had already moved the whale twice its length. Stick around and I'll explain how it happened.

We had cruised down Cook Inlet in Simeon's gas boat, the *Beachcomber*, to establish a camp at Chinitna and there await the arrival of a party of bear hunters who were going to make the trip by air. It was a dull voyage until we chugged into the gray-green bay with its overshadowing wall of snow peaks.

Here we had grandstand seats, so to speak, at a bit of marine drama typical of the western Alaska coast.

A herd of perhaps a dozen beluga whales came up from astern and began playing in our wake, rolling, blowing, and performing a variety of aquatic monkeyshines. The beluga, in case it isn't generally known, is the smallest of the true whales. It is a timid, milk-white creature which reaches a maximum length of about fifteen feet and has no special value except that it provides occasional food for the Eskimos and Aleuts.

These belugas were having a gay time and we were watching them with our glasses when all of a sudden five killer whales appeared from nowhere and closed in fast. End play hour. The belugas took off. They knew about killer whales. They scattered, regrouped, and came streaking like a torpedo spread toward their best refuge—shallow water. Behind them the dreaded killers milled and zigzagged, their sinister black dorsal fins sticking up tall as fenceposts as they tried to unravel the herd's trail.

Most small-boat skippers would have been delighted to stay out of the affair. But not Simeon. Simeon is a Russian-Aleut, a salty, burly son of the northern sea. He had cut his teeth on a chunk of beluga muktuk—the raw skin of the animal with blubber attached—and was passionately fond of the stuff, and we were currently out of fresh meat.

"You take the wheel, huh?" He said. "I'm gonna shoot us a nice beluga to eat." As I moved up beside him he added wryly, "Or one for the killers to eat."

Jacking a cartridge into his .405 bear rifle, Simeon stood at the rail balancing himself to the *Beachcomber's* roll until one of the spooked belugas surfaced fifty yards inshore. It was a bull about twelve feet long.

Simeon held on his snowy hump and hit it, midway down where the spine is, and as the mortally wounded whale made an erratic turn toward us and then lay over on his side, flukes arched up convulsively, blood jetting. Simeon shot him twice more and that did it. We could have had a bad time then with the killers who have been known to dispute possession of a whale in fine berserker fashion. But apparently they missed the blood scent. Or maybe the water was shoaling too fast for their liking. Anyway, they sheered off and vanished, and we got a line on our bull and towed him on into the bay, where we moored him to a tree in a creek mouth at high tide. This accomplished, we anchored the flat-bottomed *Beachcomber* off a sandspit a short distance up the bay and went ashore in the dinghy and made camp.

Next morning our bear friend got into the act.

Having decided that broiled beluga tenderloin with flipper muktuk on the side was just what we needed to start the day, we headed for the creek mouth at sunup with our rifles, packboards and the camp ax. The tide was out and a whiplash wind off the white Kenai peaks was in our faces. As we rounded a shaggy point 200 yards from the creek, Simeon halted abruptly, pointing. I stepped past him and behind a remarkable sight. A brown bear, a hillock of a brown bear, was dragging our whale carcass down the bed of the rocky, ankle-deep creek. He had a grip on the carcass just ahead of the tail and was backing up, tugging and straining, nervously busy as any hardworking thief making a difficult getaway with an office safe.

During the night the ebbing tide had left the whale grounded upstream as far as the mooring line would reach. The bear had now succeeded in dragging it an equal distance downstream. A total of about twenty feet—and where he thought he was going with it will forever remain a mystery to me. As to how much the whale weighed, naturally I don't know that either. But a bull beluga his length ought to go anyway 100 pounds a foot. Make it 1,200 pounds of whale.

Simeon and I weren't being paid to shoot bears, and we had long since gotten over shooting them for fun, so I hollered at the ambitious brigand toiling in the creek, inviting him to beat it while he still enjoyed good health. He got the idea. Facing us with his spade-size front feet on the whale, he bristled, snorted, and rolled his big head from side to side trying to get our scent. Then he lit out at a gallop for the alders, where he paused long enough to roar resentfully at us before disappearing. Simeon and I went on to the carcass to chop our breakfast tenderloin and muktuk.

The bear, we discovered, had eaten only a few mouthfuls from the whale's belly. He had passed up a meal in his screwball effort to corner the supply. I remarked that like some muscle characters I knew he apparently suffered from the stupids.

"Yeah," Simeon laughed, rather missing the point. "He was balmy, all right. He wasn't going nowhere with that whale. Hell, it was still tied up."

And so it was.

As a topic for campfire sagas, the strength of bears is an ancient favorite, holding up well in rough competition with blondes, barroom adventures and the pecuniary mendacity of New York fur buyers. In fact, if there was any way to prove it, I would wager a small sum that the first successful thriller related by Folsom Man after he mushed over here from Siberia had something to do with a show of brawn on the part of an Alaska grizzly or brown bear. Also I have no doubt it was true, if only because the iron strength of these outside northern brutes is difficult to exaggerate.

A bear isn't muscled like the other large carnivores. His muscles, when you've skinned him, aren't sleek, flat, and smoothly assembled. They are bunched and bulged like mats of woven wire cable. With his Titan strength concentrated in his shoulders and forearms, he can lift incredible weights, and strike with the shattering force of the hammer of Thor. In a phrase, the bear is the wilderness muscle boss of this continent, and I hear he does pretty well for himself in foreign parts too.

But a muscle boss can fall on his face. For example, the sourdoughs who brought me up used to tell me with bated breath that a bear could haul off and, with a single lethal stroke, belt an adult bull moose bowlegged—drop the critter in his tracks as if he was struck by lightning. I always wanted to see this, and by good luck one April morning I did see it. That is, I saw a grizzly stalk a bull and land his Sunday wallop. The sourdoughs, I can report, were correct only up to a point.

Due to an urgent invitation brought to me by an Indian musher, I had snowshoed over to "Banty" Jenkins' place on Spruce Creek. It seemed that Banty had bought a chain saw, the first in these parts, and he wanted me to see it work. No doubt about it, he stated in his note, the chain saw was going to revolutionize life on the frontier. Once I saw it in action, he promised, I would no more continue to cut firewood with a crosscut or bucksaw than I would arm myself for big game with great-grandpa's muzzleloading squirrel rifle. Banty is a stove-up, sample-size old-timer who abandoned trapping for sodbusting at the age of seventy because, quoting him, there was a lot more future in it. I liked him and I hadn't seen him for a spell, so I closed up the house and headed for Spruce Creek for a visit and to see the wonderful chain saw operate. I am forever glad that I did. Not for anything would I have missed the case of assault and battery I witnessed there.

Arriving toward sundown, I found Banty in a new birch-bottom clearing bordering the creek. He had just knocked off work for the day and was surrounded by felled trees, ricks of stovewood, and moose. The moose were eating the tops of downed trees. At least twenty of the huge, winter-gaunt animals were in sight, some lying in the April drifts solemnly chewing their cuds, others busily biting off frozen birch twigs with a sound like a battery of hedge clippers. If our presence worried them they didn't show it.

I have been around supposedly gentle domestic cattle that were wild-eyed and ringy by comparison. Banty said it was the free lunch of birch tops that had tamed them. Believe it or not, he said, of all the moose calls he had ever used or heard tell of, the racketing snarl of the little chain saw was the blue-ribbon best. Start the machine, and hungry moose would head for the sound from every direction. If only it worked half as well in this respect next fall when the season opened, he said wistfully, his meat-hunting problem would be solved.

"Tomorrow I'll show ya how she performs," he said. "You're gonna see something, boy, that'll make yer eyeballs pop."

He was so right. If they didn't pop, they should have.

We set out early with the saw and a can of gas and were partway to the clearing when we came to the deep-wallowed trail of a bear, apparently a grizzly, leading in the same direction we were going. As the trail was fresh, I suggested it would be prudent to go back for a rifle. Spring grizzlies can be touchy. In this part of the North they often emerge early from hibernation, presumably to feed on the carcasses of winter-killed moose and other carrion until vegetation appears. Their feet are tender, they are hungry, and their temper has a low boiling point. But Banty vetoed the suggestion. He was in a hurry to show off his chain saw. So we went on. A couple of minutes later we sighted the bear.

He was below us at the bottom of a slope, about 150 yards distant and upwind, pussyfooting through the drifts as stealthily as a big cat. His attention was riveted on three bull moose lying in the lee of a wood rick. Not an especially large grizzly, he had a gunnysack-brown pelt that rippled handsomely in the wind, and an ugly hog-snouted head with a silvery patch. A boldface. The type of a grizzly that gave the buckskin boys the creeps on the Upper Missouri and in the Sierra Nevada. Manifestly he figured to break his six months' fast with a bellyful of fresh moose meat, the heck with winter-killed carrion. And you could see that he was no amateur moose stalker. He knew the tricks.

Using every scrap of cover, hugging the snow, he ghosted straight into the wind, a brown shadow among shadows. Even so, the three bulls heard him. Their marvelously sensitive ears were semaphoring alertly but they didn't get up. I suppose they thought another hungry moose was arriving for a feed of Banty's birch tops.

In any case, they let the grizzly get close enough to make his rush. "Holy-y-y mackerel," Banty breathed. "Lookit that."

Bursting from cover with a rasping *Wagh-h!* the bear had bounded across the snow like a shaggy projectile and was alongside the nearest bull when the three suddenly panicked animals heaved to their feet. He had a setup. Everything was in his favor. This nearest bull was boxed in between his two companions and the rick of wood. To get clear he had to turn toward the bear. As the great antlerless animal pivoted, rump slamming against the bull behind him, he was wide open for what happened. The grizzly hit him.

It was a good, clean, solid haymaker delivered with the bear's left paw, and it landed on the money spot high on the bull's neck. But hard. So at last, after thirty-odd years of hearing about it, I had seen the legendary killing pawstroke of old *Ursus horribilis.* The mighty bone-busting blow that, you were told, used to lay the buffalo low, and could drop a moose as if he had been slugged by a piledriver.

This bull dropped, all right. He went to his knees with a moaning grunt audible clear up to where Banty and I stood. But he didn't stay down. In practically the same motion he lurched back to his feet. This time he wheeled in the opposite direction, toward the woodpile, and as he did so the grizzly leaped onto his back. To the desperate bull the woodpile was now no barrier at all. He went through it, bucking and floundering like a runaway truck through a picket fence. In the collision the bear was thrown off or, possibly, was knocked off by a flying chunk of frozen birch. Anyhow, the result was that the bull fled across the creek into the opposite timber, with the frustrated bear loping behind, a vain pursuit if I ever saw one.

"Well, at least he scored a knockdown," I heard myself say.

"Uh-huh," Banty said hoarsely, getting his webs crossed as he shouldered the chain saw. "But would that make you feel any better if ya hadn't et, by gosh, since last September?"

The doggondest feat of bear brawn that ever affected me personally took place here at my backwoods headquarters on Goose Creek. This particular bear was a brown bear. He had a talent for weightlifting. One night he hoisted a large cow moose out of her grave—a task better suited to a steam winch—and in due course was damn well killed for his trouble.

Old Tex Cobb and I had spent the winter running a marten line back in the Talkeetnas. In June, with our fur sold, we had come home to Goose Creek to smart up the place for a fishing party we had booked. A dandy little surprise awaited us. Two hundred yards behind the house in a stand of balm-of-Gilead cottonwoods the aforementioned cow moose had inconsiderately lain down and died, probably of old age. The carcass had ripened in the sun, a million blowflies were holding carnival on it, and a bear had taken possession.

Typically, he had ripped open the paunch before giving the carcass a token covering of earth and dead grass. Since the prevailing north wind channeled the God-awful smell directly to the house, we had a situation. Fishermen are hardened characters by and large, but still a dead moose in the back yard in hot weather would most likely, we felt, occasion protest.

The sole solution was to bury the animal. So, hating it, we set to work digging a grave. The chore proved to be an engineering project. Twelve inches down we struck frozen ground. Next we encountered a stratum of unknown depth consisting chiefly of granite boulders of the size used to ballast ships. We persevered, however, and as the midnight sun was angling down to the horizon we wearily pry-poled the carcass into its grave and covered it. Tex claimed he was a broken man.

"I tell ya, I wouldn't dig another hole in ground like that," he declared, "if I knowed there was gonna be nuggets as big as horse teeth at the bottom of hit."

He had only started digging graves.

Three mornings later I awoke with the uneasy feeling that something disastrous had occurred. In a moment I knew what it was, all right. The window between my bunk and Tex's was open. A brisk north wind was blowing the petunia-patterned trading-post curtains and it had filled the room with a familiar smell. I mean, I recognized it. There couldn't have been two such smells in the world. I dressed and then woke Tex. The big, iron-maned mountain man sat up and reached for his long pants.

Midway of the movement he froze motionless. He sniffed suspiciously, coughed, took another whiff for confirmation, and got up hastily and closed the window. That didn't help much. It just shut us in with the all-pervading smell which, I'll swear, was equal to the worst that ever was wafted from an old-time glue factory or even from a Jap whaling station. Being underground had done things to our cow moose.

"Hit'll save time." Tex groaned, "if you get the shovels while I pull on m' clothes."

Of course the bear had returned. Finding his meat cache buried, he had unburied it. Then, and I wish I might have witnessed the operation, he had muscled the cow out of her grave and dragged her fifty feet down a slope into a willow clump, where he had eaten what he wanted and again clawed earth and grass over the now rather disarranged moose carcass.

As I said, she was a sizable cow. No doubt she had been winter-gaunt, you couldn't tell much about that now, but still I estimated she would weigh close to 900 pounds. Thus to get her out of her grave, the bear had had to make a straight lift of nearly half a ton. As to the method he employed or how long it took him, your guess is as good as mine. The important thing to us was that we had to dig another grave. So we got busy. It turned out to be a worse job than before, if possible. When we stumbled back to the house in the red shadows of afternoon I had the uncanny feeling that we were caught in the toils of a nightmare. I guess Tex was a little punchy himself.

"Let's face hit," he said. "We cain't take no more chances. We gotta kill that bear. Hit's him or us."

I took the first night watch and nothing happened. But the following night Tex got action. He was sitting against a cottonwood with a blanket around his shoulders, rifle across his knees, when the bear stepped out of a thicket and came pigeon-toeing over to the new grave.

He was a big bear, about as big as brown bears grow in this part of the country. His pelt was the color of good plug tobacco and he had a yellow mane reaching from his neck to the middle of his back. He circled the grave, bristling as he got our scent. Then he swiveled around and stared toward Tex's ambush. The wind was wrong for him but he seemed to sense danger and to know where it was, Tex told me. No bear ever had a more accurate hunch. Tex laid the sights of his .30-06 Sauer Mauser on the animal's head and touched the hair trigger. The bear never knew what hit him. Awakened by the shot, I went out and helped Tex with the terrible job of taking off the pelt.

The bear was a patriarch, his teeth worn to stumps, his claws cracked and scurfy, which may have accounted for his determined appetite for carrion.

Later, at the house, Tex was stirring soda into a pan of hotcake sourdough when a thought struck him with staggering impact.

"Great gawdamighty," he moaned collapsing into a chair. "Do ya reelize what we gotta do now? We gotta dig a grave fer that blasted bear afore he starts stinkin' up the place too."

Last fall, thanks to a keg of "Wildhorse" Bob Liggett's cranberry lightnin', I got a fair working notion of the brawn stored under a black bear's glossy hide. Wildhorse is my only neighbor on Goose Creek. He is a hustling 130-pound ex-Nevada bronc stomper who aims to raise beef cattle in this wilderness despite bogs, bears, mosquitoes, and some of the worst winters north of Seattle. One September afternoon he came down to my place and said he wanted to borrow a keg. High-bush cranberries were hanging in clusters like grapes out behind his cabin, he said, and a keg of cranberry lightnin' sure would be an asset come the winter holidays. Agreeing wholeheartedly, I got a new ten gallon-oak keg out of the cache and handed it over.

"The bears are reely gonna hate me," Wildhorse laughed as he left, "for looting that beyootiful cranberry patch."

One of them didn't.

Some ten days later I made an early morning fishing trip up the creek with a pleasant elderly tourist couple from Iowa who were deeply interested in the North's wildlife. They had been here a week and were a little disappointed, they said, because they hadn't seen any moose or bears. But they saw a bear this morning. He made up for everything. As an entertainer he was equal to Walt Disney's bruins.

We were working a sunny grayling hole under a line of red-gravel cliffs half a mile upstream, not far from Wildhorse's cabin, when we heard rocks rolling ahead. Presently I spotted the cause of the racket.

It was a black bear. He stood sixty feet above the creek on the crumbling rim of one of the steeply sloping cliffs, and as we watched, he did one of the silliest things I ever saw in the wilds. He stepped deliberately over the rim, landed on his hind end twenty feet down, and slid the rest of the way to the water in an avalanche of gravel. He fanny-whopped into an eddy, and when the dust had settled he was sitting there, in three feet of water, with just his head showing.

"You'd think he could have found an easier way down," the tourist lady said.

"He did that for fun," her husband told her.

Some fun, bumping down a cliff. I slid a cartridge into the chamber of my rifle. Bears do some curious things but this act had been pretty special. I figured the bear was nuts and his next move convinced me.

Splashing ashore, the bear shook himself and came weaving down a reach of open sand bar across the creek from us. When he was a stone's throw distant a big cream-and-cinnamon meadow butterfly fluttered across his path. He made a swipe at it, missed, let go with a whistling one-two, missed again, and chased the butterfly down the bar into a willow thicket, where he vanished from our ken. The show over, we fished on up the creek. The two tourists were enchanted. They had never dreamt, they said, that wild bears were so comically playful. We fished a couple of hours, then the grayling stopped hitting and we went back to the house. An interesting bit of intelligence greeted us. My caretaker, "Starvation" Smith, told us that the strangest thing had happened. He was splitting wood, he said, when a black bear came up the trail from the creek and walked right into the yard. The bear snorted at him, he said, bit a chunk out of the clothesline post, and departed in a northerly direction at a tangle-footed gallop, whuffing like a boar hog going to war. And if I didn't believe it I could go take a look at the post.

"Was he chasing a butterfly?" I asked.

"Why—uh—I dunno," Starvation said, giving me an appraising look. "I didn't happen to notice."

By this time I had a theory about the bear and his shenanigans. After eating lunch with the tourists I went up the trail to Wildhorse's cabin. Wildhorse was sitting on the front steps cleaning his rifle. He was, he stated grimly, preparing for a bear hunt.

"Come on out to the tool shed," he gritted. "I wanta show ya what a thievin', no-good bear did there last night."

The tool shed was an open-faced spruce-slab structure that stood at the rim of the timber 100 feet behind the cabin. In it Wildhorse had been fermenting his keg of cranberry lightnin'. With loving care, he said, he had stowed the keg in a canvas-covered packing case and placed two kerosene lanterns alongside it to keep it warm. Last night it had been something to make a man's taste buds holler for more. But this morning—tragedy.

A bear had raided the place. First the animal had drunk most of the mash. Then, no doubt gloriously lit up, as he had every cause to be, he had smashed the keg. There it lay on the tool shed floor, a new oak keg reduced to a tangle of staves and hoops, testimony to the sledgehammer power behind a black bear's pawstrokes. I commented that the bear must be the Rocky Marciano of his clan. I had busted up a few oak kegs for firewood and it had taken some doing even with a heavy ax.

"Yeah. But ya gotta remember." Wildhorse gloomed, "he was loaded with my cranberry lightnin'."

But I think the best crack I ever heard on the subject of bear strength was made by my friend Wasilla Stepan. Wasilla is chief of a fading tribe of Susitna-Denna. He lives three miles north of my place and, in summer, makes his living drying salmon, which he sells to dog mushers. Tall and dignified, the only chief I ever knew who looks like one, he came down to Goose Creek one September morning to make an apology. He wouldn't be able to fill an order Tex and I had given him for a bale of dried silver salmon, he informed us, unless we could wait another ten days. There had been a little trouble at his camp, he said. Bear trouble. In fact, he said, he was going to have to build a new fish house, on account of the former one was in ruins. Over a pot of tea he told us the awful misadventure that had happened.

For several nights in a row, Wasilla said, a brown bear had prowled about the fish house obviously working up courage to enter and pull down the racks of drying salmon. A tin-roofed affair, twenty feet square and open on all sides, the fish house stood on the bank of the Susitna River 200 yards from Wasilla's summer cabin. Wasilla didn't have a watchdog, he explained, and he had been reluctant to stand guard over the fish house at night with a rifle. Like most of the Tena people, he had a strong aversion to being abroad after nightfall. Moreover, he pointed out, he was an old man, and when he had put in a hard day splitting salmon and tending his nets, needed rest.

So he did the next best thing. He set a snare for the bear. It was no ordinary snare. It was a length of quarter-inch steel cable, strong enough to have garroted a Cape buffalo. Painstakingly and with veteran trapper's skill, he set it in the brush directly behind the fish house and tied it securely to a leaning, fire-killed spruce snag. With a heap of fish gurry for bait it was a deadly contrivance, and Wasilla went home that night assuring himself that his bear troubles were practically over and done with.

Fate threw him a curve. Along toward midnight he was awakened by an astonishingly loud tinny crash in the direction of the fish house. Pulling on his pants and moccasins, he hastened out with his rifle to investigate. It was an overcast night with rain and an icy wind blowing off the glaciers of Mt. McKinley. As the old chief eased into the fish house clearing he heard the bear bawl, then saw the shadowy outline of the animal fighting the snare.

Wasilla carries a .405 and he has learned through hard-won experience that the way to kill a bear is to keep blasting as long as the bear moves and then shoot him a couple of times for luck. It prevents incidents. So tonight he emptied the .405.

Of course, the whole thing was very unsporting, but then Wasilla isn't a sportsman. He is an old man making his living on the bank of a wilderness river, and the bear was out to give him trouble. Had given him trouble. When he went over to the fallen animal, Wasilla told us, he saw for the first time that the fish house now stood in two sections. The brown bear, throwing his great weight and strength against the cable snare, had pulled over the spruce snag to which the snare was fastened. And the snag had fallen across the tin roof of the fish house—that was the crash he had heard—cleaving it in half. All the fish racks were knocked down and rain was pouring in on them.

"So that's why," Wasilla said, "I won't be able to bring you that bale of silver salmon like I said I would."

"He musta been a heck of a strong bear," Tex said.

"I guess so," Wasilla said, shrugging. "But did you ever hear of a weak bear?"

Which, I think, ties up the subject of bear strength.

Happy-Go-Siwash

Want to get more game, have more fun, and save a pile of money in the bargain? It's easy, says this man who knows, if you skip the fancy trimmings and go siwash.

"Now there," Jimmy said, genuinely awed, "is a hunting camp to write home about. My gosh, d'ya suppose they've got a post office too?"

We stood on the frost-painted Kenai hillside gazing at the spread of tents in the spruces on the bank of Resurrection Creek. We were bearded to the eyes, hatless, our clothes so grass-stained and brush-torn a rag collector wouldn't have had them. For twelve days we had been back in the September hills, living largely on the country and having the time of our lives. We had roamed among herds of rutting moose, and got close-up looks at dozens of fine trophy heads. Two days back Jimmy had found the bull he wanted—sixty-five-inch antlers, with thirty-seven points. Rather than cache the head and risk the fondness of porcupines for moose antlers, we were packing it out to the Seward-Hope highway. When we reached Anchorage we would send an airplane back for the meat.

"Honest, are these guys really hunting?" he asked. "The place looks like a town."

You could have mistaken it for a tent town. The population, we learned, consisted of five hunters, five guides, three packers, a cook, an assistant cook, and thirty-six packhorses. Strung along the creek bank were nine tents. A radio, tuned to a Seattle station, was telling the world news. Cayuse bells jangled in the timber.

From somewhere came the sound of chopping and the whine of a crosscut saw. It was a camp in the Great White Hunter tradition, typical of the clan of well-heeled sportsmen who used to come north year after year with mountains of baggage, remudas of horses and corps of assorted woodsmen, to make expeditions, not hunting trips, into the back country for big-game trophies.

Old Frank Lee, head guide of this elaborate outfit, informed us his five hunters had come to the Kenai Peninsula for moose. "Only," he said sadly, "we ain't seen none yet. An' with a circus like this, I dunno how the hell we're gonna. All we lack is a brass band an' fireworks. I sure would trade the whole shebang, an' give some boot, fer a little siwash outfit like yourn."

"Siwash" is a corruption of the French word *sauvage*, and was applied by early traders to the Northwest Indians. Hence, in Alaska, to do something siwash style is to do it in the Indian manner. When you make a siwash hunt you streamline your gear to the minimum with the idea of spending your time enjoying the wilderness instead of bossing a campaign, and of taking fine trophies as economically as possible.

The usual method is to make up a light pack of essential food and equipment for each man of the party, hire one of the many available bush pilots to fly you into a gameland, and then scout the lake-dotted forests and timberline parks, substituting hospitable trees for a tent and supplementing your food supply with natural provender, until you find the game you are seeking. The plane returns for you by pre-arrangement, thus saving you the cost of stand-by time. The advantages, aside from economy, are mobility and freedom from the noise and encumbrances of larger outfits.

Omitting airplane transportation, it is the way gran'pa and Dan'l Boone hunted. It's the way professional woodsmen have always hunted when they weren't guiding paying customers bemused by foofaraw. And sportsmen from the cities are beginning to discover it is a mighty pleasant and satisfactory way for them to hunt, too.

Last year, for example, about 2,000,000 pounds of dressed game meat was brought out of the Alaska wilds by approximately 14,000 hunters, nine-tenths of whom went into the gamelands siwash fashion, burdened only by rifle, sleeping bag, ax, a kettle or two and a few pounds of grub. If any of the goldplated, folding-bathtub expeditions came to the territory for trophies, I didn't hear about them.

Maybe wartime experience convinced sportsmen that it isn't necessary to operate in the hunting grounds like characters out of Rudyard Kipling. Perhaps when the doughfeet found they could get along all right under a bank or a good rain-shedding tree, cooking in a mess-kit over an open fire and sleeping on boughs or wild hay, it occurred to them they could do likewise in the big-game ranges. At any rate, the hunters we get up here now have vastly different tastes than the prewar boys. They don't give a hang for deluxe equipment, and when they fare forth into the gamelands they call it a hunting trip, not an expedition.

They may not impress the natives as their predecessors did, but they get the game, there is little strain on their bankrolls, and they have plenty of fun. Like the sourdoughs, they don't try to move civilization into the wilds, they just make friends with the country as they find it, and the country pays off.

Big factor in favor of the siwash method is that it enables a man to enter an area quietly. You aren't handicapped by a snorting, whickering, brush-busting herd of horses. You don't have to start the echoes ringing by cutting tent poles and slashing out a campsite. You don't even have to build a fire.

All game animals these days have had some experience with man, and when they hear you belaboring a tree with an ax, smell coffee boiling and bacon frying, and see a white tent blossom where none was yesterday, they are well capable of putting two and two together. Worst of it is that the big old mosshorns, the patriarchal trophy animals, being the smartest, always are the first to depart when you advertise your presence in their domain. It follows that the way to fool them is to tiptoe into the region, make a cold camp the first day, and keep all noise down. If game is present you'll get action. Plenty of action.

A case in point is a grizzly hunt I made with Harry Anders on the Wood River watershed, south of Fairbanks, one of the territory's better game ranges.

Our pilot landed us on a strip of pea-vine bar, and we packed upstream to an abandoned trapline cabin near the mouth of Kansas Creek. There was game sign everywhere along the stream—tracks of moose, caribou, bear—so we neither chopped wood nor built a fire. Instead, we dined cold on army "C" ration washed down with powdered milk in creek water. It wasn't delectable fare but we were thinking about the whooping big grizzly tracks we had seen. We didn't want to alarm those bear. When you spook a grizzly he starts traveling, and often doesn't stop until he has placed a mountain range, a couple of rivers and perhaps a glacier or two between you and him.

Next morning, as the first steel-gray wash of dawn touched the timber, our forbearance was dramatically rewarded. There was a sound at the door. Harry, half-asleep and not realizing where he was, sat up and mumbled, "Come in."

The sound was repeated, louder this time. Then there was a sharp *whuf-f-f!* and claws rattled across the hand-hewn planks. Heavy claws. Bear claws.

Harry and I came out of our bunks as one man and made for our rifles, which stood in a corner across the room. Before we reached the weapons a tremendous wallop flung the door open so violently it struck the wall and rebounded. In the doorway, with a front paw on each side of the frame, head bent forward to clear the lintel, stood the bear. I think I froze with one foot in the air. I couldn't tell in this light whether the bear was brown or black, but he was a big one. I didn't want any trouble with him until I could lay hands on my rifle and put on my shoes and pants. In an emergency a man feels mighty helpless unarmed, barefoot and in his shirttail.

"For the love of Mike," Harry whispered hoarsely, "do something. He's gonna come in here."

"Shut up!" I said. I must have been afraid he'd give the bear ideas.

The tableau lasted several seconds. Then the bear snorted, dropped to all fours, and vanished around a corner of the cabin. We yanked on our clothes. Harry got his shoes on the wrong feet and I buttoned my shirt to my underwear, but we were out of there before you could fill a Springfield clip.

I took one side of the cabin, Harry the other. The instant he was out of my sight he opened fire. His .300 magnum sounded like an automatic. A grizzly bawled. There was a terrific commotion in the brush, branches breaking, teeth popping, the solid thump of something heavy falling off a cutbank. When I reached Harry he was leaning against the cabin, a dazed look on his face.

"Did you get him?" I inquired.

"Which one?" he asked weakly. "Man, there were *four* grizzlies—two big ones and two monsters. I got the monsters." He pointed. "Out there in the bushes."

They were Kluane grizzlies, and apparently there had been a family of them, two adults and a pair of yearlings. Harry had killed the adults. They had handsome creamy white pelts, the underfur thick and soft, the white guard hairs uncommonly long and silky, with a sheen like prime fox fur. Probably the old cabin clearing had been one of their loafing places and they had come here for the morning sunlight. As there had been no smoke and no noise, the small amount of man scent at the cabin had only aroused their curiosity.

The episode converted Harry to the growing ranks of siwash hunters. Any time grizzlies got you out of bed and invited you to take them home as trophies, he declared, it was fair proof the siwashes had something.

To me the most attractive thing about his method of hunting is that it makes it possible for the sportsman of average means to get out into the game ranges without mortgaging the homestead or amputating his savings account. You don't have to spend fantastic sums for horses, sawbuck saddles, Humboldt pads, blankets, mantles, panniers, halters, hobbles, shoeing gear, ropes, riding saddles, bridles, belly cinches, and the hundred-and-one other items that make up a packtrain outfit. Total expense, in fact, won't equal the cost of two properly equipped packhorses landed at Anchorage.

Probably your chief trouble will be that you'll buy too much gear—most sportsmen, myself included, being suckers for the fascinating displays in the stores. The thing to do, before the clerk starts wrapping up that folding grill, the full-length air mattress and the battery-powered camp radio, is to remind yourself that what you take into the wilds on a siwash hunt goes in on your back. It is downright astonishing how few additions can cause a 50-pound pack to grow to 100 pounds.

Anguished outcries are heard each autumn in the Anchorage hotels when guides go weeding through their hunters' gear for articles to be left behind. The average sportsman puts up an impassioned plea for each discarded piece of equipment. He calls attention to its usefulness, points out that it doesn't really weigh much, and asserts that he promised the dealer on his word of honor he would field-test it. But the guides, who have heard all the arguments before, hard-heartedly cull out the excess and tell the hotel porters to place it in storage. Enough such camp gear is left behind each hunting season, I'll bet, to stock the sports department of a fair-to-middling hardware store.

Tex Cobb, dean of northern woodsmen, who enjoys a reputation as a narrator of tall but illustrative yarns, tells one about a sportsman who overruled him in the matter of taking an extraordinarily complete wardrobe into the hunting country. This man had a suit for each type of weather, each activity he expected to take part in, and each species of game he was going to hunt, Tex says. He had suits made of duck, gabardine, corduroy, water-repellent cloth, tweed and whipcord. He was the best-dressed hunter north of Seattle. They chartered two airplanes and ferried the outfit to Tustemena Lake, in the western Kenai moose country, where the dude required Tex to erect a special wardrobe tent, complete with hanger racks and a flit gun to keep out the moths.

The morning after their arrival, says poker-faced Tex, they sighted a big bull moose polishing its antlers on a hilltop snag a half-mile distant. The head was a good one, with plenty of spread and points, nicely matched brow antlers and heavy, wide palms. After studying the animal with binoculars and deciding it was the one he wanted, the dude changed into his moose suit and they began the stalk.

They had covered only a short distance when a Kenai grizzly walked out of a highbush cranberry thicket and stood gazing at them. As bull moose are many times more plentiful than grizzlies, Tex motioned for the dude to shoot the bear. But the dude only shook his head and sighed.

"Shoot, doggone hit!" Tex urged, thinking the man had buck fever. "He ain't gonna stand there all day."

"But my dear fellow," the dude protested, "I can't. I'm not wearing my grizzly suit."

Sportsmen sometimes ask if it isn't dangerous to journey into the northern wilderness with only a scanty siwash outfit. The answer is that no Alaska guide has ever lost a hunter or brought one back sick or injured.

The guides here are all licensed men (the game law stipulates that each non-resident big-game hunter be accompanied by a licensed guide) and the game commission makes certain that they are thoroughly competent. Before a license is issued to a man he must prove he is an experienced woodsman, and then must work for several years as assistant to veteran guides. Licenses expire each year and to qualify for renewal the guide is obliged to pass a stiff examination that tests him in every phase of his profession, from first-aid to throwing the diamond hitch. It has been made so difficult to obtain a full-license and hold it that many woodsmen have abandoned the trade. Sportsmen may be assured, therefore, that the guides they go hunting with will keep them out of trouble and bring them back in good order.

But you get some scares. My worst one came during a bighorn sheep hunt in the Yanert Hills with a banker who, the fifth day out, developed what we both thought was acute appendicitis. An hour after the first pain doubled him up he was the sickest dude I ever saw. He rolled on his bunk, groaning and sweating, and chewed on spruce boughs. His belly was hard as a plank.

I thought I knew what was going to happen. The confounded appendix would burst, peritonitis would set in, and in due course I would lose a hunter. I tried to remember everything I had read or heard about appendicitis. Application of an ice-pack, I recalled, was one recommended treatment. So I climbed the mountain behind camp, brought down a sack of snow, and iced the hunter from breastbone to hips. It was no use. The pain was as bad as before, he said, and would I stop trying to freeze him to death.

I took a walk and did some more thinking. By this time I was chewing fingernails. The only doctor I had known was a surgeon, famous in his profession, whom I had guided several times in the caribou country. He had once told me, with how much sincerity I don't know, that many cures are psychological and a lot of patients get well no matter what you do for them. So, with nothing to lose, I gave his idea a try.

I made a retractor by bending a spoon handle and filing it to the proper shape. I hung a kettle of water over the fire. I placed a length of gut leader in a pan to soak. Then I sat down and began whetting my skinning knife. When the significance of this struck the hunter he sat up, eyes bugged out with alarm.

"What's the idea?" he demanded. "Whad'ya think you're going to do?"

"We're going to take out that haywire appendix." I said, trying to sound matter-of-fact. "When you get back to town you can die any time you want to, but you can't ruin my reputation by doing it out here."

"No, no!" he said, edging away. "Put that damned knife up. I've felt better for the last ten minutes. Just something I ate, I guess—green blueberries, maybe. I'm going to be all right. Believe me."

Maybe it was the ice pack, or it could have been, as he said, that he was suffering from green blueberries and not appendicitis. Whichever the case, he was back in hunting trim by the following afternoon. When the hunt was over and he had returned home he wrote to me stating he had just gone to the hospital and had a perfectly good appendix removed. He was taking no further chances. He wanted his surgery performed by a man in the business, not by a wild woodsman with a skinning knife.

The length of siwash hunting trips varies, but as a general rule ten days in the field is enough. This gives you time to select a good trophy, become acquainted with the hunting area, and get in some fishing and small-game shooting on the side. If necessary, however, you can make a successful hunt in much shorter time. A couple of autumns ago, for instance, I made a moose hunt with Lurton (Count) Blassingame, the literary agent, in what must have been record time.

We had been on a salmon-fishing trip and now business made it imperative for Count to start for New York in two days. He knew he shouldn't try to make a moose hunt in this brief span. If we were delayed for any reason, his business deal would be shot to pieces. But still, he had a mighty yearning to take a moose trophy. He had a place picked out above the fireplace of his summer home, and he had thought about heavy-antlered bulls until he saw them in his dreams. Since it wasn't my business deal at stake I gave him the take-a-chance argument, and he finally agreed.

We chartered a light plane at Anchorage, loaded aboard two sleeping bags, an ax, a carton of restaurant sandwiches, a can of coffee and two kettles and a frying pan, and flew northwestward over the spruce-forested, lake-gemmed western Susitna moose country. In less than five hours' flying time we saw about a hundred moose, but they were either too far from a landable lake or the antlers weren't trophy size. At dusk we landed on a narrow lake under a chain of low hills, moored the plane to a tree, and made a cold camp in a blueberry thicket.

As we unrolled our sleeping bags a bull moose grunted a challenge from the dark wall of timber. Grayling and trout were jumping in the lake. Ducks were talking in the sedge. You could have foraged royal food here, but we held to the siwash first-day formula. No fire. No noise. It should be explained that the sound of an airplane does not disturb Alaska game animals. They hear so many that even the cagiest gun-educated veterans, taking their ease in a wild meadow, seldom get to their feet when a plane passes over.

At daybreak, finding moose sign abundant in the area, we went up on the looping crestline of the hills to reconnoiter, and presently were in the midst of a band of fifteen bulls. The great animals, just entering the madness of the rut, their antlers polished to mirror brightness, necks swollen to the size of beer kegs, were all about us in the head-high tangle of redtop grass and wild raspberry brush. If there had been time we could have had splendid sport selecting a head. As it was, we could make only rough appraisal of their merits.

The bull we took was lying sound asleep in a little tundra opening. I doubt that any game animal ever was more completely taken in by siwash technique. He wasn't aware there was a human in the district. We approached within forty feet before he heard us and stood up. We gave the meat to the pilot, took the head and cape down to the airplane, and returned to Anchorage. We had been absent from the hotel nineteen hours. Total cost of the hunt was $250.

"And I used to think," Count said, "that a northern big-game hunt was a major operation. Careful advance planning, map study, painstaking selection of equipment. . . . Yet we go out with a couple of tin cans and a box of sandwiches and have to wake a moose up to see where to shoot him. If I hadn't been there I wouldn't believe it."

In the Alaska gamelands, finest left on the continent, are nine species of big game—moose, the bighorn sheep, deer, mountain goats, caribou, and black, brown, grizzly and polar bear. On the list of small game are snowshoe rabbits, Arctic hare, three species of ptarmigan, eleven species of grouse and many species of waterfowl. In addition, nearly all the lakes and streams teem with fish. There are rainbows, cutthroats, Dolly Varden, lake trout, grayling, northern pike, the five species of Pacific salmon and the little-known giant Arctic sheefish which the Russians called "white salmon."

It is a bountiful land, one in which a gun and some fishing tackle will give you eating that celebrated restaurants can't match. It is country for the siwash hunter, because with meat, berries, fish, mushrooms and birds for the taking, why should a man overburden himself with store grub?

Guides find it remarkable how soon city-soft sportsmen can adapt to rough-and-ready ways. After a day or two they not only don't mind sleeping in the open, washing in ice-cold creeks and eating from a frying pan, they enjoy it. They take particular pride in proving that the blood of cave men runs in their veins.

Tex Cobb and I once made a grizzly hunt in the Talkeetna Range with an architect who convinced us, once and for all, that you seldom can gauge a sportsman's toughness by his behavior in town. This dude, before we got him out into the wilds, didn't like anything. He complained about the telephone service, the way the laundry ironed his shirts, and even the dust in the streets. In his opinion the local barbers were all fugitives from the hardrock mines. Waiters winced when they saw him coming, and he told the hotel manager that the lumpy mattress in his room resembled a cross-section of a terminal moraine. Weary of apologizing for him, we took him out of town as soon as we could. Alaska is still a frontier land, and complaints about service get you little save unpopularity.

"This pilgrim," Tex said grimly, "is gonna be a pain in the neck. He's the kind o' hunter that makes ya think, doggone hit, that there must be easier ways o' makin' a livin'."

We were mistaken about him. The guy was a natural—a tough, rugged, willing cookie, as easy to get along with in hunting country as he had been difficult to please in town. He ate what we gave him, bathed every morning in water that would have cooled off a polar bear, gave up shaving, and threw his hat away and went bareheaded. He was a siwash hunter from away back. But it was something that happened at our first camp that especially won him our respect.

We had flown to a lake between the north and middle forks of Montana Creek, and had packed over an open mountain to a campsite in a stand of timber on a nameless tributary stream. As we intended to hunt farther back in the ranges there was no point in taking precautions here, so Tex went out to shoot some ptarmigan while I cut wood and built a fire.

"I'll make some spruce bough beds," the architect said. "Nothing like it for a good night's sleep. Beats any of those fancy inner-spring models. It's a man's bed."

Well, he made the bough mattresses, and mine was the worst I ever tried to sleep on. There were limbs in it the size of an ax handle. They were placed crosswise, eagle nest fashion, and had knots on them. Tex and I tossed and turned, but the tenderfoot slumbered peacefully. And his bough bed wasn't any better than the ones he had made for us. I could see butt ends of saplings sticking out of it like baseball bats. If it hadn't been for this I would have suspected a practical joke, for it didn't seem possible that anybody could expect humans to sleep on such rib-jabbing, spine-corrugating piles of mismatched brush.

At last Tex gave up. He rose, placed some wood on the fire, lit his pipe, and sat down resignedly against a windfall, sleeping bag around his shoulders.

"What's the trouble?" the architect asked presently, turning over with a yawn, obviously comfortable as a cat on a cushion. "Can't you sleep?"

"I ain't decided yet," Tex said dryly. "I'll tackle hit ag'in purty soon an' let ya know. But first I'm gonna sit here a while an' rest. I reckon I ain't as tough as some o' you whang-leather fellers from the city."

It shouldn't be assumed. I hasten to point out, that to make a big-game hunt in Alaska you must be a hard-as-nails athlete. The majority of sportsmen who come North, in fact, are men past their prime. Average age is about fifty-three. Their legs aren't as good as they used to be, they puff on the upgrades, and a good many have watch-chain paunches. But they do all right. The guides estimate their capabilities and plan the hunts accordingly.

One May I made a brown bear hunt down Cook Inlet with a 72-year-old retired engineer who told me, before we left town, that doctors had warned him against the trip. His school-teacher daughter, fearful the exertion would cause a collapse, had tried to persuade him to go south instead. She wanted him to rent a cottage near the ocean and sit on the beach in the sunshine. When he refused she told him, tearfully, that he ought to have his head examined.

"Let her go sit on the beach herself," he snorted. "I tried it once and it was awful. Nothing to do, and kids with buckets fall over your feet."

We flew down the inlet to Redoubt Bay, landed on the tideflat, and the engineer made himself at home under the wide-spreading branches of the big Sitka spruce we selected as our weather shelter. During the following week he dug razor clams and cooked them, caught husky king salmon at the mouth of a nearby creek, and took giant spider crabs in a trap we borrowed from a commercial fisherman. As the season was late the brown bear weren't yet out of hibernation, but the engineer said he could wait. He said he was having a gorgeous time and would just as soon stay here all summer.

By now he was beginning to look as rough-and-tumble as a sourdough woods tramp. His pants were muck-plastered, sparks from the campfire had burnt holes in his shirt, his nose was so sunburnt that it was peeling like a frost-cracked birch tree, and he was cultivating a rakish goatee and mustache. If his doctors had placed him on a diet, he was ignoring it here. He ate whatever he pleased, whenever he was hungry, and as much as he cared to.

"Wish that red-headed daughter of mine could see me now," he chuckled one morning as he sat watching a bright ten-pound salmon broiling over a bed of coals. "She would have a Grade-A fit. One look at these wonderful pants and this marvelous shirt would give her hysterics."

A few days later, in the big crimson glow of a windy evening, he got the break we were waiting for. He had taken his rifle and fishing rod and started out to a pool in which we had seen rainbow trout jumping. Suddenly, as he topped a grassy rise, I saw him halt and jerk the rifle to his shoulder. He shot three times as I ran toward him.

Coming across the creek, splashing and bawling, was a brown bear. I will never know whether the animal was charging or only trying to reach the cover of brush on our side of the stream. It reached the near bank and bounded over the rim, a huge, shaggy apparition in the slant red light, and as it did so the engineer shot again. The animal dropped in the saw grass.

It was a very old bear, its teeth worn to yellow stumps, its claws cracked and scurfy, but it had an excellent pelt, thick and dark, beautifully prime. The engineer's delight at having taken the trophy is one of the grand memories I have of big-game hunting.

"I can't wait," he said, grinning triumphantly, "to tell my know-it-all daughter about this. Because you know what the bear was doing when I first saw him? He was sitting over there in the sunlight looking at his toes. Just shows you what's likely to happen when an old feller gets lazy and starts moping around on a beach."

The cost of a ten-day siwash-style hunt, including airplane transportation to and from the hunting country and all equipment except your rifle and binoculars, runs about $800. It is wise to make arrangements with a guide well in advance to enable him to fit your hunt into his season's schedule. If you don't know any Alaska guides, the Game Commission at Juneau will supply you with the current list of licensed men.

For a mountain sheep you should arrive in the territory not later than August 18. For moose, bear, mountain goats and caribou, August 29. There is also a spring season for bear, and you should be in the hunting area by May 20 to take advantage of it.

Bring the clothes you would wear on an autumn or spring hunt in the northern states—that is, medium-weight wool pants, shirt, underwear and socks; a light slicker; canvas jacket with a wool inner lining; leather boots or shoepacks with rubber or composition soles (hobnails are noisy and leather soles become dangerously slippery on the grassy hillsides); a pair of buckskin gloves; and your favorite shooting hat.

A good belt knife and a .22 pistol chambered for the long-rifle, high-velocity cartridge are necessary items. Binoculars are indispensable and I suggest you buy the best available. Most hunters get good results with eight-power binoculars, but some use them in ten- or twelve-power.

Most popular rifles here are the .30-06 and the .300 magnum, with the .270 a close runner-up. It would be unwise to bring a rifle of smaller caliber than the .270 as you never know in these game ranges when you will encounter a brown bear or grizzly, and Alaska bruins are difficult to stop. Sight your gun in at home so you won't have to blaze away in the hunting country. By all means buy a sturdy leather carrying case for it, for without such protection a gun takes a beating in the various traveling conveyances.

You should, before you buy your ticket North, acquire at least a fair working idea as to what constitutes a desirable game head or pelt. Often, especially when you jump game in heavy cover, your guide won't have time to decide on the animal's points as a potential trophy and give you the benefit of his advice. Moose antlers, to measure up to average trophy standard, should have a spread of sixty inches, with thirty-five points; caribou, forty-five-inch spread with fifteen points; white bighorn sheep horns, basal circumference of fourteen inches and a length of thirty-nine inches around the outside of the curl; mountain goat horns, a length of nine inches; a brown bear pelt should square nine feet, a grizzly pelt eight feet.

Tex Cobb provided a conclusion for this piece. We had returned to town from a moose hunt, and Tex had remarked to some tourists at the hotel that the moose we had killed would weigh around 1,000 pounds. One man, who apparently had done some big-game hunting, said that carrying all that meat to camp must have been a tremendous task.

"Shucks, no" Tex said. "Whad'ya think we are, dudes? We didn't pack no meat to camp. We moved camp to the meat, siwash style."

Life in a Moose Pasture

A tenderfoot's not the only hunter who can get fouled up on a moose hunt. For instance, take the case of "Wildhorse" Liggett and his $30 bedspring.

Twenty years ago, when I mushed a dog team up into the Susitna Valley and built myself a trapline headquarters cabin here at Goose Creek on the Alaska Railroad, this was as poor a moose range as a man ever camped in.

You could wear your moccasins out scouring the ridges and tundra flats without finding a fresh track. Even the Indians were seldom able to kill a moose. They subsisted chiefly on fish and beaver, while the few whites in the region ate fish and store-bought grub, of which the standard items were sow bosom, beans and sourdough bread. It was hungry country. But a big change was coming.

During the hot, dry summers of 1923-24, forest fires had swept through the valley, and in their wake was growing a dense nurse crop of aspen and birch—potential moose feed in limitless quantity. Today, thanks to this green sea of ideal browse, the valley is probably the finest moose range the world has ever seen.

An accurate moose census would be impossible, so nobody knows how many thousands of the splendid animals are in the Susitna herds. But it's a fact that at times here on our once-barren Goose Creek burns moose are almost embarrassingly plentiful.

You could ask my neighbor "Wildhorse" Liggett.

Wildhorse is a busy, 130-pound ex-Nevada bronc-twister who has homesteaded a quarter section of grassland a half-mile up the creek. He plans to raise beef cattle, possibly on the assumption that where moose can thrive critters ought to. But buying breeding stock and building fences runs into money. So Wildhorse is keenly interested in all methods of picking up an honest dollar. Last year he took a whack at dude-wrangling.

He snowshoed down to my place one frosty silver-and-blue morning just before the November season opened and announced, grinning all over, that he had booked his first hunter. The chap was a resident sportsman named Harrington who had written, Wildhorse said, that he wanted to kill a fat bull and could, if absolutely necessary, devote ten days to the project. Wildhorse was elated. The going rate hereabouts for bed, board and guide service is $30 a day. So naturally, according to Wildhorse's arithmetic, his gross take for the hunt was going to be $300 even.

His own bunk was made of spruce poles with a layer of wild hay for a mattress. But figuring that Harrington would no doubt be accustomed to softer sleeping, Wildhorse had sent to town for a set of bedsprings. The springs were going to cost him $30 landed here, but what the hell, he said, a man had to spend money to make money, didn't he?

Opening morning came in cold and violent, with a williwaw wind screaming off the glaciers of Mt. McKinley. Wildhorse and I were waiting beside the track when the snow-plastered train stopped at the bridge to deliver Harrington, his baggage, and the set of bedsprings. Harrington proved to be an amiable, elderly fellow who looked frail for a snowshoe hunt in this savage weather.

I lashed the baggage onto my packboard, Wildhorse took the bedsprings on his and we headed up the trail, which ran most of the way through a sheltering belt of timber. With our webs creaking in powder snow, and the icy wind booming overhead like a jug band playing the Hallelujah Chorus, we made good time despite the cumbersome bedsprings until we came to the rim of a frozen beaver pond.

Here Harrington halted abruptly, pointing to the trails of four moose. "Should we follow them?" "Naw. They heard us an' took off," Wildhorse said. "Let 'em go. There's plenty o' moose around here."

Hardly were the words out of his mouth when, up at the brushy inlet of the pond, there was a ringing snort and a crashing of frozen branches. Four bulls had spooked from their beds in the lee of a tangled willow thicket and were standing there staring at us, poised for flight. The hunt was over and Wildhorse knew it, but he wanted to make certain that Harrington would kill the best bull. So, motioning us to stay where we were, he stepped out onto the glare ice of the pond for an unobstructed look at the animals. He should have known better.

The birch frames of his siwash webs were polished smooth as glass, and he had taken only a few strides from the sheltering timber when a shrieking williwaw gust pounced on him. The gust grabbed the sail-like paper-wrapped bedsprings hitched on his packboard and flung him, as out of control as a wing-shot bat, fifty feet across the pond into a mess of beaver-killed snags sticking up out of the ice. He landed flat on his back with a limb speared through the bedsprings and another through the babiche of one of his webs. The four moose hadn't moved. Like Harrington and me, I guess they were too astonished to move.

Wildhorse made a valiant attempt to salvage his dignity. Wrestling himself free of the wind-whipped bedsprings, he sat up an pointed dazedly at the animals.

"Shoot the one with the big horns," he shouted across the wind. "He's got the biggest head."

Neither of us knew which bull he meant, and Harrington didn't wait to find out. His .300 blasted and the nearest bull, now in full flight, dropped with a broken neck. I helped Wildhorse butcher the kill, then took the load of baggage on to his cabin and returned home.

The following afternoon I heard the southbound passenger train stop at the bridge. A little later Wildhorse dropped in. I was having coffee with "Starvation" Smith, who lives with me and helps out on the place between prospecting trips, and Wildhorse joined us. Harrington, he stated glumly, had gone back to Anchorage with his moose meat and trophy.

"Big deal," he said. "My first perfessional hunt, an' what do I get out of it? A miser'ble thirty bucks."

"Cheer up," Starvation said. "It could of been worse. Shucks, you got them bedsprings paid fer, didn't ya?"

We don't get rich living among the moose and the moose hunters, but we have a lot of fun.

For example, consider the case of Mrs. Bradley, a comely redheaded huntress who set out to show her husband an item or two.

Starvation and I had climbed onto the roof of the lean-to back room of the house to patch a hole. It was a bitter crystalline day. Starvation had heated a can of tar and we were swabbing the stuff on the patch, when I glanced up and saw a moose walk into the clearing. It was a bull. A nice one. He sported a fair set of antlers and looked as if he had come through the rut with some tallow on his ribs.

From our elevated vantage point we watched him stalk over and begin feeding on a pile of birch tops we'd stacked to burn next spring. He could see the house, and if he had tried he could have seen us. Moreover, if he had a brain in his head he must have known that the season was open, because for days the valley had resounded with gunfire like the Aberdeen Proving Ground. But still, there he was, practically under our noses, a fine, fat bull asking for trouble.

"I'll keep an eye on him," Starvation promised in a hoarse whisper, "while you break the news to our stove-up lady hunter."

The lady hunter was the flame-tressed wife of Bill Bradley, a construction engineer with the wind and stamina of a marathon champion who had come up from town four days earlier to kill a moose for the winter larder. She'd had a rough time here. So eager was Bill to bushwhack a moose that he had inadvertently given her a workout on webs that would have made a hardened Indian musher look at his hole card. So she was now here at the house unhappily nursing a dramatic combination of snowshoe cramps, chilblains, thong-blisters and general exhaustion which, she claimed, would have interested the Mayo Brothers. Bill, still going strong, was somewhere out in the timber continuing his search for a moose.

When I hastened down off the roof I found Mrs. Bradley in the kitchen filling a hot-water bag. She was clad in pajamas and a silk robe, and looked hostile enough to have battled a jaguar barehanded. I said, "Would you like to go up on the roof and shoot a moose?" She said, "What's he doing on the roof?"

Following this cultural exchange, I explained where the moose was and told her that, if she hurried and was able to climb a ladder, now was her chance to make a kill ahead of her rugged snowshoe-artist husband.

Without lingering to put on a coat, cap or mittens, she hobbled outside and started up the ladder. I pushed while Starvation got hold of her hand and pulled. Sixty seconds later she was on the roof.

The bull was still with us. He stood on the near side of the brushpile, half facing us, chomping birch limbs as placidly as if there weren't a hunter in the whole Susitna Valley. I handed Mrs.

Bradley her .270 and she sat down and slipped the safety latch. One thing I have observed about female hunters, when they are sore about something they can shoot. Mrs. Bradley was shaking, probably from buck fever as much as the biting cold, but she still had that wounded panther look in her eye. With the whiplash bang of the shot I saw hair fly from the money spot at the point of the bull's shoulder. He raised his head, looked at us, and died on his feet, pitching forward into the brushpile that he should have bypassed in the first place.

Starvation and I were congratulating Mrs. Bradley when we noticed something that had previously escaped our attention. She was sitting in the pool of tar we had applied to the roof patch. And the tar was still slightly soft. Unaware of this, she stood up laughing and limped over to the ladder.

"Little does my husband know," she said triumphantly, "what a surprise is in store for him. He'll be positively popeyed."

"Yes'm," Starvation agreed, covertly glancing at the tar on the backside of her robe. "I expect he sure will be, at that."

I have yet to catch myself yearning nostalgically for the old days when we had Goose Creek to ourselves and there was no annual stampede of moose hunters up here. But if I ever do, I know the remedy for it. I will remind myself of the legion of characters we'd have missed knowing if this hadn't become a moose heaven. Major Walters, for instance.

The Major is a quaint, dreamy-eyed retired army dentist who visits us each autumn so he can call moose. That's right, call moose, so help me. In the opinion of most guides and experienced hunters, moose calling is strictly a stunt, useful only when nothing else will get you a shot. But to the Major it is the ultimate refinement of the sport of moose hunting. Anybody, he contends, can sneak up on a bull and dry-gulch him, but to outsmart the animal with a birch-bark horn takes talent.

Whatever it takes, the Major has plenty of it, along with persistence. He isn't especially interested in trophies, and says he can take moose meat or leave it alone. What he wants is just to get out there in the winey-smelling, frost-painted thickets by himself and grunt, wail and moan through a bark horn, waiting for some rut-simple bull to come charging up with the intention of challenging him to fight, or making love to him, depending on the call employed. As you can imagine, he has some bizarre experiences.

For our sins, Starvation and I once got suckered into one of the Major's bark-horn performances. This was on a chill, beautiful afternoon at the beginning of the September season.

Starvation and I had mushed up the creek to look for a young mulligan bull. We were out of meat, and figured to make a kill now on Starvation's ticket, then shoot another bull on my ticket in November if we needed to. But it wasn't our day to score. We sighted some cows and calves, and one venerable slat-ribbed bull who looked as if he had been around when the Russians owned Alaska. Nothing eligible for the meat house. Toward mid-afternoon we gave up and started home.

We were walking along the edge of a high bank above the creek flats, enjoying the sunshine and the brilliant aspens and birches, when below us in the timber we heard a moose making war talk. He was crosswind and close at hand, no more than 100 yards off.

As we maneuvered, trying to get a look at him, he kept sounding off in the most bellicose manner. Deep, chesty, ventriloquial grunts. Aghr-r-r-uh! Gar-r-r-oof! I mean, he was advertising to all and sundry what a hard customer he was, and what a swath he could mow among the cows. Then he sneezed. Starvation and I exchanged startled glances.

"Do moose sneeze?" Starvation asked.

I said I had never before heard one sneeze.

"I'll bet-cha," Starvation grinned as inspiration smote him, "that's the Major down there. Catchin' a cold, prob'ly, an' sneezed into his doggone horn before he could stop hisself."

It was a likely theory, only it didn't hold up. A few minutes later, as we watched and listened critically, there was a commotion in a flame-yellow wolf willow thicket and out walked not the Major, but a slab-sided, sway-bellied old bull similar to the ancient we had seen up the creek. For a bull of his advanced years, he really had ideas. He fought a sham battle with a currant bush, raking at it with his knobby antlers and rearing to strike savagely at it with his big splay hoofs. Next he pawed a hole in the ground, and after squatting over it, knelt down to rub his shoulders and antler blades in the urine-soaked mud. This bit of grooming accomplished, he charged a spruce tree a foot through and tried to push it over.

We were about to abandon him to his fun when, coming from deeper in the timber, there was a sound that brought all three of us to instant attention—an answering challenge grunt, hoarse and threatening.

"I hope this one's a mulligan moose," Starvation said. "Dammit, they can't all be ol' pelters like we been seein'."

The grunting back on the timber came closer, and the closer it got, the less warlike became the actions of our antiquated mud-smeared friend. He fidgeted nervously, and kept trying the wind, although it was blowing the wrong way to tell him anything. Finally, frightened and making no bones about it, he took off in headlong flight, plowing through the multicolored thickets like a runaway bulldozer. We made some comments about his phony courage, but it developed we were libeling him. In a moment a loud hallo sounded from a spruce thicket, and into view came the Major, bark horn slung from a thong around his neck, rifle in one hand and his hunter's red cap in the other. He had spotted us and was waving the cap energetically so we wouldn't mistake him for a moose.

"You had me fooled there for a while," he said sheepishly when he had come up the bank to us. "But then I got to thinking about that sneeze, and decided I wasn't conversing with a moose. All of us getting crossed up that way," he declared, "just shows you, by George, what a difficult sport moose calling is."

"Life in a moose pasture!" I said, shaking my head.

"Yeah," Starvation chuckled. "But you know something?" I wouldn't trade places, by gosh, with any zookeeper in the country."

Me either.

Saga of the Red One

PART 1

Beginning an exciting new Alaska serial.
The violent tale of master wolfer
against king wolf—a struggle only death could end.

The trouble started on a pretty spring day, when the Red One was yet a pup. Cottonwood buds were bursting, filling the bright air with their pungent fragrance. Golden sunshine was melting the last of the snowdrifts off the southern slopes of the great Susitna Valley, and clamorous skeins of waterfowl were winging their way across the brilliantly blue sky.

It was spring in the northern wilds, a time for gaiety and adventurous impulses. Especially it was a time for young things to try their mettle against the strange, new world that held surprises for them all.

So this spring morning the Red One, taking advantage of his mother's absence on a foraging expedition, ventured alone for the first time from the ridgeside den in which he and his eight sisters and brothers had been born.

Although he was still a milk-sucking youngster, his eyes still puppy-blue, he was the largest and boldest of the litter. When he stepped out of the den into the sunlight, the size and heft of him, the unafraid tilt of his head, foreshadowed the infamous role he was to play in this broad, birch-forested valley. In fact, before he had progressed ten feet, weaving a bit on his wobbly puppy legs, the Red One encountered an antagonist.

Though the wind in the budding trees and the brawling riffles of Goose Creek were making springtime music for him, and there were many fascinating things to see, such as clouds and butterflies, the Red One had eyes only for the creature confronting him.

From the viewpoint of a puppy, the creature was a formidable one. A rough customer indeed. Big, dangerous game, and no mistake. It was a long-tailed, profane, mountain magpie, with a sinful look in his eye and a heart full of arrogance. The bird was busily scavenging through the usual wolf-den midden of gnawed bones, grouse and ptarmigan feathers, tatters of rabbit fur and scraps of fly-blown meat. And when he saw the Red One emerge from the dark mouth of the den, he regarded the pup insolently. To him, the red-coated wolf youngster was an uncouth brat of a lesser breed, a bumpkin, a prime target for what he regarded as his infinitely sharper intelligence.

Then the Red One snarled. True, it was a falsetto snarl, but there was a savageness in it that the magpie failed to recognize. The bird squawked back jeeringly and half turned to examine a weathered marmot skull for possible scraps of sun-dried brains. As he did so, a woolly, red tornado hit him. Seconds later, the magpie took off down the hillside in a crazy, stammering flight, a flash of black and white hard put to stay in the air on account of no tail feathers. His long tail, of which he had been inordinately proud, was now clamped between the Red One's jaws. It was the pup's first victory.

This was a morning of violence. Two miles down the creek, in a grass flat, the Red One's mother, a tawny young bitch who maybe wasn't as bright as she should have been, made the mistake of stepping on the pan of one of Lobo Smith's traps.

The blunder had come about typically. A strange and fascinating scent had lured her into an innocent-appearing willow clump above the creek. As she was trying to identify the scent, the muscles of her loins rippling with delight, she had put her left front foot down precisely where Lobo Smith knew that she would. The exciting scent had come from a bottle that Lobo carried in the pocket of his caribou shirt. The secret formula was one of Lobo's chief stocks in trade. It had tolled many other bemused wolf matrons to their deaths.

What made the matter worse for the tawny bitch was that Lobo knew she was in his trap. For at the moment, he was sitting on a hillside 400 yards downwind, watching her with his binoculars. He had purpose. He wanted her to lead him to her den. Lobo well knew that he'd get as much bounty money for a wolf pup's scalp as he would for the scalp of an adult wolf—$50 a kill, whether the wolf happened to be two weeks or sixteen years old. So he hoped to find a den full of pups—a first-class financial windfall. Lobo recalled the time, up in the Talkeetnas, when old Tex Cobb had astonished himself and delighted his creditors by digging fifteen pups out of one den and scalping the lot of them. The only trouble, as Lobo knew from experience, is that wolf dens are difficult to locate. They are trickily situated for maximum concealment. The best way to find one, Lobo discovered, is to trap a bitch and let her show you the way. Sometimes the trick worked, sometimes it didn't.

So Lobo was deeply interested as he watched the actions of the tawny, young bitch down there in the sprouting grass flat. He had a special reason. Today he was going to be married, and he could use some extra honeymoon money. Right now he was feeling proud about the way things were turning out.

Ten miles distant, over the snow-patched hills, preparations for the marriage had been in progress for days at Yellowbird Village. The girl was named Maria. She was the daughter of the Yellowbird trader, white-bearded old "Ptarmigan" Dunbar, and at the age of seventeen was already a gold-bronze flame of a woman, an authentic beauty, made more beautiful by the commingled bloods of many races in her veins.

There was in Maria the blood of the wild promyschleniki sea-otter hunters, who came with Bering and Baranof from Siberia, and who had found solace in the native Alaska Indian women. There was in her the blood of the Yankee whalers, and that of the gold-stampeders who overran the land when the Klondike was struck, and also that of the Chinese and Filipinos who were brought north to harvest the sea and put salmon in tin cans. Maria was, in short, a true mestiza, a Lola Montez of the deep backwoods, with perhaps a better body, voice, and walk than the great Lola possessed at her sultry best.

But Maria was also a spitfire. Lobo himself regarded her as potentially dangerous as a grenade with the pin pulled.

So, while congratulating himself on the way things were going for him today, Lobo was nevertheless in some haste to get this den-hunting, pup-killing matter completed. For he was convinced that if anything went wrong and he was so much as five minutes late at the church, the lovely Maria would take him apart with her fingernails.

Down in the grass flat, the tawny pain-shocked wolf bitch, fighting the trap and the spruce-pole drag, went first to water, as they always do. Then, after drinking and trying to cool her crushed foreleg in the icy water, she went back across the flat to a willow thicket, with some notion of hiding while she considered her frightful predicament. She had no success here.

Lobo had contrived the drag cleverly. It was light enough so that she could move along with it at a fair pace while she was in the open. But when she ventured into cover, it caught in the brush. She attacked the trap again until her mouth was bloody and her fighting teeth were broken. Then, judgment drained out of her. She knew—as all wolf bitches with pups know from ancient instinct—that if she returned to the den she would doubtless be followed, and that this would imperil her young.

But pain and fear won over judgment, and, suddenly, she whirled and headed across the flat in a straight line toward the den. Lobo, watching with his binoculars, gave a grunt of relief and satisfaction.

At the den, meantime the Red One was exploring. Everything was new and wonderful to him: the warm, spring sunshine, the great blue arch of the sky, the duet the creek and the wind were playing, the manifold scents filling the air. But then, abruptly, he became aware of danger.

The whispering, small breeze off the creek bottoms had brought a scent that caused him to crouch instinctively. It was human scent, and while the Red One had never before winded a man, every gene and chromosome of his being warned him that a great enemy was approaching. So he crouched, and whirled back into the concealment of a shattered gray-green boulder just beyond the den's mouth.

The man-scent was that of Lobo Smith, who had got the direction line to the den, and had hastened ahead of the plodding, tawny bitch. He had prudently refrained from killing the bitch, because, if he failed to find the den on his own, he would have to return and establish the direction line from her again.

As he came up through the cottonwoods now, Lobo knew that his professional sagacity had not let him down. He smelled the den before he saw it. In spite of the stench he was glad that wolf mothers bring meat home in their bellies, and disgorge it for the pups; and then if there is a surplus, they bury it at convenient spots near the den's mouth. The half-digested meat had putrefied, and swarms of blowflies haunted the caches.

So, when Lobo's wilderness-trained nose caught the smell of the rotting meat caches, he congratulated himself. He was already, in imagination, spending a pocketful of bounty money, and spending it honeymooning with the beautiful Maria of Yellowbird.

Lobo figured there ought to be, anyhow, five pups in the den. The trapped bitch looked young, and the young ones didn't throw big litters such as the old bitches did. But still, five bounties at $50 apiece added up to $250. And then, there was the bounty he'd collect for mama, plus what he might get for mama's unprime spring pelt, if he caught some tourist in a generous mood. Maybe $350 for this morning's work. Not bad. Not bad at all.

So, happy with himself, Lobo went up through the willow brush and the high-bush cranberries, looking for a pole to twist the pups out of the den, and hoping this wouldn't be one of those damn crooked dens he'd have to dig into.

Thus the Red One, crouching behind the shattered boulder beyond the den, beheld his first human, and, in a moment, witnessed more of the day's violence.

Lobo wasted no time. To his satisfaction, he saw that the den wasn't a crooked one, and he had spotted a suitable ten-foot aspen pole. He cut the pole with his belt knife, trimmed off the limbs, and split the butt end.

He then shoved the pole into the den, and felt a squirming mass of puppy flesh crowded against the rear wall. He twisted the pole, winding the split end into the woolly pelt of the pups, and in a moment dragged the squalling wolf youngster out into the sunlight, and killed it with a blow across the head with the back of his knife.

One by one, then, he brought the wolflings out, introduced them to death, and stuffed the limp carcasses into the sack of his Indian packboard. This accomplished, he shouldered the packboard and headed back to collect the tawny, bitch wolf.

But just as he started down the hillside, a curious thing happened. In a crooked hangman's cottonwood above him, a magpie began squawking hysterically. Lobo glanced up, and observed that the bird was the only tailless magpie he could recall. Also he noticed that the magpie wasn't sounding off at him, but at something behind a shattered gray-green boulder close beyond the den, something out of his range of vision. Interested, Lobo stepped toward the rock.

There he saw a sun-cast shadow on the dusty ground at the farthest corner of the rock. It was the shadow of a wolf pup. It was immediately obvious to Lobo why the pup was there. Lobo had the entire plot figured out. Mama absent from home. Adventurous wolf pup exploring outside the den. Adventurous but too young and dumb to know that it was casting a shadow, and that you can't trust a mountain magpie. Lobo dropped the packboard, drew his old tape-handled .22 wolf pistol, and made a fast clever-footed run toward the boulder.

But Lobo didn't do any better with the Red One than had the traitorous long-tailed bird. Lobo was a fair gunhand, but the sun was in his eyes. He got in only one clear shot and saw hair fly from the Red One's forehead, and then the pup was gone into the tangled high-bush cranberry thickets.

Professional wolfer that he was, Lobo gave up hard when he was on the trail of a scalp. He scoured the thickets for an hour searching for the pup, but failed to find him. Then, cussing bitterly as he consulted his watch, he mushed back down the creek to kill and pelt the tawny bitch. Here he encountered additional trouble.

The bitch had tried to swim the creek with the trap and drag, and had been carried downstream into a right-angled jam of spruce and cottonwood logs, where she had drowned. It took Lobo another half-hour to find her.

The delay put a large flaw in his marriage plans.

By the time he arrived at the log church at Yellowbird he was two hours late, and the church was deserted. The gold-bronze Maria could not be found, and Father O'Brien, who was to have married them, informed Lobo that she had canceled the ceremony. The good father was sympathetic, but his manner indicated that a bridegroom ought to place his wedding above the matter of killing a wolf or two.

So there they were, the violent and fateful happenings of this pretty spring day. Nine wolves had died. The Red One had become motherless. Lobo was a jilted bridegroom. Maria was in seclusion, and her father, the white-bearded "Ptarmigan" Dunbar, had a grim and dangerous look in his eye.

Lobo went to his cabin and changed into what were to have been his wedding clothes. A bit later he stalked into the Yellowbird Bar. All dressed up in his new store-bought clothes, smelling of bay rum, with his shoes polished to an unprecedented gloss, he leaned against the bar and regarded himself somberly in the mirror. When the bartender came over to ask him what he would have, he heard the wolfer gritting, "I'll kill that little red s.o.b. if it takes the rest of my life."

"Huh?" the bartender asked.

"If it takes the rest of my life," Lobo repeated.

Saga of the Red One

PART 2

Lobo Smith swore he'd kill the Red one, and now he was sure how to do it. But some things you can't always figure.

On the morning of his scheduled wedding day, Lobo Smith, master wolfer, decided to get a few wolf scalps for bounty. He trapped a tawny bitch, then found her den. Here, as the Red One looked on, Lobo killed all the rest of the litter. The Red One eluded Lobo, and delayed him so much that Maria canceled the wedding.

The subarctic summer had progressed to the Moon of Foolish Wolf Puppies, the golden month of August when wolf puppies are old enough to leave their mothers, but still too awkward to keep out of trouble. And though the Red One had no mother to leave, he was finding that he had a large talent for getting into trouble.

It was midnight. The sun had just rolled behind the incredible turquoise bulk of Mt. McKinley, which loomed above the birch forests and the hammered-silver pattern of lakes and streams to the northward. This was a midnight filled with the music of wind and water, and with enough light reflecting from the glowing sky above McKinley so you could thread a buckskin needle. It was a midnight chock-full of imminent drama.

Suddenly, on the blue wall of the Goose Creek valley, wolf song arose. The baritone howls and brays began afar, then lifted to full choral volume in the middle distance. And then, seeming to shake the earth, they were picked up at the cockscomb crest of a sandstone ridge above the plunging creek. At least twenty wolves were communicating—pack members of the mightiest race of timber wolves the planet has seen since the Age of Ice. The great males have been known to weigh 175 pounds, and leave tracks five inches long.

The Red One had mourned himself to sleep. He lay curled up on the side of the sandstone ridge, near the mouth of the den where he was born. From this spot he had watched Lobo Smith, the master wolfer, kill his eight brothers and sisters, and scalp them for the bounty money the territory would pay.

Scouting from here on wobbly puppy legs, the Red One had found, down the creek, the skinned carcass of the tawny bitch who had been his mother—and had identified Lobo Smith's scent there. So the ridge held dread for him. It was haunted with terror. But, also, it was the only place of security he had ever known. He had returned to it often through the weeks, whenever he could find time from the urgent business of keeping his belly full.

But, tonight, there were other enemies.

Jerked abruptly awake when the wild chorus of wolf song echoed through the valley, the Red One stood up, shook the sand out of his pelt, and cocked his head, listening intently as the signal howls converged toward the ridge crest. Then involuntarily his puppy throat swelled, and he responded to the primeval music. His was a thin, puppy yodel, lacking in timbre and volume, but it was heard.

It was heard by the First One,. the dark, gray-muzzled matriarch of the clan, his great-grandmother. She came ghosting toward him through the twilit timber, a gaunt, ominous shadow among shadows.

She was the First One, the dowager queen. Her daughters had established their dens away from her den, and then their daughters continued the pattern, forming a society of related wolves.

The male wolves, after their first year, were the guardians of the clan's bloodline, and of its hunting rights. They were the warriors—the tough guys.

But on this spruce-fragrant midnight in the Moon of Foolish Wolf Puppies, the warriors of the Red One's clan weren't protecting their bloodline or their hunting rights. They were just being ornery. A family of four Toklat grizzlies was on the creek, and the warriors aimed to give them trouble.

Mama Grizzly came pigeon-toeing along the crest of the sandstone ridge, upwind, followed in single file by a hulking two-year-old and three fat, woolly, spring cubs. She was an ugly-looking slope-backed character. Unshed patches of last year's hair still clung to her back.

Disturbed by the encircling wolf song, she rolled her shoulders and rumbled nervously, deep in her chest. Then, from dead ahead on the ridge, the night wind brought her a gust of scent—wolf scent. She reared, wrinkling her hoglike snout and snuffling anxiously. Then she realized it was the scent of a puppy. At this same instant the Red One tried his voice again. And as he did, the she-bear spotted him.

When the Red One beheld an avalanche of grizzly fury descending upon him, he tried to dodge past her to reach the safety of the den. He wasn't fast enough.

Then down the broken crest of the sandstone ridge came the gray-muzzled matriarch wolf, covering ground like the shadow of a swooping bird. She arrowed in from the side, and seemed only to brush the she-grizzly in passing. But the poised pawstroke faltered, and missed. And the next instant the bear whirled, bellowing in pain and astonishment.

The raking teeth of the old dowager wolf had laid open her flank for six inches, as cleanly as if it had been done with a knife, so that blood was spurting and a pink bulge of intestines showed.

The Red One took advantage of the chance that fate and his great-grandmother had given him. He crawled under a windfall, and crowded into the angle of crumbling sandstone behind it.

But then, as the she-bear spun to meet the next onslaught of the matriarch, the Red One, through some deep clan instinct, flashed from under the windfall and sank his teeth into the great grizzly's paw. Death reached for him then, but found the matriarch instead.

She was old, and her reflexes were not what they used to be. But she flashed in, and the huge paw struck her out of the air. She bounced against the sandstone ledge, sobbing her life out.

The red-coated wolf puppy tried for the grizzly's throat, and missed. And as the bear lifted her piledriver paw against the youngster, a ton of wolf fury came down the ridge. Twenty warrior wolves flowed over her.

She went down on her back, popping her teeth, bawling and striking when she should have been dead. She regained her feet, shook them off, and lurched down the hillside.

Reaching the grassy cutbank of the creek, she bounded into the water and splashed 200 yards downstream into a back eddy, where she sat with only her head above the surface, the icy coldness of the glacier-fed stream soothing her many wounds.

The wolves had just finished off two litters of her grizzly tribe, and she was not certain about her own chances. Above her on the bank prowled the twenty warrior wolves.

Meanwhile the Red One had come down from the sandstone ridge to enter the fray. But before he arrived at the back eddy, where the she-grizzly was at bay, a gaunt shape drifted out of the long, red shadows of midnight, and confronted him. It was a warrior wolf, coal black, except for a dirty white patch on his chest, and he was berserk.

He stared at the puppy with his brilliant, slant, topaz eyes, set to kill—set to kill anything. But down the side of the sandstone ridge tottered the matriarch. Her life blood was pumping out; it was a miracle that she still lived. The kill-crazy warrior wolf wheeled, took one look at her, and got out of her way.

The matriarch nosed the red-coated puppy over, and caressed him with a bloody tongue. Then she curled up and died.

At Yellowbird Village during this same month, Lobo Smith—master wolfer and disappointed would-be bridegroom—spiked his store-bought wedding suit to a rough-barked balm-of-gilead poplar tree on the riverbank before his cabin, and emptied the contents of two rifles and one pistol into it. Then, wearing his woods clothes and walking with his widest snowshoe swagger, he reluctantly went over to the side door of white-bearded "Ptarmigan" Dunbar's trading post. He knocked on the door, and got precisely what he'd expected.

A voice with sugar in it said, "Enter, please."

Through pride and a great feeling of guilt about being late at the church when they were to have been wed, Lobo hadn't seen the beautiful and tempestuous Maria for three months. But the story of how Lobo had been chasing wolf scalps when he was supposed to be getting married was well known to Maria.

And now as Lobo opened the door, a barrage of crockery came through the air.

Through the bombardment of dishes he beheld the seductively lovely face of Maria. And in the instant before the door slammed in his face, and while crockery was still crashing on the gravel walk behind him, he thought: "Without her, I'm lost."

Behind the slammed door, Maria stood with her head bowed, hoping she wouldn't weep, but knowing she was going to. And she was thinking: "Maria, idiot, why did you do that? There went one of the truly good men of this frontier, and you have let him go out of your life."

Then she realized something. To herself she said: "The Red One caused this! He is my bitter enemy. . . ."

The Red One, on the morning after the fight with the grizzlies, got lonesome. He wanted to play, and he wanted to be friends with the somber black warrior wolf he'd met. So he made a playful, puppy bound toward the warrior, showing his teeth, and snarling happily.

The warrior relaxed, the kill-craziness going out of him. He nosed the puppy over, and after a moment they went down toward the creek, side by side.

They were passing through a sunny glade when the Red One turned aside to investigate a fascinating object. It was round and gray, about the size of a Japanese lantern, and it hung, swaying, from a willow branch only a couple of feet above the ground. From within it came a buzzing sound, and this so intrigued the Red One that he set his puppy teeth into the object and ripped at it, hoping to discover the source of the buzzing.

A cloud of infuriated yellow jackets hit him, all in the same instant. He fled, yelping, to the black warrior wolf, taking with him the swarm of yellow jackets. When they had outdistanced the fiery yellow jackets, they rolled in the shallow back eddy of the stream to ease the pain of the stings, and the warrior then departed.

The Red One tried to follow, and even yelped for the warrior to wait, but the warrior kept going. He'd had trouble enough for one day, and he didn't regard the red pup as a promising companion.

Back at Yellowbird that same morning, Lobo suddenly got an idea. He understood now how to kill the Red One. And he saw no reason for not making $50 today.

Lobo could think like a wolf; he could even think like a pup wolf. So he knew that, today, the Red One would return once more to the rotted carcass of his mother.

So Lobo took off over the pass to Goose Creek. He was sitting there, downwind from the grass flat in which lay the carcass of the tawny, bitch wolf, the dead dam of the Red One, when he saw the pup coming down the creek bank.

Lobo slipped the safety latch of his .300 magnum, brought the rifle up and was centering the cross hairs on the pup's chest, when the *damnedest* thing happened.

From a torn Japanese lantern of a yellow jacket nest, on a swaying willow branch, a vengeful yellow jacket whined through the air, and hit the back of Lobo's neck.

Lobo's shot went wild; then the Red One, already getting smart to many perils of this strange, new world, faded into the brush.

When Lobo returned to Yellowbird Village from his fruitless mission, he'd covered twenty miles, and he was tired. He headed into the bar again. The bartender, seeing the look on his face, poured him a double shot.

Lobo said, "He was lucky, just lucky, that's all."

The bartender said, "Huh? Who?"

Lobo said, "A wolf pup. But I'll get him—I swear I will."

Saga of the Red One

PART 3

Now the Red One faced the test that kept the clan strong. Driven by rage and hunger, he slashed into the seven well-fed pups guarding the carcass.

The only survivor of Lobo Smith's attack on the den was the Red One, but Lobo lost his girl, Maria. Even months later Lobo couldn't patch up the rift, so he decided to take it out on the Red One. In the meantime, the Red One had a brush with death when he was cornered by a grizzly. Then Lobo caught up with the Red One and lined him up in his sights. But a yellow jacket struck Lobo then and ruined his shot.

Now it was February, and the great snows had fallen upon the North. Daylight was but a brief blink at noon. The birches and cottonwoods were banging like pistol shots, as the big frost crystallized the traces of moisture in their winter hearts. This was the Moon of Hungry Wolf Pups.

The Red One, the nine-month-old, russet-coated orphan wolf pup, was plenty hungry. His lean belly was cleaving to his backbone.

During the summer and autumn he'd eaten careless field mice, birds' eggs, berries and meals stolen from the stinking carcasses of the many salmon that the fishermen-bears had carried out of Goose Creek and left in the sun to rot.

But now, he was in trouble. Now he was learning how hostile and deadly the Alaskan winter can be. Now he knew hunger—dizziness and a great despair and emptiness. He was within a few hours of starvation.

Then the Red One had a crumb of luck. Following a bull moose, he nosed out the tracks of the one-antlered monster.

In one of the posthole tracks made by the moose lay the crushed bodies of two fat field mice. The Red One gulped them. He hopefully followed the bull for another mile up the stream valley, but it was an unrewarding effort. He found no more field mice, so he went back to stalk hoarse-voiced ptarmigan in the willow thicket.

This was when the fifty-below wind, chopping and changing across the flat, brought him the scent of blood, moose—and his clan.

The Red One sat back on his haunches in the snow, pointing his frost-rimed muzzle to the bitter sky, and sounded the rallying howl. This time there was no falsetto break. Although he was only nine months old, his voice came out full and true, the voice of a timber wolf talking defiantly to the white desolation, sounding the ancient triumphs of his clan and informing them that he was arriving to share in the feast.

Through the frozen timber blasted a reply with the authority of a brazen trumpet. It said, in the old, old language of the Alaskan timber wolves: "If you are one of us, join in. If you are not, prepare to meet your death!"

The Red One plowed through the sugary drifts toward the summons and the challenge. He soon emerged upon a scene of bloody necessity that humans sometimes misunderstand. On the creek was the one-antlered bull moose. His hindquarters were down, resting upon torn hocks. He had been hamstrung.

Around him on the ice sat eight wolves. Seven were nine-month-old pups, ranging in color from white to brown-black. The eighth was a lean, silvery dowager, the mother of the others. She was also the new matriarch of this clan of Susitna Valley wolves, successor to the previous matriarch who had died several months earlier under the terrible pawstroke of a Toklat grizzly, while defending the Red One.

Now, before letting her pups assault the hapless one-antlered bull, she had prudently hamstrung him, to make him less mobile and less dangerous. The seven pups, with their fluffy new coats, now appeared to be nearly as large as their mother, and they were putting on a big, ferocious circus at the expense of the doomed bull.

With their needle-pointed puppy teeth they tore out enough of his coarse, hollow hair to stuff a sourdough's bunk pillow, but they still hadn't drawn blood themselves.

Then the old, silvery matriarch flashed in and set her blunted and time-yellowed fighting teeth in the bull's flank. She strained backward, feet braced on the ice. There was an agonized groan from the bull, and then she was standing a yard back from him, tugging the smoking guts out of his belly.

In his death throes, as he struggled to arise, the ill-starred bull fell on his side. His one antler banged against the ice, and broke off. For a moment, his panting made a white frost-fog over his head. He rolled his eyes at the seven suddenly kill-happy pups streaking at him—and that was the last sight he saw.

Then the silvery bitch forgot the dead bull. She pivoted on the ice, staring down the wind. Something was coming.

Her pups, savaging the carcass, hadn't noticed, but she had caught the ghost of a sound, in the glass-brittle frozen willows margining the creek flat. Her silvery ruff bristled, and she padded stiff-leggedly toward the oncomer.

At the edge of the creek ice she halted, her small, pointed ears cocked, her slant eyes flaring. Then, struggling wearily through the loose drifts and the willow brush, came the Red One. Because of the numbing tiredness that possessed him, he did not see the break or the ten-foot cutbank arising from the stream's edge, and so he tumbled over it and landed, sprawled out, almost at the feet of the bristling, silvery, new matriarch, who was his grandmother, although he did not know it.

Before he could recover himself she was standing over him, with death in her star-brilliant eyes. The silvery bitch shoved her blood-smeared snout between the fallen pup's hind legs. After one identifying sniff, her bristled ruff dropped, she touched noses with the pup, then she turned and trotted back toward the kill. The Red One, who had lain motionless during his introduction, trotted after her.

Nearly starved as he was, he still saw the beautiful way she held her bushy tail out straight, and he tried to imitate this timber wolf trait that distinguishes wolves at a glance from huskies and malamutes, whose tails curl upward.

But now the Red One was to learn a new lesson. In his brief life, he had already discovered, twice, the grim strength and loyalty of the old mothers of his clan. One had died for him; the other was offering him food when he was near starvation. But now came another test, the test that kept the clan strong.

Abruptly, as he followed the silvery matriarch around a bend of the frost-flowered creek ice, the Red One faced seven wolf pups of his own age. They had fed from the congealing liver and kidney fat of the dead bull moose, and were strong and confident. He had eaten only two ounces of field-mouse flesh in three days and he was weak and unsteady. But he showed his puppy teeth, and swaggered into the seven.

The new matriarch, his grandmother, sat on the ice, watching. The seven pupil pups, who up to this time had been sheltered by their mother, attacked joyously. They were defending the carcass, which they believed, as pups, that they had themselves killed.

The Red One, impelled by hunger and the sudden rage he had never known before, met them head on. His lean, starved weight was possibly ninety pounds, and his seven antagonists, who had lived well during the summer due to their mother's care, weighed at least as much, so that about 630 pounds of yapping wolf-puppy fury struck him.

Suddenly the Red One discovered why he had been born. He was in combat for the first time, and it was his natural medium. Out of the furry tangle of bodies on the ice a wolf pup staggered with his jugular cut, jetting his life blood. Another hobbled out with a broken foreleg; then another emerged from the heat with his belly split open. Then the Red One was standing alone on the creek ice. The surviving pups had retreated to their mother, who had sat motionless in the snow during the battle.

The Red One, using the last energy in him, trotted over to the moose carcass and began feeding on the freezing guts.

Meanwhile, back at Yellowbird Village, the tempestuous and beautiful Maria, the trader's daughter, had made a decision. For weeks she had understood that the people of Yellowbird believed that she was a too temperamental and hot-headed woman, and that they thought she was a fool for abandoning Lobo Smith.

Maria had reviewed, many times, the details of her parting with Lobo, and her pride was breaking down. She was in love with the tall, lean wolfer, and wanted to be with him.

Lobo was now many miles away at his trapping headquarters, engaged in his endless professional pursuit of the Susitna clan of wolves. Maria yearned toward him, and so she did the thing that any girl with Tena blood in her veins would have done. She harnessed her dogs and headed down the river to the cabin of Blind Nick, the mighty shaman of all the Tena people.

Maria stepped on the brake of her Yukon sled and brought her eight dogs to a halt before the squat, windowless cabin of Blind

Nick. She overturned the sled and tied it to a bankside spruce with a length of babiche. Then she went up the moccasin-padded snow trail to the cabin.

Because she had Tena blood in her, she was now afraid. She was on the threshold of the citadel of the religion of her people. She knocked on the hand-hewn plank door, and a deep, thudding voice said, "Enter."

She pushed the door open, and stepped inside. The one-room cabin was small, perhaps 12 by 14 feet; on the center of the earth floor an open fire burned in a ring of blackened stones, and the smoke partially escaped through a hole in the roof.

Blind Nick sat cross-legged near the fire, with a dark marten robe over his shoulders. The forty skins of the robe would have delighted any fur-buyer. Nick's hawk face turned toward Maria, and in the firelight his eyes were dead, lifeless. He had been blind from birth. But now he seemed to be studying her. He said, "Be seated."

Maria sat across the fire from him, trembling. She said, "I have come for help."

Blind Nick said, "You mean you came to me for advice, Maria. My advice is to go to him. He is a good man, but he has on him a terrible sentence; so be kind to him now. Would you like to see?"

Maria said, "Could I?"

The shaman said, "Watch! Listen!"

He reached into the flickering, red shadows behind him, and tossed a handful of sun-dried herbs onto the coals of the fire. In a moment the small cabin was filled with a strange fragrance, as the herbs crisped and burned.

Blind Nick said, "Behold!"

He spoke in Tena, a beautiful language that Maria had learned from her Indian mother, and his voice was sad.

He said, "Behold Tekunday, the Red One, and your white man lover, whom they call 'Lobo Smith'."

As Maria sat, rigid, the sweet-smelling smoke eddied and curled and then a scene emerged. It was winter and the wind screamed across a timber-lined flat at the head of Goose Creek. The williwaw gusts were scooping up clouds of crusted snow particles, and driving them like bullets through the straining, javelin spruces.

Up the flat, lunging wearily through the drifts, came a great, red wolf. He was wounded. He looked over his shoulder, and 600 yards behind him saw Lobo Smith. The Red One turned a bend of the creek onto the ice of a tributary slough, and here laid in ambush.

In Blind Nick's windowless cabin, on the snowy bank of Rabbit Slough, Maria suddenly became aware of Blind Nick's voice. She stared at him through the drift of sweet-smelling smoke. Her eyes were wide and dazed, because he had just said, "That is enough! All endings are bad; all beginnings are bad. Only a few of the things in the middle are good. Go to your man, daughter of the people."

She said, "But you did not show me the ending. Did the Red One kill him?"

The hard planes of Blind Nick's face softened in the reflected glow of the fire. He said, "Go to your man, daughter of the people!"

Saga of the Red One

PART 4

Fate lay in ambush today for both Lobo Smith and the Red One. And yet neither had any clue of the impending violence.

Now it was March, the month of the Slaughter Moon. This was the month when the clan elders would provide a great supply of meat for the nearly grown pups that still were helpless in the uncompromising subarctic wilds.

Maria had heard the most important admonition of her life. In the smoky, windowless cabin on the ice locked bank of Rabbit Slough, Blind Nick, the great Tena shaman had spoken to her. He had said, "Go to your man, daughter of the people." So now she was mushing her team of eight matched gray Kuskokwim huskies eastward over the iron-hard crust.

Lobo Smith was her man. But until Blind Nick spoke, she had been convinced that she hated the tall, lean master wolfer who had failed to arrive at the Yellowbird church for their wedding the previous May. Then, abruptly at the admonition of the shaman, whom all her mother's people held in awe, her animosity had dissolved. And that was why she was heading for Lobo's trapping cabin under giant Goose Creek snow peaks. She banged the ten-foot lash of her braided moose-gut whip over the back of her dogs, although they were doing their best. She was filled with an upsurge of tenderness and surrender that she had never before experienced.

Meantime, the Red One stood lean-bellied and hungry on the crusted crest of a nearby drift. Then he crouched, ears flattened, and showed his teeth. No longer was there a horizon. No longer could he distinguish a depression from an elevation. The mountains were gone, except for a few bare cliff faces that appeared to hang unsupported in the blue emptiness. This was that mirage of nature, Sna-ah-ga-lits.

But then the Red One's ears lifted. They had caught the thunder of many approaching hoofs. In a moment, came another sound, dramatic and thrilling. It was the high-pitched hysterical yammer of a huge pack hot on a blood trail.

The Red One's neck hair lifted, his throat swelled, and he sat on his haunches in the invisible snow and gave the series of staccato baritone brays.

Then he lunged down the side of the drift, paws skidding on the glassy crust, and suddenly halted.

Coming toward him through the luminous blue haze of the mirage, ankle joints clicking, yearlings blatting, was a flood of dun-colored animals such as he had never before seen—a herd of the superb moss-eating deer tribe, caribou.

Now a formation of wolves streaked out of the somber spruces. There were probably several thousand caribou and perhaps 100 wolves. The caribou herd was relatively small, while the wolf pack was strong, as wolf packs go.

The Red One was filled with the fervor of the big kill, which the wild pack-music of his relatives informed him was imminent. Yammering joyously, he launched himself down through the azure emptiness toward the stampeding caribou herd, fell into an invisible wash, blundered into an equally invisible cutbank, raced across a flat that was crusted so hard it would have supported even a bull moose. Now the Red One found himself on the surface of the frozen lake, directly in the path of the oncoming antlerless caribou.

Fifty feet from him at the point of the herd, driving hard through the blue trickery of the mirage, came a ribby cow. She was a veteran of many long caribou migrations, a true voyager of the tundras and the nameless mountain passes. Often in her time had she witnessed the blood assaults of timber wolves upon her family herd. So when she saw the lone yapping, russet-coated wolf pup, she headed straight toward him, and the thousands behind her followed like super-trained cavalry.

The Red One saw the gaunt cow swerve and charge at him, and the herd with her. Then the venerable, ribby cow reared and brought incongruously large hoofs crashing down at his head. He sidestepp-ed, easy as the shadow of a falling leaf. Then big trouble smote him.

The herd flowed over the Red One, tons of pounding hoofs, smashing him against the ice. Then it was over, and miraculously he was still alive.

He staggered to his feet, bloody, hurting in every bone and muscle. Dazedly he watched the drama, the most fearsome spectacle of the North.

Slashing, chopping, silent as death now, the assembled clan families of the Susitna wolves were cutting down caribou. The lake was presently strewn with struggling, hamstrung dun bodies moaning their doom and blotching the ice with their life blood. Before the slaughter was over, forty caribou were down.

Soon the bitches of this Susitna clan would bear pups in their many hidden dens. To give milk they would need meat. So the families had gathered into a mighty pack, and had intercepted the migrating caribou herd. Tomorrow the herd would be gone.

The Red One tottered toward the dying caribou, and saw his elders feeding. Many of them were feeding from the kicking and sobbing bodies of still-living, hamstrung caribou. They were going into flanks of those luckless creatures for the leaves of sweet kidney fat and the smoking purple-red livers, gorging themselves on the kill.

Each gulped at least twenty pounds of caribou flesh, and then, stupid with food, their bellies sagging, they straggled into the nearest stand of spruce and curled up on the snow, tails over their noses, and slept. The Red One had been unable to join them at the feast. The hammering he had taken from the caribou herd had made him too sick and dazed to be interested in food.

Then, as the forlorn, bruised, and humiliated wolf pup stood on the ice licking his wounds, he heard the squeal of sled runners on the snow, and he also heard the panting breaths of a team of racing malamutes. Cautiously, he retreated into a cluster of snow-bonneted spruces, and stood watching.

Lobo Smith, the sled driver, had been running a snare line on a high bench above the Goose Creek Valley when he heard the blood-yammer of the attacking wolf pack. He knew what was happening, and knew also that there would be a meat drunk and that he would profit by it.

He brought his team of ten long-legged siwash malamutes down off the bench in a careening descent, his full weight on the three-pronged brake, so the sled would not overrun the dogs. The snow mirage had now blinked out, and the valley had returned to its true white, green and blue.

When the racing malamutes took the narrow sled soaring over a snow-corniced bank and the runners banged on the frost-starred ice of the lake, Lobo yelled, "Chook!" Lobo had seen the stippling of caribou carcasses dotting the farther shore of the ice. When his lead dog halted at the Tena word of command, Lobo anchored the sled a to bankside spruce snag. He then slid his long-barreled Remington .30-06 out of its moosehide scabbard and headed across the lake, upwind, until he found the bloody paw prints and nail marks of the great pack of warrior wolves leading into the stand of snowy spruces.

Three minutes later Lobo was upon them. The wolves, suddenly awakened, were stupid and erratic, as any aggregation of drunks would have been. Lobo shot the Remington empty and made six kills. While he was reloading the other wolves vomited their gorge and loped dingle-footed into the timber.

Lobo, still stuffing shells into the magazine, ran after them, but they turned into a thicket and he lost them. Now he found himself on the margin of a spruce-encircled opening in which a dog team and its driver were standing.

Maria had heard the shots and had taken her team of huskies toward them, hoping that the rifleman would be Lobo Smith. Then, minutes later, when she saw the tall, lean wolfer emerge from the dark close-pack ranks of spruces at the rim of the frozen lake, her heart beat a wild tattoo against her ribs. She felt her knees begin to shake under the soft gray folds of her marmot parka, and she wished to shout a greeting to Lobo. She could not because her maiden throat was too full.

Lobo had not seen Maria for more than half a year. The last time they had met was when he knocked on her door at Yellowbird, repentant at having been so late for their wedding because he'd had a run-in with the Red One while trying to pick up some extra honeymoon money. At that last meeting Maria had showered him with a barrage of crockery, and then had slammed the trading post door in his face. So now he believed that this was an accidental meeting and that if he came close enough she would bang her moose-gut whip in his face

Lobo had been desolately alone in the wilds all these many months, thinking of no one but Maria. He had heard her voice in the music of the winds. He had met her in his dreams, many times. To him she was the symbol of all things good and desirable.

But he was a wolfer, a sourdough woodsman who would have been the first to admit that he was a primitive. So he acted the way any lonely, violent man would have acted.

Ducking his head against the expected crash from the moose-gut whip, he stepped into the lead dog of Maria's team. With his hard left hand he grabbed the slant-eyed gray Kuskokwim husky by the scruff of his neck and yanked him back to the bow of the Yukon sled. With his right hand he drew his belt knife and slashed the towrope. He cuffed the gray leader away from him, and yelled, "Mush!"

As the freed team of huskies departed for Yellowbird, he turned to Maria. The tempestuous and beautiful eighteen-year-old mestiza stared at him. Lobo said, "Now you're a captive bride."

When she realized what he had said, her tenderness abruptly changed to anger. With all her strength, she swung the moose-gut whip and its tasseled tip cut a patch from the shoulder of Lobo's worn caribou-fawn parka. In sudden anger he caught the lash with his hand and yanked her half across the near handlebar.

He said, "Camp is not far away—but there are many camps far beyond."

Behind Lobo and his captive bride, in a clump of spired spruces, the battered Red One sat back in the lee of a snow-hooded boulder, raised his muzzle to the steely sky and howled out the ancient wrongs and triumphs of his clan and of all living things.

Saga of the Red One

PART 5

*Badly trampled by the caribou, the Red One yearned for rest.
But instead he ran afoul of
a wire snare, an Injun devil, and the raging forest fire.*

After his pounding beneath the hoofs of the stampeding caribou herd, the Red One was sick and dizzy, aching in every joint and muscle. Making his slow, painful way up out of the Goose Creek valley, he headed toward a high bench that rose above its eastern limits.

Nearby, in the custom of wolfers of that day, Lobo Smith had shot down a number of caribou for bait in a cluster of wide-armed spruces.

When the Red One found these frozen, snow-dusted caribou carcasses, he sniffed disinterestedly at them because his appetite had not yet returned after the frightful battering he had taken from the hoofs of the herd on the lake ice four miles back. Then suddenly he whirled as the polar wind warned him of a strange animal. His ruff bristling, the Red One filled with a sense of dire urgency, hobbled toward a vantage point on the crest of a nearby boulder-studded knoll.

He never got there.

He was passing through a thin belt of alders and was holding up his right paw because of the blazing anguish of torn ligaments and bruised muscles that cramped this leg. Then he blundered, in his three-legged gait, straight into one of Lobo Smith's snares.

With the thrust of his weight the wire slipped taut about his neck and his lifted right paw. He fought and savaged the steel wire until his mouth bled and his breath came in hoarse rasps. Meantime, the snare was tightening because of a deadly lock that Lobo had invented. He had bent a two-inch iron washer back upon itself like a sandwich, and drilled a hole through it at a tricky angle, so that the wire would slide in one direction only—cinching and cinching, quarter inch by fateful quarter inch about the hopeless victim's neck.

Then, the Red One stood motionless, while he still had breath.

Once again his nose caught the scent of the strange animal. The Red One's ears picked up the rattle of claws on the crusty snow. Out of the alders came an apparition. It was a small animal by timber wolf standards; black with a pale stripe down each side and bowlegged in front. It was devil-masked, and its flat shoe-button eyes glared at the Red One with a killer's stare. It was coming straight at him, snarling.

Here was an animal accustomed to raiding the traps, snares and caches of northern woodsmen. It was the most hated and publicized of all wildlife destroyers. It was none other than the wolverine, the Injun devil.

Breathing in tortured gasps, the Red One set himself on his three free legs. He would wreak some savage destruction while the power and speed of his jaws remained with him.

Meanwhile at Lobo Smith's headquarters trapping cabin, a fourteen-by-twenty-foot log structure squatting close under the Goose Creek snow peaks, another elemental drama was happening. The cabin stood in a postage-stamp opening at the brink of a plateau. From here, Lobo with his binoculars could see ten miles of his eighty-mile trapline.

Inside the cabin, Maria sat cross-legged on a wolfskin robe that covered the wild-hay mattress of Lobo's bunk. She was pale with anger, and her dark mestiza eyes were flashing.

"I was coming to you in the advice of Blind Nick," she said. "I wanted to ask you to return with me to Yellowbird and be married, as we had planned. But you, fool, you did not wait to hear what I had to say. Instead, you cut my dogs loose and brought me here as a captive. Don't you know, idiot, that at least fifty armed mushers are searching for me now?"

Lobo gritted, "I'll take you with me to the farthest ends of the North, through the unknown passes and down the unmapped rivers and to secret places that few Indians or Eskimos, and fewer white men, have ever seen. Places that only the wolves know. I'll be kind to you and you'll help me in my trade as you agreed to do at the beginning. You'll feed the dogs, and cook, and keep the seams of my moccasins sewn tight. And you'll keep my cabin clean and be faithful in all respects." In return, Lobo made an almost pleading gesture and his deep voice broke, "I pledge you the promises made in the story of Ruth in the Bible. Have you read it?"

Maria looked at him for a long moment, and said, "Yes, I have read it. 'Wither thou goest, I will go,'" and the hot resentment in her eyes dissolved in tears.

Lobo turned in quick woodsman's embarrassment. He snatched up his binocular from a hand-hewn plank table and looked out toward his trapline.

He said to Maria, "Wait here."

Hastily, Lobo shrugged into his caribou-fawn parka, picked up the long-barreled Remington, and stepped outside. The dog team route to the snare-caught Red One would be roundabout. He could get there much faster by running alone over the crust.

But Lobo knew that if he left the dogs behind Maria would harness them and depart for Yellowbird. So he went out to the brush-roofed kennels behind the cabin and unsnapped the chains of his ten long-legged siwash malamutes. They would, he knew, head down into the nearest willow thicket to chase snowshoe rabbits, and wouldn't return to the cabin for at least an hour.

Maria watched from the cabin window, and when Lobo's tall, lean figure had disappeared down on the spruce-clad hillside, she got into her trail gear. She took one of Lobo's razor-edged skinning knives, and now, methodically, cut into short bits all the dog harness and the towrope of Lobo's sled.

Aware that her moccasins would leave no print on the cement-hard crust, Maria set out for Yellowbird. When she was a mile from Lobo's cabin, a new side of her young life arose. She leaned against the frosted, rough-barked trunk of a spruce and laughed. At first it was a laugh of triumph; then it sobered and died. She stood away from the tree and took a dozen steps on her back trail. Then she headed for Yellowbird over the crust as fast as she could travel. . . .

Meanwhile, on the Red One caught in a snare, the wolverine advanced purposefully from one side. From the other side Lobo Smith was hastening to collect his scalp.

The wolverine came in like a bulldog, unhurriedly, head down, quartz-white claws digging into the crust. The Red One backed off to the end of the six-foot snare, for fighting space. Then, as the bowlegged Injun devil rushed him with a snarl the Red One met him in timber wolf fashion.

Although he was half-strangled and on three legs, the Red One slashed a bloody furrow across the wolverine's forehead and ripped out his right eye. Then, as the wolverine flinched sidewise, the Red One grabbed him by the back and threw him crashing against the frozen alder stems. On this explosive effort, the Red One's right paw came free of the snare. This gave him two inches of slack in the noose. The Red One felt it, and eased his head out of the loop before the wire could tighten again.

A three-legged timber wolf in a snare was one thing, but this suddenly freed timber wolf, with four legs under him, was something else again. The wolverine bluffed. He bowlegged in once more, screaming in pain and rage, but floundered past; he didn't turn to resume combat.

Now the chill mountain wind brought the Red One a familiar, dreaded man-scent. He headed for cover across the opening.

Lobo had been running, and was out of breath. He'd expected to find the nearly grown russet-coated wolf pup helpless in a snare. But when he spotted the Red One crossing an opening 100 yards from the snare, Lobo sat down and put the long-barreled rifle to his shoulder. The pumping of his heart betrayed him. He tried time and again to hold steadily on the Red One, but each time the bead swung off. At last he took a chance; swinging the rifle as a shotgun-man swings his weapon, he pulled off the shot. The 220-grain slug cut a crease across the Red One's rump, and hair flew. But there was no chance for a second shot.

Cursing, Lobo started back to his cabin for Maria's unpleasant surprise.

Time wore by until it was the Fire Moon—July. It was a hot, dry summer in the Susitna Valley, and the making of trouble was in the moistureless forest floor.

At Yellowbird the half-repentant but still angry Maria had smoldered uncommunicatively for weeks. Her gold-bronze mestiza coloring had paled, and she had lost weight to the point where her father, white-bearded old "Ptarmigan" Dunbar, would have sent 200 miles for a doctor if Maria had not flashed angrily at him and said no. Maria knew in her heart that there was only one remedy for her difficulty—Lobo Smith.

So today, in the brassy glare of this hot subarctic noon, she sought relief in activity. She went down to the bank of the Susitna and slid her ten-foot birchbark canoe into the water.

Her intention was to go downstream for part of the afternoon and then find forgetfulness in the arduous task of paddling and lining her canoe back upstream to Yellowbird. But the wilderness moved against her.

Abruptly, to the eastward, thunder cannonaded across the sky. Then a blue-white streak of lightning forked down and struck a dry tangle of hillside spruce blown down.

All the dwellers of the Susitna wilderness were caught unaware. The winged ones and the strong-legged ones headed toward the Susitna River. The field mice, the shrews, the rabbits, the many species of birds who had barely begun to learn to fly—all young ones—were caught and crisped in the tide of fire.

Maria was five miles downstream when the smother of hot smoke covered the river. With charred leaves and burning branches falling about her, she blindly headed the canoe into the cottonwood-towered bank of the only island in this stretch of the Susitna. Desperately, using all the strength of her arm, she dug her paddle into the muddy current, driving the canoe in against the smoke-shrouded bank. And because she could not see she made a mistake. She hit a sawyer, one of those uprooted trees that fall into rivers and chop and churn, alternately disappearing beneath the surface and then arising unexpectedly in a froth of current. She hit it head on. The stub of a broken limb ripped a five-foot gash in the fragile bottom of the birchbark, and suddenly Maria was swimming.

She caught an overhanging willow branch and pulled herself ashore. She climbed the bank, shivering from the biting cold of the glacier-fed river, and spread her clothes across a cottonwood drift-log to dry in the sun.

Among the refugees fleeing before the wall of fire were two creatures to whom Maria's life was inexorably tied. She saw the nearly grown wolf pup, the Red One, scramble up the bank and shake the water from his russet coat.

And then she saw Lobo Smith swimming across the gray current, and suddenly she became aware of her nakedness.

Saga of the Red One

PART 6

Trapped on the island by the forest fires, the Red One faces death from the jaws of an alien warrior-wolf and the knife throwing of angry Maria.

In an easy swim across the quarter-mile channel of the Susitna River, the Red One reached the welcome sanctuary of the cottonwood island.

He waded out onto the point of an open sandspit, shook the water from his russet coat, and gazed in a kind of wild disbelief at the forest fire vaulting across the homeland of his clan of timber wolves.

Black flame-shot billows of smoke blotted out the sky. Burning spruce boughs, carbonized leaves, and hot ash were blowing across the wide reach of the muddy, many-channeled river. And already spot-fires were springing up here on the island beneath the towering cottonwoods. But so far the place was a haven.

Assembled on this smoke-shrouded haven of an island was an extraordinary cast of refugees. There were several moose—including two gaunt, frantic cows who'd lost their spring calves when a tinder-dry blowdown went up in flames as fast and fiercely as if it had been dusted with gunpowder. There were several singed and gloweringly resentful black bears. There was a high-humped, slab-sided old Toklat grizzly, who kept patrolling the beach and rumbling hoarsely as he watched the mounting wall of smoke and fire to the eastward. There was a solitary female lynx who crouched under a windfall moaning because her chest and face had been seared to the bone when she vainly sought to rescue her kittens. There was a red fox, frightened and bewildered, who never again would blunt his brush, for it had flamed like a torch and burned to a blackened stub as he streaked desperately through a blazing spruce thicket.

Also there was a venerable black warrior-wolf of the Kashwitna clan. And there was the master wolfer, Lobo Smith, and the beautiful eighteen-year-old mestiza girl, Maria of Yellowbird.

The Red One's nose was picking up a confusion of scents as the hot, crazily chopping wind eddied through the smoky cottonwoods. As he sorted them out, one by one, suddenly his back hair bristled. He had caught the scent of the trespassing black warrior from the Kashwitna. The matriarchal social system of Alaskan timber wolves is based upon family loyalty and affection—and in most cases the destruction of all invading male wolves from other clans. Technically the Red One was not yet a warrior wolf. He was only a month or two past his first year, but he had in him the undefinable qualities that might make a fighting champion.

Forgetting the menace of the forest fire, forgetting even that Lobo Smith was on the island, the Red One took the scent trail of the Kashwitna intruder. In the next few minutes he was to battle for full warrior status, and possibly establish himself by the ancient rule of fang and sinew as a princeling worthy of becoming the king wolf of this vast Susitna wilderness.

He rounded a clump of ash-whitened high-bush cranberry brush, and there was the black warrior facing him, ears flattened, lips curled in a snarl, hate-filled slant eyes flaring like chips of amber. He was a veteran warrior, but it was the younger Red One who attacked first.

Meanwhile, at the foot of the twenty-acre cottonwood island, Lobo Smith was going through what he mistakenly believed to be the deepest, most corrosive tragedy of his life. Despite the fact that most of his trapline cabins would surely burn in the forest fire, and he would lose thousands of dollars worth of gear, and have to seek a new area of operation if he continued to trap, Lobo had been happy when he pulled himself out of the water at the foot of the island. For a month now, he had a dramatic reason for being happy. It was just a month ago, at the headwaters of a nameless tributary of Goose Creek, that he'd realized the great dream of Alaska sourdoughs.

Lobo had been digging out a den of wolf pups. The den was in a crevice that ran back into the side of an iron-stained, rotten-quartz rimrock, and it was a stubborn one to get into because the crevice was crooked and the loose rock kept caving in as he laboriously worked at it with pick and shovel. He hadn't yet caught sight of the mother wolf, but this didn't disturb him. He knew the pups were in the den—he could hear them—and he knew how to get the bitch.

When he got the pups out of the den, he would keep one alive and use it as bait. He would stake the pup out, set a battery of traps about it, then depart for a day or two. From long experience he knew that no mother wolf, however wary, could resist the whimperings of a hungry pup. The bitch was probably watching him now, and possibly would know what he was doing when he set the traps, but still she would come to her staked-out pup. She would be in the traps when he returned.

Anticipating his trick, Lobo wielded his pick and shovel so vigorously that soon he was wet with sweat. A few yards to his right a streamlet plunged over the rimrock in a miniature cascade. Lobo backed out of the crevice, blinked the quartz dust out of his eyes, and went over to a bathtub-size pool for a drink. As he knelt at the water's edge he couldn't believe at first what he was seeing.

The bottom of the pool was covered with grains of reddish-yellow metal. A solid blanket of it, glinting dully in the sunlight. With a hoarse exclamation, Lobo thrust his arm into the water and scooped up a handful of the stuff. He didn't have to test it. Its weight alone told him what it was. Gold! Sunburnt gold!

Through years and years it had been gathering in this lonely spot, washed down from the rotten-quartz rimrock. A treasure, awaiting the arrival of some wayfarer blessed by the wilderness gods.

As Lobo held the gold in the palm of his hand, poking at it with a shaking forefinger, he said in a dazed whisper, "Maria, this will end the trouble between us. Now we'll really be married. You'll have diamonds and silk, and, by gosh, a castle if you want one."

But now, a month later on the cottonwood island, with the flame-filled smoke clouds rolling overhead, Lobo's triumph had dissolved into despair. The first object that had caught his woodsman's eyes as he'd waded ashore was the wreckage of a birchbark canoe speared on a deadhead snag fifty feet below the point of the island. In the muddy current, the bow of the canoe alternately rose and fell, and painted on it in the yellow pigment that the Tena Indians make with powdered limonite and melted spruce gum was the word Maria. To Lobo it seemed crushingly obvious what had happened. Maria had gone for a canoe ride on the river, and confused by the smoke had put into the island, but had missed it and hit the snag. Nobody, he knew, could have swum back upstream against that current.

Sitting down heavily, clad only in his underwear, his face soot-blackened and blistered by blowing sparks, Lobo stared at the wrecked canoe and groaned. Hating the island now, and wishing only to get away from it, he began searching for dry drift logs.

At the upper end of the island Maria was hastily putting on the clothes she had spread to dry before she saw Lobo swimming across the channel. Conflicting emotions swept through her. In a jumbled montage of memories she recalled how the tall, lean wolfer had failed to arrive at the Yellowbird church for their wedding. She recalled how Blind Nick, the shaman of shamans, had told her, "Go to your man, daughter of the people," and also she recalled with fresh resentment how she had gone to Lobo filled with tenderness and surrender, and how he had held her captive until she managed to escape.

So now as Maria finished dressing she was torn between anger and desire to run to the wolfer. While she hesitated, a wild and savage combat broke out. One hundred feet away, in an opening beyond a low screen of high-bush cranberry brush, the Red One and the trespassing black warrior wolf from the Kashwitna had engaged in their duel to the death.

The black wolf was a tough, burly customer, covered from muzzle to rump with the scars of battle. A typical warrior wolf of the giant race of timber wolves, he weighed upwards of 140 pounds. He knew all the deadly tricks and in his time had used them most successfully. But he was now fifteen years old.

He chopped at the Red One's shoulder, missed, and got a gash across his right hip that cut through the big muscle.

The Red One moved about him like a shadow, feinting, waiting for his chance. It came when the black wolf lurched off balance, betrayed by his wounded hip. Then the Red One came in from the side, fast as a wingbeat. The tremendous strength of his jaws crushed the black trespasser's right foreleg.

As the black veteran toppled with an agonized bray, the Red One split his throat. The bright gush of life-blood on the cottonwood leaves was symbolic, marking the fall of one warrior wolf and the rise of another.

Maria had witnessed this grim primeval scene. And she recognized the Red One. In the vision Blind Nick had shown her in his tiny windowless cabin on the bank of Rabbit Slough, as she sat across the dying fire from him, and the sweet-smelling smoke of the shaman's strange herbs filled the room, she had seen the Red One under the Goose Creek peaks, and she knew beyond question that the bloody-jawed, russet-coated beast before her now was the same wolf. For an instant she and the Red One glared at each other, motionless. Then Maria's hand flashed to the haft of the knife she carried.

It was a good knife, a six-inch splinter of Swedish steel, sharp as broken glass and balanced to delight a knife-fighter's heart.

Maria's hand flicked up and forward; there was a wheel of light and a sound like a giant hornet buzzing. The knife flew truly, but the Red One saw it coming and flinched aside so that it missed. Then, after holding Maria's eye for an instant with a baleful glare that she would remember all her life, he disappeared among the smoke-hung cottonwoods. Maria made the sign of the cross and fled back to the river.

Maria sat for an hour on a weather-whitened drift log, wanting to make her way down the island in search of Lobo, but afraid to do so. The spot-fires started among the cottonwoods by blazing wind-blown boughs were spreading. The eye-stinging, lung-rasping smoke was now so dense that it was impossible even to see the glossy forest canopy sixty feet overhead. Fear-crazed animals blundered about, ignoring one another in their common desire to find safety from this peril that had beset them. Then suddenly—and it made Maria's heart pound—a bull-voiced hallo sounded from the bank of blowing smoke close upriver.

Maria recognized the voice. In all the North there was only one like it. It had the character and carrying quality of a foghorn. Before she could reply, a birchbark nosed out of the swirling pall of smoke. Kneeling on the bottom, feathering his paddle as the current shot the canoe in toward her, was heavy-shouldered, iron-maned old Tex Cobb, dean of sourdoughs.

"Yer father was kinda worried about ya," Tex said. "So he asked me to take a look around and find out if ya were all right."

Maria said, "I am all right now."

Tex sat beside her on the drift log, filled his battered hook-stemmed pipe with cut plug, and remarked conversationally, "Lot of excitement today, with the fire and everything. . . . got any idea where yer boy friend Lobo Smith is hangin' out now?"

Maria said, "Why?"

"Wel-l-l, all the boys at Yellowbird is set to go on a gold stampede." He gave her an amused sidewise glance from his swamp-green eyes. "Only trouble is, nobody knows where to stampede to."

Tex lit the beat-up pipe and puffed a moment, gazing deadpan into the encircling blue shroud of fire-crimsoned smoke. "Seems as if Lobo hired and Injun to make him eight sets of dog harness, and paid him off a nugget of sunburnt gold half the size of yer thumb. When the Injun come to town to buy some grub with the nugget, he allowed that Lobo was carrying anyhow fifty pounds of nuggets and coarse gold in a coupla tin cans. So naturally," Tex said, "everybody is what ya might call extremely interested in knowing where to find yer friend Lobo."

Maria said, keeping her voice level and matching Tex's poker face, "He is at the foot of this island."

Tex said, "Hit looks like this here cottonwood island has collected some interesting characters today." He cocked an ear to a heavy crashing in the underbrush nearby, and added, "Critters an' varmints too."

Swaggering over to his birchbark, Tex slid his beautiful thin-barreled Sauer Mauser .30-06 out of its quill-decorated sealskin scabbard, and said with a courtly bow, "Jest foller close behind me."

But at the foot of the cottonwood island they found disappointment and—for Maria—heartbreak. Lobo was not there.

Tex studied the sign. He said, "Lobo left downriver maybe half-an-hour ago on a siwash raft. Two logs tied together with willer roots." Then Tex saw Maria's birchbark speared on the deadhead snag in the heavy current. He said to Maria, "How in Gawd's name did ya swim back from that?"

"I did not lose the canoe there," Maria said. "I hit a sawyer in the smoke halfway up the island, and swam ashore. The swamped canoe must have floated down and caught on that snag."

Tex's deep voice dropped an octave in sympathy as he said, "Don'tcha see? He thought you was drownded. So he didn't wanta stay here no more. Or maybe nowhere's else, if I know Lobo, and I reckon I do."

When Maria felt the full impact of this, she turned her back on Tex, and leaned her face against the ridged bark of a cottonwood and wept.

Elsewhere on the island, the Red One limped to the west shore, away from the terrible fire that was destroying his ancestral hunting ground and possibly all the other members of his clan.

The Red One knew that to the northwestward lay an enormous game land, a trackless primitive area reaching to the snow-bright Alaska Range and beyond. From many mountainsides he had seen this wild sweep of country and had tested the winds blowing to him across it. Because of the fire, it was especially a promised land.

Saga of the Red One

PART 7

Trailing an eligible mate, the Red One gets into trouble with a roar in the sky. And the plane spells a different kind of trouble for Lobo Smith.

This was a forty-below morning in late January, the Mating Moon. The Red One was sitting on the break of a great storm-carved snowdrift above the frozen Tokichitna River, at the base of Mt. McKinley. Until just now he'd been concentrating on a most serious project—that of introducing himself to a bitch wolf. But his attention had been momentarily diverted by a strange sound in the southern sky.

He tilted his head, listening to a mysterious deep-throated drone such as he'd never before heard in his four years. The airplane, a blue cabin job with skis, skimmed in over the timbered ridges, the beat of its engine swelling swiftly to a harsh roar. The Red One watched it bank over the shattered blue-green snout of Tokichitna glacier. Then it swung off northwest, upriver, and flew out of sight.

When he could no longer hear the plane, the Red One again turned his thoughts to what he'd had in mind since daybreak. He'd been following the fascinating trail of an eligible female wolf, and now he could see her 200 yards ahead. She was on the near bank of the river, intently stalking what appeared to be a barren snowdrift.

Her actions made no sense to the Red One, but she herself made plenty of sense. She was cream-yellow, only a shade darker than the snow, and very beautiful, the Red One thought.

As she stalked the snowdrift, the Red One stalked her. She neither saw, nor heard, nor winded him. So he got within sixty feet of her and sat watching her curious behavior. Minutes passed before he understood what she was up to.

A flock of willow ptarmigan was in the snowdrift. These canny white snow grouse, as he knew well from experience, would often fly headlong into a snowdrift, burying themselves, and bivouac there overnight—a safety measure on their part, as they had perfect concealment and left no tracks.

But obviously the White Bitch was unable to locate the birds exactly. While the Red One watched, she padded busily back and forth, working her nose and pausing frequently to listen. Finally impatience overrode her better judgment. She bounded up the side of the drift and thrust her head into a suspicious-looking mound.

The drift exploded, several hundred ptarmigan rocketing skyward, squawking raucously. So startled was the White Bitch that when she reared to snap at the nearest bird she lost her balance, fell backward, and rolled in undignified fashion to the foot of the drift.

Humiliated, she bounded to her feet and yapped angrily at the cloud of ptarmigan as they turned and swept back over her on whistling wings at an insultingly low altitude. Then she saw the Red One coming toward her, and salvaged her injured dignity by snarling ferociously at him.

The Red One tried to ignore this inhospitable greeting. He danced, and cavorted playfully, and tried to touch noses with her. All this got him was a spiteful one-two slash from the White Bitch's teeth which split an ear tip and tore a square-inch divot of hide off his cheek.

Trying again, he crouched on the snow, panting, and wagged his tail disarmingly. But the White Bitch still was not interested in being friendly. She turned and trotted out toward the river ice.

Now once again they both heard the strange sound in the sky. This time it antagonized the Red One. For three years, since the sad day on the cottonwood island in the Susitna when he'd watched the forest fire destroy the hunting grounds of his clan, he'd had outlaw status here in the western wilderness. And now the Red one sensed a dire threat in this unprecedented object roaring through the hard winter sky. So he loped alongside the White Bitch and shouldered her roughly downstream, away from the sound.

The Red One had never before taken a mate, because as an adolescent outlaw among hostile clans he'd been unable to get one. But now he knew that he had his mate and knew that he could hold her against all comers. No longer was the Red One a gangling, limber-jointed junior warrior. He weighed 160 pounds and was a good eight feet from muzzle to tail tip.

Not many miles away, Lobo Smith, the master wolfer, was sitting on the pole bunk of his tiny, dirt-roofed trapline cabin repairing the babiche foot-filling of a snowshoe when he heard the airplane coming in over the spruce tops. He hastened outside, staring as the pilot dived on the cabin, engine howling.

This was the first plane Lobo had ever seen, and he was open-mouthed and wide-eyed as the airman pulled out of the dive and then circled the clearing in a tight bank, headed out over the frozen river, and set down on the ice. The pilot cut the motor and stepped out.

He was a small, wiry man wearing a caribou-fawn parka and Eskimo mukluks with wolf-skin tops that reached to his hips. He had quick, smoke-blue eyes and the face of a hungry fox.

"Name's Brant," he said. "Been buying a little fur here and there, and saw your cabin and trapline trails. Thought maybe we might do some business. I'll pay . . ." he broke off, gazing at Lobo's face with suddenly sharpened interest. "Say-y-y, aren't you Lobo Smith?"

"That's what they call me," Lobo said. "If your flying machine will stand hitched, c'mon up to the cabin. I got a moose stew on and a batch of sourdough biscuits in the oven."

The wolfer ladled moose stew into two tin plates, poured coffee, and set out the pan of biscuits. As they ate, a strange tension built up between them. They both felt it but didn't understand it.

Lobo was thinking, "I've got to ask him. Either way it's gonna be rough to take, but I gotta know."

Brant was thinking, "This is the chance of a lifetime—if I play it right. There's something gnawing this guy's guts."

Lobo refilled the plates with steaming, fat-rich stew, broke a biscuit and spread it with hot marrow. Then suddenly he didn't feel like eating. "Tell me something," he said, his lean windburnt face gone taut. "Did they ever find . . ." he looked out the window a moment, ". . . did they ever find the body of Maria? You know, the trader's daughter at Yellowbird. Drowned off the tip of a cottonwood island, the day of the big fire three years ago."

"Sorry, I wouldn't know about that," Brant said. He'd managed to keep his voice level, but he was thinking exultantly, "So that's it!" Brant asked sympathetically, "Friend of yours?"

"I still like to think she was," Lobo said.

They smoked, then washed the dishes, and then Brant took Lobo out to inspect the plane. Brant knew that Maria was alive—he'd talked with her two days before at Yellowbird. That was the hand he held. And Lobo knew where there was a fabulous deposit of sunburnt gold, and that was Lobo's hand. Blue chips all over the table.

"Saw some wolves a short piece downriver," Brant said. "If you want to, we'll buzz down there and maybe blast a couple of them. There was a lone gray wolf, and a white one and a big red brute the size of a pony traveling together."

Lobo stiffened. "A red wolf?" He thought a moment. "Yeah, that forest fire might have. . . ."

The Red One and the White Bitch drifted up the ice to a moose yard. The herd of huge, grotesquely humped bulls, cows, and youngsters had been here for weeks, and the entire willow flat was trampled, urine-stained and dung-stippled like a winter cattle corral. Half-a-dozen bulls were on the ice snipping the frozen twigs of the overhanging bankside thickets. But the Red One ignored them. Today he wanted easier prey. So he edged the White Bitch to the far side of the river and went around the belligerent bulls, and presently saw what he was looking for—a ten-month-old heifer, sleek and fat, standing alone at the rim of a thicket.

With one slash the White Bitch cut a hamstring as cleanly as it could have been done with a knife. In almost the same instant the Red One set his teeth in the luckless heifer's throat and threw her so hard that her body bounced and skidded on the icy, trampled snow. Then they fed, slashing into the quivering carcass. But before they had a full gorge, they stopped.

Down the ice came a gray warrior-wolf of the Tokichitna clan. He'd caught the scent of the kill, and also the scent of his clan member, the White Bitch, in company with the alien Red One. The White Bitch stepped forward as if to greet him.

In one savage motion the Red One took her by the scruff of the neck and hurled her, end over end, fifteen feet back into a brush clump. He then advanced to meet the gray Tokichitna warrior. Then, to the northwest, the engine racket sounded again, and the Red One saw the blue airplane.

He streaked into the cover of a dense jack-spruce thicket, crowding the chastened White Bitch ahead of him. The gray Tokichitna warrior, however, being less acute, was less fortunate.

Lobo, tense, nudged Brant with his elbow. Brant pushed the stick forward and racked the plane over on its right wing. "For God's sake, don't shoot the prop off or blow a strut in two," he admonished. Lobo didn't reply. He was busy. He shoved the muzzle of the shotgun out the rolled-down window and pulled off three shots as fast as he could touch the trigger. The gray wolf somersaulted, spun as if he were chasing his tail, and fell dead. Brant said, "Nice shooting," and took the plane in a wide circle around the moose yard.

"The red wolf and the white one with him were right over there on the ice when I came in. We ought to pick them up in a minute or so."

But Brant was wrong. After quartering a square mile of terrain without spotting the Red One and the White Bitch, Brant gave up and returned to land beside the dead gray wolf.

"Beats running a trapline, doesn't it?" he asked Lobo. When Lobo allowed that it sure did, Brant said, "If you're sold on it, how about a partnership? I'll do the flying, you do the shooting."

"Don't mind, by gosh, if I do," Lobo answered. "Sounds interesting."

"You said something, pardner," Brant said enthusiastically. "But there's one detail," he added in a lower voice. "We're going to need some cash right away. This plane ain't paid for, and I'm broke. For insurance and everything, we'll need three or four thousand."

As he knelt to skin the gray wolf, Lobo said indifferently, "I know where to get it."

Saga of the Red One

PART 8

Lobo figured he could gun down the wolf from the plane. But he guessed wrong and then found that his troubles were beginning to snowball.

For days the Red One had been restless, filled with an urge that was new to him. A compelling something kept drawing him southeastward, toward the sunrise. This morning he was especially in its grip.

He and his mate, the white Tokichitna bitch, were hunting along the crest of a whale-backed timbered ridge, working into a wind that smelled of storm. Suddenly the Red One turned and gazed southeastward across the tangle that lay between him and the Susitna River. To the White Bitch's surprise and annoyance, he presently headed in that direction.

It was hard going down this side of the ridge. The snow was deep and the brush thick. She couldn't understand his motive, and neither could the Red One.

Toward noon they angled down through huge cottonwoods to a flatland bordering the river. Snow was spitting out of the leaden sky. Here the knife-sharp wind brought the Red One a familiar scent. He crouched instinctively, feeling the joyful kill-madness take him.

Somewhere close ahead, he knew, was a band of caribou. Caribou were scarce in this western wilderness. So scarce, in fact, that he had not so much as laid eyes on one during his three years of outlaw roaming. The last caribou herd he had seen was on Goose Creek, his homeland, during the Slaughter Moon when he was still a yearling pup. Remembering now the fabulous big kill that his clan members had made on that bitter crystalline day, the Red One's unaccustomed restlessness temporarily vanished.

With the eager White Bitch at his flank, he loped up the warm, ammoniac, almost tangible scent-trail that the wind was bringing him. In a moment he sighted the band. There were only seven caribou and they were winter-gaunt, weighing so little that they hardly sank into the drifts.

They were making their way out to the frozen Susitna River when one of them, a sway-bellied, discouraged-looking cow, saw the two timber wolves streaking in through the snow-plastered cottonwoods. At once her flag went up and she led the band at a gallop, the pace that caribou resort to only when they are panic-stricken.

Two hundred yards out on the river was a black band of glare ice, an overflow channel that had frozen over since the last snow. The caribou saw it, but had no possible detour. They arrived on the frost-flowered black ice all in a bunch, and then their feet went out from under them and they were floundering desperately, falling and struggling up, climbing one another's backs, being trampled.

Into this melee slammed the Red One and the White Bitch, cracking their throats in the staccato blood-yammer of their kind. The Red One tore the throat out of a silver-maned bull, and was about to kill again when he saw that the White Bitch had got herself into trouble.

She had set her teeth into the flank of the ribby leading cow, and as they both floundered on the slick ice, the cow had fallen across her. Neither could get up. With the cow's splay hoofs beating a frantic tattoo on her rump, the pinned-down White Bitch was sobbing in rage and frustration but still grimly maintaining her hold. The Red One went to work.

When the cow's flailing hoofs were quiet, the White Bitch struggled free of the carcass. She shook herself, glared at the Red One as if he had been responsible for the incident, then began feeding vindictively, snarling between mouthfuls.

As they fed, the Red One remembered how, as a starving orphaned pup, he had been welcomed to a feast such as this one fantastically cold day on Goose Creek. And with this remembrance came a crowding of sights and sounds and smells, and particularly memories of his home den on the sandstone ridge above the tumbling stream. And then, quite suddenly, he knew the cause of his restlessness of the past several days. He was homesick. He had been gone too long, and had wandered too far, from the place where he had been born. He stood up, glanced at the White Bitch, and headed southeastward across the ice, fast. Presently he heard her close behind him matching his pace.

Others were moving in the same direction today. Since the first pale flush of dawn, Brant and Lobo had been in the air, and now Brant didn't like the looks of the weather. He said gruffly, "I'm about ready to believe I never saw that damn red wolf at the moose yard. Anyhow, telling you I saw him was sure a large mistake."

For ten days they had flown from daybreak to dusk. They had seen many wolves—black, brown, gray and white wolves. They had killed four and landed to pelt them. But the Red One had been elusive as a phantom. They hadn't caught even a glimpse of him. Brant's supply of gasoline, which he had cached over on the Kahiltna River for his projected fur-buying trip, was used up. And now the weather was closing in.

Occasional snowflakes batted against the windshield and the air was rough. In all the threatening horizon-circle there was only one small patch of blue brightness. It stood where the winter sun had risen, to the southeastward. Maybe it was a pilot trap, a sucker hole, Brant told himself, but he headed toward it hopefully.

"We gotta get out of this stuff," he told Lobo. "This could turn out bad so fast you wouldn't believe it." "Hey, look" Lobo said. "Ahead there on the ice." Brant was looking. Through the veil of ghost-dancing snow, two dun objects were visible on a triangle of black ice. Caribou carcasses.

Also Lobo noticed two wolf trails on the snow. Then, as they were approaching the dark ranks of spruce timber bordering the eastern riverbank, Lobo picked up a moving dot of red. He clutched Brant's shoulder.

"That's him—the Red One. Get down there after him."

Brant shrugged, and took the plane down in a shuddering, bucking dive. He was thinking, what I ought to do is bust this wild man over the head with a fire extinguisher. But I can't. The guy has got to be humored.

They saw the Red One and the White Bitch turn and look up at the diving plane, and then saw them line out at top speed for the timber. The first spruces were only 100 yards away. The wolves made it and went in under a wide-armed tree before Brant got Lobo even close to shotgun range.

Hating it, knowing the chance he was taking, Brant circled the tree, his right wing almost brushing the spired spruce-tops, while Lobo blasted charge after charge of buckshot into the boughs.

Then Brant said sharply, "Oh-oh," and leveled the plane off fast and headed it out over the river. The controls had gone sloppy in the last turn and he knew why. Ice on the wings.

Brant said, "Partner, we bought ourselves a package. We got a glacier building up on us."

They continued downstream, fifty feet above the river, unable to climb higher. Minutes passed and then through a gap in the storm, Brant saw the rooftops of Yellowbird under his left wing.

Under the circumstances, Yellowbird was the last place Brant wanted to visit with Lobo. But he had no choice.

Brant put her down blindly, feeling for the river. She hit hard on one ski, and as Brant cut the switch, a wingtip dug in, and then there were loud sounds of screeching metal and rending fabric.

In the ten-ton silence that followed, Lobo said, "Hallelujah!"

The plane had come to rest against a cutbank at the foot of Yellowbird's one street. It would never fly again. Neither Brant nor Lobo had been injured in the crash, but Brant was painfully aware that fate had kicked him in the groin. When they had climbed out of the wreckage he turned to Lobo, a tight smile on his face. "*C'est la guerre, partner.* Do you know how a man feels when he gambles for a fortune and loses?"

"Forget it," Lobo said shakily. "I'll buy us another plane."

"If you do," Brant said unhappily, "I'll believe in Santa Claus."

They went up the moccasin-padded trail to the street, Lobo in the lead. Coming toward them was a contingent of sourdoughs who'd heard the crash. There were old Tex Cobb, Gordon Bettles, Cap Northway, the Malamute Kid, the Ragtime Kid, Caribou Jack and others whom Lobo didn't recognize in the blowing snow. Caribou Jack was in the forefront.

As usual he was the very epitome of frontier sartorial elegance. He wore knee-length Tena moccasins with a half-pound of blue and red trade beads on each one, green Mackinaw pants, and a cerise silk shirt across which was draped a nugget watch chain heavy enough to anchor a skiff. Topping this was a marten cap and a handsome silver-gray sik-sik-puk parka with hand-carved fossil-ivory buttons.

Caribou Jack halted so suddenly that gaunt, white-thatched Gordon Bettles bumped into him. "Fer gawd's sake," Caribou Jack exclaimed in an awed tone, "Is that you Lobo?

"It's me," Lobo said without enthusiasm. For him this village was haunted. Given half a chance, he'd have turned tail and headed straight across the river into the wilderness.

Guided by the pack of sourdoughs, Lobo marched up the street and turned into the Yellowbird Bar. The bartender's eyes popped, and he glanced secretly toward the back room where he'd had a stampede pack made up and ready these long three years. Lobo ordered a double shot and downed it moodily. Beating his clenched fist on the bar, Lobo said to himself, "I'll kill that red so-and-so if it takes the rest of my life."

The bartender said, "Huh?"

Lobo pushed his empty glass across the bar. "Fill it up."

By now the Yellowbird Bar had more customers than it was designed for. The sourdoughs competed to buy him drinks, but after the first two Lobo had to get out. He had to be alone like a wounded wolf, he thought. Just to get out of here was even more important than it had been that terrible day on the cottonwood island when the forest fire was raging through the valley and he'd found Maria's shattered canoe.

Lobo stepped around the sourdoughs and headed for the door. "I'll see you roughnecks later. Gotta go get myself a room."

Two blocks down the storm-swept street Brant was dickering with old man Nicholai, the dog hotel proprietor, for a team of fast sled dogs, price no object. Brant had to leave here pronto.

And two blocks up the street, at the Yellowbird trading post, Maria had left her assistant, stoop-shouldered old George Hanks, in charge of the counter while she went up to the post office. She'd heard the plane roar over the town and thought that it might have brought mail. Leaning into the storm wind, she rounded the corner to the post office—and saw ahead of her a tall, lean figure.

That long, clean woodman's stride, the set of those wide shoulders—she'd have recognized anywhere, anytime. She cried, "Lobo," and ran toward him.

Lobo spun defensively on the icy path, as a man would when beset by a ghost. Then Maria was in his arms kissing him on his mouth and it was very apparent that she was no ghost. Lobo put a hand against the front of the post office building to steady himself, and shut his eyes. In a voice that didn't sound to him like his own, he croaked, "But I thought you were. . ."

"I know," Maria said. "Don't talk about it now." She took his hand and turned back to the trading post. Making conversation, she said, "Did you come in with Brant?"

Lobo jerked his head around. The question had revived him as if he'd been hit in the face with a bucket of ice water. He said, "Why? Do you know Brant?"

Maria said, "Of course. Everyone does. He lands here every week or so with mail. He flew me to Fairbanks last month."

"Seems as if I have some unfinished business with that gentleman," Lobo gritted. "But it can wait." He ducked his head as a squall of snow whistled down the street. "Uh—where are we going?" "The trading post," Maria said. "Your father might not be happy to see me," Lobo said in sudden misery because he'd held Maria a captive in the Goose Creek peaks. "In fact, he'll probably be doggone unhappy."

"My father is in the States buying goods for the post," Maria said, looking straight ahead. "Come along, Master Wolfer."

They went in off the storm-swept sidewalk into the big lamplit business room of the post, and Maria told old George Hanks to go home. The post was closed for the day, she said, and when George had left she locked the front door and turned to Lobo. "The bathroom is down the hallway," she said. "Go shave and bathe, and find some of my father's clothes. Then come back to me."

"Am I now being held a captive?" Lobo asked with a grin. Maria said, "Yes," hands on her hips, dark mestiza eyes mocking.

Lobo gave her a long, searching look. She had taken off her parka and in the yellow radiance of the kerosene lamps, he saw a new Maria. She had become a woman, wondrous and royal-ripe. He said, "It may take some time to remove three years of wilderness shagginess, but I'll be back as soon as possible. Don't go away."

Meantime on the sandstone ridge above Goose Creek, the Red One was watching the White Bitch inspect the den in which he'd been born. She was taking great interest in it. She scratched tentatively at the litter of cottonwood leaves that had blown into it, crawled to its innermost limit, returned to survey the view it afforded, and at last curled up at the entrance. The Red One, home now and no longer restless, curled up beside her.

Back at the Yellowbird Bar Caribou Jack, setting up drinks for the house, remarked sadly, "Lobo's back again, but we still don't know where the hell to stampede to."

Saga of the Red One

PART 9

The Red One slashed across the snows at the head of a great wolf pack that terrified everything in its path. But Lobo Smith didn't stir—till the pack struck home.

Now it was April, the Moon of Wolf Pups Being Born. At Loboville, the raw new stampede camp at the head of Goose Creek, the Wolf Den saloon was jam-packed with celebrating sourdoughs, stateside newspaper reporters, and the usual motley mob of gold-camp hangers-on.

The saloon consisted of two fourteen by sixteen tents pitched end to end, with a puncheon floor, and with kerosene lanterns hung from the ridgepole. The bar itself was more picturesque and serviceable than handsome. Shrewd-eyed, paunchy Camille McGowan, the proprietor, had placed three rough spruce planks across supporting tiers of packing boxes. And on his side of this primitive dispensary he'd opened sundry cases of booze referred to by his customers as Old Busthead, Old Tomahawk, Alaska Lightnin' and similar well-deserved names.

Tonight the camp was celebrating the first month of its existence. Over in a corner a gramophone with a horn as big around as a washtub was scratchily blaring "The Rose of Tralee." A contingent of girls brought in by the Oregon Mare were grimly trying to dance with the sourdoughs without getting their French heels caught in the gaps between the puncheon floor poles. Everyone was enthusiastically convinced that history was being made here, that Loboville was certain to be numbered among

America's great, gaudy frontier camps, along with Dawson, Nome, Deadwood and Virginia City.

Lobo, resplendent and self-conscious in store-boughten clothes, was at the bar being interviewed by half-a-dozen newspapermen. He'd launched into the tale of how he had made the original strike here, when suddenly he jerked his head up, listening.

From the frosty night outside was coming a sound that cut like a knife through the Rose of Tralee, the laughter, and the confusion of convivial conversations. His scalp tingling, Lobo strode through the doorway, leaving the plank door open behind him, and stood there on the hard-packed snow facing the dark overshadowing ridge to the north. It was a night of wind and stars, maybe five below zero, and very quiet at the moment except for an owl on the ridgeside who was talking softly of hunger. Then the sound Lobo had heard came again.

It was a swelling chorus of wolf song such as probably never before had poured across the wild Susitna valley. It soared incredibly, a smooth multivoiced crescendo that climbed and climbed until at last it broke off in a thin, brittle thread of sound. Only then did Lobo observe that all of the saloon's celebrating customers had followed him outside.

"Fer gawd's sake," said Caribou Jack, one of the North's elder sourdoughs, "I never heard anything like that in my whole life before. There must be hundreds o' wolves up there on that ridge." He turned to Lobo. "What is it—a wolf convention?"

"Sounds like a king wolf has recruited himself a hunting pack," Lobo said. "Must be a real heller of a king wolf. Right now, gentlemen, I'd bet a poke of dust that I know the color of his hide." As he finished speaking, the wild chorus lifted again from the black ridge. "Listen close," Lobo advised the fascinated newspapermen, "on account of you could spend the rest of your lives on this frontier and never hear that brand of music again."

When they returned to the bar, there was one who stood alone. He was a wizened, pock-marked Russian known as "Strychnine" George. He stood listening to the gramophone, a contemplative smile parting his lips. To him the wolf chorus had sounded like money in the bank. For Strychnine George was a poisoner.

Back at his camp, hidden under his blanket, was a bottle of white crystals with the skull and crossbones label. He well knew what he could accomplish with it.

Of course, the use of poison in taking animals was illegal, and it earned the poisoner the deep contempt of all honest woodsmen.

But these were matters that Strychnine George easily shrugged off. He listened to the gramophone, smiling, and planned a campaign. But in his happy preoccupation, he never dreamt that death was grinning at his elbow.

The Red One was running tonight in the forefront of more than 100 wolves. With the frosty wash of starlight silvering the valley, and the giant turquoise peaks sheering jaggedly overhead, it was a gorgeous experience. In a single savage feat of skill he had established himself as the king wolf of both the eastern and western Susitna wilderness.

To gather wolves from the many fiercely battling clans into one hunting pack had been a bloody feat. In fact, except for the Red One's three years as an outlaw princeling when he had learned to disregard clan taboos, it would have been impossible.

Starting with twenty members of his own Goose Creek clan—all that had survived the forest fire which had raged across the eastern watershed three years ago—he had swept like a scourge through the valley. The small family hunting packs he encountered either joined him or were destroyed. It had been nightmarishly ruthless, but this was the way of a king wolf. Once, when the great pack was on the move, he found four wolves of another clan helpless in the wire snares that an Indian had set around a moose carcass. The pack flowed over them pitilessly, and when it passed on, only bloodsmears, tufts of hair, and broken bones were left on the April snow crust.

Thus the uncompromising code—the code that had prompted some men to declare that except for the eternal warfare, assassination and cannibalism that decimated the clans and kept their strength down, the timber wolves would easily dominate all the continent's wildlife and rate as the most successful of four-footed killers.

Night was yielding to daybreak when the Red One brought the pack down to the mile-long reach of Trappers' Lake, where he hoped to find a moose yard. But there were no moose. The pack was partway across the blue-glimmering ice when a dog team emerged from the dark spruces rimming the farther shore. Riding the runners, still half asleep because of the early start he'd made, was the Malamute Kid. A few days ago he had taken a contract to carry the mail from the Susitna country over the Rainy Pass to the mining camps and trading posts on the Kuskokwim. It had struck him at the time as a fine job, suited to his talents and probably quite profitable.

But now, when he saw the enormous wolf pack fanned out ahead of him on the ice, his enthusiasm abruptly dimmed. During his thirty years in the North he had heard of only one comparable pack. That one had been reported by a mail carrier like himself who encountered it on Minchumina Lake, over north of the Alaska Range. He claimed to have counted 100 wolves whereas the Malamute Kid, despite the jitters that had overwhelmed him, tallied even more in this pack.

Gee-ing his team of fourteen Siberians with a hoarse command, he headed at a racing clip back the way he'd come toward Loboville. While it was true that there was no authentic record in Alaska of wolves having attacked a human, most sourdoughs kept their fingers crossed when the big hunting packs were running.

Many men had disappeared in the Alaskan wilds, and in some cases their wolf-gnawed bones had been found. Invariably, however, biologists and laymen city folk gave the wolves the benefit of the doubt. It was assumed that the hapless wilderness-farers had perished naturally or through accident, and that the wolves had eaten their bodies after the fact. But wolves were known to be reluctant carrion-eaters, and so the sourdoughs kept their rifles ready when the packs were running, and reserved judgment.

The Malamute Kid, glancing back over his shoulders just before the spruces shut off his view, got a good look at the pack leader. A long, rosy finger of dawnlight had reached across the lake, and in its glow this wolf was a fabulous brute, half again as large as any warrior behind him, and with a coat that shone red as burnished copper.

"Hiya. Chook. Mush. You bacon-thieves," he yelled at the Siberians. And to himself he muttered, "Nobody is ever gonna believe me."

He was wrong. When he reached Loboville and told his story, newspapermen covering the new gold strike seized upon it eagerly as a colorful feature piece, and Lobo himself verified the existence of the Red One.

Then, bit by bit, from a dozen different sources, the reporters ferreted out the story of the feud between Lobo and the Red One. They had a field day with it, and in the States their stories captured the public's fancy. Within a week the Red One was notorious from coast to coast and border to border.

The Malamute Kid, defiantly insisting that it had been the smart thing for him to turn back, told the sourdoughs in the Wolf Den saloon, "I don't give one good damn if the post office department does climb onto my neck, or if those salmon-eating characters over on the Kuskokwim never get their mail. I ain't headin' out across the Susitna again while that army o' wolves is between here and Rainy Pass. I got plans for my old age, believe me."

Meantime, the White Bitch, heavy with young, was alone at the den on the side of the sandstone ridge above Goose Creek—alone by preference. This was the one time of the year when no pregnant female wolf wanted her mate near her. She had enlarged the den, digging at its walls and roof until her claws were cracked and bleeding. At its farthest end she had made a hollow to fit her body, and had lined it with the litter of cottonwood leaves which had blown into the den's mouth over the years. Now she was ready except for one thing. She needed food before her time came, needed the strength that it would give her.

So this fateful afternoon, in the bright dazzle of April sunshine, she went foraging. A half-mile upvalley from the den she cut the snowshoe trail of a human, and shied away from it. Then she came to the carcass of a wolverine who had died very hard, as its contorted position and froth-flecked mouth attested. Next, a few yards ahead in a clump of buckbrush, she sighted what she took to be a crippled magpie. The long-tailed black-and-white bird was flopping on the snow, berating erratically, uttering faint agonized squawks.

The White Bitch, of course, knew nothing of poison. Poison had never been used in the Susitna until recently, when Strychnine George had arrived here. So the White Bitch pounced upon the magpie, who had just consumed a pellet of moose tallow which enclosed a pinch of strychnine. She ate the bird gratefully—and presently was in the greatest trouble she had ever known, her heart trying to stop, her entire body tortured and convulsing. By a supreme effort she dragged herself to the creek bank and crawled in under a ledge. Then consciousness mercifully flickered out, so that she was not aware of it when she aborted her pups.

Here the Red One found her. He had brought his tremendous pack across the Susitna and up Goose Creek, and had turned aside to visit the White Bitch. Not finding her at the home den in the sandstone ridge, he had taken her trail. It was a cold trail, with only traces of her good scent lingering, but it gave him a line to the ledge under which she had sought refuge. While puzzling out her trail he several times picked up the fresh scent of a human, and the grim conviction grew in him that the man, whoever he was, had somehow been responsible for his mate's unaccountable absence from their den.

When he found the White Bitch she was again conscious and recognized him, but when he attempted to crawl in under the ledge to her, she snarled feebly and snapped at him. His nose told him how sick she was now and how close to death she had been, and loyalty and affection urged him to remain with her, but she was making it very clear that she wanted to be alone in her trouble. So he backed from under the ledge and returned to the waiting pack and led it out onto the creek ice again.

Some miles upstream he once more came to the trail of the human whom he associated with the White Bitch's sickness. And as he stood there on the ice imprinting the man's scent on his memory, a young wolf of the Kahiltna clan trotted over to a ball of moose tallow lying innocently—but incongruously—under an overhanging spray of backside alder branches, and gulped it. Within seconds the young warrior staggered, snapped at his ribs in sudden pain, moaned, and fell over in convulsions, eyes rolled back, teeth clenched and claws tearing at the ice. The pack, gathered in a circle, watched him die, and wondered.

But now the Red One knew. Arising from the dead Kahiltna warrior was a strange chemical scent that he'd detected on the breath of the half-dead White Bitch. He needed no further proof that the unknown human on the creek had brought about these tragedies. A shudder of rage ran through him, so powerful that it racked his every bone and piano-wire sinew. Red ruff lifting, his topaz eyes flaring, he pointed his nose to the sky and lifted the crazy bloodyammer of his race. For the first time in his life he was berserk, and because as a king wolf he held sway over this pack, his 100-odd followers blended their voices in the savage high-pitched howling.

Today Strychnine George was putting out another line of poison sets. It was a clever and productive type of set. He had invented it himself and was proud of it. His equipment was a gallon jar of moose blood, a tin bucket, and his cherished vial of strychnine. Working along the margin of an overflow area, he would chip a shallow trench in the ice with his camp ax, cover the bottom of the trench with moose-blood, sprinkle strychnine over it, and scatter a few clots of blood about as a scent attraction. Then he would fetch a bucket of water from the overflow and pour it into the trench, filling it level full. The water would freeze and any passing wolf, hunger aroused, would claw and gnaw through the thin covering of ice, and eat the exposed poisoned blood, and shortly would die.

The truly marvelous thing about these ice sets, in Strychnine George's opinion, was that birds, weasels, and other unprofitable small creatures could not get at the bait and steal it as they too often did when he used poisoned balls of moose tallow.

Strychnine George was making his fourth or fifth set, and was berating himself for having lost a wolf two days ago who had got only a secondary dose of poison and consequently had escaped, presumably to die in some hidden spot. He had read the sign and understood what had happened. A magpie had eaten part of a tallow ball and then the wolf had eaten the magpie. Although Strychnine George had searched an entire day, he had been unable to find the carcass of his victim. At least $50 gone, he told himself bitterly. So he'd changed his method.

He had finished chopping a hole in the two-inch-thick overflow ice, and was about to dip up water in his tin bucket, when the incredible, kill-crazy music of the Red One's pack suddenly filled the valley from rim to rim. Strychnine George spun around, mouth open, rigid. In his time he had heard some wolf talk, but never anything like this diabolical chorus. Then suddenly he saw them, scores of dark forms ghosting toward him through the timber.

He yearned to sprint for his rifle, which lay across his pack 100 feet away, between him and the unbelievable wolf pack. But his legs rebelled, refusing to carry him in that direction. Filled with panic, clutching the camp ax, he fled out across the belt of overflow ice.

Such an overflow is caused by water pressure that forces a stream channel to gush up fountain-like through the solid winter ice. This surface water in turn freezes over, but never so solidly as the layer of old ice beneath it. The result is a sort of sandwich, thick ice below, a layer of water above it, then a top layer of treacherous rubbery new ice.

Strychnine George almost made it to the far bank, where he intended to climb a tree. Almost but not quite. The overflow ice broke beneath him with a sullen crash, and in the next instant he was belly deep in the bitter current, floundering desperately for footing. He slipped and went under, came up and hooked his elbows over the ice shelf, which broke under his weight. He went under again and regained his footing only by a desperate effort. This time, uttering hoarse animal-like sounds of relief, he succeeded in dragging himself out of the water.

For April, this was a cold day, ten degrees below freezing. With his clothes turning into an icy armor, Strychnine George lumbered up the bank to the nearest spruce. Stooping in under the snow-hooded spruce, he tore off an armful of the lower dead limbs.

With the cold striking at his vitals, he broke the pitchy branches with stiffening fingers and arranged them for an emergency fire. Then he opened the waterproof metal cylinder, shook two matches into the palm of his hand, and clumsily struck the heads together. They flamed, but as he thrust them under the spruce branches, they sputtered and perversely went out. He tried again, and this time the match sticks broke in his freezing fingers.

He thought a moment, fighting off the drowsiness which he knew was death. Then he took two more matches between his teeth, managed to light them on the corrugated side of the match safe, and held his face down so that the flame was under the fuel. The matches burned down until they were blistering his lips and nose before a gob of pitch caught and flared brightly upward through the cross-piled branches.

Moaning, Strychnine George hunkered over the life-giving fire. Carefully he put on more fuel, and the heat of the crackling flames ascended through the snow-weighted boughs of the spruce. Strychnine George began congratulating himself for his woods-smartness. But loosened by the heat, a half-ton of snow cascaded off the tree, extinguishing the fire and burying Strychnine George to his shoulders.

Knowing that he couldn't do it again, he sat there unresisting. The last sound in his ears was the death music of the Red One and his pack . . . .

Lobo and Maria were sitting together on an upended crate in the new Loboville trading post, looking out the window at the mushrooming stampede camp. The post was not an imposing structure. It was a sheet-iron building with a spruce pole framework. Maria's father, white-bearded Ptarmigan Dunbar, had established it as a necessary branch of his Yellowbird post, and Maria and the venerable, stoop-shouldered George Hanks were managing it. From the window one could see the colorful beehive activity typical of a new camp, and hear the sounds that accompanied them. The white blossoms of tents going up. The blue haze of woodsmoke from the many fires the miners were burning against the frozen gravel of streambeds and benches, thawing down inch by stubborn inch to the pay streaks they hoped to find on bedrock. You could hear the good frontier sound of axes, of whipsaws cutting through knotty timberline spruce logs, of hammering and the lonesome moans of chained malamutes, of felled trees crashing down and the voices of surveyors calling the mates and bounds of claims.

Maria said, "It was a grand thing, letting your friends know," she laughed and rumpled his hair, "where the—the heck—to stampede to."

Lobo was watching an Indian runner coming up the trail from the valley. He could not quite tell yet, but he thought it was Googla Chickloosun. If it was Googla, something important must have happened. Googla was a chief's son and seldom worked as a runner.

"Seems as if there's enough gold to go around," Lobo said. "But to get back to what we were talking about . . . we'll be married in June, come whatever?"

"Will you actually be at the church in time for the wedding?"

"I'll camp overnight in the church to make sure of it," Lobo assured her.

"Then we'll be married in June, come whatever."

Lobo reached past her to the trading post counter and picked up the Sunday supplement of a Seattle newspaper, and spread it at their feet. Above the fold of the front page was an eight-column illustration. It showed a gigantic wolf, fanged jaws agape, launching himself through the air at a parka-clad woodsman who had the handsome, aquiline features of a shaving-cream model. He was armed only with a long knife, but he wore a hero's smile of confidence as he aimed a thrust at the attacking wolf's throat. The headline read, "Lobo Smith and the Red One in Dramatic Death Feud."

"Honest to gosh, do I really look like that?" Lobo asked, hopefully.

"Handsomer," Maria said, deadpan.

"Well, Well. Be doggoned," Lobo said. "So that's the secret of my life-long success with women."

Maria blazed, "Why, you conceited . . ."

Lobo scooped her onto his lap. She was still struggling and banging her heels against his shins when he saw the Indian runner top the brow of the hill and turn in toward the front door of the post. It was Googla Chickloosun, all right. Muttering at the interruption, Lobo went to the door.

Googla leaned against the stormporch, panting. "I came fast, Lobo, to tell you," he said. "Biggest wolf pack I ever heard of came through the valley maybe one hour ago. A red wolf size of a caribou was leading it. They went to your cabin. Killed your dogs—all of them. Only blood and bones left."

When Lobo returned to Maria and told her what had happened he was taut and pale with anger. "I raised those dogs from pups," he grated. "They were my friends. Now I'm gonna take that red varmint's trail and stay on it until I kill him." He picked up his long-barreled rifle and stepped out the doorway. Behind him Maria bowed her head, then vindictively ground her moccasin heel into the newspaper artist's conception of the great red king wolf.

Saga of the Red One

PART 10

Lobo was getting closer to the Red One.
And while his forgotten bride vaguely understood his desire
to kill the wolf, she was filled with foreboding.

Maria of Yellowbird touched the pilot's shoulder and pointed. A thousand feet below, sliding toward the float plane's right wing, was a narrow body of water that gleamed like hammered silver in the morning light. Between the water and a stand of brilliant yellow cottonwoods stood a squat log cabin. A wisp of smoke curled from a square hole cut in the roof's center.

"That is Rabbit Slough," Maria said. "And the cabin is Blind Nick's cabin."

The pilot nodded, and shoved the plane's nose down. New here in the Susitna country, he was an angular blond lad with freckles, a shy smile, and steady gun-blue eyes. Matt Nemick was in love, and this was hurting him plenty. He put the float plane on the water, taxied in to the mudbank in front of the cabin, and cut the switch. Then he turned to Maria.

"Sure you don't want me to go in with you?" he asked hopefully. The sultry-eyed mestiza girl shook her head.

"No. This is going to be private and personal, and you wouldn't believe anything you'd see there anyway." As she stepped down onto the float and started ashore she smiled back at him. "But you could wish me luck."

She went up the moccasin-padded trail, past chained and yowling pack dogs, past a canoe rack and a stilt-legged cache with skins drying in frames suspended from its overhang, and knocked on the plank door of the low, windowless cabin. A voice with the thudding quality of a moose-gut drum said, "Enter, daughter of the people."

Blind Nick, the Tena shaman, was sitting exactly as he had been when she'd last seen him five years ago. He sat cross-legged beside a bed of birch coals that glowed in a circle of blackened stones on the hard packed earth floor. Over his broad shoulders hung a robe of silky otter skins. His long hair was unbraided and without ornaments, but he wore an oodoochilah necklace of green burial jade from the far Kobuk, and on his right wrist was a bone bracelet with carved characters that the people who spoke Sanskrit could have read.

He motioned to a white reindeer hide on the floor opposite him, and said, "Be seated, and tell me what I can do for you."

"It is about Lobo Smith," Maria said. Her voice was low and at first the words came hesitantly because, like all her mother's people, she held Blind Nick in awe. "Hunting the red king wolf has become his whole life." Maria made the Tena sign of sorrow, the fingertips of both hands together over her heart. "I have not seen him for four months. He—he is like the man in a story my Russian-Aleut nurse told me when I was a child."

Blind Nick's lean hawk-like face was a copper mask in the ember glow, and his dead eyes were the color of chalk. "Do you want to tell me that story?" he said.

"The man was a hunter and the hero of his tribe," Maria said. "And there was a great king wolf that he regarded as his enemy. He pursued this wolf around the world. Finally he was about to loose his arrow into the wolf's heart when the animal spoke to him. 'Brother,' the wolf said, 'this matter between you and me has held the meaning of our lives. It was what we were born for. Kill me, and what will you have left?'"

"And the man agreed. He could not bear to think what existence would be like with the king wolf dead and the hunt ended forever. His tribe never saw him again."

"It is a very old story," Blind Nick said. "Older than the tablets of Moses. Once it was a song called Lament of the Hunter's Woman."

"Well, it should have a better ending," Maria said. "Maybe the hunter's woman was too tame and long-suffering. . . . Will you show me where Lobo and the Red One are now, and what they are doing?"

Blind Nick was silent so long that Maria thought he was going to refuse. Then he sighed, and reached behind him into the shadows and took a bundle of dried herbs from a beaded caribou-skin pouch. His sightless eyes held Maria's and there was compassion in his voice as he said, "In a moment, daughter of the people."

Elsewhere that day, the Red One and the White Bitch had awakened at daybreak in an alder thicket beside a plunging mountain stream. The Tenas called the stream Sky Creek, for a reason that has been lost.

The two wolves shook the dead leaves from their coats, drank at the rim of an eddy, and trotted up the stream bars. A golden eagle dived on them for practice, screaming. A hoary marmot cursed them bitterly from the mouth of its den under a lichen-shaggy boulder. On a mucky slope a black bear, digging wild onion bulbs, took one look at the pair, snorted, and fled up the canyon floor, glancing apprehensively back over his shoulder at every other bound. A typical high-country autumn morning.

Then the wind shifted, blowing down from the heights. At once the wolves halted, heads up, noses working. The Red One had killed mountain goats during other forays into the peaks, and the memory of the sweet tallow-rich meat made his stomach rumble pleasantly. The White Bitch had never seen a mountain goat, but the scent was good.

The Red One needed no urging. He turned off the creek bars, up into the belt of alders, climbing. Throughout the summer he and the White Bitch had dieted, keeping themselves lean for comfort's sake. But now the hot days were gone and it was again time to kill fat meat.

Above the brush line, on a talus slope, they came to a game trail worn by the hoofs of countless generations of goats. They followed it and presently it gave way to a three-foot cliffside ledge on which, the wind said, they would find the goats.

It was a family of goats, a billy, a female, and two four-month-old kids. The billy was an oversized patriarch, humped like a buffalo and weighing close to 300 pounds. At the moment he was puzzled. He stood with his head over the brink of the narrow ledge, gazing intently across the canyon. Over there in the rocks, 800 yards away, a point of light was winking. The billy had never seen anything like it. So, with his family behind him, he hastened down the canyon.

The winking spot of brilliance across the canyon was sunlight reflecting from the lenses of Lobo Smith's binoculars. The lean master wolfer sat with his back against a twisted timber-line spruce, muttering as he watched drama unfold on the eastern wall.

Lobo was bearded to the eyes, with a tangle of sun-streaked hair falling to his jaw line. His shirt and pants were in rags, his pacs worn through and patched with rawhide. And in 100 miles of hard hunting he had not, until the past few minutes, laid eyes on the king wolf.

And now he had the Red One and the White Bitch fair in the field of his glasses. At sunup, he'd first spotted the four goats, then a solitary black bear down in the canyon bottom. He was planning a stalk for the bear when, on a talus slope below the eastern wall, he caught a moving glint of red. His hands shook as he focused the glasses.

"Holy suffering," he groaned. "Eight hundred yards. A canyon between him and me. And me with a swell case of the starvation feebles." He watched the wolves a bit longer, then shouldered his pack, picked up the Remington, and began looking for a route down the canyonside.

Now the Red One, with the White Bitch following nervously, made his way out onto the ledge, although he hated doing it. He distrusted height. The Red One moved with exaggerated caution, and trying to keep his eyes off the 1,000-foot drop-off yawning on his left. He knew that the goats were close ahead.

As he rounded an outjutting boss of rock, the goats came slamming toward him at top speed. When the billy saw the Red One he uttered a startled grunt and skidded to such an abrupt halt that the female collided heavily with him.

The Red One was aware that of all the fighting animals in the Susitna wilderness, the clever-footed, rapier-horned mountain goat was probably the most dangerous if you had to fight him in the high rocks.

As an opening move, the Red One went in with a rush, stopping short as the billy stepped forward to meet him. Next he feinted to the right, tried for the billy's beard, missed, and took a horn-gouge across his cheek.

The billy, getting confident, moved ahead again, forefeet spread, watching the Red One with a dour-up-from-under glare. The Red One gave ground, not seeing how he could possibly get past those lightning-fast black horns.

The billy was crowding, gaining more and more confidence, when the Red One suddenly pounced. As the goat's horns thrust up wickedly at his throat, the Red One grabbed the left horn between his jaws, close down where it joined the skull, and hung on. The billy was an exceptionally powerful goat, and outweighed the Red One by more than 100 pounds, but he had never before felt the explosive strength in a king wolf's piano-wire muscles. His neck began to yield under the leverage on it. His eyes rolled. He groaned, and ground his teeth. Then, steadying himself against the cliffside, he did the unexpected. With a mighty effort he whirled in a fast quarter-pivot, so that the Red One was swung out over the brink of the ledge.

The Red One hung in space, and he knew stark fear. But he held his grip on the goat's horn, and quickly found a foothold on a point of rock, and was able to claw his way back onto the ledge.

That was the end so far as the billy was concerned. The White Bitch had raged in behind him and was cutting at his hamstrings. In a moment the two wolves stretched him out, the White Bitch ripping his belly until the guts spilled out while the Red One held him helpless. In his agony, struggling to rise, the goat kicked himself over the brink.

He turned slowly as he fell, a snow-white shape in the luminous blue morning air. Far below he crashed through a spike-armed dead spruce, struck a ledge, bounced high, then spun end over end down a shale pitch to the bank of Sky Creek. The Red One and the White Bitch went back the way they had come, heading for the canyon floor and a meal of goat meat. The female goat watched them go, blinking stupidly.

In the bottom of the canyon, under a hangman's cottonwood that glowed like a tower of yellow light, the lone black bear had curled up for a nap.

Above, up at the first sheer upslope of the cliffs, there was a rending crash of dead spruce limbs. Jerked awake, the black bear leaped up in time to see a goat carcass pinwheel down a shale slide and come to rest just thirty feet away.

After shaking the carcass to assure himself that it was really dead, he lay down across it and began feeding.

Back at Blind Nick's cabin at that moment Nick was saying, "In a moment, daughter of the people."

He dropped the bundle of dried herbs on the birch coals. The stems crackled, a pale tongue of flame arose, and blue coils of smoke climbed to the roof. The smoke had a heavy fragrance that filled the room and became almost unbearably sweet. Maria sat motionless, heart pounding, watching blue smoke-shapes eddy and drift about her. The shapes coalesced and then there was only a thin azure fog, with light trying to break through it from above. The walls of the cabin were gone, as were the shadows. Maria kept her frightened gaze on Blind Nick's face, and saw his thin lips curve in a reassuring smile. Then he was gone, too, as light struck through the blueness.

A sunlight scene was forming. There was a jumble of broken snow-topped mountains, the white shine of a glacier, and a grim gash of a canyon with a stream rushing through it. Partway down the wall of the canyon a man was descending a rock chimney. Maria caught her breath as she recognized Lobo Smith, and uttered a moan of pity when she saw his raggedness. Lobo moved with slow, rubber-kneed deliberation, obviously husbanding the strength left in him. When he reached a huge chock stone wedged between the sides of the chimney cleft, he sat down and got out his binoculars. What he saw caused him to laugh silently into his dark jungle of beard.

The scene shifted to the canyon floor on the opposite side of the stream. Here, a few yards from a spreading Indian-yellow cottonwood, a black bear was feeding on the carcass of a mountain goat. Suddenly the bear spun around, snarling. Down-canyon, at the margin of an alder thicket, there was movement, the shine of sunlight on a russet coat, and a flicker of white. Then out of the alders trotted the Red One and the White Bitch. The black bear roared at them. He reared up and made threatening gestures with his front paws. He popped his jaws like trap springs. The wolves sat on their haunches and watched the demonstration. Their mouths were open and their tongues lolling. In a human, this attitude would have been one of amusement.

Then the Red One trotted toward the bear, his ruff bristling. He went in fast the last few feet, swerved aside as the bear launched a thunderbolt pawstroke, and was in again before the bear could recover balance, slashing at an exposed flank. The bear spun, bawling, and struck with both paws. It didn't get him anything. As he half reared to try again, the White Bitch ghosted in behind him and chopped at both hamstrings. She hit the taut, straining tendons as expertly as a butcher finds a joint with his knife.

The bear stumbled, and went down on one hip. He wasn't really crippled yet, the tendons weren't severed, but he was hurt and his speed was gone, such as it had been. Sobbing, he heaved himself around and grabbed for the White Bitch with his jaws. He missed by a foot, and now the Red One was at his flank again, savaging it, seeking the life beneath the tender flank skin.

The black bear had had enough. He fled into the stream, went under, came up blowing, and swam for the bank. The millrace current carried him 100 yards, banging him against rocks and rolling him, before he was able to get his feet on bottom and limp shore. Shaking the water from his pelt, he headed down-canyon, a sorry and bedraggled bear but a lucky one, for he had fought a king wolf and his mate and was still alive.

Then Maria saw Lobo Smith come into the vision. He was cautiously picking his way toward the stream through a tumble of house-size boulders. The goat carcass and the wolves were hidden from him now by the rocks, but he had the top of the yellow hangman's cottonwood as a marker. He reached the water's edge, and was about to climb onto a great tilted slab of granite that lay with one edge in the stream, when atrocious bad luck spoiled his stalk. There was a rattle of claws and a labored grunt as the departing black bear leaped onto the rock from the opposite side. For the space of two heartbeats Lobo and the bear gazed at each other in passionate disbelief. The bear moved first. With a wild bawl of fright, he plunged into the stream again, and this time swam straight down the middle.

The Red One and the White Bitch heard the bear bawl, and were instantly alert. Obviously the bear had encountered danger, and what was dangerous to him could be dangerous to them. Fading back to the rim of the alders, they stood watching and listening. Downstream a magpie appeared from nowhere and began circling a tilted rock slab, squawking excitedly. It was telling of an alarming discovery. High in the rocks a cooperative marmot relayed the alarm in a series of shrill whistles. Then Lobo Smith eased himself onto the granite slab, pushing the Remington ahead of him. The two wolves were in motion a split second after he came into view. Lobo saw them and jerked up the rifle, but before he could line his sights the pair had vanished into a brush-masked wash. They did not reappear. Lobo sat up, cursing, then abruptly burst into laughter.

"Well, anyway, dammit," he gurgled, "I get the goat carcass."

The sunlight in the vision faded and the high mountains blurred. The scene blinked out. Then Maria was again regarding Blind Nick across the bed of birch coals. She drew in a long, shaky breath. When she trusted herself to speak, she said, "I saw what I asked to see. But there was a strange thing. I could understand what the animals were doing and why they did it. I could almost get inside their thoughts. But I could not understand Lobo. He was ragged and starved, shaggy as a wild man, and dead-tired. He failed at what he was trying to do. Still, he was happy. He laughed. Is there an answer to that?"

"There is an answer," the shaman said. "The Hunter's Woman found it. In her song she grieved because the wilderness had got into her hero's heart, and was too big to crowd out. To him the wilderness was a wolf."

"She didn't fight," Maria flared. Standing up, she went over to the door. "Will you tell me one more thing? What is the name of that stream?" "Sky Creek," Blind Nick said. "I am grateful," Maria said. "Now I will fight."

Matt Nemick had been pacing the slough-bank, chain-smoking cigarettes. When he saw Maria leave the cabin, he loped up the trail to meet her. Although he had known Maria only two weeks, he had it bad. He helped her aboard the plane, fastened her seat belt, flushing as his hand touched hers. When they were in the air, on the course to Yellowbird, he let the plane fly itself while he asked Maria the question that had been keeping him awake nights. It came out with a rush.

"Could you possibly," he asked, "consider marrying a so-so Polack bush pilot?" "What so-so Polack bush pilot?" "Me, for instance." Then he blurted. "Look, don't answer that now. It was a lousy proposal. I'll do better next time. I'm a crude guy, I guess. All I know is airplanes, and plenty of characters know more about 'em than I ever will. But think it over, will you, huh? I'm serious. I never was so serious in my whole doggoned life."

Maria was looking ahead at the emerald reach of birch forest and the broad sun-spangled channels of the Susitna River. The shadow of a smile crossed her face. "Talk to me about it," she said, "when we come back from the Sky Creek country."

"What are we going to do there?" Matt asked joyfully.

"Kill a wolf—I hope," Maria said.

Saga of the Red One

CONCLUSION

As the two came face to face, destiny stalked in single-minded determination. The air was charged with violence.

"Maria wants this wolf knocked off," pint-sized Caribou Jack was saying to the boys in the crowded Wolf-Den Saloon. "Then Lobo Smith won't have no excuse not to come home and git married like he oughta, the crazy galoot. She's in a kinda—uh—fightin' mood."

Camille McGowan broke the silence. "Just how do you figger we could kill the Red One when Lobo hisself ain't had no luck at it?" "We'll kill the varmint the scientific way, with airplanes and buckshot," Caribou Jack said. "We send a batch o' telegrams charterin' every free plane in Alaska. They could be here tomorrow. Then we recruit some extra gunners, an' take off an' fly till we locate the Red One. Maria swears she knows where the critter is hanging out." Caribou Jack tossed his poke onto the table top. "There's a starter fer expenses. Feed the kitty, gents."

Four more bulging buckskin pokes of dust thudded beside Caribou Jack's. Then green-eyed old Tex Cobb bawled to the bartender, "Hustle an armload of champagne over this way, son. Us wolf hunters aim to drink some fancy toasts to the downfall of the Red One. . . ."

The Red One and the White Bitch, had just gorged themselves full of moose meat. Now they moved downwind from the moose carcass and curled up in a warm pool of sunlight behind a time-wrecked cabin. They were lying here, drowsily licking the blood from their paws and chests, when a thin thread of vibration broke through the sighing of the forest breeze. The sound grew. It was coming out of the north, where Sky Creek pass split the purple mountain barrier. Within seconds it became recognizable as the deep-throated drone of many engines. The wolves bounded up. They knew that fateful music. Neither had forgotten the bitter day on the frozen Tokichitna when a plane roared in over the ridges, and gunfire blasted the life out of the gray Tokichitna warrior who coveted the White Bitch. Or the blizzard-threatening day on the Susitna bank when the same plane kept them crouched under a hospitable spruce while charge after charge of buckshot ripped into the shielding branches overhead.

The Red One looked about for cover. A few yards to their right was a tangle of windthrown spruces with second-growth saplings growing up through them. He headed for the place, the White Bitch at his heels, both moving heavily because of the gorge of meat and tallow in their stomachs. Crawling in under the crisscrossed fallen trees, they lay motionless while the song of the engines swelled. It was filling the sky now, racketing through the timber, closing in. . . .

Lobo Smith topped Sky Creek pass toward midafternoon. Ragged and shaggy as a wild man, he stood in the lee of a granite point, gazing at the wasteland that reached to the horizon. He was trying to make up his mind what to do. He knew beyond doubt that the Red One was out there. All day he had been seeing signs that the king wolf and his white mate had passed this way, heading south. There had been obvious signs, an occasional track, a red or a white hair caught on the stubble of rabbit-killed willow brush. Also there had been subtle signs that only a wolfer would have understood.

But Lobo was worried. More than anything else, he wanted to hang on the trail of the king wolf. It was a marvelous way to live, except for one thing.

He had to return to Loboville and Yellowbird, to Maria. He had now been four months in the wilds having a glorious time, while Maria, he told himself, had no idea where he was, or even if he were dead or alive. It would serve him damn well right, he thought, if Maria gave him the heave-ho and married some-one else.

This was when he heard the planes.

After a moment they came in low over the peaks, ten of them, spaced in a line a half-mile wide, with the canyon as its center. Lobo stared, mystified, as they passed him roaring southward. He had never before seen so many planes in a single flight. They held formation until they were over a small timbered valley with a lake in it, some six miles from the pass. Then the line became a circle, the planes banking tightly over the spruce tops. With his glasses Lobo saw the flashes of gunfire from the cockpits, and presently thought he could hear the faint popping of the many shots.

"Halleluja!" he said hoarsely as he started down the south slope at a run, hurdling boulders, scrambling across washes, "I gotta find out what that's all about. . . ."

Matt Nemick took his hands off the controls of the float plane, and searched himself for a cigarette. Maria sat beside him, holding an automatic shotgun. They were flying at the right end of the line of planes, and Sky Creek pass had just disappeared behind their left wingtip.

"Well, that's it," the blond pilot said. "We've dragged the canyon and both walls. What made you so positive we'd sight the wolves here? Something your Indian medicine-man friend told you?"

Maria said, "Yes," in a taut voice. Suddenly she felt small and foolish, almost sorry she had started this aerial hunt.

But then her back stiffened. The country ahead was open, with little cover for any animal larger than a parka squirrel. She could see only one spot where a king wolf who knew he was hunted might seek meat and sanctuary. It was a circular timbered valley with a small blue lake set in it.

"Over there, please," she said.

They both, at the same instant, sighted the moose carcass. No birds were at the carcass, which indicated that the bull had been killed probably within the hour. Matt grinned. "Salute," he said. "Your hunch was good." He waggled his wings in a prearranged signal, and the other planes came in.

It was hawk-eyed old Tex Cobb who spotted the White Bitch's tail. Only the tip showed at the side of a windfall, but it had moved as she crowded closer to the Red One. Next time around the circle, Tex shoved the barrel of his shotgun out the plane's right window and emptied it. The other sourdough gunners followed suit.

The White Bitch moaned as wood splinters, bark and earth drove against her under the impact of the barrage of shot. She felt the Red One jerk convulsively, then smelled blood, and knew that their enemies in the sky had scored against him. She herself was unhurt. But wild, unreasoning panic surged through her. She buried her nose in the Red One's ruff, and shut her eyes.

The Red One knew that what he needed most of all was a new hiding place, and it would have to be close at hand.

His gaze fell on the tumbled-down cabin. One gable of the ruined roof tilted up at a cockeyed angle, with a rotted scrap of tarpaulin hanging down over it. Maybe it would do. There was nothing better he could reach. Watching the sky, the Red One dragged himself from under the windfalls. A pellet of buckshot was lodged against his spine, and his hindquarters were numb and useless. But he reached the cabin, pulling himself with his front paws, and managed to muscle his long body up into the mold-smelling gloom behind the tattered tarpaulin. The White Bitch joined him, and they lay together, ears straining to catch the sound of any new onslaught.

"Did you see him?" Maria asked, tight-lipped, as she stuffed shells into her shotgun. "Do you think we killed him?"

"All I saw was down timber and flying splinters," Matt said. "Holy smokes, what a bombardment."

"Can you land?"

"I guess so," Matt said. "Anyhow, I'll try. I've got the best plane for it. But it's a short lake. We'll never get off again until a wind comes up. I mean, a *real* wind.

He stalled the plane onto the water and they watched the opposite shoreline swoop toward them. Matt's hands were shaking when the pontoons jarred into the sedge grass and muck. "A screwball landing," he said. "I wouldn't try that again for. . . ."

Maria was already out on the float. They went up the bank side by side, Maria holding the shotgun ready. The other planes were still circling the lake. The pilots wanted to land, but Matt's example hadn't been cheering.

The Red One and the White Bitch heard Matt and Maria coming. The White Bitch knew now what she must do. Moving silently as a leaf-shadow, she slipped from behind the tarpaulin, crawled on her belly to the nearest clump of brush, then streaked out.

Maria saw the flash of white from the corner of her eye, and to her it seemed that the wolf had come from the bombarded blowdown area. The automatic shotgun came up on line, bucking against the mestiza girl's shoulder as she pressed the trigger and kept pressing it. The White Bitch went down, snarling, skidding on the moss under the buckshot blows. She died facing away from the hiding place, her diversion accomplished.

"Now help me find the Red One," Maria said grimly. "Let's get this bloody business finished."

Leading the way to the nest of windfalls, Maria paused a moment at the fallen-in cabin to reload. She stood within four feet of the Red One. The king wolf watched her through a tear in the tarpaulin, filled with a terrible, helpless rage. Had she so much as glanced toward him, he would have hurled his crippled body upon her, and taken vengeance for the White Bitch. But in a moment Maria went on.

They searched the blowdown and the timber, and searched both again. Then it was sundown. Before the planes left, Caribou Jack dropped a note saying they would return in the morning. Matt built a fire, and broiled steaks from the wolf-killed moose.

"I should have known the Red One would escape," Maria said. "Now he will be smarter than ever—and I am lost."

Matt moved quickly, putting an arm about her, drawing her close. "Forget the wolf," he said. "Forget what you are trying to do. The whole thing is crazy. I asked you to marry me two days ago. I ask you again now."

For one fleeting second, Maria looked deep into Matt's eyes with a look he was never to forget. Then she nodded her head quickly. "All right, I'll marry you, Matt," she said.

Behind them in a dusky undergrowth there was a rustle of movement. Then Lobo Smith, a gaunt, bearded scarecrow of a man, strode near the fire and stood watching. Death was in his eyes. Finally he spoke. "Well, good night and so long. I guess I had this coming to me."

Before Maria could speak, he stepped into the timber on silent feet, and was gone.

Several weeks later, the Red One, sides bulging with the meat of mountain ram, slept in a snow tunnel. As he slept he dreamed. In his dreaming the Red One relived his escape from the tumbled-down trapline cabin the night after he had been shot. He had lived mostly as a scavenger, competing with coyotes and foxes for rotten silver salmon grounded along the sand bars of freezing streams. He foraged only at night. In daytime he hid out, for now he feared even his own people.

Then the Red One found a moose carcass lying curled up on a drift, snow-dusted, white splashes of bird dung streaking its antlers. The 800 pounds of meat was a fabulous boon, and for ten days the Red One stuffed himself. Strength seeped back into him. He regained partial use of his hindquarters. He began to feel almost his old royal self. So today he had been able to kill the ram.

Sleeping now in the blue half-light of the snow tunnel near his kill, the Red One dreamed on as the drums and pipes of the storm sounded overhead.

Lobo stood outside now, eying the tunnels that led down to an undersnow pasture of a band of mountain sheep. For fifteen hours he had fought the frozen snow to follow the Red One's trail. He had never before seen anything like the place and never expected to again. The important thing, however, was that the trail led into the tunnels. The Red One almost certainly was in one of the dark passageways. But which one? At the entrance, in the confusion of hundreds of half-obliterated sheep trails, the Red One's trail had been lost.

"All right. So I'll have to invite the devil to come out and take his medicine in the open," Lobo growled.

He thumbed the safety latch of the Remington, and fired a shot into the air. At once there was a flurry of hoofs that made the snow tremble under his webs. Sheep erupted in panic from the tunnels. They made for the creek, lunging through the drifts, falling and being trampled, climbing one another's backs.

As they wallowed past the farthest tunnel, Lobo caught a glimpse of red on the flank of the band. He tried a snap shot, missed, and cursed as he saw the Red One force his way into the center of the stampeding band, deliberately using the sheep as a shield. Lobo fired again, and a shoulder-shot ewe went down kicking, but the Red One was still on his feet. Then the sheep and their unwanted companion plunged over the creek bank in a cloud of powder snow, and disappeared.

"Gawdamighty, give me some luck now," Lobo groaned as he ran toward the frozen stream. "Just one little piece of luck, please."

The Red One, with twenty pounds of sheep meat in his belly, was incapable of flight. He landed heavily on the ice in the midst of the ewes and yearlings, picked himself up, and gazed along the ribbon of the stream. Two hundred feet above him a tributary creek came in at a right angle through a heavy growth of mountain alders. He headed for the spot, lumbering in the wake of the fear-maddened sheep.

Too well the Red One was aware of what he must do now. Since he couldn't flee, he would have to fight. He reached the point of alders and crouched behind it, waiting. He knew it was Lobo who had tracked him down and knew that this was to be the end of their long contest. But the chances were even. He had a good ambush, and the wolfer would have to pass within thirty feet of it.

Lobo did not expect an ambush, because never in his life had he known a timber wolf to attack a human. His only warning as he sprinted up the ice was a flicker of red from the corner of his eye. Twisting around on his webs, he saw the Red One coming at him in straining, belly-swaying bounds. Then, before he could bring his rifle to his shoulder, fate had its savage jest.

The tributary creek was a warm-water stream, a trap, with only a thin sheet of ice and snow crust covering it. The ice gave way under the Red One's weight, and then he was in the black water, chin and paws on the unbroken shelf of ice, the current tearing at him, trying to drag him under. He and Lobo were staring at each other, blue eyes locked with green. Then Lobo ran toward the helpless wolf. He knew not why. He yelled wildly, "No, no—not my friend!" and knelt and reached out to grab the king wolf's ruff. As he did, the ice broke under him. The sullen water closed over the two heads.

Back at Yellowbird Maria and Matt were saying, "I do."

BIBLIOGRAPHY

"Murderer in the Trees," . . . . *Sports Afield*, September 1951
"Trapping is No Way to Get Rich," . . . . *True*, February 1952
"He Wears a Black Pitchfork," . . . . *Outdoor Life*, June 1952
"Needed: A New Deal for Alaska's Bears," . . . . *Sports Afield*, June 1952
"Moose with the Gunshot Antler," . . . . *Field & Stream*, July 1952
"Viva Mayheeco!" . . . . *Sports Afield*, November 1952
"The Old Brown Bear,
She Ain't What She Used to Be," . . . . . . *Hunting Yearbook*, January 1953
"Adventure Is My Business, Part 1," . . . . *Sports Afield*, February 1953
"Adventure Is My Business, Part 2," . . . . *Sports Afield*, March 1953
"Adventure Is My Business, Part 3," . . . . *Sports Afield*, April 1953
"Adventure Is My Business, Part 4," . . . . *Sports Afield*, May 1953
"Adventure Is My Business, Part 5," . . . . *Sports Afield*, June 1953
"Adventure Is My Business, Part 6," . . . . *Sports Afield*, July 1953
"Adventure Is My Business, Part 7," . . . . *Sports Afield*, August 1953
"Adventure Is My Business, Part 8," . . . . *Sports Afield*, September 1953
"Adventure Is My Business, Part 9," . . . . *Sports Afield*, October 1953
"Adventure Is My Business, Part 10," . . . . *Sports Afield*, November 1953
"I Ought to Hate Porcupines," . . . . *True*, November 1953
"Adventure Is My Business, Part 11," . . . . *Sports Afield*, December 1953
"Brawn, As in Bruin," . . . . *Hunting Yearbook*, January 1954
"Adventure Is My Business, Part 12," . . . . *Sports Afield*, January 1954
"Adventure Is My Business, Part 13," . . . . *Sports Afield*, February 1954
"Adventure Is My Business, Part 14," . . . . *Sports Afield*, March 1954
"Adventure Is My Business, Part 15," . . . . *Sports Afield*, April 1954
"Happy-Go-Siwash," . . . . *American Rod & Gun*, August 1954
"Life in a Moose Pasture," . . . . *Sports Afield*, December 1954
"Saga of the Red One, Part One," . . . . *Sports Afield*, February 1955
"Saga of the Red One, Part Two," . . . . *Sports Afield*, March 1955
"Saga of the Red One, Part Three," . . . . *Sports Afield*, April 1955
"Saga of the Red One, Part Four," . . . . *Sports Afield*, May 1955
"Saga of the Red One, Part Five," . . . . *Sports Afield*, June 1955
"Saga of the Red One, Part Six," . . . . *Sports Afield*, July 1955
"Saga of the Red One, Part Seven," . . . . *Sports Afield*, August 1955
"Saga of the Red One, Part Eight," . . . . *Sports Afield*, September 1955
"Saga of the Red One, Part Nine," . . . . *Sports Afield*, October 1955
"Saga of the Red One, Part Ten," . . . . *Sports Afield*, November 1955
"Saga of the Red One, Conclusion," . . . . *Sports Afield*, December 1955

SAFARI PRESS